CrossCurrents

CrossCurrents

CULTURES, COMMUNITIES, TECHNOLOGIES

Kristine L. Blair
Bowling Green State University

Jen Almjeld
New Mexico State University

Robin M. Murphy
East Central University

 WADSWORTH
CENGAGE Learning·

Australia • Brazil • Japan • Korea • Mexico • Singapore • Spain • United Kingdom • United States

WADSWORTH
CENGAGE Learning

CrossCurrents: Cultures, Communities, Technologies
Kristine L. Blair, Jen Almjeld, Robin M. Murphy

Editor in Chief: Lyn Uhl

Publisher: Monica Eckman

Acquiring Sponsoring Editor: Kate Derrick

Senior Development Editor: Leslie Taggart

Development Editor: Stephanie P. Carpenter

Assistant Editor: Danielle Warchol

Editorial Assistant: Marjorie Cross

Media Editor: Janine Tangney

Executive Marketing Manager: Stacey Purviance

Marketing Communications Manager: Linda Yip

Marketing Coordinator: Brittany Blais

Senior Content Project Manager: Michael Lepera

Senior Art Director: Marissa Falco

Senior Print Buyer: Betsy Donaghey

Rights Acquisition Specialist: Alexandra Ricciardi

Production Service/Compositor: MPS Limited

Text and Cover Designer: Maxine Ressler

Cover Image: NASA

For product information and technology assistance, contact us at **Cengage Learning Customer & Sales Support, 1-800-354-9706**

For permission to use material from this text or product, submit all requests online at **www.cengage.com/permissions.** Further permissions questions can be emailed to **permissionrequest@cengage.com.**

Library of Congress Control Number: 2012938292

ISBN-13: 978-1-4130-1474-7

ISBN-10: 1-4130-1474-7

Wadsworth
20 Channel Center Street
Boston, MA 02210
USA

Cengage Learning is a leading provider of customized learning solutions with office locations around the globe, including Singapore, the United Kingdom, Australia, Mexico, Brazil and Japan. Locate your local office at **international.cengage.com/region**

Cengage Learning products are represented in Canada by Nelson Education, Ltd.

For your course and learning solutions, visit **www.cengage.com.**

Purchase any of our products at your local college store or at our preferred online store **www.cengagebrain.com.**

Instructors: Please visit **login.cengage.com** and log in to access instructor-specific resources.

Printed in the United States of America
1 2 3 4 5 6 7 16 15 14 13 12

Brief Contents

Contents

Introduction 1

> "By reading and looking at all that horrible material on Blog del Narco, we stop living in our own bubble. At least the authors plant the thought in our minds that we are in danger and we need to push the government to do something about it."

Online Resources for Chapter 1

Resources available through the English CourseMate for this text include the following:

Blogs and Videoblogs
Technorati: The Top 100 Blogs
Ask Geriatric

Mashups
The Shining as a Comedy
Sleepless in Seattle Horror Movie
Superfriends Meets *Friends*
The Grey Video
"Tick-Toxic" Mashup of Britney Spears and Gwen Stefani

Digital Arguments and Photo-Essays
A Visual Essay by Scenic America on Urban Sign Pollution
The Girl Effect

Nokia Morph Concept
China Mourns the Potential Loss of Google/ *Time Magazine*
September 12th

Online Articles and Reports
Pew Research Center for the People & the Press. "How Young People View Their Lives, Futures and Politics: A Portrait of 'Generation Next.'"
Melanie McFarland. "Young People Turning Comedy Shows into Serious News Source." *Seattle Post.*
Thomas E. Patterson. "Young People and News." *The Joan Shorenstein Center on the Press, Politics and Public Policy.*

Information Literacies 21

Online Resources for Chapter 2

Resources available through the English CourseMate for this text include the following:

Articles

David Abel. "Welcome to the Library. Say Goodbye to the Books."

Liz Dwyer. "Just Google It: How Search Engines Stunt College Students' Research Skills."

Room for Debate: "Do School Libraries Need Books?" *New York Times* Blog.

"Why Integrate Technology into the Curriculum?: The Reasons are Many." *Edutopia.*

Research Tools

Delicious
Dogpile
MetaCrawler

Information Literacy Tutorials

TILT: Texas Information Literacy Tutorial
Minneapolis Community and Technical College

RIO: University of Arizona Research Instruction Online

Information Literacy Tutorial: Five Colleges of Ohio

Web-Authoring Tools

Adobe Dreamweaver Free Trial
HTML Goodies: The Ultimate HTML Resource
Kompozer Easy Web Authoring
Web Pages That Suck

Video

Michael Wesch. *A Vision of Students Today.*

3

Shared Memories, Shared Identities 77

Edward T. Linenthal   Struggling with History and Memory   **95**

"But the presence of the *Enola Gay* established a 'commemorative membrane' around the exhibition space, within which a language of commemorative respect was expected to dominate. The exhibit was, for veterans and others, a *place of honor,* a place transformed by the aircraft into something other than a museum."

Kirk Anderson   Who Killed the Editorial Cartoon?   **104**

"I can hear you say, 'Isn't the future of editorial cartoons online? And in animation? My neighbor's daughter has an online cartoon, and people in Belize and Lithuania are reading it.'"

Carrie Coppernoll   Survivor Stories: Cecil Hawkins   **106**

"He lay on his back yard as the storm passed overhead, sucking away his home. The storm moved on, leaving Hawkins in his back yard."

John L. Esposito and Mona Mogahed   10th Anniversary of 9/11 and Muslim Americans: The Need for a New Narrative   **108**

"It is truly time for a new narrative, one that is informed by facts, and that is data-driven, to replace the shrill voices of militant Muslim bashers and opportunistic politicians chasing funds and votes."

Drew Griffin and Robert Howell   Teddy Bears, Lab Goggles, Letters Remember Virginia Tech Victims   **110**

"Tamara Kennelly is the archivist at Virginia Tech. She's responsible for documenting how everyone beyond the campus dealt with the tragedy, when the world was joined by four words: 'We are all Hokies.'"

Online Resources for Chapter 3

Resources available through the English CourseMate for this text include the following:

Websites

National September 11 Memorial and Museum at the World Trade Center

Hurricane Katrina Memorial. Biloxi, Mississippi.

"Cultural Literacy." *Engines for Education.*

Memorials

Oklahoma City National Memorial

Katrina National Memorial Park

"In Focus: The Decade Since 9/11." *The Atlantic.*

"September 11, 2001." *The Guardian.*

"The Chora of the Twin Towers." *Enculturation.*

Oral Histories

"Oral Histories." *9/11 Memorial.*

"Mississippi Oral History Project." *University of Southern Mississippi.*

TV

Aaron McGruder. "Invasion of the Katrinians." *Boondocks.*

Editorial Cartoons

"9/11." *Postroad.*

"Cartoonists Remember 9/11." *abcnews.*

Gendered Viewpoints 129

Online Resources for Chapter 4

Resources available through the English CourseMate for this text include the following:

Websites:

The Gender Ads Project
Ad Busters Magazine
Axe Body Spray ads
Dove Campaign for Real Beauty website

Videos:

Dove. "Evolution."
"Breastfeeding Dolls: Too Much, Too Soon?"
Good Morning America.
Jean Kilbourne. "Killing Us Softly."
Gunther Kress. "What Is Multimodality?"

Blogs:

Lisa Wade and Gwen Sharp. "Sociological
Images."

Podcasts:

Brad Forsythe and Ray Shilens. "The
Advertising Show."

Online Articles:

Ian O'Saben. "Visual Rhetoric Examples."
Monica Brasted. "Care Bears vs. Tranformers:
Gender Stereotypes in Advertisements."

5

Gaming Worlds 179

"My second life was much like my first, only accelerated, smaller, and more dramatic.
People married, money moved, wars began, kingdoms crumbled. Noses and lips and hair
and clothes shifted like tiny weather systems, raining images and emotions onto the
computer screens of people around the world."

"Therefore this document holds the following truths to be self-evident: That avatars
are the manifestation of actual people in an online medium, and that their utterances,
actions, thoughts, and emotions should be considered to be as valid as the utterances,
actions, thoughts, and emotions of people in any other forum, venue, location, or space."

"But suddenly we started defining ourselves by the number of followers we had and
clamored for more. Gaining a follower for me would be exciting. What will this person
think of me? Who are they exactly? But I got sucked in to the trap of wanting that
number to go up ..."

"When non-white people and people of color aren't represented in games, I wonder
what conclusion is meant to be drawn. An easy message to glean from whitewashing of
this type is that major companies don't believe that non-white folks are interested in
playing games."

Online Resources for Chapter 5

Resources available through the English CourseMate for this text include the following:

Websites

Linden Research, Inc. *Second Life* Welcome page. "What Is Second Life?"

Clive Thompson. "Scientists Remount Milgram 'Shock' Experiment Using 3D Avatars."

Official *Halo Wars* Community Site

Blogs

Ars Technica Blog: Opposable Thumbs/ Gaming & Entertainment section

Jesper Juul. The Ludologist.

The Guardian. "Games Blog."

Henry Jenkins (author of *Convergence Culture*). "Confessions of an Aca-Fan: The Official Weblog of Henry Jenkins."

Game

Juliet Davis. *Polystyrene Dream.*

Virtual Spaces

Panoramic Virtual Tour. Smithsonian National Museum of Natural History

Journals and Resources

Games Studies

Eludamos

The Digital Games Research Association Homepage

Online Articles

Clive Thompson. "Me and My Big Dwarf Nose: A *Wired News* Column on Race in Online Games," *Collision Detection blog*.

Harold Goldberg. "How Video Games Have Shifted the Culture."

6

Community Engagement and Relations 225

Online Resources for Chapter 6

Resources available through the English CourseMate for this text include the following:

Websites

Hasbro's Community Relations page
Best Buy's Community Relations page
Nationwide's Community Relations page
"Social Capital." *CDC*.
"Social Capital." *Infed*.
"Library." *Learn and Serve America*.
"Kids in Action." *Learn and Serve Idaho*.

Higher Education Network. "The Social and Physical Capital of Women in Higher Education." *The Guardian*.
Fran Smith. "Learning by Giving Community Service as Classwork." *Edutopia*.
Emma Zink. "An Outsider's Mentality: Community Projects Scream for Engaged Volunteers." *The Daily Utah Chronicle*.

Articles

Beth A. Covitt. "Middle School Students' Attitudes toward Required Chesapeake Bay Service-Learning," *Corporation for National and Community Service*.
Kimberly Fornek. "Even with Running Start, State Struggles with Mandate," *Catalyst*.

Videos

The Service Learning Channel. YouTube.com
"The Difference Between Service Learning and Community Service." *Volunteer Global*.
Katherine Fulton. "You are the future of philanthropy." *TED*.

Social Networks 263

"We are tethered to our 'always-on/always-on-us' communications devices and the people and things we reach through them: people, Web pages, voice mail, games, artificial intelligences (nonplayer game characters, interactive online 'bots'). These very different objects achieve a certain sameness because of the way we reach them."

"Social media has a strange role in America as both kingmaker and career wrecker. For every social media success story like President Barack Obama's 2008 grassroots campaign there is another of a career-crippling gaffe, like Weinergate, where New York Representative Anthony Weiner accidentally tweeted a picture of his crotch."

"What happens when I expected a phone call about something and read about it in a status update instead? What's the polite response to a distant friend posting bad news on Facebook? What to do with sensitive information? Making matters trickier, good etiquette on Facebook might not apply on Twitter or in an email."

"Sarah Wells makes an unlikely cyber-vigilante. But the middle-aged mother in Virginia was outraged when she read a Saint Charles Journal article on Megan Meier, a 13-year-old Missouri girl driven to suicide by relentless online bullying. The fact that the bullying appeared to be instigated by the mother of one of Megan's friends…enraged Wells all the more."

Online Resources for Chapter 7

Resources available through the English CourseMate for this text include the following:

Videos

CNN YouTube Republican Debates

CNN YouTube Democratic Debates

Kitchen: Cyberbullying Prevention commercial, Ohio Commission DRCM

Think Before You Post, Ohio Commission DRCM

Sarah Phillips. Tribute to her dying mother, "Autumn by Paolo Nutini."

Olga Kay. My Ford Fiesta Story

Blogs and videoblogs

"Twitterquette: Rules of Conduct on Twitter," Buzzle.com

Online Articles and Reports

A Day Without Media, International Center for Media & the Public Agenda (ICMPA)

Scott Michels. "Teachers' Virtual Lives Conflict With Classroom"

Mary Helen Miller. "East Stroudsburg U. Suspends Professor for Facebook Posts," "East Stroudsburg U. Professor Returns After Suspension for Facebook Posts"

"Twitter Therapy: Cancer Patients Tweeting Through Chemo," Huffington Post

Websites

Nation Master: World Statistics/Country Comparisons

mGive Mobile Donations via Text Message

Vimeo Homepage

Deviant Art Homepage

Human Ecologies 311

The Real Costs of Digital Technologies 312

Online Resources for Chapter 8

Resources available through the English CourseMate for this text include the following:

Online Articles:

Ecycling: From the Environmental Protection
   Agency
Grist: Environmental News, Commentary,
   Advice
Interview with Emmanuel Dogbevi
Edward Wong. "Outrage Grows Over Air
   Pollution and China's Response."

Resources:

Design Crave: Earth Day Graphics:
   30 Creative Environment Ads
GoodGuide
TagCrowd
Wordle

Websites:

Climate Reality Project
EarthDay
Ecogamer
Enviromedia Greenwashing Index
Gardening SuperFund Site
Greenpeace Guide to Greener Electronics
MyFarm
Story of Stuff Project

Preface

In many ways, popular culture has become digital culture.

It seems there is very little that we do not do online now—we do everything from paying bills and ordering furniture to going to school and learning to write. This changing technological landscape also changes concepts of literacy: in an era of Web 2.0, new media, and cloud computing, being digitally and culturally literate is essential to being a successful student, writer, and professional.

CrossCurrents: Cultures, Communities, Technologies is a cultural-studies and technology-based rhetoric and reader that foregrounds writing and reading activities about contemporary cultural contexts, issues, and artifacts. *CrossCurrents* asks students to consider ways texts and contexts are distributed and redistributed within a wide range of traditional and new media technologies—magazine advertising, television, and the Internet. *CrossCurrents* also challenges students to see how the technologies interact to create dominant cultural messages about the relationships among individuals, communities, and cultures.

More and more, instructors are asked to implement electronic writing pedagogies in their classrooms. These pedagogies emphasize the role of computers in the writing process; the role of discussion boards, chat rooms, wikis, and blogs in fostering a social view of writing through electronic peer review; the role of Web-authoring tools in expanding audiences and redefining elements of development, organization, and style through Web and document design; and the role of new media such as digital video and audio as vital parts of a composing process that is inherently multimodal. Because of changing technologies and expectations for literacy, *CrossCurrents* provides readings and activities in *both print and online venues*. These readings and activities encourage students to critically examine mass culture and also the media that circulates within it. The readings and activities simultaneously engage rhetorically with electronic communication, presentation, and Web-authoring and digital imaging technologies, ultimately balancing consumption and production of such texts.

Although students may be familiar with contemporary technoculture, they often are not used to writing and reading about such cultural artifacts and social processes within undergraduate courses. We have found that students can develop critical reading and writing practices through a consistent pedagogical apparatus that emphasizes the role of technology and media in their literate lives. *CrossCurrents*, as the title suggests, seeks to counter the dominant emphasis on print reading and writing genres by creating a robust digital approach to the teaching of writing in a new media era. To that end, *CrossCurrents* combines a variety of traditional alphabetic texts and multimodal texts—including blogs and microblogs, wikis, podcasts, videos, images, and social networking sites—to allow students a fuller picture of what it means to "write" and "read" in the twenty-first century.

Finally, we believe that a real emphasis on producing one's own texts is key to critical engagement. This book will improve students' academic reading and writing skills while providing experience in analyzing the genres and formats of mass media and the popular arts to determine their influence on self and society. *CrossCurrents* offers students ample opportunity to develop a multitude of traditional and less traditional compositions, from digital photography assignments, podcasts, and Web design to research papers, rhetorical analysis of online and offline artifacts, and research bibliographies.

Organization of *CrossCurrents*

CrossCurrents includes eight chapters: one introductory chapter exploring intersections between the topics in the text, and seven thematically organized chapters.

- **Chapter 1: Introduction** guides students in critical reading and writing, situating these rhetorical practices in the context of information and electronic literacy skills. The opening chapter also provides a student example of a blog analysis.
- **Chapter 2: Information Literacies** examines the role of the Internet as a primary source of literacy and learning, with emphasis on what it means to be critically literate.
- **Chapter 3: Shared Memories, Shared Identity** explores connections between cultural literacy practices, memory, and place.
- **Chapter 4: Gendered Viewpoints** foregrounds visual literacy practices, utilizing print and television advertising to focus on issues of gender identity.
- **Chapter 5: Gaming Worlds** investigates social norms and subcultures in gaming environments. The chapter strongly focuses on the use of digital-image, video, and audio elements to create "in game" identities.
- **Chapter 6: Community Engagement and Relations** focuses on community literacy and its relationship with engagement and service learning, asking students to consider what constitutes valuable community service.
- **Chapter 7: Social Networks** balances the pros and cons of living life and making friends online, including topics such as digital identity, virtual citizenry, and cyberbullying.
- **Chapter 8: Human Ecologies** engages with environmental issues, emphasizing climate change, the role of green technologies, and the media coverage and advocacy of more social responsibility for sustaining the earth.

Each chapter consistently presents the following elements:
- Image(s) to introduce and frame each chapter
- Five to seven reading selections (academic, popular, print, and online)
- Related media artifacts (cartoons, advertisements, photographs, screen captures of websites)
- Questions and/or exercises at the end of readings and artifacts
- Technological Beginnings:
  - Special projects involving the use of multimedia for invention
  - Computer-tip sections about Web design, digital imaging processes, presentation software, and so on
- Additional Writing and Composing Activities:
  - Issues and questions for virtual and face-to-face discussion and other forms of individual and collaborative invention
  - Opportunities for narrative, persuasive, expository, and research projects in both print and electronic writing formats

How to Use *CrossCurrents*

Because this text is thematically organized around cultural moments and movements, it is not meant to be used chronologically. Instructors can select themes that best resonate with their own course content. Many of the assignments are multimodal; however, their rhetorical purpose allows instructors to assign a range of print or digital genres that suit their curriculum and classroom practices.

Although the text is intentionally technology rich, it does not presume expert knowledge on the part of the instructor or the student. We have built in a range of activities, some that make use of very basic technologies and others that take advantage of more advanced digital composing tools. The technology tips are meant to ease the transition into new digital spaces and communities.

Similarly, although many of the activities in *CrossCurrents* have an electronic component, students can complete assignments and exercises without technological access, through activities such as small group work, whole-class discussion, in-class or out-of-class journaling, and on-site library research.

Unique Pedagogical Features

- **An introductory chapter** gives students a method for reading and writing critically about cultures, communities, and technologies. Students can return to these rhetorical considerations as they work through the thematic chapters.
- **Engaging themes** explore issues of identity (Chapter 5, Gaming Worlds), what it means to be literate in a digital age (Chapter 2, Information Literacies), and cultural memory (Chapter 4, Shared Memories, Shared Identity), among other issues related to cultures, communities, and technology. Each chapter provides historical and cultural context for the theme, along with specific strategies for studying the media texts in light of the theme.
- **A rich sampling of texts** includes scholarly and popular readings in print and electronic forms alongside visual texts including photography, advertising, and screen captures of websites. This diversity helps students develop critical literacy with media and genres both familiar and unfamiliar.
- **Cultures, Communities, and Technologies activities** woven into each chapter reinforce the key topics of cultural studies. These three elements provide opportunities for students to compose while working through the chapter, rather than only at the end of the chapter or in response to readings. This approach ensures that students have multiple opportunities to produce texts, not just consume them.
- **Technological Beginnings sections and Technology Tips** make strong connections between writing activities and the technologies used to produce such projects.
- **Additional Writing and Composing Activities** at the end of each chapter draw on students' work throughout the chapter to help them develop essays and other compositions.

Additional Resources

English CourseMate for *CrossCurrents*

The online component of *CrossCurrents* provides rich resources for both students and instructors:

- A variety of student writings, ranging from traditional text to multimodal work, give students and instructors ideas for possibilities well beyond the print essay.
- A collection of links to online technology tutorials aid students who are less familiar with specific technologies. The tutorials provide easier entrance into technological discourse communities.
- A wide array of additional live, online resources feature everything from blogs to online archives and other digital research tools.
- Additional composing activities address cultures, communities, and technologies.
- Reading comprehension questions follow each selection in the book and each selection online.

Go to *login.cengage.com* to access these resources. This icon 🖥 denotes a resource available within CourseMate.

Interactive eBook

Printed Access Card:
Instant Access Code:

CrossCurrents is available as an interactive ebook! The ebook provides students with the full text of the print version; interactive exercises; user-friendly navigation; a search, highlighting, and note-taking tool; and links to videos that enhance the handbook content. The ebook requires an access code.

Online Instructor's Manual

Located on a password-protected faculty companion website, our interactive online resource manual provides instructors resources and discussion points for the readings and student essays.

Acknowledgments

We first want to acknowledge the joy it has been to work on this project together—as former students and faculty, now colleagues and friends. Additionally, Kristine Blair wishes to thank especially her mother, Angela P. Blair, and her husband, Kevin D. Williams. Similarly, Jen Almjeld is grateful for the endless support of her friends in Las Cruces and her mother, Annette Almjeld. Finally, Robin Murphy thanks her husband, Kaleb Murphy.

As an authorial team, we owe tremendous gratitude to our editors, publisher, and others who worked tirelessly to help manifest our ideas for best practices for the multimodal English classroom in this book project. Of all the people with whom we had the pleasure to work on *Cross-Currents*, several deserve our utmost thanks. First, we wish to sincerely thank Kate Derrick, acquisitions editor, who was instrumental in bringing this project to fruition. We are grateful for Kate's encouragement, her support, and her vision from the very first conversation we had with her at the 2009 Computers and Writing Conference. We also owe special thanks to Stephanie Pelkowski

Carpenter, our fearless and amazing development editor. Without Stephanie's ability to help us stay on schedule, sift through revisions, and juggle our many, many tasks, *CrossCurrents* would still be just an idea. We also extend our gratitude to Leslie Taggart, senior development editor, for her tremendously helpful feedback and good humor throughout the process. Together, these individuals comprised the best editorial team we could have ever hoped for.

We are also immensely grateful to Lyn Uhl, publisher, and Monica Eckman, executive editor, for their wonderful support in the project's early stages; to Cara Graff, senior media editor, for working to produce our essential online component; to Michael Lepera, senior content project manager, for guiding us through the production process; to Danielle Warchol, assistant editor, and Marjorie Cross, editorial assistant, for managing the details so well; and to Stacey Purviance and Jason Sakos and their marketing team for making sure *CrossCurrents* reaches our audience.

Finally, we wish to thank the many reviewers of *CrossCurrents*, whose insights and collective wisdom helped us ground the project in contemporary composition theory and practice:

Tanya Allred, *New Mexico State University at Alamogordo*
Evelyn Beck, *Harrisburg Area Community College*
Lynn Beene, *University of New Mexico*
Carol Britt, *San Antonio College*
Patricia Cullinan, *Truckee Meadows Community College*
David Elias, *Eastern Kentucky University*
Benjamin Emery, *Central New Mexico Community College*
William Etter, *Irvine Valley College*
Kevin Garland, *Palm Beach State College*
Sue Hum, *University of Texas at San Antonio*
Bruce G. Johnson, *Curry College*
Patricia Leaf-Prince, *North Carolina Central University*
Leanne Maunu, *Palomar College*
David McCracken, *Coker College*
Antonio Menendez, *Butler University*
Teresa Mercsak, *The Art Institute of California –San Diego*
John Miller, *National University*
Bryan Moore, *Arkansas State University*
Stephen Morrow, *Ohio University*
Yvonne Prather, *Austin Peay State University*
Shelley Rees, *University of Science and Arts of Oklahoma*
Vanessa Ruccolo, *Virginia Tech*
Molly Scanlon, *Virginia Tech*
Leslie St. Martin, *College of the Canyons*
Jim Wilkins-Luton, *Clark College*

Introduction

Figure 1.1 Library bookshelf depicting increasing importance of Google in society

The cartoon in Figure 1.1 speaks not only to shifts from print to digital but also to the shift in value associated with certain technologies and media. In our media-dense society, the number of hits one receives online is perhaps as significant or more significant than being singled out in a Who's Who sort of publication. As more people access textual material online, ebook readers such as the Kindle, Nook, and the iPad are changing our understanding of what a book is and how we read it.

CrossCurrents itself addresses the intersection of old and new media by connecting print and online materials. This ensures that the texts and contexts throughout the book can not only be accessed online but also discussed and responded to through various social networking and digital composing tools. These options for responding allow you to create a powerful message that integrates image and text—just like the cartoon—and to contribute to this collaborative idea-sharing process.

Defining CrossCurrents

As the title suggests, *CrossCurrents: Cultures, Communities, and Technologies* explores the intersections among a number of twenty-first-century "currents," including the following:

The relationship between larger national and global cultures and local subcultures

The relationship between these cultures and the values and alliances that circulate within them

The relationship between these values and the communication genres and technologies we use to share the values and thus create and sustain local and global communities

Finding Common Ground

Often the daily communication tools we use seem invisible to us; we can't remember a time when we didn't have iPhones and Blackberries, Google, YouTube, or academic research databases, all of which help us access and share information. The purpose of *CrossCurrents: Cultures, Communities, and Technologies* is to help you more critically think about these intersecting

COMMUNITIES   Because *CrossCurrents* relies on communication technologies for online dialogue about the issues and texts in print and online, it is important to develop an online communication policy for appropriate dialogue as classroom citizens so that your instructor may include it as part of the other classroom policies about attendance and participation. In a group, come up with two or three things you feel must be covered in your classroom communication policy and explain why. These suggestions can be added to other students' suggestions. Distribute your collaboratively written policy on your online discussion forum.

communication modes and contexts common to today's society. Part of this process involves establishing "common ground," or a type of mutual understanding about current events and social issues and shared spaces for reflecting upon them.

One way this text attempts to establish that common ground involves selecting contexts that have a real-world connection to our daily lives as students, as consumers, as political citizens, and as members of multicultural communities. Another way involves providing strategies for defining and understanding the contexts in which we take on these varied identities and the ways that various media and technological contexts help to shape those identities, whether we intend them to or not. As you will see in Chapter 7, "Social Networks," specific commonplace genres allow us to reflect on these relationships. In today's digital age, such genres can range from the weblogs we establish to record private and public reflections, to the YouTube video we share with a mass audience. Developing reading, listening, and viewing strategies help make us critically informed citizens, able to evaluate the cultural, political, and professional messages we receive every day.

Finally, finding common ground also includes our understanding of how these cultures, communities, and technologies can both unite and divide us as citizens. It may require us to develop our own critical voices, in the editorial in the campus paper, in the logo we develop for a local organization, or in the groups we join on Facebook. In this way, accessing information through technological means is a social and political process. The distinction among news, history, and entertainment isn't necessarily clear and thus contributes to another type of crosscurrent.

In fact, a 2008 Pew Research Center publication reports that many Americans now consider themselves "integrators," who receive news both from traditional sources like TV and newspapers and also from the Internet. The same study reports about a third of those twenty-five and younger get no news each day. This study, however, does not take into account less-traditional news sources like entertainment news shows (*The Daily Show, The Colbert Report*) and social networking spaces (Facebook status update alerts, Twitter news cycles). Some argue, then, that young people are not paying less attention to news but instead are relying on "a different distribution system" (Patterson, 2007). Similarly, although some may presume that only younger people are relying on tools such as iTunes or YouTube, older generations are becoming as wired as younger ones, as the recent YouTube videoblog geriatric1927 suggests.

Given this shift in news and media distribution, educators and political watchdog groups have advocated a more critical literacy. Indeed, an Internet search will reveal dozens of sites from around the world advocating media literacy, information literacy, the study of popular culture, and media's influence on individuals and society. By promoting the study of these areas, educators hope students become more able to parse the messages embedded in the media tools they use. By learning to view the world around them with a more critical eye, students should be equipped to make better informed decisions about the roles media plays in their lives and thereby their citizenry.

As we write this introduction, in early 2012, just as we have left a decade that began with the 9/11 attacks on the World Trade Center and the Pentagon, Hurricane Katrina, and wars with Iraq and Afghanistan, we now begin the decade with the earthquake in Haiti, protests in Egypt, stopping Osama bin Laden, launching the first solar-powered spacecraft, the Arab Spring, the Occupy movements, the repeal of the "Don't ask, don't tell" policy, and several natural disasters in the United States. Our knowledge and understanding of these events are shaped by the media in which we access information, whether that be cable news media with television and online information, a political blog, Facebook groups, or other forums such as Twitter, in which we are encouraged not only to read about these events but to join in a dialogue about them as well.

Questioning Crosscurrents

The overall theme of *CrossCurrents* is that media and multimedia messages should always be subject to a critical analysis that acknowledges the cultural and community context in which the message is produced, distributed, and consumed. Often gaps between the larger culture and particular subcultures create conflicts and debates among shared assumptions. With this theme in mind, we offer the following questions to help foster critical reading and thinking about the materials you will encounter in this book and in your daily lives:

Cultures

Who owns or produced the message, whether it be a website, a television commercial, or even a hairstyle or mode of dress?

Under what contexts or conditions (historical, political, or cultural) was the message created?

How does the text relate to these contexts or conditions?

How do the producers or creators establish their sense of purpose or reason for communicating?

Communities

What is the intended impact on the reader, viewer, or listener? What is the audience "supposed to do"?

How does the text affect how viewers think about content? How does the content change their cultural assumptions?

How does the message help shape membership within a community or create common goals and values?

How does the text appeal to diverse groups or interests, including ethnicity, gender, sexual orientation, class, or age?

Does the text encourage social action or civic responsibility? How?

Technologies

What technology does the producer rely on to create the message?

Why is this technology preferable to or more appropriate than others? Does the technology have limits?

How are the visual and the textual related? Why is this relationship important to the message? What types of strategies (such as color, placement, size, or hyperlinks) help create the overall persuasive point?

What are the technology's social or cultural associations or values?

Each chapter of *CrossCurrents* provides a specific context for questioning and understanding the connections and currents between cultures, communities, and technologies. Whether considering "real" social networking and shared memories or created gaming worlds, the chapters and related readings, images, and technological examples reframe familiar subjects and the literacy practices that help create and sustain cultural values and community goals. In addition, each chapter provides a representative strategy for finding common ground among the cultural, communal, and technological currents.

Although many of the communication forms we discuss in *CrossCurrents* are social, we define *communication* broadly; it occurs in many different forms. For example, with the recent popularity of the *Twilight* series, both books and films, some fan communities have created tattoos (see **Figure 1.2**) honoring their devotion to the series, thus creating a subculture with shared interests, values, and modes of expression. *Twilight*'s fan base represents itself in a range of formats, including the Facebook community group Team *Twilight* (**Figure 1.3**), which has been "liked" by nearly 11 million Facebook members. Although it may be unusual to study tattoos and Facebook pages, applying the questions on p. 5 to these items can help you gain an understanding of that subculture.

Figure 1.2 *Twilight* tattoo

REX FEATURES VIA AP IMAGES

Figure 1.3 Facebook group for Team *Twilight*

COURTESY OF TEAM TWILIGHT

COMMUNITIES Based on your understanding of fan communities in general and the *Twilight* fan group represented here and elsewhere, engage in an online dialogue with your classmates that relies on some of the foregoing questions to explore the cultural values and media tools used to establish a community and express its values.

Technological Beginnings

Another feature of *CrossCurrents* is Technological Beginnings tips. These sections introduce readers to emerging technologies and offer strategies for successfully taking up a new tech tool. Given the changing political, modal, and literacy landscape, for example, we are interested in ways blogs might be useful to students.

TECHNOLOGIES Visit one of the popular blog sites such as WordPress.com or Tumblr.com and sign up for an account to create your own blog in relation to the readings and activities in this class. Throughout the book you will be asked to use your blog as a form of free writing in preparation for research topics and media projects. In the event you do not always have reliable Internet access, you can still participate by keeping an electronic journal on your personal computer or storage disk or by keeping a print journal in a notebook.

Blogs, like the one pictured in **Figure 1.4**, offer individuals flexibility in developing an online persona. Whereas some individuals treat blogs as private diaries written primarily for themselves, others use blogs as a blend of both private and public. These are forums for journaling about shared interests or identities. Still others maintain them on behalf of organizations, whether commercial or not-for-profit. Blogs, thus, may be an important site for beginning research and for gaining a general understanding of local and national conversations on any number of topics. Many classes include blogs to facilitate writing and communication, and although your current course may not have a blogging component, you may choose to experiment with a social or academic blog just to see what all the hype is about.

COURTESY OF WORDPRESS.COM

Figure 1.4 WordPress.com blog site

Reading Image-Texts and Contexts

Just as blogs are changing our concept of writing and composition by providing new formats and forums within which you can privately journal and/or publicly dialogue about important issues, digital photography, video, and audio are becoming new tools of "composition." You can experiment with these technologies to help document cultural and community values.

One major distinction between older media of television, newspapers, and film and new media of blogs and YouTube is the difference between passive viewing and active participation. *CrossCurrents* provides you with ample opportunities for producing texts, media, and multimedia that reflect your own identities, values, and roles within your various cultures and communities. Whereas larger culture, as reflected in the mass media and the popular arts, has always had access to the tools of film, television, advertising, and the news media, the advent of the desktop computer and increased public access to digital communication tools in many cases expand an individual's power to speak and to be heard. With newer media you can use technology to express yourself, exchange information, and persuade others to your viewpoints in just the same way you would in a purely print document.

As an example, consider the following two images. The first, **Figure 1.5**, is a 1937 photograph by acclaimed photographer Margaret Bourke-White, published in *Life Magazine*. The photo portrays victims of the Louisville

Figure 1.5 "The American Way," by Margaret Bourke-White

Flood waiting in line at a Red Cross Relief station. Using some of the questions on page 5 about cultures, communities, and technologies, discuss with your classmates the message you believe this image conveys and the historical and cultural context behind its implied meaning. What aspects of the image lead to your particular reading of it? Also, do some searching on your own. Have you seen a similar image in recent years? Does your opinion differ when you view the more modern image? What has changed or is the same?

Now let's "read" the next figure. The original image from *Life Magazine* has recently been reappropriated by various political groups to engage in critical commentary about a particular administration's response to economic crisis and recent national disasters (including George Bush's response to Hurricane Katrina). The second image (**Figure 1.6**), for example, appears on the site RevLeft.com, one of the world's largest leftist forum communities. The image invites critical commentary about the Obama administration's response to the unemployment crisis. Take a moment to discuss how various aspects of the original image have been revised to create new arguments and to explore the larger context behind those arguments.

This new argumentation and expression through the combining of existing media and content to create new meaning is increasingly prevalent in music, entertainment, and social organizations. It is often referred to as *mashup*. Perhaps one of the best-known examples of musical mashup is Danger Mouse's 2004 *The Grey Album*.

Figure 1.6 *The Louisville Flood* on RevLeft.com

Looks clean, doesn't it?

NASA/JPL; VISUAL ARGUMENT USED BY PERMISSION OF ANNGEE LEE

Figure 1.7 A visual argument

■■
■
■■ **TECHNOLOGIES** Often the success of visual arguments, such as those presented in Figures 1.5 and 1.6, occur through using or reusing an image to convey an ironic or satirical point that contrasts images themselves or images and texts. Bourke-White's photo contrasts the phrase "There's no way like the American Way" with the plight of flood victims. In **Figure 1.7**, a student's visual message about environmental issues depends equally on both image and text. With this process in mind, select an existing image to create, through the contrast of visual and/or textual images, your own new visual argument about the issue you explored in the Cultures exercise on page 4, or another issue or topic that interests you.

Notice that the text in Figure 1.7 indicates an implicit argument. In this example, the author's argument isn't spelled out directly, but you know as an audience member that the author's intent is to argue that the world isn't as clean at it appears. So the author's thesis for this image, if stated directly or explicitly, might be something like one of the following statements:

Broad

Thesis: The world is not as clean as it seems.

Thesis: Our environment is not as clean as you might think.

Thesis: We should do more to keep our environment clean.

Narrow

Thesis: The United States should have stricter air pollution laws.

Thesis: Countries that pollute should be sanctioned more stringently by the United Nations.

Thesis: The Kyoto Protocol Act has failed to curb carbon dioxide emissions.

In these broad and more narrowed statements, the overall idea is clear to the audience. This should be the case with all thesis statements. In an academic essay, thesis statements are usually explicitly stated, and they usually indicate, in one to three sentences or even an entire paragraph (depending on the length of the essay), what the audience can expect to read about in the essay. For instance, in the thesis statement "The Kyoto Protocol Act has failed to curb carbon dioxide emissions," the audience expects the essay that follows to argue, with support, how the Kyoto Protocol Act has failed to curb carbon dioxide emissions. The essay might begin with an introduction that explains the Kyoto Protocol Act, defines its intentions, or even gives background about why the Kyoto Protocol Act was established.

Often the thesis is found at the end of the introduction paragraph, but it can be placed anywhere in the organization of the essay. However, the essay's content must correlate with the thesis precisely or the audience will become confused. Although the thesis doesn't have to be stated directly, an author should always have a thesis in mind in order to keep the idea focused.

If you were going to use the image in Figure 1.7 to make an explicit argument in favor of the condition of the environment, how would you change the text?

Whether you agree or disagree with arguments of these images, or any other image you may encounter in print or online, it is clear that newer technologies of communication are allowing individuals from varied backgrounds to participate in social and political dialogue, contributing to both the crosscurrents of ideas and the crosscurrents of technologies to express them. The English CourseMate for *CrossCurrents* provides more examples of mashup, and we encourage you to search YouTube and other online sites for sources to share and discuss.

Student Sample: Draft of Blog Analysis

In the following analysis of a blog, student Lorena Beltram uses the "Questioning CrossCurrents" questions on page 5 of this chapter to examine a particular community, culture, and technology.

Lorena Beltram
Dr. Jen Almjeld
English 326
16 March 2012

El Blog del Narco: Anonymous Voices Bring Truth

The Internet had a worldwide impact in the workplace, leisure time, and knowledge in general. Thanks to the Web, millions of people have easy and fast access to any type of information online. We can send emails and instant messages, watch movies, play games, do research, create a Facebook profile, and use weblogs. In many countries, any person can create many different things online to transmit their ideas, information, and identities, and one example is the *Blog del Narco*. This website was created to inform readers about what really happens in Mexico, a country of insecurity, violence, and drug trafficking. Most of the information on the blog comes from anonymous sources, and it can really have an impact on our political, social, and individual views due to the strong material provided.

Drug dealers (cartels) participate in an international illegal industry that grows, manufactures, distributes, and sells illegal drugs. This illegal business has generated violence between cartels for the control over new "plazas," and now we have access to videos, photos, interviews, and comments about these dangerous people and their crimes in the *Blog del Narco* ("About Us"). This web page was created about a year ago and contains historic records of the drug dealers in Mexico that no other source dares to publish due to the constant threats of violence against reporters, police, and government officials. There have been people killed, such as radio anchors and news reporters, who revealed important names and information.

Two young men who fight to objectively publicize what happens in Mexico created this blog (Cardenas). A key factor for the creation of this blog was that other media wanted to hide the terror that the country suffers. The bloggers unveil violent acts without alterations and in a transparent way, not seeking to offend anyone. We can also find the bloggers on social networks like Twitter, Facebook, and YouTube.

The *Blog del Narco* has become so popular around the world that it has been translated into different languages, including English, French, German, Chinese, and Japanese. On the main page we find the most recent news about shootings, arrests, and acts of corruption, with their respective photographs. We can also see commercial ads, and on the left side of the blog is a column with a list of links of interest such as movies, forums, and popular sites. At the top are seven tabs that take readers to other windows: Home, About Us, Contact, Press, Forum, Twitter, and Index.

In the "About Us" window we can find a brief description of when, how, why, and who created this web page; and on the bottom is a link to a form that people can fill out to contact the authors or send them information. To do so, readers must write their name and email address, the subject, and a message, and they can attach files. But at the top of the form we ironically read: "100% anonymous." Obviously, no one writes his or her real information.

On the "Press" window we find all the news, articles, videos, pictures, and more from press such as LaRazon.es, Milenio.com, and *La Jornada*. The information on these related sites is not as explicit when you compare it with the unaltered news of the *Blog del Narco*. This is an example of how media can be controlled by the government. According to Luis Cardenas in a video from *Noticia Digital* posted on YouTube, "The world and the truth are created and recreated by the media, specially television and radio; and Televisa, the largest media company in the Spanish world and the most corrupt, is in alliance with the Mexican government to not publish certain news that brings negative consequences to the country" (*Anonymous*).

In the "Forum" section people can comment and have conversations about the articles and news, or just share their point of view about any issue.

Some people think the material is too strong, but others believe this is pure reality and there is no purpose to hide it. It is very sad to recognize that Mexico is one of the most dangerous countries in the world.

Another communication space is the "Twitter" window that takes us to the Twitter page where there is a list of links with all the most relevant news. And last, but not least, we have the "Index," the window that lists all the exclusive videos, interviews, and pictures by date.

Due to the blog's popularity, people know how violent and harsh the content of this website can be, even though there are no warnings on the home page. The audience can get some hints by looking at the blog's main title; it's a big red rectangle with white letters that read: "Blog del Narco." Behind the letters there is a black ribbon with smaller letters that read: "more than 30,000," and at the sides there are images of two AK-47s, sending a clear message of violence. The only thing that directly warns the audience of its high content of violence is the videos.

People who navigate this website really want to know what is going on in the country. To me, people who read and post to this blog are people who are not afraid of reality and want to get involved in letting everybody know the awful and indescribable things that are happening in Mexico. This blog is created mostly by the audience, which anonymously gathers a lot of information because audience members happen to be at certain places when a shooting takes place and they take video or pictures. Thirty-five years ago, people reading newspapers in this part of the world did not face such images or even real mention of drug-related violence (Castro). Unfortunately, these are things that happen in everyday life; it's not rare anymore.

The language used in this technology is "journalese" for the articles and news, but there is also a lot of popular language on the video and forum sections. In these two sources there is no censure of words. In the forum, for example, people use nonsense language to express their anger and disappointment, mainly toward the Mexican government. There are very dramatic discussions between members of the audience who share different opinions, and they are not afraid to publish their thoughts, because they have created false identities. By "false," I mean they use different names and ages to let the world know their true feelings and ideas about the situation in Mexico. It's very important to remain anonymous for security reasons. People kill for many reasons; let's not give them our real information, otherwise they could kill us too for practicing our right of freedom of expression.

This type of website is very useful and important for society on- and offline because it brings us back to reality. According to a post on the importance of online news outlets, "The advent of online news sites has been extremely beneficial for people who lead a hectic life and have to spend long hours in front of computers" (Brian8). By reading and looking at all that horrible material on

Blog del Narco, we stop living in our own bubble. At least the authors plant the thought in our minds that we are in danger and we need to push the government to do something about it. The *Blog del Narco* transmits the message to the entire world that has access to the Internet, and thanks to this, many countries are taking an interest in helping Mexico. There are people who want to censure this website, but it won't do any good because we will only be hiding the corruption and violence that has taken possession of a once beautiful country.

Personally, I think the *Blog del Narco* is hard to view due to its bloody and violent material, but it's a very important source because it's the only place I can see what really is going on in my country. TV news doesn't even tell you half of what we can find in this blog: the videos of interviews and random shootings are shocking, but they alert us to be more careful of where we go and whom we hang out with. We have to be very careful while the war between cartels continues. An example of a video found on this blog is one of an unknown man who is hanging nude from his feet alive. There is a group of unknown men who holds the man with their faces covered and wearing military-style clothing. One of the guys cuts the nude man with a knife, another cuts his throat, others take pictures with him, and then they start cutting his arms and legs and throwing them in a bucket. Viewers can hear background music the whole time. There is no censure in this video, so it is extremely hard to watch.

Those with access to technologies such as the Internet are very lucky because they get more than a source of information; they get a source that alerts society to all the events and violent acts that happen in specific areas of Mexico. The *Blog del Narco* can give us information about who the drug cartels are, where they are, whom they are going for, and who is in jail already. The only warning is that if a person is very sensitive to strong images, it won't be a very good idea to watch it, because viewers will find a picture of a head, arms, legs, and other body parts in a big pot, cooking with *pozole* and other ingredients, with a big sign that says: "This is what is going to happen to your people if you don't obey my orders."

Works Cited

"About Us." *Mundo Narco*. Blog del Narco, n.d. Web. 12 Feb. 2012.

Anonymous. *Blog del Narco*, 2012. Web. 5 Feb. 2012.

Brian8. "The importance of online news sites and RSS feeds." *Article Dashboard*. ArticleDashboard.com, n.d. Web. 10 Feb. 2012.

Cardenas, Luis. "El Blog del Narco." *Notícias Digital*. YouTube. 19 Aug. 2010. Video. 15 Feb. 2012.

Castro, Jesus. "Cuando el narco no era noticia" ("When the drug trafficking wasn't news"). *Vaguardia*. 9 Sept. 2010. Web. 10 Feb. 2012.

Revising a Blog Analysis

If you were giving revision advice to the author of the blog analysis, what would you tell her? What kinds of questions do you have for the author? Consider the following:

- Does the author seem to be missing anything in the analysis? What should be added?

- Is the topic analyzed in a way that makes sense?

- How could she improve the organization of the essay? Should any of the paragraphs be moved around?

- Is all of the content important and helpful in understanding the website? What can be deleted without losing the purpose of the essay?

- Is the author's thesis clearly stated or is it implicit? How might she improve the impact of the thesis?

- Does the essay appeal to you? Why?

Contributing to the Crosscurrents

In addition to the wide range of media and multimedia included in the print and online components of *CrossCurrents*—including photographs and art-work, references and stills from television programs, music videos and song lyrics, software, video games, advertisements, cartoons, tattoos, logos, and websites—many of the exercises, activities, and writing and research projects provide an opportunity for you to "compose" your work in ways that integrate written and visual texts. Although many projects allow you to write a print-based response, still other assignments may ask that you represent your ideas visually through the creation of a photograph, a video-essay, or a website that has life beyond your class. In some instances, such as Chapter 6, "Community Relations," you may be asked to create projects for an organization as a way of developing your technological literacy skills and using them to support the values of a particular culture or community. Regardless of the context, each chapter will provide a range of print and electronic activities as well as help-ful hints for using technology to create media artifacts, including the use of digital cameras; video recorders; web authoring, digital imaging, and podcast-ing software; as well as CDs, DVDs, and desktop-published and web-based delivery options.

You may already be very accustomed to electronic communication tools in your personal and professional lives; instant messaging, text messag-ing, and access to information and people are a natural part of daily life.

Not surprisingly, many writing classrooms take advantage of the latest communication technologies for prewriting, drafting, and revising activities. Each chapter of *CrossCurrents* features at least one online writing or communication tool to assist you in your composing processes. These tools include presentation software such as Microsoft PowerPoint, image storage software such as Flickr, blogging and microblogging tools such as WordPress (see Figure 1.4 (p. 7), web-based discussion boards on free and commercial sites, and course management tools such as Blackboard.com. Course management tools, for instance, provide not only discussion boards but also chat forums, virtual classrooms, and private email, all to maximize the opportunity for collaboration and dialogue about the cultures, communities, and technologies profiled within this text. Although the contexts in which you communicate online may be very informal, often the classroom community creates a higher standard of communication, stressing courtesy and collegiality, especially during discussions of controversial issues.

CrossCurrents profiles a range of digital technologies and literacy practices that you may effectively and appropriately integrate into existing course assignments, research topics, and community projects. Although you may be unable to publish your own images on the same scale as some of the projects on display, you can use some of the same tools to create them.

Whether you begin with a regular camera, a disposable one you buy at the grocery store, the camera setting on your cell phone, or the popular array of digital cameras or video cameras on the market, you can use images to tell a story or take a stand.

TECHNOLOGY TIP   **Digital Imaging and Storing Options**

You can choose from a range of options to incorporate digitized images into your assignments. For instance, the first version of this chapter was initially completed in Microsoft Word, with most images downloaded from the Web and inserted directly into the document. You can use software such as Apple iPhoto (on a Mac) or the My Pictures feature (in Windows), to both organize and display your photos in a slideshow presentation format, a possible option for a photo-essay assignment. On sites such as Facebook and Flickr, you can display and store photos online. Microsoft PowerPoint and Apple iMovie are popular options for presentation purposes. We address these tools in later chapters, where they are introduced as options for completing particular assignments and projects.

Just as we provided some guiding questions about reading texts within the contexts of cultures, media technologies, and communities, we offer the following questions to help you produce your own texts in response to those contexts:

Cultures

What issues does your text respond to?

What are the larger cultural assumptions about this topic?

What are the divergent viewpoints?

What is the modal purpose (argument, narrative, and so on) of your text?

What genres and media are typically used to communicate within the culture?

How does your design promote your intent?

Communities

What specific audience are you trying to reach?

How might they react to your response?

How does your text add to the conversation about the topic?

How might it encourage future dialogue or community action?

How does your text make you or your audience more critically aware of the issue?

How will you present or store the final product? How does the audience influence this choice?

Will the audience have access to the technologies you choose to deliver the product through?

Will your audience be able to engage with your ideas?

Technologies

What genre is your text: report, website, photo-essay, blog, podcast, video- or audio-essay? Why have you made this choice?

What tools will you use to produce your text?

What research, training, or knowledge do you need to design your text?

How much time do you need?

What rhetorical devices do you want to apply in your text?

What values are associated with your chosen media?

What colors and organization do you want to use?

What can you change to make your text more persuasive?

Additional Writing and Composing Assignment

Whether you recognize it or not, you are a member of various cultures and communities. Your membership begins very early with your own families and continues through to adulthood. As college students, you are also part of a university culture. Depending on your interests and activities, you are part of campus and community organizations, as well as workplace or social cultures, that use a range of communication and literacy practices to sustain the existing community and often to recruit others into it.

Identify at least one community in which you consider yourself a regular member, whether it be on or off campus. What are the community's goals and values, and in what ways does it use a range of technologies to communicate those values?

Bring one sample text—a brochure or newsletter, a website, a blog, a logo or image, or another promotional tool—to share with the class. If you were to design a text that represents this community, what might you do, and why?

Apply the questions on page 5 to your text to help describe the culture, community, and technologies that give the text meaning.

Take several digital photographs on your campus, at your home, or if possible and appropriate, your workplace or volunteer community organization. Based on those images, what message can you communicate to viewers about the lifestyles, community values, and social roles of students, of individuals, or of professionals in those spaces? How can you arrange the images to create this essay? What written captions or oral narration can or should you provide to help structure the essay? Are such accompaniments necessary? As you begin to arrange or storyboard your images (a process we will discuss more in later chapters), what additional images may help tell your story or make your point? Be prepared to discuss why you made particular choices.

Online Resources

Resources available through the English CourseMate for this text include the following:

Blogs and Videoblogs

Technorati: The Top 100 Blogs

Ask Geriatric

Mashups

The Shining as a Comedy

Sleepless in Seattle Horror Movie

Superfriends Meets *Friends*

The Grey Video

"Tick-Toxic" Mashup of Britney Spears and Gwen Stefani

Digital Arguments and Photo-Essays

A Visual Essay by Scenic America on Urban Sign Pollution

The Girl Effect

Nokia Morph Concept

China Mourns the Potential Loss of Google/ *Time Magazine*

September 12th

Online Articles and Reports

Pew Research Center for the People & the Press. "How Young People View Their Lives, Futures and Politics: A Portrait of 'Generation Next.'"

Melanie McFarland. "Young People Turning Comedy Shows into Serious News Source." *Seattle Post*.

Thomas E. Patterson. "Young People and News." *The Joan Shorenstein Center on the Press, Politics and Public Policy*.

Figure 2.1 Cartoon depicting student reliance on the internet for information

Information Literacies

Just as the Information Age influences increasingly more aspects of professional and social interaction, reading and writing processes change as well. The term "Information Age" is likely not a new one to you. Whereas Chapter 1 suggests that all media play a part in creating and sustaining our cultural identity, this chapter focuses on access to Web-based information and on the need for developing online reading and writing strategies. For instance, Chapter 1 profiles the rise of weblogs and their role in providing news and information, and as you likely know, your campus library has many Web-based resources for locating information from both scholarly and popular publications, regardless of whether they are in print or online. Because of this increasing dependence on the Web to access information, it is vital to develop strategies for retrieving information, assessing its reliability, and producing our own online content as well.

In some cases the view that online information may be more suspect than traditional print information has its own set of cultural biases. Clearly, one advantage of Web publishing is that many, though not all of us, can access Web-publishing tools to broadcast our views, whether through a personal or professional website, a discussion post, or a blog entry. For those of us who have been raised in this digital era, these options seem natural, not necessarily supplemental to what we obtain from the newspaper, the evening news, or a library book.

Even so, print sources often continue to carry more authority than electronic ones. The distrust of new technologies is nothing new: 2,500 years ago, the Greek philosopher Socrates lamented the role writing—used instead of oral philosophical debate—played in deceiving audiences. As a tool, writing was once a new and frightening technology, just as electronic texts can be today. Modernly, the question "Which is better, print or electronic text?" may be beside the point: technology breaks down barriers between print and electronic information every day. Information is everywhere, and the easier it is to access from your home or school computer, the better . . . right? That is likely the perspective the search engine corporation Google had in mind when it announced the plan to digitize the libraries of several major American universities, including the University of Michigan and the Massachusetts Institute of Technology (MIT).

Print publication processes often involve peer-review procedures in which experts in a field evaluate the quality of the author's work prior to its publication. Thus, there is often a presumption that books and other print-based materials are more credible than digital sources. Although many of us regularly retrieve information and conduct research online, we can't always be as sure of the reliability of online information as we generally are of the materials we retrieve from a

CULTURES   What does the cartoon in **Figure 2.1** presume about students and technology? How does this cartoon relate to Liz Dwyer's "Just Google It: How Search Engines Stunt College Students' Research Skills," available online and through the English CourseMate for this text.

CULTURES What does the sign in **Figure 2.2** assume about the term "library"? What are your own library usage habits? How have they changed over time?

traditional library. As this chapter stresses, values and biases about the quality of online information are not only generational but also cultural.

Data access and retrieval will continue to depend on technology to sustain and archive information from print format. Equally important, data access and retrieval skills contribute to your success across the curriculum by helping you determine the validity of various visual, verbal, and written arguments; synthesize multiple points of view; come to your own conclusions; and effectively articulate those conclusions.

© ALAN SCHEIN PHOTOGRAPHY/CORBIS

Figure 2.2 Street sign indicating a nearby library using a symbol for reading a print book

Defining Information Literacies

The title of this chapter, "Information Literacies," refers to "the ability to define problems in terms of their information needs, and to apply a systematic approach to search, locate, apply, and synthesize the information and evaluate the entire process in terms of effectiveness and efficiency." Indeed, this definition is brought to you courtesy of a Google search, which generated multiple definitions from multiple resources, including BusinessDictionary .com, from which the definition was ultimately taken. (see **Figure 2.3**).

In the context of contemporary reading and writing practices, the structure, format, and design of information and the tools used to locate it require new technical and critical literacies, often lumped under the term "Information Literacy." As some readings and activities for this chapter indicate, the ability

to both produce and consume usable, valuable information is key to academic, professional, and commercial success.

It is important to consider the ways digital tools both limit and enable information access. Although particular tools may organize and disseminate information, they may also overwhelm us with the possibilities and the responsibilities of consuming and producing data, as you might notice from the 100,000 hits you might get back on a Google search for the term "information overload." Given the increasing number of emails we are expected to read and respond to every day, often including spam (online ads, gimmicks, and offensive content), some of us may be nostalgic for the days of "snail mail" junk mail. Even as our tools advance to allow us to automatically filter the data trash from the data treasure, technology alone cannot resolve our sense of overload. We need a toolkit of literacy competencies to retrieve and interpret information not just online but from other forms of media and the popular arts. This chapter can help you build that toolkit.

Often media-saturated texts, whether print or electronic, call for a blended literacy, something symbolized in **Figure 2.4**. This hybrid notion of literacy holds true in our various metaphors for digital communication: the web *page*, the *iPad*, and the *tablet* PC, for example.

Figure 2.4 Illustrator John S. Dyke's depiction of the reading process

© IMAGES.COM/CORBIS

CULTURES In what way is John Dyke's artwork in Figure 2.4 a commentary on reading and literacy? What aspects of the image reflect contemporary social habits?

COMMUNITIES Dyke's image is not unfamiliar to us. Whether in the dining areas on our campus or the coffee houses in our communities, the act of reading print or electronic texts is a common one. Where, how, and what do you read regularly? Describe how new technologies foster or inhibit your preferred reading processes.

Strategies for Reading and Writing Online

Regardless of what one thinks of online information—that somehow it is less or more reliable than print—it is clear that, as scholar Jay David Bolter contended more than fifteen years ago in his canonical book *Writing Space*, the computer is not the death of print. Rather the computer carries print into a new medium. For that reason, it is vital that we question the validity of *all* texts, print or electronic. How do we know that information is reliable in any format? To address this question, this chapter encourages critical reading and writing, focusing on criteria for evaluating the reliability, validity, and accessibility of online information.

Equally important to remember is that despite some of the skepticism about online information, print texts have as much potential to contain bias and misinformation, thus lacking as much credibility as electronic texts. However, online information does have its own set of formatting and content conventions that influence validity, usability, and accessibility. These content and format strategies combined are essential to making online information you consume and online information you produce more readable, accessible, and usable.

Critically Reading the Web

Unlike other media such as television, commercial film, and newspapers, the World Wide Web allows individuals who can access it to create a digital life for their political beliefs and viewpoints, their pets, their businesses and organizations, and so on.

Purpose

To determine a website's purpose, first look at its domain:

.gov for government

.com for commercial

.org for nonprofit

.edu for educational

.net for network

Although these domains may generally identify purpose, even educational sites have commercial purposes in recruiting students or encouraging financial donations by alumni. Thus, domain type alone does not limit a website's function.

Ask yourself, "What does this site want me to do or want to do for me?" Some possibilities include the following:

Buy a product

Support a cause through a particular action

Make a donation

Consume information or news

Seek entertainment

Content

Because a site's purpose will greatly affect its content, when you evaluate a site's reliability, consider these specifics:

Accuracy: How factual are the site's claims? What evidence is cited to support claims?

Objectivity: What viewpoints or affiliations with causes, positions, or political parties are evident? Does the site display advertising or links to organizations that support the authors or content?

Credibility: Who is the site's author or sponsoring organization? How might this personal identity or group affiliation impact the accuracy and the objectivity of the site's content? What contact information does the site provide?

Currency: Does the site possess a "last updated" date? Do the quality of information and design suggest a frequently updated page? Are links to other relevant information up to date?

Format

Often our understanding of what makes a website good or bad (see the "Technological Beginnings" section later in this chapter) is instinctive. Certain colors, fonts, images, and layouts are more appealing than others, and certain organizational and navigation structures make for easier online usability. To more formally evaluate websites, consider the following:

Navigation: How does the site provide navigation from one page to another? Navigation can be accomplished by textual links, buttons and bars, as well as menus and placement (consider side, top, or bottom navigation).

Design: How does the site provide a sense of visual theme and design? What dominant images, color schemes, and fonts help create an organizational image or personal identity?

Text: How does the site avoid making the user scroll down or across the page? Does it offer internal links, or does it limit the text on individual pages?

Readability: Do the contrasting backgrounds and text color make the information readable? What might improve this relationship?

Visuals: Where and how are visuals placed on the page? Are they aligned with text? How are the visuals sized in relation to the text?

Levels of Interaction: What options exist for interaction? Does the site provide email links or use scripts and codes that permit chat or submission of data in forms?

Media:	If video and other forms of multimedia are present, does the site provide information about the players and plug-ins necessary to access these features?
Links:	How relevant are the links that are provided? Do they connect to useful, related sources that define, exemplify, or provide further background?

 COMMUNITIES Find a website for each type of domain—.com, .gov, and so on. What similarities and differences in language, tone, content, and design features do you notice about each?

TECHNOLOGY TIP Managing Your Information

A common practice in writing computer instructions or documentation includes the use of screen captures, which are pictures of windows on your computer or the entire desktop. Although you need specific programs to assist in creating high-quality images of your computer screen, you can create basic screen captures such as the ones included in this chapter by using built-in features on a Mac or a PC.

On a Mac, hold down SHIFT, COMMAND, and the number 3 on your keyboard to automatically take a picture of your entire screen. Press SHIFT + COMMAND + 4 to select a specific window or section of your screen by clicking and dragging. On a PC, screen captures are just as easy to create. You can use the PRINT SCREEN key on your keyboard, which just like the Mac OPTION key, selects the entire screen. To "capture" a specific window, press ALT + PRINT SCREEN. Once you capture the screen shot you want, simply "paste" the capture (on a PC) or use the Insert menu (on a Mac) to insert the image directly from the file that is created through the screen capture process.

 TECHNOLOGIES Locate one research database related to your major. Write a brief set of instructions on how to use this resource. Consider your audience to be students in your area who might not know about this resource or how to access and utilize it. Rely on screen captures to guide your readers.

Readings

The readings in this chapter ask what it means to be literate and knowledgeable. They also consider the possibilities and constraints of various tools in our literacy practices. Even in ancient Greece, as Western culture was shifting from oral to written literacy, there were concerns about the impact of writing upon critical thinking and knowledge development, as we see in Plato's *Phaedrus*. Nicholas Carr's "Is Google Making Us Stupid" and Christine Rosen's "People of the Screen" suggest that in the age of the Internet, tools like Google are similarly impacting our ability to engage in deep reading and deep thinking. Still others, such as Marc Prensky in "Digital Natives, Digital Immigrants" and Kathleen Tyner in "Splintered Literacies," argue that the age of information requires a broadened definition of literacy to account for the multiple media forms we encounter each day. These varying perspectives are also complemented by resources from the English CourseMate for this text website, including the Room for Debate series from the *New York Times*, which addresses the Cushing Academy's 2010 decision to get rid of hard copies of its books in favor of a completely digital library. Ultimately, we encourage you to consider your own definitions of literacy based on your current habits in accessing and researching information online and offline and how this chapter's definitions of literacy align with your literate activities.

● Plato

Excerpts from the *Phaedrus*

Plato, the classical Greek philosopher who lived from 427 to 347 BC, helped shape Western thought and is read across the disciplines. With more than thirty dialogues to his credit, he was the student of Socrates and the teacher of Aristotle. He founded the Academy, the first institution of higher learning in the Western world. A proponent of dialectic, a way of establishing truth from reasoned oral exchange, Plato nevertheless committed his dialectical treatises, such as the *Phaedrus*, to written form. In this excerpt from the *Phaedrus*, Socrates dialogues with the younger Phaedrus about the limitations of writing and its presumed impact on memory and truth seeking. The full text of the dialog is accessible through a link on the English CourseMate for this text.

Socrates: At the Egyptian city of Naucratis, there was a famous old god, whose name was Theuth; the bird which is called the Ibis is sacred to him, and he was the inventor of many arts, such as arithmetic and calculation and geometry and astronomy and

Plato, "Phaedrus," in Patricia Bizzell and Bruce Herzberg, eds. *The Rhetorical Tradition: Readings from Classical Times to the Present*. Boston: Bedford/St. Martin's, 2001.

Figure 2.5 Statues of Plato and Aristotle outside Academy of Athens, Greece

draughts and dice, but his great discovery was the use of letters. Now in those days the god Thamus was the king of the whole country of Egypt; and he dwelt in that great city of Upper Egypt which the Hellenes call Egyptian Thebes, and the god himself is called by them Ammon. To him came Theuth and showed his inventions, desiring that the other Egyptians might be allowed to have the benefit of them; he enumerated them, and Thamus enquired about their several uses, and praised some of them and censured others, as he approved or disapproved of them. It would take a long time to repeat all that Thamus said to Theuth in praise or blame of the various arts. But when they came to letters, This, said Theuth, will make the Egyptians wiser and give them better memories; it is a specific both for the memory and for the wit. Thamus replied: O most ingenious Theuth, the parent or inventor of an art is not always the best judge of the utility or inutility of his own inventions to the users of them. And in this instance, you who are the father of letters, from a paternal love of your own children have been led to attribute to them a quality which they cannot have; for this discovery of yours will create forgetfulness in the learners' souls, because they will not use their memories; they will trust to the external written characters and not remember of themselves. The specific which you have discovered is an aid not to memory, but to reminiscence, and you give your disciples

Phaedrus: not truth, but only the semblance of truth; they will be hearers of many things and will have learned nothing; they will appear to be omniscient and will generally know nothing; they will be tiresome company, having the show of wisdom without the reality.

Phaedrus: Yes, Socrates, you can easily invent tales of Egypt, or of any other country.

Socrates: There was a tradition in the temple of Dodona that oaks first gave prophetic utterances. The men of old, unlike in their simplicity to young philosophy, deemed that if they heard the truth even from "oak or rock," it was enough for them; whereas you seem to consider not whether a thing is or is not true, but who the speaker is and from what country the tale comes.

Phaedrus: I acknowledge the justice of your rebuke; and I think that the Theban is right in his view about letters.

Socrates: He would be a very simple person, and quite a stranger to the oracles of Thamus or Ammon, who should leave in writing or receive in writing any art under the idea that the written word would be intelligible or certain; or who deemed that writing was at all better than knowledge and recollection of the same matters?

Phaedrus: That is most true.

Socrates: I cannot help feeling, Phaedrus, that writing is unfortunately like painting; for the creations of the painter have the attitude of life, and yet if you ask them a question they preserve a solemn silence. And the same may be said of speeches. You would imagine that they had intelligence, but if you want to know anything and put a question to one of them, the speaker always gives one unvarying answer. And when they have been once written down they are tumbled about anywhere among those who may or may not understand them, and know not to whom they should reply, to whom not: and, if they are maltreated or abused, they have no parent to protect them; and they cannot protect or defend themselves.

Phaedrus: That again is most true.

Socrates: Is there not another kind of word or speech far better than this, and having far greater power—a son of the same family, but lawfully begotten?

Phaedrus: Whom do you mean, and what is his origin?

Socrates: I mean an intelligent word graven in the soul of the learner, which can defend itself, and knows when to speak and when to be silent.

Phaedrus: You mean the living word of knowledge which has a soul, and of which the written word is properly no more than an image?

Socrates: Yes, of course that is what I mean. And now may I be allowed to ask you a question: Would a husbandman, who is a man of sense, take the seeds, which he values and which he wishes to bear fruit, and in sober seriousness plant them during the heat of summer, in some garden of Adonis, that he may rejoice when he sees them in eight days appearing in beauty? At least he would do so, if at all, only for the sake of amusement and pastime. But when he is in earnest he sows in fitting soil, and practises husbandry, and is satisfied if in eight months the seeds which he has sown arrive at perfection?

Phaedrus: Yes, Socrates, that will be his way when he is in earnest; he will do the other, as you say, only in play.

Socrates: And can we suppose that he who knows the just and good and honourable has less understanding, than the husbandman, about his own seeds?

Phaedrus: Certainly not.

Socrates: Then he will not seriously incline to "write" his thoughts "in water" with pen and ink, sowing words which can neither speak for themselves nor teach the truth adequately to others?

Phaedrus: No, that is not likely.

Socrates: No, that is not likely—in the garden of letters he will sow and plant, but only for the sake of recreation and amusement; he will write them down as memorials to be treasured against the forgetfulness of old age, by himself, or by any other old man who is treading the same path. He will rejoice in beholding their tender growth; and while others are refreshing their souls with banqueting and the like, this will be the pastime in which his days are spent.

Phaedrus: A pastime, Socrates, as noble as the other is ignoble, the pastime of a man who can be amused by serious talk, and can discourse merrily about justice and the like.

Socrates: True, Phaedrus. But nobler far is the serious pursuit of the dialectician, who, finding a congenial soul, by the help of science sows and plants therein words which are able to help themselves and him who planted them, and are not unfruitful, but have in them a seed which others brought up in different soils render immortal, making the possessors of it happy to the utmost extent of human happiness.

Phaedrus: Far nobler, certainly.

Socrates: And now, Phaedrus, having agreed upon the premises we may decide about the conclusion.

Phaedrus: About what conclusion?

Socrates: About Lysias, whom we censured, and his art of writing, and his discourses, and the rhetorical skill or want of skill which was shown in them—these are the questions which we sought to determine, and they brought us to this point. And I think that we are now pretty well informed about the nature of art and its opposite.

Phaedrus: Yes, I think with you; but I wish that you would repeat what was said.

Socrates: Until a man knows the truth of the several particulars of which he is writing or speaking, and is able to define them as they are, and having defined them again to divide them until they can be no longer divided, and until in like manner he is able to discern the nature of the soul, and discover the different modes of discourse which are adapted to different natures, and to arrange and dispose them in such a way that the simple form of speech may be addressed to the simpler nature, and the complex and composite to the more complex nature—until he has accomplished all this, he will be unable to handle arguments according to rules of art, as far as their nature allows them to be subjected to art, either for the purpose of teaching or persuading;—such is the view which is implied in the whole preceding argument.

Phaedrus: Yes, that was our view, certainly.

Socrates: Secondly, as to the censure which was passed on the speaking or writing of discourses, and how they might be rightly or wrongly censured—did not our previous argument show—?

Phaedrus: Show what?

Socrates: That whether Lysias or any other writer that ever was or will be, whether private man or statesman, proposes laws and so becomes the author of a political treatise, fancying that there is any great certainty and clearness in his performance, the fact of his so writing is only a disgrace to him, whatever men may say. For not to know the nature of justice and injustice, and good and evil, and not to be able to distinguish the dream from the reality, cannot in truth be otherwise than disgraceful to him, even though he have the applause of the whole world.

Phaedrus: Certainly.

Socrates: But he who thinks that in the written word there is necessarily much which is not serious, and that neither poetry nor prose, spoken or written, is of any great value, if, like the compositions of the rhapsodes, they are only recited in order to be believed, and not with any view to criticism or instruction; and who thinks that even the best of writings are but a reminiscence of what we know, and that only in principles of justice and goodness and nobility taught and communicated orally for the sake of instruction and graven in the soul, which is the true way of writing, is there clearness and perfection and seriousness, and that such principles are a man's own and his legitimate offspring;—being, in the first place, the word which he finds in his own bosom; secondly, the brethren and descendants and relations of his idea which have been duly implanted by him in the souls of others;—and who cares for them and no others—this is the right sort of man; and you and I, Phaedrus, would pray that we may become like him.

Phaedrus: That is most assuredly my desire and prayer.

Socrates: And now the play is played out; and of rhetoric enough. Go and tell Lysias that to the fountain and school of the Nymphs we went down, and were bidden by them to convey a message to him and to other composers of speeches—to Homer and other writers of poems, whether set to music or not; and to Solon and others who have composed writings in the form of political discourses which they would term laws—to all of them we are to say that if their compositions are based on knowledge of the truth, and they can defend or prove them, when they are put to the test, by spoken arguments, which leave their writings poor in comparison of them, then they are to be called, not only poets, orators, legislators, but are worthy of a higher name, befitting the serious pursuit of their life.

Phaedrus: What name would you assign to them?

Socrates: Wise, I may not call them; for that is a great name which belongs to God alone,—lovers of wisdom or philosophers is their modest and befitting title.

Phaedrus: Very suitable.

Socrates: And he who cannot rise above his own compilations and compositions, which he has been long patching and piecing, adding some and taking away some, may be justly called poet or speech-maker or law-maker.

Phaedrus: Certainly.

Socrates: Now go and tell this to your companion.

Phaedrus: But there is also a friend of yours who ought not to be forgotten.

Socrates: Who is he?

Phaedrus: Isocrates the fair:—What message will you send to him, and how shall we describe him?

Socrates: Isocrates is still young, Phaedrus; but I am willing to hazard a prophecy concerning him.

Phaedrus: What would you prophesy?

Socrates: I think that he has a genius which soars above the orations of Lysias, and that his character is cast in a finer mould. My impression of him is that he will marvelously improve as he grows older, and that all former rhetoricians will be as children in comparison of him. And I believe that he will not be satisfied with rhetoric, but that there is in him a divine inspiration which will lead him to things higher still. For he has an element of philosophy in his nature. This is the message of the gods dwelling in this place, and which I will myself deliver to Isocrates, who is my delight; and do you give the other to Lysias, who is yours.

Phaedrus: I will; and now as the heat is abated let us depart.

Socrates: Should we not offer up a prayer first of all to the local deities?

Phaedrus: By all means.

Socrates: Beloved Pan, and all ye other gods who haunt this place, give me beauty in the inward soul; and may the outward and inward man be at one. May I reckon the wise to be the wealthy, and may I have such a quantity of gold as a temperate man and he only can bear and carry.—Anything more? The prayer, I think, is enough for me.

Phaedrus: Ask the same for me, for friends should have all things in common.

Socrates: Let us go.

READING REACTIONS

1. What point does Socrates attempt to make in his tale of Theuth and Thamus?

2. What examples does Socrates use to make his case? Are these examples effective?

3. What is the relationship between writing and knowledge? According to Socrates, how is writing like painting?

4. Research the classical distinction between rhetoric and dialectic. How is the term "rhetoric" used today and in what context?

5. The exchange between Socrates and Phaedrus represents a teaching approach referred to as the "Socratic method." Explain this method and consider whether this approach or alternative teaching styles mesh with your own learning styles or your expectations of teaching and learning.

6. Socrates represents an early classical view of writing when compared to speaking. How does this view hold up today? Can you point to examples in your academic experience where either speaking or writing is preferable? Is it an either/or situation, or can both work well in some contexts?

7. How is Plato's argument about writing similar to others' arguments about the Internet?

● Nicholas Carr

Is Google Making Us Stupid?

A graduate of both Dartmouth and Harvard, Nicholas Carr is the author of *The Shallows: What the Internet Is Doing to Our Brains*, a *New York Times* best seller and a nominee for the Pulitzer Prize. He has written for the *New York Times, The Wall Street Journal,* and *Wired.* In his widely anthologized essay, "Is Google Making Us Stupid?," which appeared in *The Atlantic Monthly* in 2008, Carr laments the supposed loss of "deep reading," claiming that "Once I was a scuba diver in the sea of words. Now I zip along the surface like a guy on a Jet Ski." He currently has a website at http://www.nicholasgcarr.com.

"Dave, stop. Stop, will you? Stop, Dave. Will you stop, Dave?" So the super-computer HAL pleads with the implacable astronaut Dave Bowman in a famous and weirdly poignant scene toward the end of Stanley Kubrick's *2001: A Space Odyssey.* Bowman, having nearly been sent to a deep-space death by the malfunctioning machine, is calmly, coldly disconnecting the memory circuits that control its artificial brain. "Dave, my mind is going," HAL says, forlornly. "I can feel it. I can feel it."

I can feel it, too. Over the past few years I've had an uncomfortable sense that someone, or something, has been tinkering with my brain, remapping the neural circuitry, reprogramming the memory. My mind isn't going—so far as I can tell—but it's changing. I'm not thinking the way I used to think. I can feel it most strongly when I'm reading. Immersing myself in a book or a lengthy article used to be easy. My mind would get caught up in the narrative or the turns of the argument, and I'd spend hours strolling through long stretches of prose. That's rarely the case anymore. Now my concentration often starts to drift after two or three pages. I get fidgety, lose the thread, begin looking for something else to do. I feel as if I'm always dragging my wayward brain back to the text. The deep reading that used to come naturally has become a struggle.

I think I know what's going on. For more than a decade now, I've been spending a lot of time online, searching and surfing and sometimes adding to the great databases of the Internet. The Web has been a godsend to me as a writer. Research that once required days in the stacks or periodical rooms of libraries can now be done in minutes. A few Google searches, some quick clicks on hyperlinks, and I've got the telltale fact or pithy quote I was after. Even when I'm not working, I'm as likely as not to be foraging in the Web's info-thickets—reading and writing e-mails, scanning headlines and blog posts, watching videos and listening to podcasts, or just tripping from link to link to link. (Unlike footnotes, to which they're sometimes likened, hyperlinks don't merely point to related works; they propel you toward them.)

For me, as for others, the Net is becoming a universal medium, the conduit for most of the information that flows through my eyes and ears and into my mind. The advantages of having immediate access to such an incredibly rich store of information are many, and they've been widely described and duly applauded. "The perfect recall of silicon memory," *Wired*'s Clive Thompson has written, "can be an enormous boon to thinking." But that boon comes at a price. As the media theorist Marshall McLuhan pointed out in the 1960s, media are not just passive channels of information. They supply the stuff of thought, but they also shape the process of thought. And what the Net seems to be doing is chipping away my capacity for concentration and contemplation. My mind now expects to take in information the way the Net distributes it: in a swiftly moving stream of particles. Once I was a scuba diver in the sea of words. Now I zip along the surface like a guy on a Jet Ski.

I'm not the only one. When I mention my troubles with reading to friends and acquaintances—literary types, most of them—many say they're having similar experiences. The more they use the Web, the more they have to fight to stay focused on long pieces of writing. Some of the bloggers I follow have also begun mentioning the phenomenon. Scott Karp, who writes a blog about online media, recently confessed that he has stopped reading books altogether. "I was a lit major in college, and used to be [a] voracious book reader," he wrote. "What happened?" He speculates on the answer: "What if I do all my reading on the web not so much because the way I read has changed, i.e. I'm just seeking convenience, but because the way I THINK has changed?"

Bruce Friedman, who blogs regularly about the use of computers in medicine, also has described how the Internet has altered his mental habits. "I now have almost totally lost the ability to read and absorb a longish article on the web or in print," he wrote earlier this year. A pathologist who has long been on the faculty of the University of Michigan Medical School, Friedman elaborated on his comment in a telephone conversation with me. His thinking, he said, has taken on a "staccato" quality, reflecting the way he quickly scans short passages of text from many sources online. "I can't read *War and Peace* anymore," he admitted. "I've lost the ability to do that. Even a blog post of more than three or four paragraphs is too much to absorb. I skim it."

Anecdotes alone don't prove much. And we still await the long-term neurological and psychological experiments that will provide a definitive picture of how Internet use affects cognition. But a recently published study of online research habits, conducted by scholars from University College London, suggests that we may well be in the midst of a sea change in the way we read and think. As part of the five-year research program, the scholars examined computer logs documenting the behavior of visitors to two popular research sites, one operated by the British Library and one by a U.K. educational consortium, that provide access to journal articles, e-books, and other sources of written information. They found that people using the sites exhibited "a form of skimming activity," hopping from one source to another and rarely returning to any source they'd already visited. They typically read no more than one or two pages of an article or book before they would "bounce" out to another site. Sometimes they'd save a long article, but there's no evidence that they ever went back and actually read it. The authors of the study report:

> It is clear that users are not reading online in the traditional sense; indeed there are signs that new forms of "reading" are emerging as users "power browse" horizontally through titles, contents pages and abstracts going for quick wins. It almost seems that they go online to avoid reading in the traditional sense.

Thanks to the ubiquity of text on the Internet, not to mention the popularity of text-messaging on cell phones, we may well be reading more today than we did in the 1970s or 1980s, when television was our medium of choice. But it's a different kind of reading, and behind it lies a different kind of thinking—perhaps even a new sense of the self. "We are not only *what* we read," says Maryanne Wolf, a developmental psychologist at Tufts University and the author of *Proust and the Squid: The Story and Science of the Reading Brain*. "We are *how* we read." Wolf worries that the style of reading promoted by the Net, a style that puts "efficiency" and "immediacy" above all else, may be weakening our capacity for the kind of deep reading that emerged when an earlier technology, the printing press, made long and complex works of prose commonplace. When we read online, she says, we tend to become "mere decoders of information." Our ability to interpret text, to make the rich mental connections that form when we read deeply and without distraction, remains largely disengaged.

Reading, explains Wolf, is not an instinctive skill for human beings. It's not etched into our genes the way speech is. We have to teach our minds how to translate the symbolic characters we see into the language we understand. And the media or other technologies we use in learning and practicing the craft of reading play an important part in shaping the neural circuits inside our brains. Experiments demonstrate that readers of ideograms, such as the Chinese, develop a mental circuitry for reading that is very different from the circuitry found in those of us whose written language employs an alphabet. The variations extend across many regions of the brain, including those that govern such essential cognitive functions as memory and the interpretation of visual and auditory stimuli. We can expect as well that the circuits woven by our use of the Net will be different from those woven by our reading of books and other printed works.

Sometime in 1882, Friedrich Nietzsche bought a typewriter—a Malling-Hansen Writing Ball, to be precise. His vision was failing, and keeping his eyes focused on a page had become exhausting and painful, often bringing on crushing headaches. He had been forced to curtail his writing, and he feared that he would soon have to give it up. The typewriter rescued him, at least for a time. Once he had mastered touch-typing, he was able to write with his eyes closed, using only the tips of his fingers. Words could once again flow from his mind to the page.

But the machine had a subtler effect on his work. One of Nietzsche's friends, a composer, noticed a change in the style of his writing. His already terse prose had become even tighter, more telegraphic. "Perhaps you will through this instrument even take to a new idiom," the friend wrote in a letter, noting that, in his own work, his "'thoughts' in music and language often depend on the quality of pen and paper."

"You are right," Nietzsche replied, "our writing equipment takes part in the forming of our thoughts." Under the sway of the machine, writes the German media scholar Friedrich A. Kittler, Nietzsche's prose "changed from arguments to aphorisms, from thoughts to puns, from rhetoric to telegram style."

The human brain is almost infinitely malleable. People used to think that our mental meshwork, the dense connections formed among the 100 billion or so neurons inside our skulls, was largely fixed by the time we reached adulthood. But brain researchers have discovered that that's not the case. James Olds, a professor of neuroscience who directs the Krasnow Institute for Advanced Study at George Mason University, says that even the adult mind "is very plastic." Nerve cells routinely break old connections and form new ones. "The brain," according to Olds, "has the ability to reprogram itself on the fly, altering the way it functions."

As we use what the sociologist Daniel Bell has called our "intellectual technologies"—the tools that extend our mental rather than our physical capacities—we inevitably begin to take on the qualities of those technologies. The mechanical clock, which came into common use in the 14th century, provides a compelling example. In *Technics and Civilization*, the historian and cultural critic Lewis Mumford described how the clock "disassociated time from human events and helped create the belief in an independent world of mathematically measurable sequences." The "abstract framework of divided time" became "the point of reference for both action and thought."

The clock's methodical ticking helped bring into being the scientific mind and the scientific man. But it also took something away. As the late MIT computer scientist Joseph Weizenbaum observed in his 1976 book, *Computer Power and Human Reason: From Judgment to Calculation*, the conception of the world that emerged from the widespread use of timekeeping instruments "remains an impoverished version of the older one, for it rests on a rejection of those direct experiences that formed the basis for, and indeed constituted, the old reality." In deciding when to eat, to work, to sleep, to rise, we stopped listening to our senses and started obeying the clock.

The process of adapting to new intellectual technologies is reflected in the changing metaphors we use to explain ourselves to ourselves. When the mechanical clock arrived, people began thinking of their brains as operating "like clockwork." Today, in the age of software, we have come to think of them as operating "like computers." But the changes, neuroscience tells us, go much deeper than metaphor. Thanks to our brain's plasticity, the adaptation occurs also at a biological level.

The Internet promises to have particularly far-reaching effects on cognition. In a paper published in 1936, the British mathematician Alan Turing proved that a digital computer, which at the time existed only as a theoretical machine, could be programmed to perform the function of any other information-processing device. And that's what we're seeing today. The Internet, an immeasurably powerful computing system, is subsuming most of our other intellectual technologies. It's becoming our map and our clock, our printing press and our typewriter, our calculator and our telephone, and our radio and TV.

When the Net absorbs a medium, that medium is re-created in the Net's image. It injects the medium's content with hyperlinks, blinking ads, and other digital gewgaws, and it surrounds the content with the content of all the other media it has absorbed. A new e-mail message, for instance, may announce its arrival as we're glancing over the latest headlines at a newspaper's site. The result is to scatter our attention and diffuse our concentration.

The Net's influence doesn't end at the edges of a computer screen, either. As people's minds become attuned to the crazy quilt of Internet media, traditional media have to adapt to the audience's new expectations. Television programs add text crawls and pop-up ads, and magazines and newspapers shorten their articles, introduce capsule summaries, and crowd their pages with easy-to-browse info-snippets. When, in March of this year, *The New York Times* decided to devote the second and third pages of every edition to article abstracts, its design director, Tom Bodkin, explained that the "shortcuts" would give harried readers a quick "taste" of the day's news, sparing them the "less efficient" method of actually turning the pages and reading the articles. Old media have little choice but to play by the new-media rules.

Never has a communications system played so many roles in our lives—or exerted such broad influence over our thoughts—as the Internet does today. Yet, for all that's been written about the Net, there's been little consideration of how, exactly, it's reprogramming us. The Net's intellectual ethic remains obscure.

About the same time that Nietzsche started using his typewriter, an earnest young man named Frederick Winslow Taylor carried a stopwatch into the Midvale Steel plant in Philadelphia and began a historic series of experiments aimed at improving the efficiency of the plant's machinists. With the approval of Midvale's owners, he recruited a group of factory hands, set them to work on various metalworking machines, and recorded and timed their every movement as well as the operations of the machines. By breaking down every job into a sequence of small, discrete steps and then testing different ways of performing each one, Taylor created a set of precise instructions—an "algorithm," we might say today—for how each worker should work. Midvale's employees grumbled about the strict new regime, claiming that it turned them into little more than automatons, but the factory's productivity soared.

More than a hundred years after the invention of the steam engine, the Industrial Revolution had at last found its philosophy and its philosopher. Taylor's tight industrial choreography—his "system," as he liked to call it— was embraced by manufacturers throughout the country and, in time, around the world. Seeking maximum speed, maximum efficiency, and maximum output, factory owners used time-and-motion studies to organize their work and configure the jobs of their workers. The goal, as Taylor defined it in his celebrated 1911 treatise, *The Principles of Scientific Management*, was to identify and adopt, for every job, the "one best method" of work and thereby to effect "the gradual substitution of science for rule of thumb throughout the mechanic arts." Once his system was applied to all acts of manual labor, Taylor assured his followers, it would bring about a restructuring not only of industry but of society, creating a utopia of perfect efficiency. "In the past the man has been first," he declared; "in the future the system must be first."

Taylor's system is still very much with us; it remains the ethic of industrial manufacturing. And now, thanks to the growing power that computer engineers and software coders wield over our intellectual lives, Taylor's ethic is beginning to govern the realm of the mind as well. The Internet is a machine designed for the efficient and automated collection, transmission, and manipulation of information, and its legions of programmers are intent on finding the "one best method"—the perfect algorithm—to carry out every mental movement of what we've come to describe as "knowledge work."

Google's headquarters, in Mountain View, California—the Googleplex— is the Internet's high church, and the religion practiced inside its walls is Taylorism. Google, says its chief executive, Eric Schmidt, is "a company that's founded around the science of measurement," and it is striving to "systematize everything" it does. Drawing on the terabytes of behavioral data it collects through its search engine and other sites, it carries out thousands of experiments a day, according to the *Harvard Business Review*, and it uses the results to refine the algorithms that increasingly control how people find information and extract meaning from it. What Taylor did for the work of the hand, Google is doing for the work of the mind.

The company has declared that its mission is "to organize the world's information and make it universally accessible and useful." It seeks to develop "the perfect search engine," which it defines as something that "understands exactly what you mean and gives you back exactly what you want." In Google's view, information is a kind of commodity, a utilitarian resource that can be mined and processed with industrial efficiency. The more pieces of information we can "access" and the faster we can extract their gist, the more productive we become as thinkers.

Where does it end? Sergey Brin and Larry Page, the gifted young men who founded Google while pursuing doctoral degrees in computer science at Stanford, speak frequently of their desire to turn their search engine into an artificial intelligence, a HAL-like machine that might be connected directly to our brains. "The ultimate search engine is something as smart as people—or smarter," Page said in a speech a few years back. "For us, working on search is a way to work on artificial intelligence." In a 2004 interview with *Newsweek*, Brin said, "Certainly if you had all the world's information directly attached to your brain, or an artificial brain that was smarter than your brain, you'd be better off." Last year, Page told a convention of scientists that Google is "really trying to build artificial intelligence and to do it on a large scale."

Such an ambition is a natural one, even an admirable one, for a pair of math whizzes with vast quantities of cash at their disposal and a small army of computer scientists in their employ. A fundamentally scientific enterprise, Google is motivated by a desire to use technology, in Eric Schmidt's words, "to solve problems that have never been solved before," and artificial intelligence is the hardest problem out there. Why wouldn't Brin and Page want to be the ones to crack it?

Still, their easy assumption that we'd all "be better off" if our brains were supplemented, or even replaced, by an artificial intelligence is unsettling. It suggests a belief that intelligence is the output of a mechanical process, a series of discrete steps that can be isolated, measured, and optimized. In Google's world, the world we enter when we go online, there's little place for the fuzziness of contemplation. Ambiguity is not an opening for insight but a bug to be fixed. The human brain is just an outdated computer that needs a faster processor and a bigger hard drive.

The idea that our minds should operate as high-speed data-processing machines is not only built into the workings of the Internet, it is the network's reigning business model as well. The faster we surf across the Web—the more links we click and pages we view—the more opportunities Google and other companies gain to collect information about us and to feed us advertisements. Most of the proprietors of the commercial Internet have a financial stake in collecting the crumbs of data we leave behind as we flit from link to link—the more crumbs, the better. The last thing these companies want is to encourage leisurely reading or slow, concentrated thought. It's in their economic interest to drive us to distraction.

Maybe I'm just a worrywart. Just as there's a tendency to glorify technological progress, there's a countertendency to expect the worst of every new tool or machine. In Plato's Phaedrus, Socrates bemoaned the development of writing. He feared that, as people came to rely on the written word as a substitute for the knowledge they used to carry inside their heads, they would, in the words of one of the dialogue's characters, "cease to exercise their memory and become forgetful." And because they would be able to "receive a quantity of information without proper instruction," they would "be thought very knowledgeable when they are for the most part quite ignorant." They would be "filled with the conceit of wisdom instead of real wisdom." Socrates wasn't wrong—the new technology did often have the effects he feared—but he was shortsighted. He couldn't foresee the many ways that writing and reading would serve to spread information, spur fresh ideas, and expand human knowledge (if not wisdom).

The arrival of Gutenberg's printing press, in the 15th century, set off another round of teeth gnashing. The Italian humanist Hieronimo Squarciafico worried that the easy availability of books would lead to intellectual laziness, making men "less studious" and weakening their minds. Others argued that cheaply printed books and broadsheets would undermine religious authority, demean the work of scholars and scribes, and spread sedition and debauchery. As New York University professor Clay Shirky notes, "Most of the arguments made against the printing press were correct, even prescient." But, again, the doomsayers were unable to imagine the myriad blessings that the printed word would deliver.

So, yes, you should be skeptical of my skepticism. Perhaps those who dismiss critics of the Internet as Luddites or nostalgists will be proved correct, and from our hyperactive, data-stoked minds will spring a golden age of intellectual discovery and universal wisdom. Then again, the Net isn't the alphabet, and although it may replace the printing press, it produces something altogether different. The kind of deep reading that a sequence of printed pages promotes is valuable not just for the knowledge we acquire from the author's words but for the intellectual vibrations those words set off within our own minds. In the quiet spaces opened up by the sustained, undistracted reading of a book, or by any other act of contemplation, for that matter, we make our own associations, draw our own inferences and analogies, foster our own ideas. Deep reading, as Maryanne Wolf argues, is indistinguishable from deep thinking.

If we lose those quiet spaces, or fill them up with "content," we will sacrifice something important not only in our selves but in our culture. In a recent essay, the playwright Richard Foreman eloquently described what's at stake:

> I come from a tradition of Western culture, in which the ideal (my ideal) was the complex, dense and "cathedral-like" structure of the highly educated and articulate personality—a man or woman who carried inside themselves a personally constructed and unique version of the entire heritage of the West. [But now] I see within us all (myself included) the replacement of complex inner density with a new kind of self—evolving under the pressure of information overload and the technology of the "instantly available."

As we are drained of our "inner repertory of dense cultural inheritance," Foreman concluded, we risk turning into "'pancake people'—spread wide and thin as we connect with that vast network of information accessed by the mere touch of a button."

I'm haunted by that scene in *2001*. What makes it so poignant, and so weird, is the computer's emotional response to the disassembly of its mind: its despair as one circuit after another goes dark, its childlike pleading with the astronaut— "I can feel it. I can feel it. I'm afraid"—and its final reversion to what can only be called a state of innocence. HAL's outpouring of feeling contrasts with the emotionlessness that characterizes the human figures in the film, who go about their business with an almost robotic efficiency. Their thoughts and actions feel scripted, as if they're following the steps of an algorithm. In the world of *2001*, people have become so machinelike that the most human character turns out to be a machine. That's the essence of Kubrick's dark prophecy: as we come to rely on computers to mediate our understanding of the world, it is our own intelligence that flattens into artificial intelligence.

READING REACTIONS

1. According to Carr, how is the Internet impacting our reading and thinking processes? What is happening to our brains?

2. What types of evidence does Carr use to support his argument? Which set of evidence has the most credibility for various audiences?

3. Why does Carr focus on Google? What difference would it have made if he had chosen another tool?

4. According to Carr, how is older media influenced by newer media?

5. Carr uses the term "Luddite." Who were Luddites, and why is this term important to Carr's argument?

6. Is it natural to have a fear of various tools as their significance increases? Consider this question from a historical perspective by researching cultural reactions to a past era's technological innovations, such as the printing press, the radio, or the television.

● Marc Prensky

Digital Natives, Digital Immigrants

As his website marcprensky.com indicates, Marc Prensky is as "speaker, writer, consultant, and designer in the critical areas of education and learning." His concept of "Digital Natives" that he defines in his classic article "Digital Natives, Digital Immigrants" has become part of our current understanding of the gap between youth culture and literacies and academic practice. He has published multiple books on technology and learning, including his recent *Teaching the Digital Natives*.

It is amazing to me how in all the hoopla and debate these days about the decline of education in the US we ignore the most fundamental of its causes. *Our students have changed radically. Today's students are no longer the people our educational system was designed to teach.*

Today's students have not just changed *incrementally* from those of the past, nor simply changed their slang, clothes, body adornments, or styles, as has happened between generations previously. A really big *discontinuity* has taken place. One might even call it a "singularity"—an event which changes things so fundamentally that there is absolutely no going back. This so-called "singularity" is the arrival and rapid dissemination of digital technology in the last decades of the 20th century.

Today's students—K through college—represent the first generations to grow up with this new technology. They have spent their entire lives surrounded by and using computers, video games, digital music players, video cams, cell phones, and all the other toys and tools of the digital age. Today's average college grads have spent less than 5,000 hours of their lives reading, but over 10,000 hours playing video games (not to mention 20,000 hours watching TV). Computer games, email, the Internet, cell phones and instant messaging are integral parts of their lives.

It is now clear that as a result of this ubiquitous environment and the sheer volume of their interaction with it, today's students *think and process information fundamentally differently* from their predecessors. These differences go far further and deeper than most educators suspect or realize. "Different kinds of experiences lead to different brain structures," says Dr. Bruce D. Perry of

Baylor College of Medicine. As we shall see in the next installment, it is very likely that *our students' brains have physically changed*—and are different from ours—as a result of how they grew up. But whether or not this is *literally* true, we can say with certainty that their *thinking patterns* have changed. I will get to *how* they have changed in a minute.

What should we call these "new" students of today? Some refer to them as the N-[for Net]-gen or D-[for digital]-gen. But the most useful designation I have found for them is ***Digital Natives***. Our students today are all "native speakers" of the digital language of computers, video games and the Internet.

So what does that make the rest of us? Those of us who were not born into the digital world but have, at some later point in our lives, become fascinated by and adopted many or most aspects of the new technology are, and always will be compared to them, ***Digital Immigrants***.

The importance of the distinction is this: As Digital Immigrants learn— like all immigrants, some better than others—to adapt to their environment, they always retain, to some degree, their "accent," that is, their foot in the past. The "digital immigrant accent" can be seen in such things as turning to the Internet for information second rather than first, or in reading the manual for a program rather than assuming that the program itself will teach us to use it. Today's older folk were "socialized" differently from their kids, and are now in the process of learning a new language. And a language learned later in life, scientists tell us, goes into a different part of the brain.

There are hundreds of examples of the Digital Immigrant accent. They include printing out your email (or having your secretary print it out for you—an even "thicker" accent); needing to print out a document written on the computer in order to edit it (rather than just editing on the screen); and bringing people physically into your office to see an interesting web site (rather than just sending them the URL). I'm sure you can think of one or two examples of your own without much effort. My own favorite example is the "Did you get my email?" phone call. Those of us who are Digital Immigrants can, and should, laugh at ourselves and our "accent."

But this is not just a joke. It's very serious, because the single biggest problem facing education today is that ***our Digital Immigrant instructors, who speak an outdated language (that of the pre-digital age), are struggling to teach a population that speaks an entirely new language***.

This is obvious to the Digital Natives—school often feels pretty much as if we've brought in a population of heavily accented, unintelligible foreigners to lecture them. They often can't understand what the Immigrants are saying. What does "dial" a number mean, anyway?

Lest this perspective appear radical, rather than just descriptive, let me highlight some of the issues. Digital Natives are used to receiving information really fast. They like to parallel process and multi-task. They prefer their graphics *before* their text rather than the opposite. They prefer random access (like hypertext). They function best when networked. They thrive on instant gratification and frequent rewards. They prefer games to "serious" work. (Does any of this sound familiar?)

But Digital Immigrants typically have very little appreciation for these new skills that the Natives have acquired and perfected through years of interaction and practice. These skills are almost totally foreign to the Immigrants, who themselves learned—and so choose to teach—slowly, step-by-step, one thing at a time, individually, and above all, seriously. "My students just don't _____ like they used to," Digital Immigrant educators grouse. I can't get them to _____ or to _____. They have no appreciation for _____ or _____. (Fill in the blanks; there are a wide variety of choices.)

Digital Immigrants don't believe their students can learn successfully while watching TV or listening to music, because they (the Immigrants) can't. Of course not—they didn't practice this skill constantly for all of their formative years. Digital Immigrants think learning can't (or shouldn't) be fun. Why should they—they didn't spend their formative years learning with *Sesame Street*.

Unfortunately for our Digital Immigrant teachers, the people sitting in their classes grew up on the "twitch speed" of video games and MTV. They are used to the instantaneity of hypertext, downloaded music, phones in their pockets, a library on their laptops, beamed messages and instant messaging. They've been networked most or all of their lives. They have little patience for lectures, step-by-step logic, and "tell-test" instruction.

Digital Immigrant teachers assume that learners are the same as they have always been, and that the same methods that worked for the teachers when they were students will work for their students now. ***But that assumption is no longer valid.*** Today's learners are *different*. "Www.hungry.com" said a kindergarten student recently at lunchtime. "Every time I go to school I have to power down," complains a high-school student. Is it that Digital Natives *can't* pay attention, or that they *choose not to*? Often from the Natives' point of view their Digital Immigrant instructors make their education *not worth* paying attention to compared to everything else they experience—and then they blame them for not paying attention!

And, more and more, they won't take it. "I went to a highly ranked college where all the professors came from MIT," says a former student. "But all they did was read from their textbooks. I quit." In the giddy Internet bubble of a only a short while ago—when jobs were plentiful, especially in the areas where school offered little help—this was a real possibility. But the dot-com dropouts are now returning to school. They will have to confront once again the Immigrant/Native divide, and have even more trouble given their recent experiences. And that will make it even harder to teach them—and all the Digital Natives already in the system—in the traditional fashion.

So what should happen? Should the Digital Native students learn the old ways, or should their Digital Immigrant educators learn the new? Unfortunately, no matter how much the Immigrants may wish it, it is highly unlikely the Digital Natives will go backwards. In the first place, it may be impossible—their brains may already be different. It also flies in the face of everything we know about cultural migration. Kids born into any new culture learn the new language easily, and forcefully resist using the old. Smart adult immigrants *accept* that they don't know about their new world and take advantage of their kids to help them learn and integrate. Not-so-smart (or not-so-flexible) immigrants spend most of their time grousing about how good things were in the "old country."

So unless we want to just forget about educating Digital Natives until they grow up and do it themselves, we had better confront this issue. And in so doing we need to reconsider both our methodology and our content.

First, our methodology. Today's teachers have to learn to communicate in the language and style of their students. This *doesn't* mean changing the meaning of what is important, or of good thinking skills. But it *does* mean going faster, less step by step, more in parallel, with more random access, among other things. Educators might ask "But how do we teach logic in this fashion?" While it's not immediately clear, we do need to figure it out.

Second, our content. It seems to me that after the digital "singularity" there are now *two kinds* of content: "Legacy" content (to borrow the computer term for old systems) and "Future" content.

"Legacy" content includes reading, writing, arithmetic, logical thinking, understanding the writings and ideas of the past, etc.—all of our "traditional" curriculum. It is of course still important, but it is from a different era. Some of it (such as logical thinking) will continue to be important, but some (perhaps like Euclidean geometry) will become less so, as did Latin and Greek.

"Future" content is to a large extent, not surprisingly, digital and technological. But while it includes software, hardware, robotics, nanotechnology, genomics, etc. *it also includes the ethics, politics, sociology, languages and other things that go with them.* This "Future" content is extremely interesting to today's students. But how many Digital Immigrants are prepared to teach it? Someone once suggested to me that kids should only be allowed to use computers in school that they have built themselves. It's a brilliant idea that is very doable from the point of view of the students' capabilities. But who could teach it?

As educators, we need to be thinking about how to teach *both* Legacy and Future content in the language of the Digital Natives. The first involves a major translation and change of methodology; the second involves all that PLUS new content and thinking. It's not actually clear to me which is harder—"learning new stuff" or "learning new ways to do old stuff." I suspect it's the latter.

So we have to invent, but not necessarily from scratch. Adapting materials to the language of Digital Natives has already been done successfully. My own preference for teaching Digital Natives is to invent computer games to do the job, even for the most serious content. After all, it's an idiom with which most of them are totally familiar.

Not long ago a group of professors showed up at my company with new computer-aided design (CAD) software they had developed for mechanical engineers. Their creation was so much better than what people were currently using that they had assumed the entire engineering world would quickly adopt it. But instead they encountered a lot of resistance, due in large part to the product's extremely steep learning curve—the software contained hundreds of new buttons, options and approaches to master.

Their marketers, however, had a brilliant idea. Observing that the users of CAD software were almost exclusively male engineers between 20 and 30, they said "Why not make the learning into a video game!" So we invented and created for them a computer game in the "first person shooter" style of the consumer games *Doom* and *Quake*, called *The Monkey Wrench Conspiracy*. Its player becomes an intergalactic secret agent who has to save a space station from an attack by the evil Dr. Monkey Wrench. The only way to defeat him is to use the CAD software, which the learner must employ to build tools, fix weapons, and defeat booby traps. There is one hour of game time, plus 30 "tasks," which can take from 15 minutes to several hours depending on one's experience level.

Monkey Wrench has been phenomenally successful in getting young people interested in learning the software. It is widely used by engineering students around the world, with over 1 million copies of the game in print in several languages. But while the game was easy for my Digital Native staff to invent, creating the content turned out to be more difficult for the professors, who were used to teaching courses that started with "Lesson 1—the Interface." We asked them instead to create a series of graded tasks into which the skills to be learned were embedded. The professors had made 5–10 minute movies to illustrate key concepts; we asked them to cut them to under 30 seconds. The professors insisted that the learners do all the tasks in order; we asked them to allow random access. They wanted a slow academic pace, we wanted speed and urgency (we hired a Hollywood script writer to provide this). They wanted written instructions; we wanted computer movies. They wanted the traditional pedagogical language of "learning objectives," "mastery", etc. (e.g. "in this exercise you will learn . . ."); our goal was to completely eliminate any language that even *smacked* of education.

In the end the professors and their staff came through brilliantly, but because of the large mind-shift required it took them twice as long as we had expected. As they saw the approach working, though, the new "Digital Native" methodology became their model for more and more teaching—both in and out of games—and their development speed increased dramatically.

Similar rethinking needs to be applied to all subjects at all levels. Although most attempts at "edutainment" to date have essentially failed from both the education and entertainment perspective, we can—and will, I predict—do much better.

In math, for example, the debate must no longer be about *whether* to use calculators and computers—they are a part of the Digital Natives' world—but rather *how* to use them to instill the things that are useful to have internalized, from key skills and concepts to the multiplication tables. We should be focusing on "future math"—approximation, statistics, binary thinking.

In geography—which is all but ignored these days—there is no reason that a generation that can memorize over 100 Pokémon characters with all their characteristics, history and evolution can't learn the names, populations, capitals and relationships of all the 101 nations in the world. It just depends on how it is presented.

We need to invent Digital Native methodologies for *all* subjects, at *all* levels, using our students to guide us. The process has already begun—I know college professors inventing games for teaching subjects ranging from math to engineering to the Spanish Inquisition. We need to find ways of publicizing and spreading their successes.

A frequent objection I hear from Digital Immigrant educators is "this approach is great for *facts*, but it wouldn't work for "my subject.'" Nonsense. This is just rationalization and lack of imagination. In my talks I now include "thought experiments" where I invite professors and teachers to suggest a subject or topic, and I attempt—on the spot—to invent a game or other Digital Native method for learning it. *Classical philosophy?* Create a game in which the philosophers debate and the learners have to pick out what each would say. *The Holocaust?* Create a simulation where students role-play the meeting at Wannsee, or one where they can experience the *true* horror of the camps, as opposed to the films like *Schindler's List*. It's just dumb (and lazy) of educators—not to mention ineffective—to presume that (despite their traditions) the Digital Immigrant way is the *only* way to teach, and that the Digital Natives' "language" is not as capable as their own of encompassing any and every idea.

So if Digital Immigrant educators *really* want to reach Digital Natives— i.e. all their students—they will have to change. It's high time for them to stop their grousing, and as the Nike motto of the Digital Native generation says, "Just do it!" They *will* succeed in the long run—and their successes will come that much sooner if their administrators support them.

READING REACTIONS

1. What is the distinction between Digital Native and Digital Immigrant? Why do you think Prensky uses these particular terms? Prensky is writing in 2001; do you believe this distinction holds true today?

2. Who is the audience for Prensky's essay? How do you think they would react after reading it?

3. Prensky quotes a high school student as saying, "Every time I go to school I have to power down." How is technology used or not in your current courses?

4. What does Prensky mean by "Legacy" and "Future" content?

5. Prensky mentions gaming strategies as a way to engage learners, a topic covered in a later chapter. As an example, view the game "September 12," available through the English CourseMate for this text. How does this game's social theme engage and teach players?

6. What other types of tools you use might bridge the presumed gap between Digital Natives and Digital Immigrants?

7. Review Marc Prensky's website at http://marcprensky.com. What content and design strategies from his website might you use if you were developing your own digital presence on a blog or other online space?

TECHNOLOGY TIP   **Managing Your Information**

As we become increasingly dependent on the Web for accessing and storing information in our academic and social lives, we can use a range of online resources to manage and share that information across the tools we use to retrieve information, from our computers to our smart phones and back again. Delicious.com is a popular bookmarking site where you can save bookmarks, share them, and learn from others who are bookmarking information on topics that interest you. In addition, tools such as Evernote.com allow you to not only save and share websites but also to take notes in a text or audio form that can be accessed on computer or phone, regardless of the platform (Mac or PC).

● Christine Rosen

People of the Screen

Christine Rosen is a senior editor of *The New Atlantis*, a journal devoted to the political and ethical implications of technology in our larger culture. The author of the books *Preaching Eugenics: Religious Leaders and the American Eugenics Movement* and *My Fundamentalist Education*, Rosen's articles have appeared in such venues as *The New York Times Magazine*, *The Wall Street Journal*, and *The New England Journal of Medicine*. She received her Ph.D. from Emory University.

The book is modernity's quintessential technology—"a means of transportation through the space of experience, at the speed of a turning page," as the poet Joseph Brodsky put it. But now that the rustle of the book's turning page competes with the flicker of the screen's twitching pixel, we must consider the possibility that the book may not be around much longer. If it isn't—if we choose to replace the book—what will become of reading and the print culture it fostered? And what does it tell us about ourselves that we may soon retire this most remarkable, five-hundred-year-old technology?

We have already taken the first steps on our journey to a new form of literacy—"digital literacy." The fact that we must now distinguish among different types of literacy hints at how far we have moved away from traditional notions of reading. The screen mediates everything from our most private communications to our enjoyment of writing, drama, and games. It is the busiest port of entry for popular culture and requires navigation skills different from those that helped us master print literacy.

Enthusiasts and self-appointed experts assure us that this new digital literacy represents an advance for mankind; the book is evolving, progressing, improving, they argue, and every improvement demands an uneasy period of adjustment. Sophisticated forms of collaborative "information foraging" will replace solitary deep reading; the connected screen will replace the disconnected book. Perhaps, eons from now, our love affair with the printed word will be remembered as but a brief episode in our cultural maturation, and the book as a once-beloved technology we've outgrown.

But if enthusiasm for the new digital literacy runs high, it also runs to feverish extremes. Digital literacy's boosters are not unlike the people who were swept up in the multiculturalism fad of the 1980s and 1990s. Intent on encouraging a diversity of viewpoints, they initially argued for supplementing the canon so that it acknowledged the intellectual contributions of women and minorities. But like multiculturalism, which soon changed its focus from broadening the canon to eviscerating it by purging the contributions of "dead white males," digital literacy's advocates increasingly speak of replacing, rather than supplementing, print literacy. What is "reading" anyway, they ask, in a multimedia world like ours? We are increasingly distractible, impatient, and convenience-obsessed—and the paper book just can't keep up. Shouldn't we simply acknowledge that we are becoming people of the screen, not people of the book?

TO READ OR NOT TO READ

Every technology is both an expression of a culture and a potential transformer of it. In bestowing the power of uniformity, preservation, and replication, the printing press inaugurated an era of scholarly revision of existing knowledge. From scroll, to codex, to movable type, to digitization, reading has evolved and the culture has changed with it. In *A History of Reading*, Alberto Manguel reminds us that the silent reading we take for granted didn't become the norm in the West until the tenth century. Far from the quiet contemplation we imagine, monasteries were actually "communities of mumblers," as critic Ivan Illich once described, where devotional reading was constant and aloud. Just as our styles of reading have changed, so too have our reasons for reading and the amount of time we devote to it. "Read in order to live," Flaubert wrote. Critic Harold Bloom views reading from the other end of the human lifespan. "One of the uses of reading is to prepare ourselves for change," he argues in *How to Read and Why*, "and the final change alas is universal." But however much we read and for whatever reasons, literacy has long been prized as a marker of civilization and a measure of a society's success. Literacy is now nearly universal in the United States and the rest of the developed world—a remarkable historical achievement, and yet one that has sparked more complacency than comment.

That may be changing. In 2007, the National Endowment for the Arts (NEA) published a report, *To Read or Not To Read: A Question of National Consequence*, which provided ample evidence of the decline of reading for pleasure, particularly among the young. To wit: Nearly half of Americans ages 18 to 24 read no books for pleasure; Americans ages 15 to 24 spend only between 7 and 10 minutes per day reading voluntarily; and two thirds of college freshmen read for pleasure for less than an hour per week or not at all. As Sunil Iyengar, director of the NEA's Office of Research and Analysis and the lead author of the report, told me, "We can no longer take the presence of books in the home for granted. Reading on one's own—not in a required sense, but doing it because you want to read—that skill has to be cultivated at an early age." The NEA report also found that regular reading is strongly correlated with civic engagement, patronage of the arts, and charity work. People who read regularly for pleasure are more likely to be employed, and more likely to vote, exercise, visit museums, and volunteer in their communities; in short, they are more engaged citizens.

Not everyone endorses this claim for reading's value. Bloom, for instance, is not persuaded by claims that reading encourages civic engagement. "You cannot directly improve anyone else's life by reading better or more deeply," he argues. "I remain skeptical of the traditional social hope that care for others may be stimulated by the growth of individual imagination, and I am wary of any arguments whatsoever that connect the pleasures of solitary reading to the public good."

Whether one agrees with the NEA or with Bloom, no one can deny that our new communications technologies have irrevocably altered the reading culture. In 2005, Northwestern University sociologists Wendy Griswold, Terry McDonnell, and Nathan Wright identified the emergence of a new "reading class," one "restricted in size but disproportionate in influence." Their research, conducted largely in the 1990s, found that the heaviest readers were also the heaviest users of the Internet, a result that many enthusiasts of digital literacy took as evidence that print literacy and screen literacy might be complementary capacities instead of just competitors for precious time.

But the Northwestern sociologists also predicted, "as Internet use moves into less-advantaged segments of the population, the picture may change. For these groups, it may be that leisure time is more limited, the reading habit is less firmly established, and the competition between going online and reading is more intense." This prediction is now coming to pass: A University of Michigan study published in the *Harvard Educational Review* in 2008 reported that the Web is now the primary source of reading material for low-income high school students in Detroit. And yet, the study notes, "only reading novels on a regular basis outside of school is shown to have a positive relationship to academic achievement."

Despite the attention once paid to the so-called digital divide, the real gap isn't between households with computers and households without them; it is the one developing between, on the one hand, households where parents teach their children the old-fashioned skill of reading and instill in them a love of books, and, on the other hand, households where parents don't. As Griswold and her colleagues suggested, it remains an open question whether the new "reading class" will "have both power and prestige associated with an increasingly rare form of cultural capital," or whether the pursuit of reading will become merely "an increasingly arcane hobby."

There is another aspect of reading not captured in these studies, but just as crucial to our long-term cultural health. For centuries, print literacy has been one of the building blocks in the formation of the modern sense of self. By contrast, screen reading, a historically recent arrival, encourages a different kind of self-conception, one based on interaction and dependent on the feedback of others. It rewards participation and performance, not contemplation. It is, to borrow a characterization from sociologist David Riesman, a kind of literacy more comfortable for the "outer-directed" personality who takes his cues from others and constantly reinvents himself than for the "inner-directed" personality whose values are less flexible but also less susceptible to outside pressures. How does a culture of digitally literate, outer-directed personalities "read"?

MY OWN DIGITAL DICKENS

In A.D. 1000, the Grand Vizier of Persia, an avid reader, faced a peculiar logistical challenge when he traveled. Unwilling to leave behind his precious collection of 117,000 books, as historian Alberto Manguel tells us, he hit upon a unique strategy for transporting them: four hundred camels trained to walk in an alphabetically-ordered caravan behind him on his journey.

What the Grand Vizier needed was a Kindle. Since its much-hyped launch in 2007, Amazon's portable electronic reader (if *it* is the "reader," what does that make *you*?) has received outsized media attention. In a characteristically enthusiastic article about the device in *Newsweek*, Amazon founder Jeff Bezos was quoted as saying, "This is the most important thing we've ever done. . . . It's so ambitious to take something as highly evolved as the book and improve on it. And maybe even change the way people read." The market for e-books, although growing rapidly, is still less than 1 percent of the total publishing business: perhaps 400 million paper books will be sold in the United States in 2008, and Amazon expects to sell 380,000 Kindles in 2008, resulting in an unknown number of book downloads.

Much has been written about the Kindle's various features: wireless service that allows for rapid delivery of e-texts; the ability to search the Web; a service called "NowNow" that performs real-time searches (using human beings!) to answer questions; a dedicated "Search Wikipedia" function. These features are remarkable—and remarkably distracting.

The screensaver on the Kindle I used featured literary personages of British descent: Oscar Wilde tricked out in fur-trimmed velvet, for example, and the ghostly visage of Virginia Woolf. Another more self-serving screensaver popped up later with a definition of "kindle" and the cloying explanatory sentence—*By reading to me at bedtime when I was a child, my parents kindled my lifelong love for reading*—in a weird evocation of childhood nostalgia for the very printed page the e-book's pushers mean to supplant. (Kindle users have already figured out how to hack the Kindle screensaver function to use images other than the default ones, of course.)

A friend of mine who was an early Kindle user noted how much he enjoys the fact that the Kindle delivers the day's newspapers to his device overnight, so he can read them first thing in the morning. He uses his Kindle for work travel a lot as well, and as one of those people who always ambitiously packed too many books for long plane flights, now enjoys the convenience of being able to bring dozens of books stored on one device. The Kindle also appeals to people who deal with a lot of paper in their jobs; publishers such as Random House are now distributing e-readers to editors to read manuscripts.

When Amazon sent me a Kindle to try, I had been reading a worn copy of Dickens's *Nicholas Nickleby*—a Penguin classic edition from the 1970s, with its distinctive orange paperback spine (and a list price of $3.95). Dickens seemed a good choice to read on the Kindle—after all, he was one of the great serial novelists, and the Kindle seems to lend itself to serial reading. Dickens's adoption of monthly serialization—approximately thirty-two pages per month, sold in cheap editions for a shilling apiece (at a time when most Victorian novels were several volumes long and a great deal more expensive) represented a gutsy experiment in marketing and mass publishing—not unlike the Kindle. And his novels are all still in print.

The Kindle and other similar devices, such as Sony's e-Reader, train users to read on screens intended to replicate the readability of paper and minimize eye strain; unlike bright computer monitors, the screens on these e-books are dull gray with black lettering, using a sophisticated "E Ink" display developed by M.I.T.'s Media Lab. Although mildly disorienting at first, I quickly adjusted to the Kindle's screen and mastered the scroll and page-turn buttons. Nevertheless, my eyes were restless and jumped around as they do when I try to read for a sustained time on the computer. Distractions abounded. I looked up Dickens on Wikipedia, then jumped straight down the Internet rabbit hole following a link about a Dickens short story, "Mugby Junction." Twenty minutes later I still hadn't returned to my reading of *Nickleby* on the Kindle. I found that despite the ability to change the font size and scroll up and down the screen, reading was much slower on the Kindle than in book form. I'd want it on a long trip, but not for everyday use.

There are practical concerns as well: Despite Kindle's emphasis on accessibility—get any book, anywhere, instantly—this is true only if you can afford to own the device that allows you to read it. You can't share the books you've read on your Kindle unless you hand the device over to a friend to borrow. There are other drawbacks to the Kindle, more emotional than practical. Unlike a regular book, where the weight of the book transfers from your right hand to your left as you progress, with the Kindle you have no sense of where you are in the book by its feel. It doesn't smell like a book. Nor does the clean, digital Kindle bear the impressions of previous readers, the smudges and folds and scribbles and forgotten treasures tucked amid the pages—markings of the man-made artifact. The printed book is the "transformation of the intangible into the tangibility of things," as Hannah Arendt put it; it is imagined and lived action and speech turned into palpable remembrance. Such feelings of partiality to the printed book are impossible to quantify, and might well strike the critic as foolish attachment to an outmoded medium, as rank sentimental preference for the durable over the delible and digital. To be sure, "I just like the feel of it" is hardly firm intellectual footing from which to launch a defense of the paper book. But it is at least worth noting that these tactile experiences have no counterpart when reading on the screen, and worth recalling that for all our enthusiasm about the aesthetics of our technologies—our sleek iPhones and iPods—we are quick to discount the same kind of appreciation for printed words on paper.

KIDS AND KINDLES

It is also worth questioning what role the Kindle will play in the lives of younger readers. If there is such a thing as a culture of reading, it begins in the home. Regardless of their parents' educational background or income level, children raised in homes with books become more proficient readers. Does this apply to the Kindle? Sven Birkerts, author of *The Gutenberg Elegies* (1994), describes how our screen technologies exert a "conditioning impact" on all of us who use them; that is, "they make it harder, once we do turn from the screen, to engage the single-focus requirement of reading." This seems a particular danger for children. We already know that electronic books marketed for children, far from being helpful in teaching literacy, can hamper it. Researchers at Temple University's Infant Laboratory and the Erikson Institute in Chicago who studied electronic books aimed at children described a "slightly coercive parent-child interaction as opposed to talking about the story," and concluded, "We shouldn't use e-books to replace traditional books." Anyone who has read a book to a toddler knows that one experience with an e-reader would yield more interest in the buttons and the scroll wheel than the story itself.

Meanwhile, older children and teens who are coming of age surrounded by cell phones, video games, iPods, instant messaging, text messaging, and Facebook have finely honed digital literacy skills, but often lack the ability to concentrate that is the first requirement of traditional literacy. This poses challenges not just to the act of reading but also to the cultural institutions that support it, particularly libraries. The *New York Times* recently carried a story about the disruptive behavior of younger patrons in the British Library Reading Room. Older researchers—and by old they meant over thirty—lamented the boisterous atmosphere in the library and found the constant giggling, texting, and iPod use distracting. A library spokesman was not sympathetic to the neo-geezers' concerns, saying, "The library has changed and evolved, and people use it in different ways. They have a different way of doing their research. They are using their computers and checking things on the Web, not just taking notes on notepads." In today's landscape of digital literacy, the old print battles—like the American Library Association's "Banned Books Week," held each year since 1982—seem downright quaint, like the righteous crusade of a few fusty tenders of the Dewey Decimal system. Students today are far more likely to protest a ban on wireless Internet access than book censorship.

Not every librarian is pleased with these changes. Some chafe at their new titles of "media and information specialist" and "librarian-technologist." One librarian at a private school in McLean, Virginia, described in the *Washington Post* a general impatience among kids toward books, and an unwillingness to grapple with difficult texts. "How long is it?" has replaced "Will I like it?" he says, when he tries to entice a student to read a book. For an increasing number of librarians, their primary responsibility is teaching computer research skills to young people who need to extract information, like little miners. But these kids are not like real miners, who dig deeply; they are more like '49ers panning for gold. To be sure, a few will strike a vein, stumbling across a novel or a poem so engrossing that they seek more. But most merely sift through the silty top layers, grab what is shiny and close at hand, and declare themselves rich.

The Kindle will only serve to worsen that concentration deficit, for when you use a Kindle, you are not merely a reader—you are also a consumer. Indeed, everything about the device is intended to keep you in a posture of consumption. As Amazon founder Jeff Bezos has admitted, the Kindle "isn't a device, it's a service."

In this sense it is a metaphor for the experience of reading in the twenty-first century. Like so many things we idolize today, it is extraordinarily convenient, technologically sophisticated, consumption-oriented, sterile, and distracting. The Kindle also encourages a kind of utopianism about instant gratification, and a confusion of needs and wants. Do we really need Dickens on demand? Part of the gratification for first readers of Dickens was rooted in the very anticipation they felt waiting for the next installment of his serialized novels—as illustrated by the story of Americans lining up at the docks in New

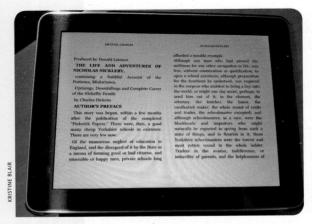

KRISTINE BLAIR

Figure 2.6 Apple iPad displaying Charles Dickens' novel *Nicholas Nickleby*

York to learn the fate of Little Nell. The wait served a purpose: in the interval between finishing one installment and getting the next, readers had time to think about the characters and ponder their motives and actions. They had time to connect to the story.

We are so eager to explore what these new devices do—particularly what they do *better* than the printed book—that we ignore the more rudimentary but important human questions: the tactile pleasures of the printed page versus the screen; the new risks of distraction posed by a device with a wireless Internet connection; the difference between reading a book in two-page spreads and reading a story on one flashing screen-display after another. Kindle and other e-readers are marvelous technologies of convenience, but they are no replacement for the book.

THE BOOK IS DEAD. LONG LIVE THE BOOK!

A parallel debate about the meaning of texts and the future of reading is going on with regard to the efforts of Google (and others) to digitize the world's libraries (a debate wherein, oddly, the word "bibliophile" is often hurled as an epithet but the word "technophile" is rarely uttered). John Updike's *cri de coeur* at the 2006 BookExpo called on booksellers to "defend your lonely forts" against these and other challenges to the book, reminding his listeners, "For some of us, books are intrinsic to our human identity."

Perhaps the most excitable dispatch from this front came from former *Wired* magazine editor Kevin Kelly in a 2006 article in the *New York Times Magazine*. This ode to gigajoy included the obligatory prediction that paper books would be replaced with handheld devices. "Just as the music audience now juggles and reorders songs into new albums," Kelly writes, the universal digital library that Google is bringing into the world "will encourage the creation of virtual 'bookshelves'—a collection of texts, some as short as a paragraph, others as long as entire books, that form a library shelf's worth of specialized information." Kelly anticipates the day when authors will "write books to be read as snippets or to be remixed as pages." But what would a mash-up of George Eliot's *Middlemarch* and the latest best-selling mystery look like? There are some extraordinary lines in Eliot's novel. Writing of Lydgate and Rosamond, for example, Eliot says, "He once called her his basil plant; and when she asked for an explanation, said that basil was a plant which had flourished wonderfully on a murdered man's brains." But devoid of the complicated context of the rest of the novel, how can we understand why this observation is poignant, apt, and true?

Kelly's hope for the book is to turn it into a kind of digital Frankenstein monster, a contextless "text" that is no more than the sum of its scattered and remixed parts: "What counts are the ways in which these common copies of a creative work can be linked, manipulated, annotated, tagged, highlighted, bookmarked, translated, enlivened by other media and sewn together into the universal library," he writes. And he is confident that "in the clash between the conventions of the book and the protocols of the screen, the screen will prevail." Perhaps it will, but Kelly might want to include in his own future e-book another snippet from Eliot's masterpiece, one which might serve as a warning for us all: "We are on a perilous margin when we begin to look passively at our future selves, and see our own figures led with dull consent into insipid misdoing and shabby achievement."

If reading has a history, it might also have an end. It is far too soon to tell when that end might come, and how the shift from print literacy to digital literacy will transform the "reading brain" and the culture that has so long supported it. Echoes will linger, as they do today from the distant past: audio books are merely a more individualistic and technologically sophisticated version of the old practice of reading aloud. But we are coming to see the book as a hindrance, a retrograde technology that doesn't suit the times. Its inanimacy now renders it less compelling than the eye-catching screen. It doesn't actively *do* anything *for* us. In our eagerness to upgrade or replace the book, we try to make reading easier, more convenient, more entertaining—forgetting that reading is also supposed to encourage us to challenge ourselves and to search for deeper meaning.

In a 1988 essay in the *Times Literary Supplement*, the critic George Steiner wrote,

> I would not be surprised if that which lies ahead for classical modes of reading resembles the monasticism from which those modes sprung. I sometimes dream of *houses of reading*—a Hebrew phrase—in which those passionate to learn how to read well would find the necessary guidance, silence, and complicity of disciplined companionship.

To those raised to crave the stimulation of the screen, Steiner's houses of reading probably sound like claustrophobic prisons. For those raised in the tradition of print literacy, they may seem like serene enclaves, havens of learning and contentment, temples to the many and subtle pleasures of the word on the page. In truth, though, what Steiner's vision most suggests is something sadder and much more mundane: depressing and dwindling gated communities, ramshackle and creaking with neglect, forgotten in the shadow of shining skyscrapers. Such is the end of the tragedy we are now witness to: Literacy, the most empowering achievement of our civilization, is to be replaced by a vague and ill-defined screen savvy. The paper book, the tool that built modernity, is to be phased out in favor of fractured, unfixed information. All in the name of progress.

1. "People of the Screen" appears in the journal titled *The New Atlantis*. Research the significance of the term "New Atlantis" for the content of Rosen's essay.

2. How does Rosen define literacy? In what ways does her presumed definition contrast with your own? What does it mean to "read"?

3. According to Rosen, what are the advantages and disadvantages of e-readers such as the Kindle?

4. Rosen notes that "Every technology is both an expression of a culture and a potential transformer of it." What does she mean by this statement? Can you provide both historical and contemporary examples?

5. Rosen cites a National Endowment for the Arts study indicating that "Nearly half of Americans 18 to 24 read no books for pleasure; Americans ages 15 to 24 spend only between 7 and 10 minutes per day reading voluntarily; and two thirds of college freshmen read for pleasure for less than an hour per week or not at all." Do you believe this to be accurate? Why or why not?

6. In response to Rosen, view Michael Wesch's YouTube video: *A Vision of Students Today*, available through a link on the English CourseMate for this text. How do Wesch and his students' survey data respond to Rosen's use of the National Endowment for the Arts data?

Kathleen Tyner

Splintering Literacies

Kathleen Tyner is Associate Professor in the Department of Radio-Television-Film at the University of Texas at Austin. She is author and editor of several books and numerous articles for media educators, including *Media Literacy, Literacy in a Digital World: Teaching and Learning in the Age of Information,* and *Visions/Revisions: Moving Forward with Media Education.* In this excerpt form *Literacy in a Digital World,* Tyner introduces the concept of "multiliteracy."

New approaches to literacy teaching and learning suggest that instead of approaching literacy as a monolithic concept, for example, a "Good Thing" with sanctioned, printed texts and lofty purposes, it is more useful to break literacy down into any number of multiple literacy modes, each with distinctive characteristics that reveal a variety of social purposes: good, useful, and otherwise. These multiple literacies have been called *technology literacy, information literacy, visual literacy, media literacy,* and so on. The foundations for these literacies are rooted in literacy traditions of oral/aural, visual, and

---

Kathleen Tyner, "Splintering Literacies," *Literacy in a Digital World: Teaching and Learning in the Age of Information,*" New York: Routledge, 1998. Copyright © 1998 by Taylor and Francis Group LLC. All rights reserved. Reproduced by permission.

alphabetic/text modalities. As contemporary communication media converge into a sensory soup, the peculiar features of each of these literacies also converge and overlap to combine alphabetic with oral and visual literacy traditions and practices. And because information consumers increasingly use new tools both to receive and transmit messages, it is helpful to get a fix on some competencies and purposes for each of the literacies and then, in jigsaw puzzle fashion, to attempt to put the literacy pieces back together again.

An examination of these literacies in isolation from one another does little to promote either clarity or utility. Such a specialized look at each literacy only serves to reflect the tautology and polemic of its constituents. In practical terms, the various multiliteracies have not been advanced long enough to have a sufficient body of evidence, research, and tradition to make sufficient predictions about the promising practices of literacy that might accompany new and emerging media in educational settings.

The key to understanding the changing landscape of contemporary literacy is to study the areas where the rationale, skill sets, and purposes of various literacies converge and overlap for clues to the common features, competencies, and pedagogies of literacy at this point in time. Only then can a new vision of literacy in its myriad forms begin to take shape.

A NEW LITERACY FOR A NEW AGE

The abundance of information has been called an "information explosion," and it is almost as if the cornucopia of digital and analog technologies shocked literacy scholars into reevaluating popular assumptions about oral and alphabetic literacy practices. The sudden profusion of mass media led researchers into a confusing morass of new and untested theories about the nature of literacy in the electronic age. In a 1946 book on audiovisual teaching, author Edgar Dale defined his vision of this new kind of literacy:

> What do I mean by the term "literacy" and the "new" literacy? I mean by literacy the ability to communicate through the three modes: reading and writing, speaking and listening, visualizing and observing—print, audio, and visual literacy. This literacy, broadly speaking, can be at two levels. First, is at the level of training, initiative reaction. Here we communicate the simple, literal meaning of what is written, said or visualized. . . . Or second, we can have creative interaction, can read between the lines, draw inferences, understand the implications of what was written, said or spoken. We thus learn what the speaker, writer or visualizer "meant to say" which requires a greater degree of literacy. And finally, we learn to read beyond the lines, to evaluate, and apply the material to new situations. We use the message in our own varied ways.
>
> I would also classify responses as uncritical or accepting, or as critical and evaluating. The new literacy involves critical reading, critical listening, and

critical observing. It is disciplined thinking about what is read, heard, and visualized. (pp. 92–93)

As technology continues to impinge upon familiar textual/alphabetic literacy practices, literacy researchers and constituents for specific literacy modes are still groping toward workable definitions for the new version of literacy—not that they had any consensus about the definition of alphabetic literacy to begin with.

And definitions are important. Philosophers quibble about the relationship between thought, word, and deed, but there seems to be a consensus that words can be the catalyst for action. In the name of rationalism, great value is placed on naming and classification, specialization, epistemology, and isolation of words. Therefore, the power to name a thing, or better yet, to designate an entire concept or class of things, is a mark of respect in Western intellectual circles, resulting in prominence and wielding influence. Whether the act of defining leads to broad consensus about meaning is another matter entirely.

Naming represents an intellectual process that is as exclusionary as it is inclusive, with the implicit goals of sanctioning some definitions over others, establishing universally accepted classification schemes and then situating oneself within the boundaries of the definition for purposes of identity, resource development, and involvement in spheres of influence. It is by the decidedly circuitous route of definition and classification that words can lead to activity in cultures rooted in classical, western traditions. The hope is that once an entity is named, it becomes manifest. It is also why definitions can cause such *sturm* and *drang* in academic circles.

Librarian Lawrence J. McCrank addressed the problematic process of establishing definitions for emerging concepts in an essay about the historical significance of library competencies defined as *information literacy:*

> What is in a name, then? Everything! . . . The naming of new concepts or coining neologisms is always fraught with problems. Some usage dissolves quickly into jargon, some catches on for short fads, and some is deliberate propaganda, but other words last because they are substantive, are meaningful to more than their inventors, and are sustained by users who give the term life. (McCrank, 1992, p. 485)

Definitions may be sustained, but obviously they don't last forever. This is especially true for "umbrella" terms that shelter a host of related, sprawling ideas. This is apparently the case for the word *literacy*. For some time, it has been of concern to a diverse and growing number of people that traditional notions of alphabetic literacy, that is, the reading and writing of print, do not begin to encompass the wide range of real and perceived literacy needs for contemporary times. To critics and change agents, literacy, as currently practiced in school settings, does not seem to take into account the glut of information available to people, or the amount of electronic information they use, or the new interactive nature of mediated experience, or converged/multiple modalities, or the confluence of digital media forms and content. The all-purpose word *literacy* seems hopelessly anachronistic, tainted with the nostalgic ghost of a fleeting Industrial Age.

> In ancient Rome (literacy) referred to the letters of the alphabet and, by extension, to the epistles of earliest times. With the passage of the years, however, it came to be identified with literature and the increasingly crucial skills required in written communication. Little more than a decade ago, the term "universal literacy" simply meant the hope that all men could have made available to them the skills of reading and writing. But the term continues to change as the means of communication change. Today literacy [consists of] the skills with which man manipulates the many media of mass communication. (Postman, 1971, p. 26)

Operative definitions for the broad term *literacy* have become so mired in cultural politics and theoretical hairsplitting that a constellation of multiple kinds of literacy has emerged to represent addenda to literacy, or aspects of literacy that are felt to be missing in its common usage. Perhaps this is an inevitable trend at the end of one century marked by the tangible commodities of industry and another century that is synonymous with the more abstract and less tangible concept of information. It is becoming increasingly obvious that there is a disconnect in the old adage, "Knowledge is power." In fact, the relationship between the two gets murkier by the day: Data is certainly not information and information is not, in itself, knowledge and knowledge does not, necessarily, lead to power. And so, what good does it do to live in an age of information? And furthermore, where does literacy fit in? There is a widely held perception that society needs a "new and improved" literacy that is responsive to the times at hand.

> The writers and educators who have used terms like "media literacy" and "visual literacy" do so with that usage in mind. Both terms are, in a sense, analogies; they are used to say that an audiovisual learning experience can be like a reading experience. Clearly, "literacy" has been stretched beyond the definition of reading and writing letters, not necessarily out of irreverence towards print but as a reaction to technological advancements in communication. Perhaps "literacy" is the wrong word to associate with media and visual learning, but lament over the literacy meaning of somewhat oxymoronic terms is too late. Visual literacy and media literacy have become established educational jargon. (Johnson, 1977, p. 7)

A CASE FOR MULTILITERACIES

Literacy theorist David Olson (1977) welcomed the contributions of electronic media to literacy: "To take explicit written prose as the model of a language, knowledge and intelligence has narrowed the conception of all three, downgrading the general functions of ordinary language and common sense knowledge" (p. 75). A more expansive view of literacy has been presented by scholars from a variety of disciplines as "literacies," or "multiple literacies," or "multiliteracies" (The New London Group, 1996, p. 63).

These literacies have been called *computer literacy* (Horton, 1983, p. 14), *information literacy* (Farmer & Mech, 1992; Sutton, 1994), *technology literacy* (Thomas & Knezek, 1993; U.S. Department of Education, 1996), *visual literacy* (Considine, 1986; Considine & Haley, 1993; Messaris, 1994; Moore & Dwyer, 1994), and *media literacy* (Considine, 1990, 1995a, 1995b; Considine & Haley, 1993; Hobbs, 1994; Lloyd-Kolkin & Tyner, 1991; Silverblatt, 1995; Silverblatt & Eliceiri, 1997). There are others:

> . . . the many literacies in addition to or "beyond" "traditional" alphabetic literacy—from those of science and numeracy, to the spatial literacy that some geographers term "graphicacy," to the loudly touted and seemingly highly vulnerable "cultural literacy," "historical literacy," and "moral literacy." Some among the lengthening lists are long established in presumption but much more novel discursively or semantically: ecological literacy, "teleliteracy" and other media literacies, food literacy, emotional literacy, sexual literacy. (Graff, 1995, p. 321)

As previously mentioned, the current impetus for changing definitions of literacy is a wide perception of roiling institutional change brought about by technology. Attempts to define various literacies represent a complex multiplicity of purposes for literacy that reflect changing social and economic realities: frequent intercultural interaction; rapid use and combinations of a variety of discursive modes; availability of a wide variety of popular texts; converging, multimedia forms; a proliferation of communication channels for both commercial and personal purposes; enhanced opportunities for individual expression outside of commercial media industries; changing ideals and expectations for public schooling; the influence of new media on the political process; and shifts in job roles and opportunities caused by a global, free market economy.

Multiliteracies related to communication and information, notably media literacy, computer literacy, visual literacy, information literacy, network literacy, and technology have stepped forward to define the changing, amorphous shape of communication needs for a society awash in electronic sounds, images, icons, and texts. Indeed, these neologisms have contributed some defining characteristics that might be considered for literacy needs within contemporary contexts.

Little research has been done to link them to the ground breaking concept of multiple intelligences developed by Harvard educational psychologist Howard Gardner (Gardner, 1991, 1993; see also Armstrong, 1994), or the related uses of digital communication to leverage the preferred learning modalities of individuals. The term *multiliteracy* resonates and rides on the name recognition factor of Gardner's theories of multiple intelligences—theories that are increasingly popular with educators.

Multiliteracy practices insinuate a need for a range of modalities that seem to be compatible with Gardner's work in incorporating a wider range of learning modalities in the classroom. In brief, Gardner's theory has been abridged to at least "seven ways of knowing" that include the following intelligences: logical/mathematical; visual/spatial; bodily/kinesthetic; musical/rhythmic; interpersonal; intrapersonal; and linguistic. Later, Gardner added an eighth "way of knowing" he calls "naturalist."

Gardner's compelling theory of multiple intelligence has run into problems of oversimplification when teachers "mis-diagnose" students or when the theory is misused to label, categorize, and pigeonhole students into their preferred modalities. Instead, the theory can be used to structure educational environments that offer students the opportunity to become proficient in all the categories of intelligence. Nonetheless, when encouraged to become proficient in as many "intelligences" as possible, the sensory range provided by multimedia experiences holds the possibility to integrate and expand a learner's preferred approaches to learning to include at least a cursory understanding and some experience with each of the "ways of knowing." This may be especially true of young learners who have not yet mastered alphabetic literacy practices, but who have strong visual and verbal comprehension skills (Robertson Stephens & Company, 1993, p. 9).

Just as oversimplification is a problem found in practical application of the theory of multiple *intelligences*, the tendency to oversimplify the concept of *multiliteracies* can be similarly problematic. Multiliteracies suggest a splintering of literacy into discrete parts that belie the true nature of literacy as a complex and intersecting set of social actions. Multiliteracies also carry the unfortunate connotation that one literacy is as good as the next, when the operant question should instead be, "good for what?" Because their competencies and characteristics overlap, multiliteracies are not necessarily discrete from one another, although there may be discrete facets to each articulation of literacy. This is particularly true in the focus each might have on specialized tools, such as bibliographic search engines for information literacy, video cameras and image-manipulation software for media literacy, computer graphics for visual literacy, statistical software packages and calculating engines for mathematical literacy, and so forth. Furthermore, the goal of the teacher is to expand the number of choices available to students. An understanding of the many literacies and their uses offers opportunities for students to become as proficient in as many literacies and learning styles as possible—not only those with which the student finds an affinity.

The discussion of multiliteracies that center on the use of communication technologies provides some focus to examine the relationship between traditional notions of literacy and multiliteracies. There are more common features to each of the emerging communication multiliteracies than not. It is fair to say that—at least in theory—all of the technology-related multiliteracies strive for some version of critical literacy. Furthermore, multiliteracies are inseparable from and supportive of the many principles associated with the research-base for literacy. For example, no one would suggest that a media literate person would not also be able to critically read novels, or to write letters; or that a person who is numerically literate might not also want to know how to construct a Web page, or to participate in an online chat.

In spite of its potential usefulness, little has been done to highlight the links between various literacies in a cross-disciplinary way. Multiliteracies can be better conceptualized as elements subsumed under the broad and flexible umbrella of literacy. Proponents of new literacies hope to have a positive influence on literacy policies and then get down to the intricate business of literacy teaching and learning by incorporating some effective methodologies. Unfortunately, beyond their respective attempts at definition, even the substance of these hybrid areas of literacy study are still speculative and formative and their methodologies and optimum pedagogies largely untested.

Although their very names—information literacy, visual literacy, computer literacy, media literacy, and especially technology literacy—hint at an important sense of urgency as proponents clamor for inclusion in the circle of literacy, multiliteracies appear more reactionary than responsive to a world in flux. Just as the research base moves from theory building to field-based research and back again as it informs the historical boundaries between oral and print cultures, each multiliteracy must go through a number of rigorous research phases in order to prove its credibility and utility. With the exception of the enthusiastic McLuhanists, who gamely make pronouncements about nearly any communication technology, alphabetic literacy researchers are still as tentative about the nature of multiliteracies as they are about electronic literacy.

The extent to which the newly proliferating literacies signify little more than a semantic "name game" or a feature of the politics of literacy and education or professional specialization raises hard questions. . . . An enormously important set of critical developments, whose potentially revolutionary consequences for learning and teaching are largely unappreciated, thus far remain prisoner to scholarly, cultural, and pedagogical fragmentation. (Graff, 1995, p. 321)

At present, multiliteracies have proven to be not much more than defensive shields in the face of the rapidly changing societal needs of a technological, information-glutted, increasingly consumerist global village. To be sure, this apparent superficiality does not mean that it is not viable to examine the many facets of literacy, but rather that evidence of their viability is not available. As seen in its broader uses throughout history, literacy can be used to entrench the *status quo* as easily as it can be used to accommodate change. New versions of literacy deliberately set themselves apart from the old monolithic concept of literacy by grafting special tags— qualifying adjectives (media, visual, information, computer)—that attempt to push the boundaries of literacy to address a host of needs and purposes that presumably are not currently represented by operative notions of alphabetic literacy. These hybrids hope to create a synergistic definition from the sum of the parts in a way that one word alone would not. As often happens, the qualifiers themselves are so confusing and jam-packed with purpose that they overreach and obfuscate as much about literacy as they clarify. For example, *media literacy* reacts and sets itself apart from the presumed print bias of literacy in order to nudge a consideration of electronic forms of communication and popular texts into formal educational settings. *Visual literacy* reacts to a relative neglect of design, aesthetics, and graphics in the teaching of literacy. *Network literacy, computer literacy,* and *technology literacy* react to the astonishing proliferation of computerized technology and its influence on education, work, and lifestyles. *Information literacy* is a reaction to the changing nature of libraries and the role of librarians at the turn of the 20th century. *Cultural literacy* reacts—often with anxiety—to the need for cross-cultural understanding in a diverse, global, environment—or conversely, to entrench a dominant cultural perspective. *Numerical literacy* reacts to the perception that ordinary citizens cannot fathom the complex economic, scientific, and technical information that confronts them daily.

Finally, because of the inseparable relationship between literacy and schooling, each new iteration of literacy must also react to the dramatic, cyclical calls to dismantle and overhaul contemporary public schooling. School reform carries with it an urgency that pressures the new ideas for literacy to consolidate quickly in order to define their place in the "schools of tomorrow." Beleaguered teachers are already pressured by special interest groups to insert a mind-boggling array of lessons and units into the existing curriculum. Without a sound rationale about the usefulness of multiliteracies across the curriculum, the call to expand literacy can only add to the classroom teacher's burden.

Because of the paucity of research on the subject, the relationship that multiliteracies have with one another, or even with traditional notions of alphabetic literacy, remains to be seen. Before multiliteracies can demonstrate significant influence on what it means to be literate, a review of the literature on the subject suggests that each needs more time to "cook," that is, interested professionals must have opportunities for discourse around definitions and core competencies and these theories must be field-tested in authentic learning environments in order for the ideas to be credibly served up for general consumption. Teachers must have the room to experiment with literacy in relationship to the needs of their students, and then to reflect on the practice.

This of course takes time, and the public has run short of patience with educational tinkering, no matter how sensible and well-intentioned. It is increasingly difficult to gin up public enthusiasm for educational reform campaigns, especially for literacy, a subject in which most people like to consider themselves expert. Although each of the multiliteracies has its champions, the implementation of new literacy ideas looks less like a traditional literacy campaign and more like an ad hoc revolution already in play, school by school, teacher by teacher, and parent by parent.

> Recognition of the multiple meanings and varieties of literacy . . . argues for a diversity of educational approaches, informal and community-based as well as formal and school-based . . . effective literacy programs are those that are responsive to perceived needs, whether for functional skills, social power, or self-improvement. . . . The road to maximal literacy may begin for some through the feeder routes of a wide variety of specific literacies. (Scribner, 1989, p. 81)

People will certainly try to find the literacy they need, and over time it is probable that the boundaries of literacy will eventually collapse to include many of the goals and strategies being promoted by the definers of *multiliteracies*. In spite of alarmist rhetoric that prods educators to keep up with the tumultuous changes in technology with corresponding changes in literacy, a patient and measured approach to the theory and practice of literacy, in all its manifestations, is still in order.

"This one, when you open it, smells like the Times."

Figure 2.7 Cartoon commenting on the e-reader trend

© LEO CULLUM/THE NEW YORKER COLLECTION/ WWW.CARTOONBANK.COM

CULTURES In **Figure 2.7**, what is the relationship between the cartoon's image and caption, which reads, "This one, when you open it, smells like the Times."? What does the cartoon presume about reading and literacy?

Compare the message and tone of Cullum's cartoon with Christine Rosen's "People of the Screen."

READING REACTIONS

1. According to Tyner, what is multiliteracy? What are some of the disadvantages of this term?
2. Why is attempting to define literacy important in the first place? What are the implications for academic and professional development?
3. Tyner mentions "enthusiastic McLuhanists," referring to Marshall McLuhan. Who was Marshall McLuhan, and how was his work important to the concept of multiliteracies?
4. How does an enthusiastic McLuhanist differ from a Luddite?
5. In what ways has your high school and/or college experience fostered a particular type of literacy profiled in Tyner's chapter?
6. Explain Tyner's comment that "Teachers must have the room to experiment with literacy in relationship to the needs of their students, and then to reflect on the practice."

Technological Beginnings

Effective and usable Web design is an important aspect of being professionally successful online, whether it be in establishing a digital identity for yourself, your organization, or your business. As an experiment, find three websites: for an individual, a campus organization, and a corporation. What are these sites' common features? What aspects of the sites do you like or dislike? Be prepared to share these "reactions" with your classmates in an effort to generate some criteria for what constitutes an effective "Web presence."

The guidelines you may use to evaluate a website's purpose, content, and format are in fact the same guidelines you should use to create your own Web-based materials. Whereas the concerns of effective writing—audience, purpose, development, organization, style, tone, and grammatical acceptability—apply to online documents as much as they do print documents, the manner in which these features manifest themselves online is completely different.

You can create a website in several ways without much technical knowledge:

- Save your document as a web page. You can turn a document file into an HTML or Web-based file in your word-processing program. This option is typically found in the File menu as "Save as Web Page." Although this approach does create an instant web page, it limits your control over how your page looks.

- Use Web-authoring software. You can create a website using software such as Adobe Dreamweaver (see **Figure 2.8**), which provides many of the same menus and tools you use to create print documents. Because Dreamweaver is not a free application and thus may not be available on your home campus, you may want to consider a free thirty-day trial of the software or the use of a free web-authoring tool such as Kompozer, available at http://kompozer.net.

- Learn HTML. More technical approaches include learning HTML, or Hypertext Markup Language. HTML is the basic language of most websites. You can use HTML to develop a website in a text editor such as TextEdit for the Mac or Notepad for Windows. An online HTML resource, HTML Goodies, is available through a link on the English CourseMate for this text.

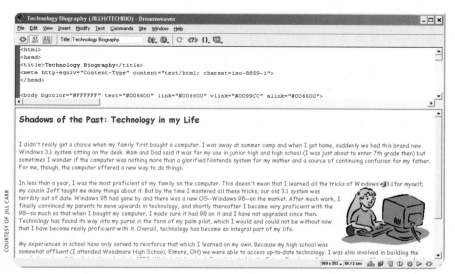

Figure 2.8 Jill Haar's website in Adobe Dreamweaver's code and design view

- Use a blog site such as Blogger, Tumblr, or WordPress. With a blog, you can choose from a range of template designs.

Whatever your approach, it is important that you plan your web page or site in advance to make your design choices look creative but not haphazard. Whereas for a print essay assignment, you might "outline" your major points and subpoints, or even use visual clusters, Web design commonly involves "storyboarding" a site. To storyboard, you create empty templates on paper or on screen to guide to the relationship between text and visuals, navigation throughout the site, and overall placement and format of content. Other considerations include how much content to place on a particular page to maximize both access and readability and the use of specific fonts and color contrast between background, text, and links. As you begin to design your site, you should experiment with different options to compare overall design quality.

Once you create a website with text, a color scheme, links, and images, preview it on multiple Web browsers, such as Internet Explorer, Firefox, and Safari to get a sense of how it will appear to the users of these different browsers. Although in some cases, Web-authoring tools are referred to as WYSIWGs ("what you see is what you get"), testing your page by previewing it in a browser often proves this not to be the case; different window sizes and different screens often alter the design you are trying to achieve.

In addition to previewing your site, it is important that you ask users to navigate your site. In professional design settings, this is often referred to as usability or beta testing. Getting feedback about your online writing and communication is as important as getting feedback about your printed work.

TECHNOLOGY TIPS ✳ Serif vs. Sans Serif Fonts

Web designers are often aware that some online information—particularly long passages of texts in course syllabi, or online essays—is often printed for better readability. Yet, in just as many cases, material produced for the Web is designed to be read on the Web. To facilitate on-screen reading, designers use sans serif fonts, which lack "feet." Sans serif fonts like Helvetica, Geneva, and Arial are easier to read online than fonts with feet, such as Times New Roman, Century, and Courier. For that reason, many well-designed sites typically use sans serif fonts for content, reserving serif fonts for headings, subheadings, navigation, and banners.

Regardless of your typeface choices, keep in mind that one strong contributor to professional design is consistency of typeface throughout a site. Most Web-authoring software will provide style sheets to help you create a standard type style, size, and color scheme for headings and content throughout your website (see "Technological Beginnings" in this chapter).

As you develop a site, consider not only your site's usability but also its accessibility to diverse audiences. For example, the Americans with Disabilities Act (ADA) attempts to ensure that in addition to providing other types of equitable access to facilities and services, state and local government websites must comply with ADA guidelines. For more information about these guidelines, visit the ADA's discussion of accessible websites at http://www.ada.gov/websites2.htm. Many personal, organizational, and commercial websites are not necessarily required to be ADA compliant. However, the continuing importance of the Web as a universal information literacy tool suggests that if you fail to consider Web design that allows impaired users to access your site, you could potentially reduce the overall impact of your message on potential audiences.

Because many impaired users rely on assistive technologies such as screen readers and text-to-speech software, many Web designers use "alt" tags, which provide text "alternatives" to images or even give a streamlined textual version of a media-intensive site. Web designers can also increase their overall site accessibility by observing accessibility guidelines such as those provided by the Web Accessibility Initiative at http://www.w3.org/WAI.

COMMUNITIES   Use Web accessibility guidelines to analyze a website for a campus or community organization to which you belong. Share your results with other members of your organization, and prepare a list of revisions that will make your site more accessible to a wider range of users.

Additional Writing and Composing Activities

1. **Literacy Narrative.** A literacy narrative is a common composing activity in which you summarize your past and present reading and writing experiences. This can help you understand your attitudes about reading and writing. Because reading and writing so often occur in digital environments, literacy narratives can also include discussions of technology and social media and may even be composed in audio or video form. For this assignment, compose a literacy narrative. What do you remember about learning to read and write? Who were your teachers? What methods did they employ to help you develop your literacy skills? How relevant are those skills today?

2. **Evaluation of a Tutorial.** Visit your library's website to see whether it has an information-literacy tutorial, or look at the examples available on the English CourseMate for this text. Take the tutorial, noting the definitions of information literacy and skills and competencies for becoming information literate. How does the tutorial help users achieve such skills? How well does it allow you to assess your own level of information literacy? For your classmates, write an evaluation of the tutorial, indicating whether you would recommend it to others.

3. **Personal Website.** Using tools of your choice, create the introduction to a website about yourself and your interests. What colors and fonts best represent you? How will your color choices give a sense of the persona or ethos you wish to convey? What types of images do you wish to include? Portraits? Logos? To what extent is your proposed website personal, professional, or both? Based on your purpose, what types of content should you include? A resume, biographical statement, or samples of your academic and professional work? Whom do you want to view your site and why? Visit several personal websites to determine the types of content and format available to you. Finally, don't forget to storyboard your page, planning where images and text and navigation tools will go on the page. Such planning will help you develop a more consistent digital theme throughout your entire site.

Online Resources

Resources available through the English CourseMate for this text include the following:

Articles

David Abel. "Welcome to the Library. Say Goodbye to the Books."

Liz Dwyer. "Just Google It: How Search Engines Stunt College Students' Research Skills."

Room for Debate: "Do School Libraries Need Books?" *New York Times* Blog.

"Why Integrate Technology into the Curriculum?: The Reasons are Many." *Edutopia*.

Research Tools

Delicious
Dogpile
MetaCrawler

Information Literacy Tutorials

TILT: Texas Information Literacy Tutorial
Minneapolis Community and Technical College

RIO: University of Arizona Research Instruction Online
Information Literacy Tutorial: Five Colleges of Ohio

Web-Authoring Tools

Adobe Dreamweaver Free Trial
HTML Goodies: The Ultimate HTML Resource
Kompozer Easy Web Authoring
Web Pages That Suck

Video

Michael Wesch. *A Vision of Students Today*.

Shared Memories, Shared Identities

Do you have a favorite memory from a family tradition, a family trip, the prom, an athletic event, or even a favorite place to visit? When you gather with people who experienced the same event, do you feel like you've shared something important with them? Perhaps this is why we have school and family reunions, memorial services, and even parties—to reconnect with people who have shared histories.

Shared histories, or "citizen identities," can be with people who are close to us. Or as **Figure 3.1** shows, our memories of historical or cultural events can be with people from our town, our state, our country, and even the entire world. Cultures need shared moments; they often shape our

Figure 3.1
Oklahoma City memorial fence

R. MURPHY

77

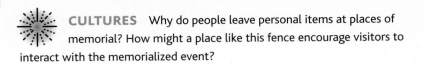

history and our identity. Our remembrances of such moments are called "collective memories." They are memories a group shares and passes on to others. In his work "Collective Memory," Pierre Nora says contributions like those on the fence in Figure 3.1 are significant to the role of place and spaces of shared memory. Note that the fence contains all sorts of items, from the personal to the common.

Memory and Memorial

Thousands of memorials across the United States serve as architectural memories commemorating historical moments or influential people. These spaces become important to our collective social identity and memory as citizens. They also act as rhetorical places for examining and producing individual and community narratives.

In "Transcendence at Yellowstone," Gregory Clark claims that "individual and collective identity" is associated with "place" in our culture. He believes that such spaces allow for a place of discourse—private and public—that promotes civic responsibility. Clark further calls the education allowed for by these rhetorical places "functional civics." Overall, Clark's article makes a significant point about rhetorical places: "when individuals share experiences that have been rendered symbolic of their community, those experiences themselves—whether of language or of landscape—wield considerable rhetorical power."

Another scholar, S. Michael Halloran, writes that public knowledge of place initiates public discourse, or the act of publicly discussing a situation or event. In "Writing History," Halloran calls the rhetorical knowledge of place a "historical perspective." This knowledge is similar to Clark's idea of "individual and collective identity" but within the context of a "place." For instance, Americans can both individually and collectively identify with the rhetorical and historic place of traumatic events such as the sinking of the

Gregory Clark, "Transcendence at Yellowstone," *Rhetorical Education in America*. Cheryl Glenn, Margaret M. Lyday and Wendy B Sharer, eds. Tuscaloosa: University of Alabama Press, 2004, pp. 145–159.

Titanic, places of remembrance like Pearl Harbor, or even places of historical significance like Gettysburg. We even make movies and devote television series to these events. It is in the experience of these historic places, materials, and artifacts that we can build on a tradition of community, which is vital to a citizen's sense of identity. Take for example the fence that surrounded the Alfred P. Murrah Federal Building in Oklahoma City, Oklahoma, after the bombing in 1995. People from all over the world left and continue to leave material mementos for the victims and their families. In Figure 3.1, you can see a New Mexico license plate and a British flag among the artifacts. As this photo shows, after more than fifteen years, the fence is still an important part of the Oklahoma City National Memorial public experience; its artifacts are even archived in the museum. Years later, when the towers fell at the World Trade Center (WTC) site, a similar fence was erected and covered with personal items, letters, and other mementos. Artifacts collected at the Vietnam Veterans Memorial wall are archived as well.

The act of interaction with a site of historic importance makes people feel like they've participated in something, whether in remembrance, honor, camaraderie, or even as a token of hope. In "Collective Memory," historian Pierre Nora suggests that the act of interacting with a place of memorial adds to the memorial's significance. As our culture continues to memorialize historic events, they become a part of our cultural identity and thereby become significant pieces of our collective and shared memories as citizens. Our participation with them adds to our practice of citizen literacy, which includes valuing the shared memories of common cultural events. The idea of citizen literacy might sound new to you, but you've participated in a kind of citizen literacy or shared cultural identity all of your life. In fact, to share a memory of any event—familial, community, and so on—is to share a part of your identity.

Though you might be unfamiliar with the Oklahoma City National Memorial, you probably know of or have seen one of the many national memorials in Washington DC. The Vietnam Veterans Memorial is one site that also encourages participation, much like the Oklahoma City fence, as

CULTURES   Have you ever visited a memorial? Perhaps a local memorial or even a national memorial in Washington DC? What about the memorial made you feel like you were a part of its history? What aspects of the memorial might have shaped your identity as a person or as a citizen of the United States? Explain why the memorial was significant, or not, to you.

you can see in **Figure 3.2**. A common way people interact with the wall is to take a rubbing of names. Often, visitors leave memorabilia as well. To place something at the wall and to take the pencil rubbing allows people to participate and reflect by using the physical place of the wall. Likewise, **Figure 3.3** shows the newly opened World Trade Center Memorial. Much like the Vietnam Veterans Memorial, the World Trade Center Memorial is designed to encourage visitors to interact with the memorial.

Figure 3.2 The Vietnam Veterans Memorial wall

JÖRG HACKEMANN/SHUTTERSTOCK.COM

REX FEATURES VIA AP IMAGES

Figure 3.3 Wall of names at the WTC memorial

CULTURES   In what ways do the memorials in Figures 3.2 and 3.3 look similar? Do they memorialize in similar ways? Do they encourage interaction in similar ways? In what ways do they differ? Does the sense of place matter? The Vietnam War did not occur on the National Mall in Washington DC, but the attack on the WTC did occur at the site of the memorial. Does location reduce or increase the significance of either memorial in any way?

TECHNOLOGIES   Visit the website of a memorial of your choice. (This can be something like one of the 9/11 memorials, the Martin Luther King, Jr. National Memorial, the Oklahoma City National Memorial, or the Massacre of Wounded Knee National Memorial.) How might the shift in place or space from the physical to the virtual affect your interaction with the memorial? Do we need to visit a memorial physically to gain or share in a collective memory?

Other memorials are not so participatory, but they do mark a place where something cultural or historic occurred. Consider the Wounded Knee National Memorial, where more than one hundred Lakota Indians died, including the iconic Chief Big Foot. Many Native Americans consider this place sacred ground. It is not used to participate in the history of the event, necessarily, but the marker helps the place of the massacre retain its significance in Native American history.

Figure 3.4 Image of Crazy Horse Memorial with scale model

NORTH WIND PICTURE ARCHIVES VIA AP IMAGES

Often historic places are marked by a monument. Crazy Horse Memorial (see **Figure 3.4**) is a monument in the making not far from Mount Rushmore, an iconic U.S. monument. The Crazy Horse Memorial is meant to represent Native American culture and its heroes in general. So it's not just the space and place of these memorials and monuments that are significant. The story, or narrative, that is told to keep cultural and shared memory alive is just as, or perhaps even more, important.

Storytelling as Memorial

Geary Hobson, in his introduction to the anthology *The Remembered Earth*, says that "in the remembering of heritage, there is strength, continuance, and renewal." He goes on to reinforce the role of place to Native American culture: "Heritage is people; people are earth; earth is heritage. By remembering these relationships—to the people, the land, the past—we renew in strength our continuance as a people." Hobson claims that the act of storytelling nurtures "the sense of remembering" for a people or a culture. Storytelling is as old as communication itself, and the role of orality, or *verbal literacy*, is just as important as physical space to our shared memories. For instance, Holocaust survivors are asked to archive their stories for museums. Similarly, for many Native American tribes, as Hobson suggests, the act of storytelling is vital to their retaining their culture. Their culture, then, is kept alive by the stories they pass down generation by generation; this oral literacy is part of their shared identity within their tribe's citizen literacy practices. Though the stories are often about sacred places, they also tend to include animal characters or focus on a significant material item. Read the following story, a Choctaw Nation story, and pay close attention to how the story is told and how cultural values and memory are embedded within it.

PAS FALAYA: As Told by Cynthia Clegg

CYNTHIA: This story is about my hokni. Do you know what "hokni" means?

CHILDREN: Yes, yes—"grandma."

CYNTHIA: Grandma is "pokni." Pokni.

CHILDREN: Pokni.

CYNTHIA: My hokni had died. "Hokni" is "aunt."

She told me. She passed away years ago. And she told me this story when I was little. See, I'm from Tucker and my aunt was from Tucker. So then, she said to me, she had been sick and her "icokasat" was not well. Do you all know what "icokas" is?

CHILDREN: No.

CYNTHIA: "Icokas" is your heart.

And her heart was not well. And that's what my grandparents died from. They died of a heart attack. So we were scared because she was sick.

So, anyway she lived in this old wood frame house. And the house was like this [motions with her hand]. Door—"okkisa" means door—the door stood like this, and the living room was like this. And what was supposed to be the dining room, a table was supposed to stand there, they put her bed there. So that's where she slept. And the door was like this, the wall, and the window was here [she motions with her hands to describe the layout of the house].

From the dining room you could see whoever came over toward the door.

So anyways what she told me was that one night, "qbatoh" [it rained].

What is "qba"?

CHILDREN:	"Rain."
CYNTHIA:	Hilohatoh [It was thundering].
	What is "hiloha?"
CHILDREN:	"Thunder."
CYNTHIA:	Malattatoh [It was lightning].
CHILDREN:	"Lightning."
CYNTHIA:	Lightning. It said, "Boom."

She was asleep. It was almost dawn.

So then she said she woke up. Then she said something went "Boom, boom, boom" at the door. And she said she wondered, "What am I hearing?" Then she laid there.

Someone knocked again. It came to the door.

And it rained hard, it was raining so hard that you just couldn't see good outside.

So she said she sat up, then stood up. And she said it seemed as if someone arrived.

"Who would be so crazy to come out in this rain?" she thought.

Then she went to the window. And there was a curtain on the window, so she quietly opened, like this [pantomimes pulling a curtain to the side], and she looked out.

And at the front door, from the sideways, she said she could see this way. And she said a tall man was standing there. And he was wearing a black hat, and his hair was long hair.

So when she said "pasi falaya," I thought she was talking about my grandma's great-uncle, because he died long, long time ago. But he was a medicine man and his name was Pas Falaya.

What is "pas falaya" in Choctaw?

CHILDREN:	"His hair is long."
CYNTHIA:	"Long hair," yes.

That's who I thought she was talking about. I wondered was it him who came and revealed himself to her.

But, she said that when she looked, with the curtain this way [she pantomimes pulled to the side], he stood there. And when a tall man with a long black coat to his knees, was standing there, when she looked at him in this way, his eyes were like this. [Cynthia rolls her eyes back into her head so only the whites show].

Only the whites of his eyes were showing. And it was like this [repeats gesture: kids all scream]. Only the whites of his eyes were showing. He didn't have no pupils.

It was said that when she saw that, she was frightened.

But she wondered, "What will I do?"

She said that when she wondered, "Why is he showing himself to me?" she went back to bed and she was laying there.

She said that the knock stopped and she just fell asleep.

Then when it was morning, she said she didn't tell anyone about it.

It was several days later, she told me about it.

Her son was certainly sick. So it was he who was possibly going to die, she said. Maybe that is the message he is bringing, she said. But, but he never passed away.

It was several months later when it was she who passed away.

And she passed away, she died.

CHILD: How?
CYNTHIA: Her heart, her heart was not good.
CHILD: Who died?
CYNTHIA: My aunt.

After she told me that, when she told me only the whites of his eyes were showing, she said, "I was scared, and I could not go to sleep that night."

So when I see movies today and if it is about ghosts I get scared when I see it.

CHILDREN: Do it again!
CYNTHIA: One last time. [She rolls her eyes back into her head and the kids scream]
CHILDREN: Do it again one more time.
CYNTHIA: It was like this. [She does it again and the kids scream]

But that's my story and that's a true story, because it was my aunt who told me. That's a true story.

CHILD: That was true?
CYNTHIA: It was a true story.

We often use storytelling to build or share memories. When a story is *written*, it's called a *narrative*. Narrative is a primary mode of essay-writing and composition practices because writers like to write about what they know. We commonly tell our experiences through stories in order to share what we know about our culture or history or even to share our opinions about something. And while stories help keep our shared memories and heritage alive, they also help people remember certain points of information.

The audience for any essay needs help to remember what point the author means to make. An author helps the audience remember, often, through a narrative or an *anecdote* (a really short story, usually used as an example) in the essay. When an audience member can relate to a story or recall a similar story, a shared connection is made. Like Native American tribes, our culture, and therefore our essay audience, responds to the emotional appeal (or *pathos*) of a story.

Most narratives are written chronologically. This means the story is organized by time. Much like the fairy tales from our childhood, narratives are often told from beginning to end. Of course, sometimes people tell the end of the story first in order to encourage their audience to read on to find out how the story ended the way it did. Sometimes a flashback within the story explains a past event or episode, and sometimes a flash forward attempts to interest the reader in what is to come. Either way, the narrative is told according to time, even if the time is scrambled.

CULTURES   How might a story's venue affect any shared memories it utilizes for appeal or effect? For instance, is telling the story orally better than writing it down? Does the story gain or lose something in either way? Is culture affected when an oral story is recorded and not just told around the kitchen table or at a public event? What happens to a story when it's put in print? What happens when it's put online? How might these different environments or venues affect the audience?

 TECHNOLOGIES   You may have heard of someone posting a newscast or interview to the Web in the form of a podcast. Using your smart phone or a digital audio recording device, record one of your friends, family, or fellow students telling a story. If you built a website in Chapter 2, post the recording as a link on the site.

If you do not have access to a recording device, write the story by hand or type it and print a hard copy. Attach the story to a poster board and find images that are relevant to the story. Check old magazines, online, or even your own photo albums to tell the story through a collage of sorts on the poster board.

You can also try inserting all your relevant images and the story, in segments, into a Microsoft PowerPoint (or equivalent) slideshow. This would be a great way to practice alternative organization structures as well as slideshow options, such as configuring slides to appear on the screen for a certain amount of time. You could also add a digital audio file of the story to the slideshow. If you built a website in Chapter 2, post this slideshow as a link on the site.

CULTURES   **Write a comparison** of one of the stories you found in your earlier research to a story you've seen in a Disney, or similar, movie.

Rewrite a story you remember from your childhood that included a moral. Change the moral.

Write a screenplay that includes dialogue, characters, and a moral. For an example, see the student screenplays available through the English CourseMate for this text.

Figure 3.5 Editorial cartoon of flag raising at the WTC

Images as Memorials

Shared memories and cultural identity aren't found only in memorials and the stories we tell. We can also share a cultural or collective memory through the narrative of an image or even an editorial cartoon. To get the full story of the cartoon in **Figure 3.5**, for example, the audience must have a large range of historical and social knowledge.

To even begin discussing the shared memory of the cartoon in Figure 3.5, the reader must be familiar with the famous image from the World Trade Center tragedy and the components of the iconic image from the Battle of Iwo Jima during World War II. Similarly, a more recent cultural memory recorded in **Figure 3.6** asks the reader to recall the significant role of a marketing logo in order to make sense of it. Finally, **Figure 3.7** asks the reader to combine the understanding of a cultural artifact, the military headstone, with the image of a child as emotional appeal or pathos.

CULTURES What else did you recognize in the images in Figures 3.5, 3.6, and 3.7? How did you relate to them? Do you think seeing them in this textbook affects you differently than seeing them on the day they were published online or in a newspaper would have? How might editorial cartoons or images help us archive our shared memories?

Figure 3.6 Profile of Steve Jobs in apple

THANK YOU

Figure 3.7 Editorial cartoon of child hugging military headstone

Argument and Memorial

Since memories are such an important part of our culture and being a critical citizen, many people exert great effort to justify building a monument or funding a place for memorial. To do this, they can use another typical form of essay: argument.

Toulmin Argument

Stephen Toulmin developed a standard argumentative technique that usually includes a *claim*, *support* for the claim, and a *warrant*. A claim is the statement of your position in an argument. The most common kinds of claims are claims of policy (changes in rules and regulations), claims of fact (the use of a fact to build an argument), and claims of value (changes based in beliefs and morals, judgments of good or bad and right or wrong). Support might include things like the grounds and backing for your argument and relevant evidence. This evidence usually uses audience appeal, which is commonly understood to involve ethos, pathos, and logos. Simply put, ethos = credibility of character, pathos = emotion, and logos = logic. (You'll practice audience appeal more in Chapter 4.) An argument can also include a shared assumption, or *warrant*. Shared assumptions are a lot like a shared memory or a common place. We, as a culture, assume some things to be true. In an argument, these assumptions are called warrants. They are usually the unstated ways in which we view or approach a problem. Because of their basis in shared values, argument warrants are often the key to identifying weak reasoning or to countering the argument.

Toulmin Argument Example

Claim
Online memorials are not as effective as physical places of memorial.

Support

1. Even though media-based memorials can be interactive, they don't allow the same kind of interaction as physical memorials.

2. The screen eliminates the emotional intimacy associated with the memorial by removing the physical interaction.

3. The screen removes the ability of the visitor to fully experience the memorial because the memorial space isn't shared in the same way with other cyber visitors.

Warrant
The foregoing evidence assumes all people visit and experience memorials in the same way and for the same reasons. (However, we know that different ages and cultures experience and value physical memorials in different ways, so this warrant gives us room for a counterargument.)

Rogerian Argument
An alternative to the Toulmin argument strategy is the Rogerian strategy. Young, Becker, and Pike outline a Rogerian argument in *Rhetoric: Discovery and Change with Communication: Its Blocking and Its Facilitation*. They clarify that a strong Rogerian argument:

- Eliminates threat in language and structure.

- Uses a voice of neutrality.

- Understands the idea, attitude, point of view, feelings, and content of opposition.

Young, Becker and Pike, "From Rhetoric: Discovery and Change, with Communication: Its Blocking and Facilitation," *Teaching Argument in the Composition Course*. Bedford/St. Martin's.

- Shows complete understanding of the opposing argument.
- Realizes the circumstances or context of the validity in the opposing viewpoint.
- Always shows the opposition's argument *first*, and accurately.
- Addresses both denotation and connotation.
- Indicates a sincere, mutual trust from both sides.
- Is participatory and strives for common ground.
- Indicates genuine discourse or dialogue.
- Considers alternatives, or "plays" with ways to understand the opposition.
- Restricts its ties to traditional argumentative techniques.

Imagine the counterargument to the thesis given in the preceding Toulmin argument (Online memorials are not as effective as physical places of memorial).

In a Rogerian argument, you would first present the opposition's side. You would start your essay with an accurate summary of the opposition's points, in a nonthreatening manner. You would use appropriate language and try to find points of contact where you can express that the opposition is valid. In this section of the essay, you would also indicate in what situations the opposition's points might be valid and where it is possible to compromise with some of the points. You would try to show mutual trust and genuine consideration for your opponent's position on the matter at hand. You would then go on to state your side of the issue in a nonthreatening manner. In the end, your essay would likely lack the Toulmin argumentative format, with its structure of claim, support, warrant because Rogerian argument restricts its use of these more traditional structures.

Rogerian Argument Example

The following is a short example of the structure a Rogerian-style paper might take:

> I can see the validity in your claim that online memorials might not be as effective as physical places of memorial. In fact, it's true that though media-based memorials can be interactive, they can't allow the same kind of bodily interaction as physical memorials. Although a website can be interactive through pop-ups and the ability to leave a comment or respond to another visitor, because the visitor can't touch the memorial, a certain level of intimacy is removed.

(Student Samples of complete Rogerian arguments are available on the English CourseMate for this text.)

Popular Culture and Memorial

Like stories, images, cartoons, and memorials, films and television also commemorate shared cultural moments. In his *Amusing Ourselves to Death*, Neil Postman says that "Television . . . encompasses all discourses . . . [and] is our culture's principal mode of knowing about itself." Likewise, Steven Johnson claims that the modern television narrative asks viewers not just to remember but also to analyze. In *Everything Bad Is Good for You*, he says, "this is the difference between intelligent television shows and shows which force you to be intelligent." This narrative Johnson discusses is found in many modern television shows, and these shows are sometimes just as culturally complicated as the physical memorials discussed earlier. In fact, many shows require viewers to have a high level of cultural literacy to understand their nuances. By exerting the effort to understand those nuances, we become critical participants in the shows.

Stephen Johnson, *Everything Bad is Good for You*, Penguin, 2005, pp. 121, 64.

For instance, one popular post-9/11 television series that recently enjoyed a cultlike following was FOX Network's *24*. Each season dealt with a new terrorist action that the members of the Counter Terrorism Unit (CTU) were called to defuse—from nuclear threats to government official–kidnappings and assassinations to drug running. For instance, in one season, a plane was stopped from being used as a bomb, and in another, a bioterrorism plot was foiled. In each season the only way to stop terrorism was through a complicated, shared effort of the CTU community and its governmental and familial counterparts. Family and friends sacrificed for the larger good of the country or the community, a common ideological theme and sociological reaction following traumatic and historic social events. Viewers had to actively participate in several literacy practices to understand the full story of each episode. This was not the type of show an audience could watch passively; it required previous social knowledge.

Other television shows have been born from shared memories and relied on the characters' collective memory to not only build the plot but also keep the memory of the historical event significant. These shows were *about* the event and its aftermath. Three examples of this kind of television show are *Saving Grace*, *Rescue Me*, and the more recent *Homeland*.

Saving Grace is about a female Oklahoma City detective who lost her sister in the bombing. Grace had been too hungover to take care of her nephew the day before the bombing, so her sister put off her trip to the Murrah building until the next day. She was killed; Grace blamed herself. Grace's guardian angel, Earl, attempts to help her through her journey of remorse and remembrance. Among the many episodes that deal with Grace's guilt, the stories of the bombing, the memorial, or the survivors are always present.

The television show *Rescue Me*, like *Saving Grace*, was born from social tragedy. The plot revolves around a firehouse, the firefighters, and the way they deal with the trauma of the World Trade Center attack. Many of the episodes address the firefighters' reactions, reflections, and memorials, but the main story is of Tommy, who lost his cousin when the WTC fell. Among Tommy's many flaws is alcoholism, and Tommy often sees and talks with his dead cousin. *Rescue Me* also deals with heavy subjects like which group of rescuers did more at the WTC—the police or the firemen—whether or not there should be a memorial, and several conspiracy theories.

Homeland is about a Missing-in-Action Marine who suspiciously returns to the United States after being lost for eight years. Brody, the Marine, appears to be a hero, but the CIA thinks differently. He's accused of being turned into an al-Qaeda operative. Still in its infancy, the show asks viewers to see war's effects on soldiers from a new angle. The show is a mix of mystery, intrigue, and social and cultural commentary, which requires the viewer to reconsider his or her views on war, the military, the government, and the ideological concept of threat.

All of these television shows tell the story of how citizens, ordinary and extraordinary, respond to moments in our history that become part of our shared identity. Many of them argue that an ordinary citizen can be extraordinary in times of trauma. All of them respond to our shared memories and help keep our literacy of civic events current.

Televised cartoons, too, often respond to and utilize shared memories and historic events. If you watch *Family Guy*, you might remember the episode where Lois won an election by referring to 9/11. She didn't have to debate her opponent; she simply said, "9/11." Similarly, the televised cartoon *Boondocks* did an episode in response to Hurricane Katrina, where Grandpa didn't want to take in relatives affected by the hurricane. The episode showed how some victims abused the government aid they were receiving. References to historic events and our shared memories of them are all over the television, and our citizen literacy is stronger if we can understand and critically analyze the political and pop-culture responses to such events.

CULTURES   Think of a documentary you've seen that was made in response to a historic moment in our culture or another culture. What types of stories were told? What kinds of arguments were made? Do you think the documentary did a good job of memorializing the event for future generations? Why or why not? What was the film's best attempt at facilitating collective memory? Why did you choose this aspect of the film?

Readings

Some of the readings for this chapter are narrative and some are argumentative. Each touches on, in some way, the role of collective or shared memories. Edward T. Linenthal's article discusses how historical artifacts affect memory in his "Struggling with History and Memory." Kirk Anderson's "Who Killed the Editorial Cartoon" argues that editorial cartoons are dying for numerous reasons, along with the print newspaper. Carrie Coppernoll's "Survivor Stories: Cecil Hawkins" reports on Mr. Hawkin's memory of a tornado which destroyed his home. John L. Esposito and Mona Mogahed argue for a change in context in their "10th Anniversary of 9/11 and Muslim Americans: The Need for a New Narrative." Drew Griffin and Robert Howell's "Teddy Bears, Lab Goggles, Letters Remember Virginia Tech Victims" discusses the memorial archive established for the Virginia Tech victims. Christian Davenport's article about the Arlington National Cemetery focuses on its visitors' modern participatory practices. Dr. Murray's short fiction, "The Last Indian Summer," not only epitomizes the historical conflict of white and "red" relations, it signifies the importance of memory, place, and people in the life of a young boy. Along with Murray's narrative, the two subsequent Native American myths show how storytelling practices can make an argument or uphold cultural identities. You can find more resources about shared memories and identity on the English CourseMate for this text.

● Edward T. Linenthal

Struggling with History and Memory

Professor Linenthal teaches religion and American culture at the University of Wisconsin, Oshkosh. He sat on the advisory board for the Enola Gay exhibition. His latest book is The Unfinished Bombing: Oklahoma City in American Memory (2001).

I wish to speak about the components of the controversy at the National Air and Space Museum (NASM): (1) the presence of the *Enola Gay* itself; (2) the evolution of the museum, from the nation's "Valhalla of the Air" to a place that investigates the "interrelationship between aerospace technology and modern warfare"; (3) commemorative expectations at fiftieth anniversaries; and (4) the grotesque caricature of script, curatorial motive, and interpretive purpose that dominated media coverage. (This stands in striking contrast to the thoughtful critique by military historians of the infamous first script.) I conclude with a few comments about the implications of this controversy.[1]

The *Enola Gay* may stir more passions than any other relic in the culture. For some, it carried a weapon that saved countless lives—perhaps theirs—and ended the war. Brig. Gen. Paul Tibbets, who piloted the *Enola Gay* on its mission to Hiroshima, said it should be displayed as a "peacekeeper . . . the harbinger of a cold war kept from going hot." For others, however, it was a harbinger of a new and more indiscriminate holocaust—a term appropriated purposefully from its traditional usage to impress people with the gravity of the predicament.[2]

There has been ambivalence regarding the appropriate location in American memory and on American soil of the *Enola Gay*. There were scattered objections in 1946 when Sen. Carl Hatch of New Mexico introduced a bill to display the *Enola Gay* in a special museum to be part of an Atomic Bomb National Monument near Alamogordo, New Mexico. There was outrage from some veterans when the *Enola Gay*, already the property of the Smithsonian Institution, languished near a runway at Andrews Air Force Base in Maryland from 1953 to 1960. A 1956 newspaper account reported that "the once bright aluminum exterior is dull. The propellers are rusting, windows have been broken out, instruments smashed and the control surface fabric torn." Yet even aviation enthusiast Barry M. Goldwater—who pushed hard for funding a new air and space museum building in 1970 to tell a "patriot's history"—said, "what we are interested in here are the truly historic aircraft. I wouldn't consider the one that dropped the bomb on Japan as belonging to that category." During the same hearings, Congressman Frank Thompson wondered aloud if the *Enola Gay* should go to the United States Air Force museum in Dayton, Ohio. "I don't think we should be very proud of [the use of atomic weapons]," he said. "At least it would offend me to see it exhibited in the museum."[3]

Martin Harwit became NASM's director in 1987 and decided that the *Enola Gay* would be the centerpiece of an exhibit on the history of strategic bombing, an idea that eventually evolved into the plan for "The Last Act: The Atomic Bomb and the End of World War II."

[1] The phrase "Valhalla of the Air" was used when the Smithsonian Institution took possession of the *Enola Gay*. See Paul Garber, July 3, 1949 (National Air and Space Museum, Washington, D.C.); Martin Harwit to Robert McCormick Adams, Oct. 22, 1991, memo, *ibid*.

[2] [Paul W. Tibbets], "Statement Offered by Brigadier General Paul W. Tibbets (USAF Retired) at the Airmen Memorial Museum on June 8, 1994 Upon the Acceptance of the Air Force Sergeants Association's Freedom Award," *ibid*.

[3] *Evening Star*, July 6, 1956, n.p., ibid. For the remarks by Barry M. Goldwater and Frank Thompson, see Michael McMahon, "The Romance of Technological Progress: A Critical Review of the National Air and Space Museum," Technology and Culture, 22 (April 1981), 294.

But the presence of the *Enola Gay* established a "commemorative membrane" around the exhibition space, within which a language of commemorative respect was expected to dominate. The exhibit was, for veterans and others, a *place of honor*, a place transformed by the aircraft into something other than a museum. In October 1994, during the raging debates over the exhibition, American Legion national commander William Detweiler told an ABC *Nightline* audience, "if the *Enola Gay* is going to be included . . . we are concerned that the valor of those people [the crew members] is going to be dishonored, and that's our major concern. If they pull the *Enola Gay* out . . . then that may be another exhibit that we can talk about." Discussion of the decision to drop the bomb, he said, "belongs somewhere else, in a . . . seminar or in some educational event." Earlier that year, Sen. Nancy Kassebaum told Robert McCormick Adams, then secretary of the Smithsonian, it was a "travesty that when the *Enola Gay* is finally exhibited, it will be in a manner that many veterans find objectionable." She wanted it displayed with "understanding and pride in another museum" and suggested three, all located in her home state of Kansas. Tibbets said the exhibit was a "package of insults" that would "engender the aura of evil in which the airplane is cast."[4]

Historian Greg Mitchell, who coauthored *Hiroshima in America*, read the presence of the *Enola Gay* differently. "Because of its size and visual impact, [the section in which the aircraft appears] overwhelms the rest of the exhibit. It does more than justify the bombings—it glorifies them. And because of [its] central role in the exhibit, this glorification becomes the central (if unintentional) message of the entire script." In November 1994, over eighty historians signed a letter to the new Smithsonian secretary, I. Michael Heyman, noting that "the Smithsonian is taking fastidious care to make sure that each bolt, each gauge and detail of the *Enola Gay* is a perfect reflection of the true artifact," an activity that "stands in extraordinary contrast to the disregard of historical documents and the scholarly literature on the atomic bombings."[5]

The NASM's attempts to present its artifacts, including the *Enola Gay*, in other than their traditional exhibit style angered many, including the editor of *Aviation* magazine, who believed that "a new order is perverting the museum's original purpose from restoring and displaying aviation and space artifacts to presenting gratuitous social commentary on the uses to which they have been put."[6]

---

[4]"The Fight over the Enola Gay," *Nightline* (ABC, Oct. 25, 1994); Nancy Kassebaum to Adams, March 30, 1994 (National Air and Space Museum); [Tibbets], "Statement . . ."
[5]Robert Jay Lifton and Greg Mitchell, *Hiroshima in America: Fifty Years of Denial* (New York, 1995); Greg Mitchell to Michael J. Neufeld, Nov. 22, 1994 (National Air and Space Museum); Martin Sherwin et al. to I. Michael Heyman, Nov. 17, 1994, *ibid.*
[6]Arthur H. Sanfelici, "Is NASM Thumbing Its Nose at Congress While No One's Watching?," *Aviation*, 3 (July 1993), n.p.

The NASM, however, thought it had prepared the way for this exhibit. For example, the V-2 rocket, displayed in a section on civilian space activities, had originally been described in the exhibition label as a

> milestone in the progress of rocket technology. . . . The V-2 held the promise of much larger rockets which could fulfill the dreams of pioneers of space flight. . . . Four thousand of these rockets were fired against Allied targets in England and on the continent in 1944 and 1945. . . . Thus after World War II, missiles which caused much death and destruction pointed the way to development of rocket boosters for launching satellites.

The new description—characterized as a breakthrough in "truth in labeling" in *Science and Government Report*—reads:

> Concentration camp prisoners built V-2s under unimaginably harsh working conditions. Thousands perished in the process. . . . More than 1500 V-2s hit southern England alone, causing over 2000 deaths. . . . V-2s killed a total of 7000 people and terrorized millions. . . . Because the V-2 could not be precisely guided, anyone within miles of the general target could be hit without warning.

Photographs restored a discomfiting past to American rocket hero Wernher von Braun, shown chatting with Nazi officers; a photograph of the body of a V-2 victim in Antwerp, Belgium, was the first corpse shown in a NASM photo. The lack of substantive controversy over this display, over the display of a Soviet SS-20, over a four-minute film at the entrance to a World War II exhibit that discussed the restoration of the *Enola Gay* and the destruction caused by the atomic bomb, or over the exhibit "Legend, Memory and the Great War in the Air"—which contrasted the heroic mythologies of World War I's air war with the horror of trench warfare—all combined with the lack of controversy over a sixteen-month series of lectures, panels, and films on the history of strategic bombing to convince the museum staff that they could successfully mount what they knew would be a controversial exhibit.[7]

But none of these programs had to confront the presence of the *Enola Gay* or to make more complex the orthodox interpretation of the dropping of the bomb on its fiftieth anniversary in *the* major NASM exhibition about the end of World War II. Such anniversaries privilege the commemorative voice, one that speaks with the authority of the witness. And many witnesses of World War II believed that the bomb had saved their

[7]For lengthy excerpts from both old and new labels, see Daniel S. Greenberg, "New Candor on a Nazi Aerospace Legacy," *Washington Post*, Dec. 8, 1990.

lives. In 1993, curator Tom Crouch wrote Martin Harwit, "Do you want to do an exhibition intended to make veterans feel good, or do you want an exhibition that will lead our visitors to think about the consequences of the atomic bombing of Japan? Frankly, I don't think we can do both." While the media accused him of being devious, Crouch recognized the tension between the commemorative voice and the more impersonal historical voice of the exhibition, which seeks to discern motives, understand actions, and discuss consequences that may have been difficult to analyze during the event itself.[8]

There are, in fact, two clashing historical narratives and two commemorative agendas at work in this controversy. One story entailed an exhibition that portrayed the use of the bomb as the culmination of the bloody Pacific war, saving many lives. The appropriate historical context was the pre-bomb horror of the war. The commemorative message was: "Remember what we did and what it cost." The other, proposed by the museum, sought to freeze a moment it considered a turning point in world history, the first use of atomic weapons. While acknowledging the bomb's role in ending the war, this second narrative's historical context was the postwar legacy of the nuclear arms race; its appropriate intellectual context a host of controversial issues that had occupied historians for fifty years. The commemorative message was: "Never again."

Privately, museum personnel received mixed signals about their plans. In the summer of 1993, the Air Force Association conveyed to Harwit its ringing denunciation of an exhibit proposal, but these warnings were not taken seriously. At our February 1994 advisory committee meeting, the only substantive criticisms came from historian Martin Sherwin, author of *A World Destroyed,* who worried whether a museum exhibit could do justice to the historical controversies and whether the presence of the *Enola Gay* would make the exhibit too celebratory. Air force historians Richard Hallion and Herman Wolk—both members of the advisory committee—sent the curators a list of criticisms but prefaced their comments by saying, "Overall, this is a most impressive piece of work, comprehensive and dramatic, obviously based upon a great deal of sound research, primary and secondary. While little is left untouched, no mean feat in itself, there are places and themes which require either more, or less, emphasis in order to give the exhibit a better contextual balance." A handwritten note at the end of the list of criticisms reads, "Again—an impressive job! A bit of 'tweaking' along the lines discussed here, should do the trick." In subsequent correspondence with curator Tom Crouch, Hallion said this was merely a "polite and supportive

---

[8]Tom Crouch to Martin Harwit, July 21, 1993 (National Air and Space Museum).

introduction of encouragement." Hallion also passed a handwritten note to curator Michael Neufeld that read, "Mike—chin up—you've got a great script, and nobody—except Marty— is out to emasculate it." In an August 1994 letter to Crouch, Hallion complained that this "friendly 'bridge building' note I passed to Mike Neufeld during our meeting in early February in an effort to maintain a useful dialogue has even been cited out of context." Responding to Hallion, Crouch wrote, "If you are telling me that you simply wanted to be polite, I can only respond that we were looking for an honest reading—not polite chit-chat. If you really saw a problem, you should have indicated it. We might not be in this situation today." Hallion answered, "We trusted you, and believed that you would take our comments seriously. Since you did not 'big trouble' naturally resulted." He became a prominent critic of the exhibit, complaining that none of his criticisms had been taken seriously.[9]

Also responding positively to the first script was the only Pacific war combat veteran on the advisory committee, former chief historian of the National Park Service, Edwin C. Bearss. He wrote to Crouch that "as a World War II Pacific War combat veteran, I commend you and your colleagues who have dared to go that extra mile to address an emotionally charged and internationally significant event in an exhibit that, besides being enlightening, will challenge its viewers."[10]

The first major critique of the exhibition script appeared in the pages of *Air Force Magazine* in April 1994. The focus was less on the specifics of the script than on the philosophical bent of the museum, which had led to what editor John Correll believed was an unbalanced exhibit. He complained about existing exhibits, including "Legend, Memory and the Great War in the Air," characterizing them as "politically correct curating." Although it was ignored in the subsequent condemnation of the exhibition as an offense to all veterans, *Air Force Magazine* did note that the 509th Composite Group was covered "extensively and with respect."[11]

As criticism intensified in the spring of 1994, Harwit appointed another review body, the "Tiger Team," which included several air force veterans and was chaired by retired air force Brig. Gen. William Constantine. Contrary to all press accounts, of the 42 specific recommendations this review body made,

[9] Martin J. Sherwin, *A World Destroyed: The Atomic Bomb and the Grand Alliance* (New York, 1975); Richard Hallion and Herman Wolk, Feb. 7, 1994, critique (National Air and Space Museum); Hallion to Crouch, Aug. 9, 1992, *ibid.*; Crouch to Hallion, Aug. 12, 1994, *ibid.*; Hallion to Crouch, Aug. 15, 1994, *ibid.*

[10] Edwin C. Bearss to Crouch, Feb. 24, 1994, *ibid.*

[11] John T. Correll, "War Stories at Air and Space," *Air Force Magazine*, 77 (April 1994), 28.

30 were fully implemented, 7 were partially implemented, and only 5 were not by the fall of 1994. Despite these alterations, media criticism became both more venomous and more reckless. A few examples: an opinion piece in a small-town North Carolina newspaper asked and answered, "how bleeding are some hearts? One Smithsonian exhibit is Japan's Hiroshima Memorial Peace Museum," thereby "proving" to readers that the Smithsonian was pro-Japanese. *USA Today*'s Tony Snow informed his readers of the "consensus" view that "six million or more people would have died during an allied invasion of Japan" and dismissed any arguments that postwar concerns about the Soviet Union were a factor in the decision to drop the bomb as "crackpot theories." In the *Washington Times,* R. Emmett Tyrrell Jr. railed against the "politically correct pinheads . . . at the Smithsonian Institution" and declared that had one million Americans died in an invasion of Japan, "surely that would have left some of the present pinheads . . . fatherless or even, oh bliss, unborn." And, in the most egregious example of journalistic irresponsibility, the *Wall Street Journal* spoke of the "oozing romanticism with which the . . . show's writers describe the kamikaze pilots . . . , These were, the script elegiacally relates, 'youths, their bodies overflowing with life.'" The *Journal* has taken a quotation from a kamikaze pilot in the script and implied that these are the curators' words, although the curators included this to provide "insight into [the kamikazes'] suicidal fanaticism, which many Americans would otherwise find incomprehensible." Ken Ringle of the *Washington Post* quoted the *Journal*'s paragraph, repeating for his readers the false accusation.[12]

Each subsequent draft of the script brought a new round of media denunciation, even while Alfred Goldberg, historian at the Office of the Secretary of Defense and a veteran of World War II, wrote of the August 1994 script, "the first three sections of this draft should dispose of most of the negative criticism. . . . The issues of racism, strategic bombing policy, [the] decision to drop the bomb, and invasion plans and casualties are handled with acceptable objectivity. . . . The section on the effects of the atomic bombs . . . will no doubt continue to draw critical comment as being too long, too detailed, and too sympathetic to the Japanese, but the exhibit would be incomplete and much less meaningful without it." He did, however, suggest cutting the section on effects by another 25 percent.[13]

---

[12]Johnny Morrow, "From Where I Sit," *Mooresville* [North Carolina] *Tribune,* May 18, 1994; Tony Snow, "Sanitizing the Flight of the Enola Gay," *USA Today,* Aug. 1, 1994; R. Emmett Tyrrell Jr., "Hiroshima and the Hectoring Herd," *Washington Times,* Sept. 24, 1994; "War and the Smithsonian," *Wall Street Journal,* Aug. 29, 1994; Ken Ringle, "A-Bomb Exhibit Plan Revamped," *Washington Post,* Aug. 30, 1994.
[13]Alfred Goldberg to Neufeld, Sept. 19, 1994 (National Air and Space Museum).

As script after script deleted material about historical controversies regarding the decision to drop the bomb, added photographs both of mushroom clouds and of structural damage, and removed most photographs of dead Japanese, historians and peace activists met with museum officials to argue for what they believed should be restored or newly incorporated. They wanted to restore the statements of military figures who expressed reservations about the use of atomic weapons, to revise a statement that Hiroshima was a military target, to revise casualty figures, to restore photographs of Japanese victims, to include documentation "of religious, moral, and political protest," and to treat adequately the legacy of the bomb. The exhibit scripts became a kind of Rorschach test. People were concerned with different questions, paid attention to different "facts," and interpreted the same facts differently.

In the end, all the groups involved believed their history had been "stolen," resulting either in a "revisionist" exhibit or in one showing a callous disregard for historical integrity. Most disturbing, the media assumed that critics were objective in their view of history and that only anti-American museum curators and revisionist historians brought a point of view to the exhibit. Many who contemptuously dismissed historians as revisionists are no doubt pleased when Russian historians revise *their* memory of World War II—to confront, for example, the Molotov-Ribbentrop pact, the Finnish-Russian War of 1939–1940, and the murder by Soviet secret police of approximately 21,000 Polish officers in the Katyn Forest in 1940—or when the Japanese recall their role as perpetrators in the Pacific war. In each country there is opposition from those who look upon revisionists as subversives who demean military sacrifice and national honor.[14]

Very troubling is the ignorance and arrogance of certain members of Congress, for whom completely unfamiliar historical debates about the bomb registered as un-American activity. Rep. Sam Johnson, recently appointed to the Smithsonian Institution Board of Regents, said, "We've got to get patriotism back into the Smithsonian. We want the Smithsonian to reflect real America and not something that a historian dreamed up." On May 11 and May 18, 1995, the Senate Committee on Rules and Administration, chaired by Sen. Ted Stevens, held hearings on the exhibition. Questions the American Legion asked to be raised indicate the vindictive atmosphere: "Has it been Harwit's intent since his hiring to 'radicalize' and 'redirect' NASM?" "Why was Michael Neufeld, a Canadian national, hired by NASM?" "What

---

[14]For a recent discussion of the massacre in Katyn Forest, see Nina Tumarkin, *The Living and the Dead: The Rise and Fall of the Cult of World War II in Russia* (New York, 1994), 176–81.

are his philosophical and political underpinnings?" During my testimony, Senator Stevens asked why taxpayers' funds should be used to "support a book or a museum exhibit on the basis of scholarly enterprise, despite the fact that it goes against the commonly accepted viewpoint as to the interpretation of the history of the event." In this view, the responsibility of historians and curators working in public institutions is to support "commonly accepted viewpoints" and, further, to celebrate the American experience. If they do, their work is "factual." If they do not, their work is subversive and "revisionist." While there were real errors of judgment, if not stunning examples of political naïveté, in the creation of the exhibit, none was a dereliction for which the jobs of museum curators should be threatened. If museums are forced to shape exhibits merely to satisfy benefactors, the result will be propaganda. A dangerous precedent is set when an interest group representing only one voice—be it the American Legion or the Fellowship of Reconciliation—becomes the arbiter of public history.[15]

Rep. Peter I. Blute of Massachusetts, one of twenty-four congressmen who complained about the exhibit in a letter to Martin Harwit in August 1994, told Andrea Stone of *USA Today*, "I don't want sixteen-year-olds walking out of there thinking badly of the U.S."[16] History, however, should not be confused with therapy, used to puff up the self-esteem of individuals or nations. If Congressman Blute believes the patriotic litmus test of a public museum in the nation's capital is that young people should not be confronted with the complexities of history, would he then want to oppose federal funding for the United States Holocaust Memorial Museum? There, visitors learn that Americans encountered and liberated the camps and that many Holocaust survivors found a home in the United States. They also learn, however, about prewar anti-Semitism in the State Department that kept thousands of European Jews from legally emigrating to this country. They learn that the ss *St. Louis* was turned away from American shores in 1939, resulting in the deaths of many passengers in the Holocaust. At that museum, visitors are judged to be mature enough to be able to engage a story that is more than a heroic American narrative. Surely they had the ability to do the same at the NASM.

[15]"A Museum in Crisis," *U.S. News and World Report*, Feb. 13, 1995, p. 74. For the questions from the American Legion, see Johnson to Heyman, March 22, 1995 (National Air and Space Museum); and Rowan Scarborough, "Congressman Keeps Asking about Enola Gay Exhibit," *Washington Times*, April 11, 1995. U.S. Congress, Senate, Committee on Rules and Administration, *Hearings on the Smithsonian Institution Management Guidelines for the Future*, 104 Cong., 1 sess., May 11, 18, 1995, p. 65.

[16]Andrea Stone, "Wounds of War Still Color Enola Gay's Place in History," *USA Today*, Oct. 5, 1994.

1. What role do history and memory play in society?
2. What does Linenthal argue?
3. What is the story behind the *Enola Gay*?
4. How might an artifact like an airplane help a museum visitor understand an important event?
5. How might the emotion associated with an artifact complicate how we view history or encourage a memorial?
6. How might writing a reflection about an artifact help an author tell a story of an event?
7. How might writing a reflection about an artifact help an author make an argument?

● Kirk Anderson

Who Killed the Editorial Cartoon?

Kirk Anderson is an editorial cartoonist. His often controversial cartoons have appeared in *The New York Times*, *The Washington Post*, and *Newsweek*, among other publications.

The profession of editorial cartooning isn't so much dying as it is simply entering a new phase in the circle of life—the phase where the corpse is eaten by maggots and turned into dirt.

This nutrient-rich soil will help future generations of satire to grow and prosper, and the cycle continues. Pessimists are fond of looking at maggot-infested corpses and seeing only the negative; I see helpful maggots hell-bent on progress.

Motivational speakers remind us that the Sanskrit word for "opportunity" is the same as the one for "loss of job, profession, life savings and health care." We editorial cartoonists know that when one window closes, another one opens, even if it leads onto the ledge of the 41st floor.

True, cartoonists are just above mimes and poets in social significance; is the nation really losing anything?

Editorial cartoons used to have power and influence. This was back in the days of Thomas Nast, when the corrupt politician Boss Tweed famously said of Nast's blasts, "Stop them damn pictures! I don't care what the papers write about me. My constituents can't read. But, damn it, they can see the pictures!" (True quote.) Editorial cartoons might still carry such power today, were it not for the destructive rise in literacy.

But now there is enormous competition for the public's attention. Back in the late 1800s, if you weren't looking at an editorial cartoon, you were checking out hog scrapers in the Sears-Roebuck catalog. This was back when people went to church just for something to do, as preachers were about the only available form of entertainment next to bear-baiting.

Editorial cartoons must have spoken to people like a burning bush. Today we find a burning bush in every commercial, a burning train wreck on every news broadcast and an inferno on every AM radio show. An editorial cartoon must blow up bridges, flash breasts and teach your child Spanish, just to be noticed.

Or maybe not. People still read books. Books! Some books are still in black and white, and some don't even have pictures.

Similarly, people still enjoy live stand-up comedy. In a world where we demand the latest and the fastest, people still pay to see a mortal simply stand on stage and talk to them. Just a guy.

No different from Caveman Dave telling stories around the campfire. We've had satire ever since Cavewoman Bernice drew a buffalo stampede on a cave wall, trampling Caveman Dave. We will always have and will always need satire, whether it comes in a 2D drawing or a Zenga Bot X9000.

One of my favorite editorial cartoons is George Orwell's "Animal Farm," which is not an editorial cartoon at all in the traditional sense, but an editorial cartoon in the form of a novel, with its brilliant use of metaphor, humor, insight and outrage.

Satire may come in the form of Mark Twain, Jonathan Swift, Shakespeare or Stephen Colbert's scorching and divine presentation at the White House correspondents' dinner.

We satirists in the editorial cartoonist cult have long referred to ourselves as "buggy-whip makers," with newspapers playing the role of buggies. That would be a problem, if the death of the horse and buggy had rendered the nation devoid of transportation.

But the horse and buggy were just one form of travel, and editorial cartoons are just one form of satire, to be replaced by something better when it comes along. Unless there's a government bailout.

I can hear you say, "Isn't the future of editorial cartoons online? And in animation? My neighbor's daughter has an online cartoon, and people in Belize and Lithuania are reading it."

The pessimists reply, "But how do you make money?" The optimists say, "*Volume!* Sure, people don't pay for content, but if *enough* people don't pay for content, surely you reach a *critical mass* of nonpaying customers!" The pessimists say, "People don't pay for content."

Editorial cartoons are dying because newspapers are dying, or perhaps "adapting." Or "entering a new phase in the circle of life." Some of the damage is self-inflicted. Some newspapers want safe cartoons that won't bring phone calls from advertisers, and safe cartoons are as fascinating as safe NASCAR.

To the extent we cartoonists oblige, self-censor and draw nonthreatening gag cartoons about swilling beers at the White House, we're part of the problem and deserve our enforced dirt nap.

Life will go on without editorial cartoons, just as it will without bank regulation. The death of newspapers is not so different from the death of any other commodity: eight-track tapes, perhaps.

That is, if eight-track tapes were fundamental to a functioning democracy.

READING REACTIONS

1. What is the role of the editorial cartoon according to Anderson?
2. What are the primary characteristics of the editorial cartoon?
3. What aspects of the editorial cartoon are no longer necessary? Why?
4. Why is the newspaper dying? Why is the editorial cartoon dying?
5. How does Anderson appeal to his audience?
6. Does his argument have a strong claim? Support? Evidence? Why or why not?
7. What warrant underlies Anderson's argument? How would you counter his points?

Carrie Coppernoll

Survivor Stories: Cecil Hawkins

As a columnist and reporter for *The Oklahoman*, Carrie Coppernoll has won several awards, including being named 2008 Journalist of the Year by the Oklahoma City Chapter of the Public Relations Society of America. She also writes for the Red Dirt Ruckus Blog at blog.newsok.com/red-dirt-ruckus.

DEL CITY—Cecil Hawkins lay flat on his stomach in the grass, eyeing the maple tree in his back yard as the tornado ripped off all the branches. If the tornado didn't knock that tree on him, he thought, he'd survive. The tree was still standing and Hawkins lived, though the storm ripped apart the Del City home he'd lived in for nearly 50 years. "After losing all the things, the Lord gave me a peace of mind that he was going to take care of me," said Hawkins, who is now 84. "I usually cry about anything that amounted to anything, but that tornado, I didn't cry."

Hawkins grew up in Harmon County, where he met his future wife, LaFern. They married in March 1947 and soon after moved to their home in Del City. He repaired lawnmowers and appliances for a living, and he and his wife spent a decade as Baptist missionaries in Mexico. LaFern died in 1998, so Hawkins was living alone the night of May 3, 1999.

He heard the tornado coming, and ran to the back yard to get into the cellar. The wind was too strong, and Hawkins couldn't pull the door open. He gave up and headed back for the house, but the wind knocked him over. He lay on his back yard as the storm passed overhead, sucking away his home. The storm moved on, leaving Hawkins in his back yard. Debris surrounded him—lumber, branches, a metal beam from the construction supply yard nearby. A round piece of metal half the size of his body lay inches away. "If it had landed on top of me," he said, "it would have killed me."

Hawkins was treated for a cut on his head and spent the night with a friend in Del City. The next day, he returned to the remains of his home. He found some tools, an air conditioner, a garden tractor and some sheets of tin. Looters took it all, except for lumber and Bibles.

"I was not angry about losing my house," he said. "It made me mad to think them robbers had come and cleaned me out." Where his house stood is now the Sheraton Hotel. He was able to buy a new home with insurance money, federal assistance and small gifts from strangers. "I was surprised to get that kind of help," he said, wiping away tears. "People are really good to me to help me. I was surprised."

READING REACTIONS

1. Who is Cecil Hawkins and why is his story important?
2. What role does the tornado play in his memory?
3. What role does the tornado play in his cultural, community, or family history?
4. What kind of details does Hawkins use to make his story interesting enough for Coppernoll to use in her article? Think about audience appeal (ethos, pathos, logos).
5. Does Hawkins's story make an argument or have a moral?
6. What is the role of the image (**Figure 3.8**) that accompanies the story?

COURTESY OF THE OKLAHOMAN

Figure 3.8 Elderly man who survived tornado clutches Bible.

● John L. Esposito and Mona Mogahed

10th Anniversary of 9/11 and Muslim Americans: The Need for a New Narrative

John L. Esposito is a professor of religion and international affairs at Georgetown University. He is author of more than forty-five books and monographs, and his articles and interviews have appeared in publications such as *The New York Times* and *The Economist*. Mogahed is a Conference Organizer at Georgetown and received her bachelor of arts in Rhetoric, Religious Studies, and Middle East Studies from the University of Wisconsin–Madison.

While post-9/11 resulted in necessary Western government responses to counter international and domestic terrorism, this tragic event has been widely exploited by far-right neocons, hardline Christian Zionist Right and xenophobic forces. Islam and mainstream Muslims have been brush-stroked with "terrorism," equated with the actions of a fraction of violent extremists. Major polls by Gallup, PEW and others reported the extent to which many Americans and Europeans had and have a problem not only with terrorists but also with Islam and all Muslims.

Islamophobia grew exponentially, as witnessed in America's 2008 presidential and 2010 congressional elections, Park 51 and post-Park 51 anti-mosque and so-called anti-Shariah campaigns, as well as increased hate speech and violence. The massacre in Norway is a tragic signal of this metastasizing social cancer. Anders Behring Breivik's 1500-page manifesto confirmed the influence of the hate speech spread by American anti-Muslim (Islamophobic) leaders, organizations and websites.

It is truly time for a new narrative, one that is informed by facts, and that is data-driven, to replace the shrill voices of militant Muslim bashers and opportunistic politicians chasing funds and votes. Key findings from the recently released Abu Dhabi Gallup Report, "Muslim Americans: Faith, Freedom, and the Future," offer data that provide a good starting point—a very different picture of Muslims in America today.

Far from the image of a fifth column of foreign, terrorist sympathizers and shariah-imposing boogeymen, data indicates that Muslim Americans are actually among the most integrated, optimistic,

Figure 3.9 American flag used as hijab, or head covering

ISTOCKPHOTO.COM/DIETER SPEARS

thriving, and loyal citizens of this country. Astonishingly, despite the hate speech, discrimination and erosion of their civil liberties, American Muslims remain optimistic about their status and future in America. Muslim Americans report being better off and more optimistic in 2011 than they were in 2008. Their life evaluation ratings have increased more than any other American religious group: 60% are thriving in 2011, up 19 percentage points from 2008. They are also more hopeful about their future than any other major religious group. They rate their lives in 5 years at 8.4 on a scale of 0 to 10, compared with 7.4 to 8.0 among other major religious groups and are more likely to see their standard of living getting better in 2011 (64%) than they were in 2008 (46%). More than other groups, Muslim Americans believe the economy in 2011 vs. 2008 has improved more than that of other groups. They tend to vote Democrat and are happier with the political climate since the election of Obama (8 in 10 Muslim Americans approve of Obama's job performance, the highest of any other major religious group).

In contrast to their critics who question their loyalty and charge that Muslim Americans do not reject terrorism, Muslim Americans (78%) are most likely to reject violent military attacks on civilians and are most likely (89%) to reject violent individual attacks on civilians versus other major U.S. religious groups. 92% say Muslims living in this country have no sympathy for Al Qaeda.

Yet, despite data that indicates Muslim Americans are loyal to the U.S., 10 years after 9/11 significant minorities of their fellow citizens continue to question their loyalty. Thus, while 93% of Muslim Americans believe they are loyal to America, 80% of Jews, 59% of Catholics, and 56% of Protestants believe this to be the case. Not surprisingly, 60% of Muslim Americans believe that most Americans are prejudiced toward Muslims and data shows that roughly half (between 47%–66%) among other religious groups agree. 48% of Muslims (by far the highest of any other group) say they have personally experienced religious or racial discrimination in the past year.

At the same time, 57% percent of Muslim Americans have confidence in the honesty of elections, the highest of all other major U.S. religious groups, and are among the most open group to other faith communities, with 44% classified as "integrated," 48% as "tolerant," and only 8% as "isolated."

For many, one of the most astonishing findings of the Gallup poll may well be the common ground that Muslims share with Jewish Americans in their political and social views. After Muslim Americans themselves (93%), Jewish Americans (80%) are more likely than Catholics, Protestants, and Mormons (59% or less) to see U.S. Muslims as loyal to America. They say that there is prejudice toward U.S. Muslims in higher numbers (66%) than do Muslims (60%). Jews (74%) and Muslims (83%) in America are the most likely to say the Iraq war was a "mistake." And perhaps most surprising, a substantial majority of Jewish Americans (78%) and Muslim Americans (81%) support a future in which an independent Palestinian state would coexist alongside of Israel.

This September 11th provides an opportunity to remember the past but also to recognize that truth is stranger than fiction, the fiction constructed by preachers of hate whose fear-mongering has infected our popular culture and society. Now is the time to reassess and rebuild our national unity on the facts.

READING REACTIONS

1. What does this article argue?
2. How does the article define "Muslim Americans"?
3. Does the article argue a claim of fact, value, or policy? How do you know?
4. What is the article's most surprising statistic?
5. Does the article rely most on ethos, pathos, or logos for audience appeal?
6. What three words in the article affected you most? Why?
7. Would you categorize this as a Toulmin or Rogerian argument?

Drew Griffin and Robert Howell

Teddy Bears, Lab Goggles, Letters Remember Virginia Tech Victims

Drew Griffin and Robert Howell wrote for CNN/US. Griffin is currently a correspondent writer and worked as an investigative reporter in Los Angeles. Howell now works as a television news producer.

Erin Sheehan was a freshman last year when Seung-Hui Cho peeked through the door of her German class. The next hour of her life would become a struggle for survival. "The gunman entered my room. He shot my German teacher and then proceeded to shoot the students in the classroom pretty thoroughly," she said. Sheehan was only one of four students in the room not to get shot. She jumped on the floor and remained quiet while Cho went on his rampage. "I thought if I played dead then he hopefully would think I was already hit." She listened as the killer left her Norris Hall classroom to attack another room. She and the other survivors barricaded the door to keep Cho from coming back. "I tried to use a podium at the front of the classroom to block the door, because the gunman was shoving at the door and started firing through the door. We didn't think we were going to be able to hold it," she said.

Sheehan is now a sophomore at Virginia Tech. Like so many on campus, April 16, 2007, marks the worst day of her life, when Cho killed 32 students and professors in the deadliest school shooting in U.S. history.

Sheehan recently accompanied CNN to what is known as the Virginia Tech April 16, 2007 Prevail Archive—an office space on the edge of campus where mementoes sent from across the world are temporarily warehoused. The university is cataloging and documenting every item it can save in order to create a permanent collection as well as an online archive that the public can access.

Teddy bears, an American flag from the U.S. Embassy in Afghanistan, painted eggs, the hood of a race car, condolence posters signed by Koreans and a letter from President Bush are housed there. Thousands of other letters are also kept in the archive.

"This is making me feel super bad. Because a lot of people died at Blacksburg. I love VT," wrote one young child. Walking through the archive for the first time, Sheehan was overcome with emotion. She stopped and held a picture of all the victims, pointing out her slain German teacher and another classmate. "I believe this is Nicole White, she sat right next to me. And I think I would credit her with taking bullets for me," she said in a muted tone. Of the entire archive, she added, "I don't ever remember seeing it all together like this before. I think it is really remarkable that so many people cared to reach out to us like this." Tamara Kennelly is the archivist at Virginia Tech. She's responsible for documenting how everyone beyond the campus dealt with the tragedy, when the world was joined by four words: "We are all Hokies." "People at other places have really identified with us and felt all of this with us," she said. "I think it's very heartening, it's very moving to me."

They've received just about anything, from condolences books from funeral homes to messages from prisons to letters from elementary students.

"There are always people who really have their own story to tell or a powerful way of putting it. And when you find those letters, they stay with you—all day, all week," said Amy Vilelle, the manuscript archivist. "There are a few that I will not ever forget reading." Some are very personal, like a pair of goggles from a lab partner. "Mike may you rest in peace. You will forever be remembered as my favorite lab partner. We'll be missing you," it says on the goggles. Fighting back tears, Kennelly said, "This job is very moving because you get something and you read it and you think, 'oh gosh, they want to share something with us somehow. They want to reach out and give some kindness.'" Gail McMillan, the director of digital archives, says it's especially difficult to read material from children. "It's hard to know what kind of impact this may have on them."

Their job is not only to remember, but to preserve, an archival collection for the university. For those who lived it, the tragic events of April 16, 2007, are still too fresh to put into the past.

"I still have trouble sleeping some days," Sheehan said. "It really does bother me because I still understand I could have been killed so easy, and there is no explanation why I wasn't."

READING REACTIONS

1. What makes this eyewitness account interesting?
2. What is the emotional difference between an eyewitness account of an event and a story told at second hand?
3. How is the Prevail Archive like any other archive? How might the archive be useful or important in fifty years?
4. Why is having the archive important?
5. What types of artifacts listed in the article seem to most effectively convey memories?
6. In what ways is the archive participatory?

● Christian Davenport

At Arlington National Cemetery, Mementos for Latest War Dead Get More Personal

Christian Davenport is a reporter for *The Washington Post* and a finalist for the 2005 Pulitzer Prize for his work on the scandal of the Abu Ghraib prison in Iraq. He is also author of *As You Were: To War and Back with the Black Hawk Battalion of the Virginia National Guard.*

The headstones wear Hawaiian leis and Mardi Gras beads. They are festooned with bottles of Yuengling, flasks full of Jack, boxes of cigars.

In Arlington National Cemetery's Section 60, where those killed in Iraq and Afghanistan lie, the graves aren't just markers of remembrance; they are canvases decorated with stones, shiny balloons and handwritten notes. In this corner of the nation's most sacrosanct military burial ground, all manner of ornamentation abounds—one headstone is covered in lipstick kisses—bringing a colorful poignancy to an otherwise monochromatic place of mourning.

Above all there are faces. Arlington may officially consecrate the fallen by marble and etched lettering, but the families of Section 60 have rejected those

Figure 3.10 Military headstone with memorabilia

protocols, covering the graves with photos of the dead. Here they are as children. Here they are with their battle buddies. Here they are with their families.

One note reads, "Dear Daddy, I know it seems impossible but I'm going to be a junior in high school . . ."

Many of these mementos are gathered by curators from the U.S. Army Center for Military History who descend on Section 60 every week. To preserve what is left behind, they add the items to a collection they hope will one day become a museum exhibit to help tell the story of the wars, and their cost.

On Friday, Veterans Day, the cemetery will again be full of mourners who will leave in their wake new graveside gifts. And sometime next week, the curators will sweep through with their plastic bags.

Since the program began about two years ago, after news outlets reported that the cemetery was regularly trashing items left at graves and leaving others to rot in the rain, the curators have collected more than 4,500 objects. They are catalogued and stored at a climate-controlled facility at Fort Belvoir, where the air is recycled four times daily.

Flowers and other organic materials are not kept.

"Items that are not collected by the Center for Military History are removed when they become faded and unsightly or pose a hazard to groundskeepers," said cemetery spokeswoman Jennifer Lynch. (She would not say how the uncollected objects are disposed of.)

At the Vietnam Veterans Memorial, visitors have been leaving objects for many years, and they are collected daily by the National Park Service. Some have been displayed at the Smithsonian's National Museum of American History. They also are kept at a Park Service facility in Landover.

At Arlington, before the wars in Iraq and Afghanistan, "the expression of grief was confined to wreaths and flowers—that's all people brought by," said Chris Semancik, acting chief of the Army's Collections Branch. "It's now changed to be much more personal in nature."

At Christmas there are wrapped presents. At Halloween, pumpkins. At Valentine's Day, hearts and cupids. At St. Patrick's Day, many graves are covered with Guinness bottles and four-leaf clovers.

The Army has gathered all sorts of knickknacks: poker chips, a Martha's Vineyard snow globe, bullets, a Superman Pez dispenser. Some items are deeply personal: ultrasound images, poems, Purple Hearts, Bronze Stars.

So much of the cemetery is for everyone else, the 4 million annual visitors who make it one of the most frequented stops on the Washington tour loop. They gather at the eternal flame at John F. Kennedy's grave, the stately Memorial Amphitheater and, of course, the Tomb of the Unknowns.

But Section 60 is unlike any place else at Arlington. It's a place for the living as much as the dead, both mournful and celebratory.

On a recent visit, Roderick Gainer, a curator with the military history center, scooped up a Coast Guard flag. U.S. flags, he leaves. They've already collected plenty.

"It's unusual to get a Coast Guard flag," he said. Into the bag it went.

On a nearby grave was a small plaque that said, "We love you."

"That wasn't here last week," Gainer said. "So let's leave it for another week."

He left a bullet casing. "Those are becoming more and more common," he said.

He took a family photo, a Marine Corps Marathon medal, a note that read, "For my love, Paul."

"It's an evolving process," Gainer said. "We're balancing sentimentality with documentation."

Taking items from veterans' graves could be hazardous duty. Gainer and his colleagues wear jackets that clearly identify them as Army staffers, in thick yellow lettering. At first, he said, families wanted to know what they were doing.

"They were never hostile, just curious," he said. "Word spread very quickly, and then it was, 'Are you the guys from the Center of Military History?'"

Overall, families are supportive of the program, but some are concerned that they "left a private note and it's collected and then it's in a museum somewhere," said Amy Neiberger-Miller, a spokeswoman for TAPS, a nonprofit organization for families of fallen service members.

"There is awareness on all our parts that some things are personal and not for public dissemination," said Charles Cureton, the director of Army

Museums. But he said the notes are vital to the country's understanding of the people who fought and died.

"Twenty years from now, 100 years from now, that's the record of what people thought about those individuals, and it gives us connection to them," he said. "And it makes that person who died timeless."

The curators start collecting toward the rear of Section 60, from the graves of those killed in the wars' early days. They move forward through the rows of headstones, and through recent history, from the days after Sept. 11 to the invasion of Iraq, to those killed in the surges of both wars, until they get to where the dirt has just been recently turned.

They've been doing it so long now that they know many of the families, and they are getting to know more each week. Since they've started, about 10 new rows of graves have been added.

Finishing up their recent visit, the collectors reached the last row of Section 60, where the fresh graves did not yet have headstones, only temporary markers. At one there was a photograph of a soldier. A smiling face, peering up from the dirt.

READING REACTIONS

1. How is the cemetery like an archive? How might the cemetery's archived items be useful or important to future visitors?
2. Of the artifacts listed, which seem to most effectively convey memories?
3. Which items seem to correlate with items left at the Vietnam Veterans Memorial wall or the Oklahoma City Bombing fence?
4. How do you think visitors choose which items to leave?
5. How is the cemetery participatory to visitors? To history? To memory making?

● Jason Murray

The Last Indian Summer

Dr. Jason E. Murray, an American Indian, (Chickasaw and Choctaw) is the Associate Chief Diversity Officer, Director of Indian University of North America, and Assistant Professor of English at the University of South Dakota. Dr. Murray has published short fiction and poetry in the *Yellow Medicine Review*, the *Oklahoma Review* and the *Red River Review*.

It's been almost twelve years since I've been home. I'm sure my family is waiting on me to show up at my parent's house for Thanksgiving, but I find myself feeling a bit nostalgic. And so I end up driving around—visiting old haunts and recalling times before marriage, before college, and some even before manhood. I visit the high school, where our football team won state during my senior year. I visit Van's Hamburger Stand, where my cousins and I used to devour mountains of cheeseburgers and curly-Qs. I even visit the home of my first real girlfriend, Lisa Jefferies, who broke my heart when she ran off to Dallas with some twenty-seven-year-old used car salesman named Larry Coker. It feels good to visit these places, but the one place I really long to visit, no longer exists. Instead, in its place stands a large cedar and stained glass building crowned with an oversized decorative sign that reads, "Shawnee Garden Club."

"Twelve years is a long time, buddy," the man at the door explains. "They tore the remnants of that drive-inn down a few years back. They would have done it sooner, a couple years after that old Indian hobo died, but the city end up having to fight the damned Indians over the deed to the land."

"That Indian Hobo," I explain through clenched teeth, "was named Chitto Harjo . . . and those damned Indians are the proud Muscogee Nation."

The man shoots me a nervous glance.

"Whatever you say, man . . . I've got to get back to work." He rushes away. Some things never change, I think, as I load back into my pick up and head down number nine highway toward the Deep Fork River Dam.

"Stay away from that damned Indian!" My mother yelled after me as I burst out the front door with my fishing pole and tackle box in tow. Seemed like she was always on me these days—wanting to know who I was hanging out with, exactly what we were doing, if there were any drugs or drinking going on. It was like since I turned thirteen, she didn't trust me or thought I was automatically going to do something stupid. And she really didn't like the idea of me hanging out with old Chitto. She didn't think he was a good influence.

Most of the townsfolk didn't hold a very high opinion of Chitto Harjo. But most of them, including my mother, had never even met him. What little they knew came from their periodic bingo-game chatter and cigarette gossip. Of course, there were those who disliked Chitto simply because he was Indian. But the reason most people didn't like Chitto was because neither he nor his home quite fit into their vision of small town Shawnee, Oklahoma.

Chitto was Creek. He was in his late sixties, tan-faced, and brown. His eyes were olive and he had a thick, round, slightly-poxed nose that sat squarely above a smooth stony chin. The skin on his neck and hands was weathered through like the red Oklahoma clay that lined the banks of the Deep Fork River. He wore only Wrangler blue-jeans. A single salt and pepper braid snaked its way down the back of those thin long-sleeved plaid pearl-snap button shirts that he was so fond of. And he always carried a red bandana in his back left jeans' pocket and sported a pair of gray, well-worn Roper boots.

Chitto's house was just off of the Federal and Union junction on a dead-end road that the county refused to pave because only he lived there. But it wasn't a big deal to Chitto. He preferred earth over pavement. The old man stayed in what used to be the concession stand of the Starlight Drive-Inn Theater. And although all of the speaker stands had been knocked down, the towering white screen still stood outside his back door—a reminder of Friday and Saturday nights past, when Hollywood Indians whooped savagely, threatened white women, and finally lost their lives to the likes of heroic-tough cowboys and blue-coated Calvary men.

There was no electricity in the large one-room cement-block building or anywhere on the premises for that matter. Certainly, Chitto did not mind. He used kerosene lamps for light, took cold showers, ate out of an ice-chest, and cooked on a charcoal grill. Chitto didn't watch television or listen to the radio.

"Never picked up the habit," he explained.

Mostly, Chitto sat out in his front yard. He would sit for hours in a beat up old metal patio chair that was spray-painted green. He always sat facing east—as if he was waiting for something or someone. If it was raining or snowing, he would sit in that patio chair under the makeshift front porch awning, which in all actuality was a hastily hung twelve-foot blue tarp with frayed corners and torn eye-hooks. The porch, too, is where Gino, Chitto's old cow-dog, lounged during the heat part of the day.

As I continued to peddle my bicycle toward Chitto's, I recalled the first time I met the old man. I had been to the river searching for insects for a class science project. He was sitting out like he does and I came riding slowly up.

"Whatcha doing?" I asked.

"Studyin' the first church . . ." he replied.

Immediately I assumed this was some type of Indian thing. Curious, I questioned further. "Nature?"

"No," he said. "The First Baptist church there . . . across the field." Extending a finger and pointing across the way, the old man started to chuckle. With this, I felt stupid. But soon, I started laughing too. In that moment, Chitto and I became friends.

Next to his house sat a rusted out 1959 Ford pick-up with no hood, only one wheel, and a cracked wind-shield. Scattered across the porch were various parts of the pick-up's engine and front-end, along with a number of shoes, sticks, and coke bottles that Gino had dug up. Also, sitting on the porch were ten or twelve clear plastic Piggly Wiggly milk jugs. "Some for sun-tea . . . some for juggin'," Chitto explained.

Juggin', I later found out, was a type of fishing, in which an empty plastic jug is cast out into the water and acts as a large counter float to hook any fish that strikes the bait strung to it.

"You can really catch some big ones this way," encouraged Chitto.

Chitto also taught me about tree lines—a fishing line is tied to a tree branch and then baited and thrown into the river. When a fish strikes, the tree flexes only so far, until it hooks the fish.

"My grandpa would set lines like these here every morning. He would tell us kids, 'I catch the fish, you clean the fish.' He meant it, too. Every evenin' he would bring in fish, sometimes a whole mess of 'em. Us kids would clean 'em and our grandma would fry 'em up with some bread and onions. Wish I had some right now."

"Me too," I'd respond, rubbing my belly. Chitto would laugh. He also taught me about noodeling—using your hands to seek out catfish holes and grabbing them up by their gills.

"Me too," I'd respond, rubbing my belly. Chitto would laugh. He also taught me about noodeling—using your hands to seek out catfish holes and grabbing them up by their gills.

"Got to be careful," he warned. "Don't want to get hold a no beaver . . . that beaver would tear you up!" He was serious. Chitto knew about all different types of fishing, but he loved to fish best with his old cane pole. It had been a gift from his father, before Chitto was taken away to boarding school at Concho. "The last thing father ever gave me," Chitto explained. "Father died at the Indian Health Services in Lawton after I was taken away to Concho."

"But that was a long time ago . . . ," Chitto would always say.

Folks used terms like "Redskin," and "Injun" to refer to Chitto. Likewise, they used terms such as "eyesore" and "dump" when referring to his house. Mr. Bowen, my eighth-grade American History teacher, was one of these folks.

Once, I heard him talking to the vice-principal about American Indians protesting Columbus Day as a national holiday. Mr. Bowen was saying how it was like "that damned Redskin who lives in the old theater coming down here to picket the school system—as if we didn't all benefit from it . . . in Columbus's time, he brought civilization to the savages that's all . . . why shouldn't we celebrate that? Why shouldn't they want to celebrate that?" I remember being so mad that I was shaking, but I didn't do or say anything out of fear of my mother finding out.

Truth be known, old Chitto was here long before anyone else. His family had been allotted land here by the Dawes Act, before Oklahoma was even a state and before the government bought it back for one tenth of its worth—leaving Chitto's family with no land and little money to purchase decent housing. And so, Chitto's family lived in town—in a trailer—on a rented lot.

Chitto remembered. "We had no land. Nowhere to plant a garden or keep stock. Not even a yard to sit in. Just a cement driveway for the car we didn't have . . . mother and father made sure we ate, had blankets, and didn't spend a night out in the rain though." Chitto grew up in that trailer, but when he got back from Vietnam, he bought the awkward five acres that the defunct Starlight Drive Inn Theater sat on, moved into the old concession stand, and sold most of the surrounding acreage to a development company out of Tulsa that was looking to build a Wild West theme park.

"Them white men from Tulsa was really gonna make it big with their park," Chitto laughed. "Until this here Deep Fork showed 'em who was in charge. Floodin' worst as ever been round here. Not long after that, they gave me back the land I had sold 'em . . . called it a write off. Funny folks—them white men from Tulsa." I laughed until I cried every time Chitto told that story.

Chitto and Gino were waiting on me when I arrived. Without a word, we made the quarter-mile trek down the back hill, through the tall willows, and out onto a sandy bank of the Deep Fork. Chitto used bits of hot dogs soaked in strawberry pop for bait. He had soaked some the night before in an old Styrofoam ice-chest. As Gino took his usual place atop the cool limestone rocks along the near bank, Chitto and I baited our lines and began fishing.

During that first day of fishing, Chitto told me that he was named after a Creek Leader, who had fought against the advancement of the whites and had spoken out on many occasions against the government's treatment of American Indians. Chitto also told me that he had fought in Vietnam and had won a great many medals. Chitto told me too that he never had a driver's license and really never wanted to drive, except for a few years between 1968 and 1974. These were the years of the Red power movement and Chitto was much younger. He wanted to live up to his name's sake and drive out to San Francisco to join his brothers and sisters out on Alcatraz, and then in Washington, and at The Knee.

"It was a good time to be Indian," Chitto explained. "We was takin' back the land and shakin' things up. Lettin' the government know that we were still here and not gonna take to being ignored anymore. Trudell, Banks, Means, the Bellacourts . . . that whole bunch inspired me and so I quit my job rough-neckin' in the Anadarko oil-fields. I bought that old Ford truck with my last pay-check and headed out to make war on the government."

Old Chitto only made it as far as Albuquerque. This is where the truck gave up the ghost and left young Chitto stranded. Luckily, he was fortunate enough to meet up with a Navajo family headed east from Santa Fe. They gave him a lift and towed his truck with a tow dolly all the way back to Oklahoma. "Indians helpin' Indians," he would say. The pick-up had been sitting ever since.

Still, Chitto did get out and about at times. His niece would come and take him to stomp dances and pow-wows every so often. Chitto seemed to enjoy these times because he would talk for days about the different people he had seen, the bread and sofki he had eaten, and the drumming he had heard. Chitto smiled when he talked of these times—the same way he smiled when he talked of the Red Power Movement and fishing.

As I rode my bike up the dirt path to his front porch, I noticed Gino was inside, whining and bouncing anxiously.

"Chitto!" I hollered.

"Hey you old *stijaati* (red man) . . . where are you?" I hollered again.

Opening the screen door, I saw Chitto slumped over in a chair and struggling for breath. For just a moment, I stood paralyzed. After realizing the direness of the situation, I eased Chitto to the floor, unbuttoned his shirt, and checked his pulse. It was weak. Trying not to appear upset, I told him to just hang on a little while and that help would be on the way. He kept his eyes fixed on me the entire time. Chitto did not have a phone and so with Gino running and barking right beside me, I rode my bicycle as fast as I could. I did not stop peddling until I reached our house, where I burst through the front door and yelled, "Mom . . . mom! Chitto . . . something is wrong . . . I found him slumped over in his chair . . . he needs help! Quick!"

She looked me over quickly. I guess to see if I was hurt in any way and then she picked up the phone and dialed 911. Grabbing her keys and rushing out the door, my mother told me to stay put and then she sped off toward Chitto's house. It wasn't long before both an ambulance and a fire-truck went speeding by—with sirens ablaze. Standing there, looking out the front door, all I could seem to think about was stomp dances, the Red Power Movement, and fishing.

I was not allowed to attend the burial. Since it was a traditional ceremony—only family and clan members were allowed to attend. However, my mother, realizing that I needed closure of some type, made up a large casserole, drove me to Chitto's niece's house some fifty miles away, and allowed me to drop the dish off and pay my final respects.

Chitto's niece met me at the front door and welcomed me in—thanking me for the casserole and waving to my mother, who stayed in the van. Immediately, I was surrounded by more Indians than I had ever seen. Of course I had seen Indians on television and in movies, but these were real Indians. As Chitto's niece introduced me, everyone in the house stood up and came toward me. Each of them—old and young alike—shook my hand and thanked me for being Chitto's friend. After shaking the last person's hand, my attention turned toward the smoke in the room. Chitto's niece must have noticed my curiosity.

"Sage and Cedar," she explained. "Part of our tradition . . ."

"Smells nice," I responded.

She smiled. "Pull up a chair. Let me fix you a plate."

"Oh, thank you, but my mother is waiting in the car . . . I've got to get going."

"Then, I'll fix you two big plates to go," she insisted.

As she began putting the plates together, I noticed the kitchen table was full of all kinds of food—fried chicken, biscuits, potato salad, beans, green onions, corn, squash, and many other dishes that I did not recognize, but suspected to be traditional Creek dishes.

"Everything ok?" My mother asked, as I climbed back into the van.

"Chitto's niece loaded us up," I showed her the two huge plates.

"That was nice. How are they all doing?" She asked genuinely concerned.

"Pretty well, I guess. They were eating, laughing, and visiting with each other like it was a family reunion or something."

"They probably don't get to see too much of each other," mom explained. "It's terrible that it takes something like a death to bring family together." With this my mother looked over at me in a strange way. I think she was trying to find a way to apologize for not wanting me to hang out with Chitto, but at the time, I was not sure. Regardless, I told her I loved her and she responded with the same, "I love you."

After old Chitto passed, the county decided to tear his house down. Before they started the demolition, though, they cleared it of Chitto's few belongings, which, interestingly enough, among them was a Chester drawer full of military awards and war medals. Turns out old Chitto was not lying about his military service. He had actually been one of the most decorated American Indians in the history of Oklahoma. After discovering this, the local papers ran articles celebrating Chitto's service and all of the town's folk gathered and held their glasses up to him in a toast of appreciation. What a bunch of phonies!

There was another interesting item among the stuff that was cleared away. Sometime before his kidneys failed, old Chitto had written as best he could in English—though he spoke English well enough, he had difficulty writing it—a note on a brown paper sack. The sack was wrapped around the old cane fishing pole that his father had given him. The note said, "For my young *stijicti* (white man) friend who likes to fish . . . thank you."

Mother never did fully comprehend how an old Indian man and a white teenage boy could have such a friendship as Chitto Harjo and I had, but in time she came to appreciate the positive influence that the old man had on me. She even apologized to me one day a few months after the burial.

"I'm sorry I didn't want you hanging out with your friend . . . I see now that he really was your friend. I should have trusted you . . . you've always been a good son. But you understand how it is my job to protect you . . . don't you?"

"I do mom . . . I do. And I'm sorry that I disobeyed you . . . but Chitto really was my best friend," I began to tear up. We hugged and made things right. And although my mother never completely understood what Chitto and I had between us, she did come to accept and respect it. Ultimately, she was sorry that Chitto had to pass on so soon. I was sorry too—even though in a strange way, Chitto's passing had brought my mother and me closer together.

The gravel pops and cracks under the weight of the thick black radials, as I pull off of the highway and into the dam-site. There are no other vehicles in the parking lot. I have the river to myself. And so, I decide to fish with Chitto's pole. After parking the truck, I reach behind the bench-seat and pull out an old worn green Army blanket. Inside is a red cane pole with wooden eyes. They don't make them like this anymore, I think. They don't make them like Chitto anymore either, I smile. As I cast out my line, I begin to recall more and more about that summer. And with each memory, Chitto's voice becomes clearer and clearer. After a short while, it's as if he is right there with me again—on the banks of the Deep Fork—where stories once flowed like the waters in that river—from an old man to a young boy.

READING REACTIONS

1. What is the role of storytelling within this narrative?
2. How is memory used in the story?
3. What material items seem to hold significance for the characters?
4. What traditions or ceremonies are upheld in the story?
5. How might the site of the Drive-Inn be a place of memorial?
6. What does this story argue? Is the argument subtle or obvious?
7. Does it affect the ethos of the story to know Murray is an American Indian?
8. What is Murray's commentary on Native American traditions?

Two Native American Myths: "Guardian of Yosemite" and "Chief Mountain"

"Guardian of Yosemite" is a Native American Myth from the Miowok Nation. Here, it is transcribed as retold by S. E. Schlosser. The Miowok are of the California area and consist of about eleven tribes. Known as cultivators of tobacco, the Miowok are also hunter-gatherers. Their population now is about 3,500. S. E. Schlosser is an author and editor of http://americanfolklore.net.

"Chief Mountain" is a Native American Myth of the Blackfeet Nation. The Blackfeet are of the Rocky Mountain area and are a warrior people. Their population now consists of four tribes numbering more than 25,000 in the United States and Canada.

"GUARDIAN OF YOSEMITE," A NATIVE AMERICAN MYTH (MIOWAK TRIBE), RETOLD BY S. E. SCHLOSSER

For many nights and many days, the guardian spirit of Tisayac watched over the beautiful valley of Yosemite. Often, the gentle spirit would drift invisibly among the good folk of the valley, and it was during one of these visits that she noticed a tall, proud man named Tutokanula. He was a strong leader who greatly enhanced the lot of his people, and Tisayac came more often to the valley so that she could watch him.

One day, Tutokanula was hunting near the place where Tisayac had laid down to rest. When she realized the proud leader was close by, the shy spirit peered out at him from among the trees. Seeing the beautiful woman with her golden hair and ethereal appearance, Tutokanula fell in love. Realizing it was the guardian of the valley, he reached out his hands to her, calling her by name. Confused by the rush of feelings inside her, Tisayac flew away, leaving a brokenhearted warrior behind. Tutokanula spent many days searching for Tisayac. Finally he left the valley and his people in despair. Without his wise guidance, the valley fell into ruin and most of the good folk left to find a new home.

When Tisayac returned again to her valley, she was horrified to find it barren and her people gone. When she learned that Tutokanula had forgotten his people, had left them to fend for themselves without the benefit of his great wisdom, and had spent many days and nights searching and longing for her, she cried out in despair. Kneeling upon a mighty dome of rock, Tisayac prayed with all her heart that the Great Spirit would undo this wrong and would restore to this land the virtue which had been lost.

Hearing her prayer, the Great Spirit took pity on the plight of her people. Stooping down from on high, he spread his hands over the valley. The green of new life poured forth over the land; trees blossomed, flowers bloomed, birds sang. Then he struck a mighty blow against the mountains and they broke apart, leaving a pathway for the melting snow to flow through. The water swirled and washed down upon the land, spilling over rocks, pooling into a lake and then wandering afar to spread life to other places. In the valley, the corn grew tall again, and the people came back to their home.

Then Tutokanula himself came to the valley when he heard that Tisayac had come home. Upon his return, he spent many hours carving his likeness into the stone so his people would remember him when he departed from this earth. When the carving was finished, Tutokanula sat down wearily at the foot of the beautiful Bridal Veil Falls the Great Spirit had created. Tisayac drifted into the spray of the falls, watching him. He was ready to depart from his people, from his valley. Would he go with her? She moved forward through the falling water and made herself visible. When Tutokanula saw Tisayac, he sprang to his feet with a cry of joy and she held out her arms to him. The brave warrior leapt into the falls and took his love into his arms at last. For a moment, there were two rainbows arching over the water. Then Tisayac drew him up and up into the clouds and away as the sun sank over Yosemite.

S.E. Schlosser, "Guardian of Yosemite," (Retold from Miowak Tribe), *AmericanFolklore.net*. Copyright © by Sandra E. Schlosser. All rights reserved. Reproduced by permission.

"CHIEF MOUNTAIN," A NATIVE AMERICAN MYTH (BLACKFEET TRIBE), RETOLD BY LORI FULLER

Many years ago, a young Piegan warrior was noted for his bravery. When he grew older and more experienced in war, he became the war-chief for a large band of Piegan warriors.

A little while after he became the war-chief, he fell in love with a girl who was in his tribe, and they got married. He was so in love with her that he took no other wives, and he decided not to go on war parties anymore. He and his wife were very happy together; unusually so, and when they had a baby, they were even happier then.

Some moons later, a war party that had left his village was almost destroyed by an enemy. Only four men came back to tell the story. The war-chief was greatly troubled by this. He saw that if the enemy was not punished, they would raid the Piegan camp. So he gave a big war feast and asked all of the young men of his band to come to it.

After they had all eaten their fill, the war-chief arose and said to them in solemn tones: "Friends and brothers, you have all heard the story that our four young men have told us. All the others who went out from our camp were killed by the enemy. Only these four have come back to our campfires. Those who were killed were our friends and relatives.

"We who live must go out on the warpath to avenge the fallen. If we don't, the enemy will think that we are weak and that they can attack us unhurt. Let us not let them attack us here in the camp."

"I will lead a party on the warpath. Who here will go with me against the enemy that has killed our friends and brothers?"

A party of brave warriors gathered around him, willing to follow their leader. His wife also asked to join the party, but he told her to stay at the camp.

"If you go without me," she said, "you will find an empty lodge when you return."

The Chief talked to her and calmed her, and finally convinced her to stay with the women and children and old men in the camp at the foot of a high mountain.

Leading a large party of men, the Chief rode out from the village. The Piegans met the enemy and defeated them. But their war-chief was killed. Sadly, his followers carried the broken body back to the camp.

His wife was crazed with grief. With vacant eyes she wandered everywhere, looking for her husband and calling his name. Her friends took care of her, hoping that eventually her mind would become clear again and that she could return to normal life. One day, though, they could not find her anywhere in the camp. Searching for her, they saw her high up on the side of the mountain, the tall one above their camp. She had her baby in her arms. The head man of the village sent runners after her, but from the top of the mountain she signaled that they should not try to reach her. All watched in horror as she threw her baby out over the cliff, and then herself jumped from the mountain to the rocks far, far below.

Her people buried the woman and baby there among the rocks. They carried the body of the Chief to the place and buried him beside them. From that time on, the mountain that towers above the graves was known as Minnow Stahkoo, "the Mountain of the Chief," or "Chief Mountain."

If you look closely, even today, you can see on the face of the mountain the figure of a woman with a baby in her arms, the wife and child of the Chief.

READING REACTIONS

1. What is the significance of place for both of the myths?
2. In both myths, someone dies. Why is this important to the myth?
3. The narrative of both myths shows repetition and a conscious choice to use nature as a primary character. Why?
4. In both stories, characters become a part of nature or part of a place. How is this concept similar to that of the participatory memorials discussed earlier in this chapter?
5. What are the main differences between the Miwok and Blackfeet myths? How might these differences reflect cultural histories?

Technological Beginnings

Telling a story or sharing a memory through video is a popular function of media. If you have smart phone, a digital camera that takes short videos, or a pocket-size video camera, it's easy to record a video. The trick is learning how to edit the video or even add music or an audio file. This takes time, patience, and practice. Don't worry about failing—just try!

For the purposes of this exercise, you need some sort of video recorder. Team up with at least one other person who has access to a video recorder of some sort, and learn the rest together.

Make a video that tells a story in two minutes or less. In this case, you don't need any audio except what you record while filming. Maybe you can ask the people in your group to retell a fairy tale or a memorable event. It doesn't matter—as long as you tell a story with video.

For helpful video-editing instructional sites, see those available through the English CourseMate for this text.

Additional Writing and Composing Activities

1. **Profile of a Place.** Choose an episode in your life that involves a place or space that is important to you. Do three things: (1) Tell a story or anecdote (narration) about the place. (2) Describe the place spatially in general and specific detail. (3) Explain why this place is important to your identity. If you have an image that represents the event, copy it, document where you found it if it's not your property, and include it on the last page of the paper.

2. **Analysis of a Visual Argument.** Find a cartoon or advertisement that makes an argument about a social issue, or consider Figure 3.5, 3.6, or 3.7 (p. 86). Then do two things: (1) Describe the cartoon or ad in general and specific detail. (2) Explain the social issue and the artist's argument about the issue. Next, discuss the purpose and the audience of the cartoon or ad, and evaluate how well the image addresses purpose and audience. Organize your paper to include all of these requirements in a way that makes sense to you and your audience.

3. **Cause-and-Consequence Analysis.** Think about a type of contemporary American popular-culture media (television, movies, video games, etc.) or social event (parties, concerts, etc.) and what causes trends in the media or social event. Why is a specific trend occurring? What are the trend's effects? In other words, why do we like the things we like, what are some possible consequences of the trend, and what does the trend say about our identity as citizens?

4. **Poster or Advertisement as Memorial/Advocacy.** Divide into groups of at least three. One member of your group should have experience with some sort of design or photo-editing software. Using **Figure 3.11** as a reference, create a poster or advertisement to advocate for a local community organization or to make a memorial sign for something that has occurred in your community.

Figure 3.11 Poster of Oklahoman support for New Yorkers

Online Resources

Resources available through the English CourseMate for this text include the following:

Websites

National September 11 Memorial and Museum at the World Trade Center

Hurricane Katrina Memorial. Biloxi, Mississippi.

"Cultural Literacy." *Engines for Education.*

Memorials

Oklahoma City National Memorial

Katrina National Memorial Park

"In Focus: The Decade Since 9/11." *The Atlantic.*

"September 11, 2001." *The Guardian.*

"The Chora of the Twin Towers." *Enculturation.*

Oral Histories

"Oral Histories." *9/11 Memorial.*

"Mississippi Oral History Project." *University of Southern Mississippi.*

TV

Aaron McGruder. "Invasion of the Katrinians." *Boondocks.*

Editorial Cartoons

"9/11." *Postroad.*

"Cartoonists Remember 9/11." *abcnews.*

4

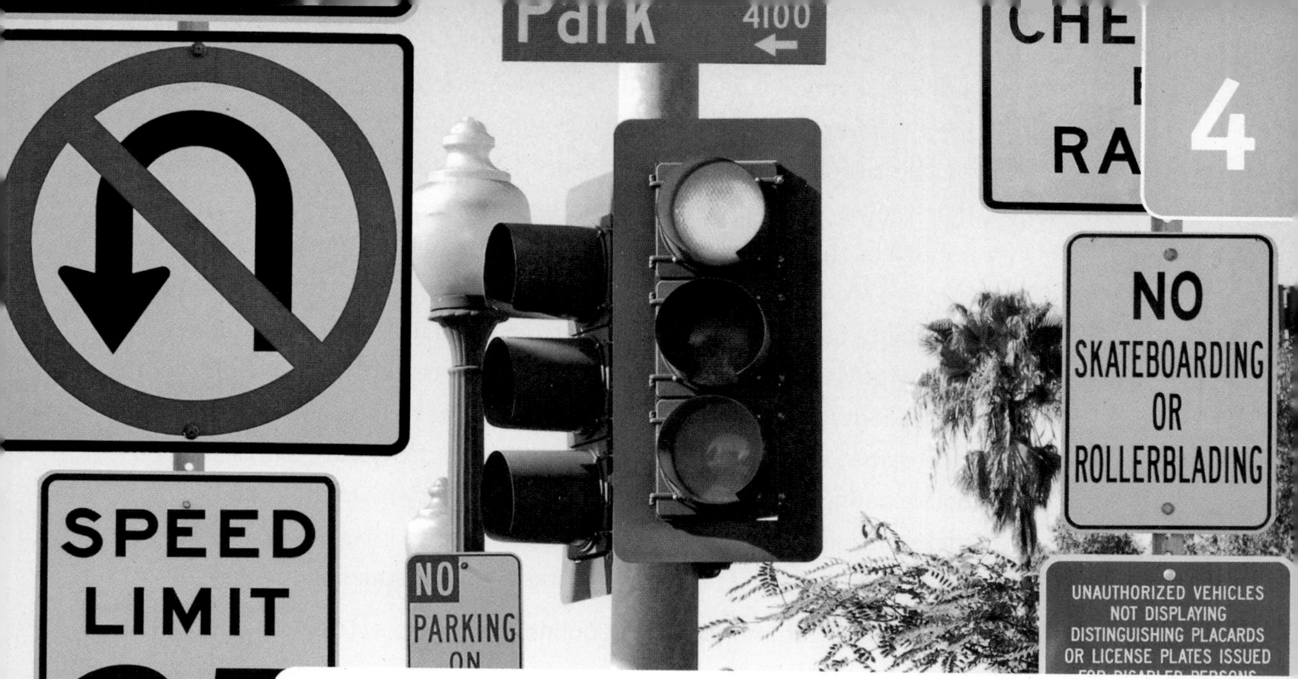

Gendered Viewpoints

How do we receive information? Think about your day so far. Did you pass speed limit signs and interstate exit markers like the ones in **Figure 4.1** on the way to campus? Is the parking lot coded by color to let you know where commuters, residents, and faculty should park? Consider also those around you. How do you "read" them? Can you spot an instructor based on his style of clothing and the stack of papers to be graded under his arm? Does a band logo on a classmate's T-shirt allow you to strike up a conversation with her?

You have already encountered, decoded, and processed a great deal of information today, maybe before you ever picked up and read an alphabetic text like this one. John Jennings, a professor of graphic design at the University of Illinois, says that our population is inundated with more images daily than ever before in history. In fact, according to

JAMES STEIDL/SHUTTERSTOCK.COM

Figure 4.1 Street intersection congested with street signs

Jennings, a modern person will see more images in a day than someone in the Victorian era would have seen in a lifetime.

This suggests that the skills needed to be literate today are different than they were for previous generations. The term *literacy* is common enough in our schools and workplaces, but in our daily lives being literate involves more than the ability to read and write. Cultural literacy requires the ability to decode, identify, understand, and use information from a variety of visual, audio, print, and multimodal texts.

Modern readers may need specific literacies to locate YouTube videos, read billboard advertising, navigate virtual worlds, and decipher online dating profiles. Visual literacy is the ability to interpret and make meaning from information presented as an image. Your visual literacy skills are increasingly important in understanding the ways cultures and communities work online and offline. Being visually literate requires not only skills in decoding and constructing images, but also an understanding of how context and culture contribute to visual meaning.

Figure 4.2 Pedestrian-crossing sign altered with a skirt and the caption "why not a woman"

© DAVID H. WELLS/CORBIS

CULTURES Think about the importance of context for the example of visual rhetoric in **Figure 4.2**. Where would you expect to find this sign (near a college, in a particular part of the country, in a big city or small town)? What clues from the image suggest where this sign might be located?

What message does the author convey, and what issue does this text respond to? What audience is the author trying to reach?

What cultural assumptions about gender and what sort of divergent viewpoints might this sign represent? Look around your campus or neighborhood. What other seemingly gender-neutral signs do you see? List the larger cultural messages you could decode from the signage.

Literacy in a Visual World

Literacy requires an awareness of rhetorical concepts. Audience awareness (as discussed in Chapter 2) impacts the sorts of emotional and logical appeals an author uses to support an argument or make a point. These appeals must then be purposefully arranged to best persuade listeners, readers, and, in this case, viewers. A working knowledge of traditional rhetorical approaches to crafting an argument is vital to producing and decoding visual communication, but visual literacy also requires additional skills and considerations. Scholar Gunther Kress believes we live in a visual culture in which the "grammar of the image" has replaced or at least joined more traditional grammars. Where punctuation and capitalization rules are important in regulating and transmitting meaning in alphabetic texts, features like color, shade, tone, and contrast help us decode—or read—visuals.

Building meaning in an image, video, or other multimodal text begins with an awareness of things like arrangement, tone, and point of view—things understood as part of all texts. Additionally, color, shade, contrast, and perspective—terms taken from the visual arts—are also important in understanding how to read and write visually. Consider the following rhetorical concepts in relation to **Figure 4.3**.

- **Arrangement** is the spatial organization of elements of an image. Arrangement cues viewers in to what to value and how the elements of an image interrelate.

© DUNCAN SMITH/CORBIS

Figure 4.3 Sneaky woman grasping apples

- **Tone** reveals the author's attitude toward the subject and message that is being presented visually.
- **Point of view,** or **perspective,** is the way an image asks viewers to see it. Looking down on, straight at, or up to a focus point suggests things about power, meaning, and ways to empathize (or not) with the image.
- **Color** has social and cultural meanings. White often stands for good, red for danger, blue for tranquility, and so on.
- **Shade** adds dimension and rhetorical meaning to color. Often related to mood and tone, a darker shade might be regarded as menacing while a lighter shade might read as energetic.
- **Contrast** is the difference in color and brightness between objects.

Consider the arrangement of elements in Figure 4.3. As the only person in the image, the woman takes up a lot of space in the shot. Her position just left of center suggests that she is the main focus of the image. For alphabetic texts, authors often emphasize ideas by using *chronological* arrangement, whereas in still images artists use *visual* arrangement to indicate something's importance—the emphasized object might occupy a large amount of space in the frame or be placed at the top or center of the shot.

Note also the point of view of Figure 4.3. We see the subject head-on, but she does not return our gaze. Her glance to the left suggests that she expects someone and is anxious that the person might catch her. The image's perspective—looking straight on—invites us to judge the subject. We are equals with her. Color intensifies the presumption of guilt: the woman wears black, the opposite of white, which is associated with innocence and goodness.

Think too about the associations of the color red. Red, in U.S. culture, often signifies violence, danger, or passion. Further, the apple itself has many associations: good health (an apple a day keeps the doctor away), knowledge (an apple for the teacher), and—most relevant for this image—sin (the apple in the Garden of Eden). Finally, consider the photographer's choice to cast a woman for this shoot. What female stereotypes does this woman conjure in your mind? The wicked stepmother handing Snow White the poisoned apple? A wealthy crone taking what she wants? How might this image's message differ if the subject were a man?

By analyzing discrete pieces of images, we learn to read visuals in much the same way we read literature and academic writing. By breaking down the rhetorical components of visuals, viewers see how a unified meaning emerges from carefully chosen and arranged visual elements and how visual and multimodal texts work to impact readers, speak to specific cultural and historical contexts, and take advantage of cultural associations that allow meaning to be transmitted.

Figure 4.4 *War*

✳ **CULTURES** Using the reading of Figure 4.3 above as a model, analyze the image titled *War*, which is shown in **Figure 4.4,** by Caitlin Szinegh, to reveal the rhetorical strategies the photographer uses to create meaning.

First, in a paragraph or two, read this image attending to color, point of view, tone, arrangement, and other strategies for creating meaning in visuals. Next, respond to the following questions regarding the cultures, communities, and technologies influencing this image.

- **Under what contexts** or conditions (historical, political, or cultural) was this 2004 image created?

- **What is the** intended impact on the viewer? What are you "supposed" to do or feel when you see this image?

- **Does this visual** text encourage social action or civic responsibility? How does the photographer make that sort of plea?

- **What are this** image's social or cultural associations or values?

- **Why is photography** a particularly effective medium for this message? What strengths does this technology offer? What limitations?

Think about the questions from Chapter 1, page 5. How is this image intended to affect the viewer? How are you supposed to feel about this woman? What cultural associations persist relating to the ways gender and class roles are presented here?

Cultural Cues

Understanding the culture in and for which you are producing texts is critical to encoding visual texts and to understanding the visual texts surrounding you. The meaning of an image depends on cultural context. Cultural context takes into account the set of circumstances that surround the creation of meaning—whether through images or words—and acknowledges that images do not have intrinsic meaning. For example, a picture of a round, red object with a green stem attached at the top does not yet mean apple—much less health or sin—until those in a given culture decide it does. Meaning, then, is negotiated between producers and audiences and is rooted in the time the image is created and also viewed. Consider the newspaper photographs in **Figure 4.5**.

Although the composition of these images from Hurricane Katrina–ravaged New Orleans is very similar (people submerged to chest-level in water, dragging bags behind), and information about the people depicted is limited (all are unnamed), cultural context shapes the way the audience and the journalist read the images. The caption accompanying the picture of a young African-American man reports "looting," while the caption for the second image reports that the Caucasian man and woman were "finding" items. How can we explain the difference in meaning? What role do race, class, and gender play in these readings?

Our own stories are impacted by our cultural stories. We are programmed to read—or decode—images and other texts in certain ways thanks to our communities, cultures, and ideologies. An ideology is a body of beliefs that guides our behaviors and values as individuals and as societies. We often demonstrate our ideologies with visuals that stand for larger concepts. For

Figure 4.5 Dueling photo captions

AP PHOTO/DAVE MARTIN

AP **Associated Press** AP • Tue Aug 30, 11:31 AM ET

A young man walks through chest deep flood water after looting a grocery store in New Orleans on Tuesday, Aug. 30, 2005. Flood waters continue to rise in New Orleans after Hurricane Katrina did extensive damage when it

Email Photo   Print Photo

RECOMMEND THIS PHOTO   • Recommended Photos
Recommend it   Average (138 votes)
☆ ☆ ☆ ☆ ☆   ★ ★ ★ ★ ☆

CHRIS GRAYTHEN/GETTY IMAGES

AFP   3:47 AM ET

Two residents wade through chest-deep water after finding bread and soda from a local grocery store after Hurricane Katrina came through the area in New Orleans, Louisiana. (AFP/Getty Images/Chris Graythen)

Email Photo   Print Photo

RECOMMEND THIS PHOTO   • Recommended Photos
Recommend it   Average (211 votes)
☆ ☆ ☆ ☆ ☆   ★ ★ ★ ★ ☆

RELATED
• Katrina's Effects, at a Glance AP • Tue Aug 30, 1:26 PM ET

Hurricanes & Tropical Storms

example, the Stars and Stripes connote freedom and patriotism, and a gold cross necklace suggests faith, Christianity, and belief.

The use of visuals as symbols is common, but it's not free of challenges. Because images have no inherent rhetorical meanings, communicators must shape images in ways that members of specific communities can understand and agree upon. Such "unfixed" meanings require those who use visuals for rhetorical purposes to think carefully about the multiple meanings images may carry.

Culture sets the exact meanings and values of images, and thus these meanings shift over time. In the 1940s, for example, World War II propaganda posters were designed to mobilize a country and a military force. They tapped into prevailing political ideologies of patriotism and American "might and right" as well as subtler belief systems, including the importance of family, certain class expectations, and beliefs about gender and racial norms. Though certainly not everyone shared these ideologies at the time, cultural norms dictated the meanings of these images. Creators used cultural norms to negotiate meanings with audiences.

Using subtle design choices like color, tone, lighting, and point of view, the posters in **Figures 4.6 and 4.7** have lots to say about femininity and images of women during the 1940s. The posters manage this even while using very few words. In Figure 4.6, viewers engage with an iconic image of the blonde, slender all-American girl. She is slim and clean-cut and is pictured in a very gendered role, seated behind a typewriter. Although red is the main color in both posters, the color is coded differently in each. For "Miss U.S.A." red denotes energy and is a patriotic symbol of an allegiance to the United States' red, white, and blue. But in Figure 4.7, red is used to punctuate danger and starkly contrasts the colorless face above. The woman's face in Figure 4.7 is

Figure 4.6 Victory waits on your fingers

Figure 4.7 Wanted! for murder

partially obscured by shadows, and her dark eyes and hair are accentuated by the low lighting. All these elements combine to create a menacing tone and to set this woman in direct opposition to the blonde "girl next door." What can we learn from these images about gender norms in the United States in the 1940s? What stereotypes of womanhood do these posters sell or condemn?

> **TECHNOLOGIES** The posters in the Powers of Persuasion online exhibit were created with a specific purpose and audience in mind. However, as discussed earlier, image meaning comes not only from the creator but also from the audience. Select an image from the Powers of Persuasion site (http://www.archives.gov/exhibits/powers_of_persuasion/powers_of_persuasion_home.html), and rhetorically analyze the image. Refer to compositional elements like color and tone. Address rhetorical concepts like intended audience, purpose, and context, as well as ideological assumptions about things like gender, family, and patriotism. Post the image and your analysis on a blog or wiki. Respond to your readers' comments, considering alternate readings of the image you may see that they did not.

Selling Gender

All images are persuasive and ask us to do something. An image of you as a child may ask you to feel nostalgic, and a bumper sticker with a picture of Barack Obama may ask you to vote. Images seek to persuade us to feel, to agree, to think, to act, and often to buy. Although the World War II posters weren't selling a product, they were most certainly selling a feeling and an ideology. Advertisers' use of visuals and socially agreed-upon symbols is a complicated and effective way to sell any number of things, from social agendas to floor wax. Although not all product ads appeal explicitly to gender, tacit gender (as well as race and class) norms pop up in most advertisements we encounter daily.

On the surface, the Dove and Axe Body Spray advertising campaigns seem to posit very different images of womanhood: Dove is selling "real beauty" and "real women" while Axe positions women as hypersexualized accessories for men. Both campaigns tap into cultural shorthands about heterosexuality and gender norms. Coincidentally, both brands are also owned by the multi-national parent company Unilever.

Figure 4.9 features a Dove ad that seems to push back against cultural stereotypes and the temptation to reduce women to their body parts, but it simultaneously presents the female body as an object to be judged on "sexiness." The Axe women in **Figure 4.8** are similarly defined as objects to be viewed but make no pretense at being average or "real." Instead they are overtly sexual and very slender and explicitly defined by sexual aggression leading them to disrobe in public. Whereas this display of women as objects of sexual desire may seem more overt in this Axe ad, Dove frequently portrays women naked and therefore at least somewhat sexualized. And no matter how they are displayed,

IMAGE COURTESY OF THE ADVERTISING ARCHIVES

Figure 4.8 Women in Axe Body Spray advertisements are often positioned as sexual objects and sexual aggressors

Figure 4.9 Half empty?
half full?

half empty?

half full?

Does sexiness depend on
how full your cups are?

IMAGE COURTESY OF THE ADVERTISING ARCHIVES

women in both Axe and Dove advertisements are expected to be beautiful, and that beauty is assumed to come not from within but from products.

Consider both of these images as they demonstrate ways cultures, communities, and technologies intersect to create meaning for viewers. What is the intended impact of these ads on viewers? How do the producers of the Dove and Axe Body Spray campaigns establish their purpose and reason for communicating in this way? Both ad campaigns—though targeted at radically different audiences—are selling heterosexuality and normative beauty along with their products. These ads identify the women pictured as attractive and inspire viewers either to become like the woman in the Dove ad or to attract her with Axe Body Spray. Additionally, these ads celebrate consumption. According to the advertisers, we are all—men and women—improved by products.

What social or cultural associations or values do these sorts of images of women have? Dove products make women more beautiful and confident, and it can be inferred that Axe, though a body spray for men, is a product that leads to sexually aggressive and desiring women. In both cases, the female body is regulated by and powerless to products. Women's bodies are "cleaned up" and made beautiful by Dove while Axe Body Spray frees the female body to express natural sexual desires. Playing on the familiar rhetorical question inquiring whether one sees a glass as half full or half empty, the text tells the viewer to make a judgement call about the "sexiness" of the model's breasts. In doing so, she becomes an object of sexual desire, not just a gendered body. Both ads depend on the cultural message that women are and should be sexualized.

Gender for All Ages

Dove's Real Beauty campaign went a step beyond print ads and commercials to include a documentary-style video called "Dove Evolution," accessible through the English Coursemate for this text. To understand this video, you must not only understand the cultural stereotypes and agreed-upon assumptions about gender, but you must also realize that such gender standpoints are often critiqued. This film, which is an advertisement masquerading as a public service announcement, is selling both the company as well as ideas about gender and womanhood to girls. While some argue the ad does positive things by revealing unrealistic representations of the female body, others may point out that the ad continues to assume that all girls want and need to feel beautiful. They argue that the ad is simply a new twist on traditional values and views of female bodies as objects of desire.

Another gender image frequently seen in advertising is motherhood. Consider the magazines and television commercials you've seen that feature well-dressed, lovely, and patient soccer moms passing out juice boxes and purchasing vitamins. Girls and boys alike are exposed to such images from a very young age. Consider the breastfeeding doll controversy. While many parents and consumer groups were troubled by the apparent sexualizing of the childhood baby doll, and the accompanying advertising campaign seen in **Figure 4.10**, the product is also interesting to consider from a marketing standpoint: Who is the intended audience for this ad? What does the ad want you to do? What values are associated with the doll and, therefore, with motherhood and femininity? How might this ad differ if a little boy were pictured caring for the doll? What role might race and socioeconomic status play in this ad?

One way to analyze the ad is to consider the rhetorical situation of the ad and the appeals to pathos, ethos, and logos. The rhetorical situation identifies the *rhetor*, or speaker; the *audience*; and the *text*. For the print advertisement shown in Figure 4.10, the advertiser, Berjuan Toys, is the rhetor, and the intended audience is children and their parents.

How do the ad creators build *pathos*, or an emotional response? Think about how the doll itself is a signifier for family and the sanctity of childhood. Is the fact that the ad is aimed exclusively at little girls

COURTESY OF BERJUAN TOYS, LLC

Figure 4.10 The Breast Milk Baby ad image

an appeal to *logos*—or logic—because only a female body is capable of breast-feeding? Now think about the *ethos*, or trustworthiness, of the author, in this case the company selling the doll. The company builds its credibility by selling "wholesome" toys like dolls and by portraying the consumers in the advertisement in safe, clean, inviting environments. While Berjuan Toys is clearly selling a plastic toy, the company is also selling family, femininity, and gender roles associated with motherhood.

Technological Beginnings: Images as Artifacts

Most of us remember show-and-tell from grade school. You would bring your favorite stuffed animal or a rock you found while hiking and use it as a story starter and visual aid. It's important to recognize the power of visuals in our adult lives when it comes to making meaning.

For your own writing, consider finding a print advertisement and using it as a story prompt. Who are the main characters in the ad, and what story do they tell? Another writing strategy might be to pay special attention to targeted advertisements on Facebook and other sites in order to identify culturally significant trends that might make good topics for research papers. For example, when a Facebook ad prompts you to consider getting an online degree in public relations, it may lead to writing projects about online education, job trends, the economic downturn forcing people back to the classroom, and definitions of job "success" and satisfaction. Similarly, an ad urging you to join an online dating service may prompt investigation into virtual dating communities and the fiscal components of finding love.

Readings

Gender stereotypes clearly persist in our culture. The ability to decode visual images is an important literacy skill because much of what we have come to accept as "gender norms" are transmitted, reinforced, and sometimes challenged in the visuals we encounter every day.

Margaret Matlin's "Bimbos and Rambos" offers an introduction to specific ways mass media manifests these gender stereotypes. The piece, though important as a foundation, is somewhat dated (first appearing in the late 1990s), so we also include a more recent look at advertising in "Europe Takes Aim at Sexual Stereotyping in Ads." Gail Tom and Anmarie Eves then discuss "The Use of Rhetorical Devices in Advertising," demonstrating strategies for rhetorical analysis of print ads.

After you have read the foregoing articles, you can apply what you have learned to three specific ad campaigns: the Dove Real Beauty campaign in "Learn to Love Your Tree, Baby," the Axe Body Spray advertisements taken up in Julie Bosman's "How to Sell Body Sprays to Teenagers," and finally the Breast Milk Baby. Mandy Van Deven's *Bitch Magazine* commentary on the breastfeeding doll controversy not only alludes to cultural assumptions about women's bodies but also considers the power of image and viewers' responsibility to question and possibly resist advertising and media coverage. Finally, because female bodies are not the only ones regulated and reproduced in advertising campaigns, we also include Michael A. Messner and Jeffrey Montez de Oca's study of beer and liquor ads in major sports media events and the ways such ads construct modern masculinity.

● Margaret W. Matlin

Bimbos and Rambos: The Cognitive Basis of Gender Stereotypes

> Matlin received her MA and PhD in experimental psychology from the University of Michigan and works at the State University of New York Geneseo, though she is on leave writing textbooks currently.

In the 1990s, a major theoretical framework for explaining stereotypes is called the social cognitive approach. According to this approach, stereotypes are belief systems that guide the way we process information, including information

Margaret Matlin, "Bimbos and Rambos: The Cognitive Basis of Gender Stereotypes," *Eye on Psi Chi*, Winter 1999, Vol. 3, No. 2, pp. 13–14, 16. Copyright © 1999 by Psi Chi International Honor Society in Psychology. All rights reserved. Reproduced by permission.

about gender. In my presentation at the Southeastern Psychological Association convention, I focused on two questions: how gender stereotypes influence cognitive processes and how the media contribute to these stereotypes.

HOW DO GENDER STEREOTYPES INFLUENCE OUR COGNITIVE PROCESSES?

Our cognitive processes perpetuate and exaggerate stereotypes. In addition, stereotypes tend to encourage inaccurate cognitive processes. Let's examine four representative examples of these inaccurate thought patterns.

Gender Polarization

According to psychologists such as Sandra Bem (1993), one cognitive process that seems nearly inevitable in humans is to divide people into groups. We can partition these groups on the basis of race, age, religion, and so forth. However, the major way in which we usually split humanity is on the basis of gender. This process of categorizing others in terms of gender is both habitual and automatic. It's nearly impossible to suppress the tendency to split the world in half, using gender as the great divider. In fact, after finishing this article, try ignoring the gender of the first person you meet!

When we divide the world into two groups, male and female, we tend to see all males as being similar, all females as being similar, and the two categories of "male" and "female" as being very different from each other. In real life, the characteristics of women and men tend to overlap. Unfortunately, however, gender polarization often creates an artificial gap between women and men.

Different Expectations for Males and Females

The second way in which gender stereotypes are related to cognitive processes is that we have different expectations for female and male behavior. A classic study focused on adults' interpretations of infants' behavior. Condry and Condry (1976) prepared videotapes of an infant responding to a variety of stimuli. For example, the infant stared and then cried in response to a jack-in-the-box that suddenly popped open. College students had been led to believe that the infant was either a baby girl or a baby boy. When students watched the videotape with the jack-in-the-box, those who thought the infant was a boy tended to judge that "he" was showing anger. When they thought that the infant was a girl, they decided that "she" was showing fear. Remember that everyone saw the same videotape of the same infant. However, the ambiguous negative reaction was given a more masculine label (anger, rather than fear) when the infant was perceived to be a boy.

The Normative Male

According to a third principle, we tend to believe the male experience to be normative. A gender difference is therefore typically explained in terms of why the female differs from that norm. For example, research often shows a gender difference in self-confidence. However, these studies almost always ask about why females are low in self-confidence, relative to the male norm. They rarely speculate about whether females are actually on target as far as self-confidence, and whether males may actually be too high in self-confidence (Tavris, 1992).

Consider another example. In recent U.S. Presidential elections, many commentators remarked about various gender gaps. For example, women are more likely than men to vote in elections. Interestingly, commentators typically spoke as if the male turnout rate was standard, the norm. In contrast, they provided many explanations for why the females were different. Only rarely did they consider the females to be the norm, trying to explain why male turnout was low (Miller, Taylor, & Buck, 1991).

Remembering Gender-Consistent Information

In general, people recall gender-consistent information more accurately than gender-inconsistent information. Selective recall is especially likely when people are faced with too many simultaneous tasks (Macrae, Hewstone, & Griffiths, 1993).

For example, Arnie Cann (1993) found that students recalled sentences like "Jane is a good nurse" better than "Jane is a bad nurse." When someone is employed in a gender-consistent occupation, we recall this person's competence. In contrast, students recalled sentences like "John is a bad nurse" better than "John is a good nurse." When someone is employed in a gender-inconsistent occupation, we recall this person's incompetence. Notice that when we combine selective recall with the other cognitive factors—gender polarization, differential expectations, and the normative male—we strengthen and perpetuate our existing stereotypes.

HOW DO THE MEDIA CONTRIBUTE TO GENDER STEREOTYPES?

Television, movies, and the printed media help encourage people to develop and maintain the gender stereotypes we have been examining. Let's consider four general trends.

Women Are Underrepresented in the Media

Research suggests that women are underrepresented in the media, even during the 1990s. For example, music videos feature roughly twice as many males as females (Sommers-Flanagan, Sommers-Flanagan, & Davis, 1993).

Women are not seen much, but they are heard even less. For example, the next time you see a television advertisement, notice whose voice of authority is extolling the product's virtues. Males constitute between 85% and 90% of these voice-overs. Furthermore, only 5% of radio talk-show hosts are female (Flanders, 1997).

Women's and Men's Bodies Are Represented Differently

If you glance through magazine advertisements, you'll notice that women are much more likely than men to serve a decorative function. Women recline in seductive clothing, caressing a liquor bottle, or they drape themselves coyly on the nearest male. They bend their bodies at a ludicrous angle, or they look as helpless as 6-year-olds. They also may be painfully thin. In contrast, men stand up, they look competent, and they look purposeful (Jones, 1991).

Women and Men Are Shown Doing Different Activities

In magazine advertisements, men are rarely portrayed doing housework. Instead, men are more likely than women to be shown working outside the home. The world of paid employment is not emphasized for women. For example, an analysis of the articles in *Seventeen* magazine demonstrated that only 7% of the contents concerned career planning, independence, and other self-development topics. In contrast, 46% of the contents concerned appearance (Peirce, 1990). In the magazine advertisements, men are rarely portrayed doing housework. Basically, the media world often represents men and women as living in separate spheres.

Women of Color Are Represented in an Especially Biased Way

When Black women are shown at all, they are likely to appear in stereotypical roles. They are portrayed in an exaggerated way, with body positions even more exaggerated than those of European American women. Other women of color—Hispanics, Asians, and Native Americans—are virtually invisible (Andersen, 1993).

Fortunately, however, we are finally beginning to see some progress in the representation of men and women in advertisements and other visual media. One of my favorites is a poster for the graduate program in cognitive psychology at Indiana University. Instead of the traditional European American male head—complete with gears and other mechanical devices in the brain to illustrate thinking—this poster features the head of an African American woman. This example leads us to wonder whether our gender stereotypes would be more flexible if we were exposed to more positive images of this nature. With less rigid stereotypes, we might indeed find an important impact on the accuracy of our cognitive processes.

REFERENCES

Andersen, M. L. (1993). *Thinking about women: Sociological perspectives on sex and gender.* New York: Macmillan.

Bem, S. L. (1993). *The lenses of gender: Transforming the debate on sexual inequality.* New Haven: Yale University Press.

Cann, A. (1993). Evaluative expectations and the gender schema: Is failed inconsistency better? *Sex Roles, 28,* 667–678.

Condry, J. C., & Condry, S. (1976). Sex differences: A study in the eye of the beholder. *Child Development, 47,* 812–819.

Flanders, L. (1997). *Real majority, media minority: The cost of sidelining women in reporting.* Monroe, ME: Common Courage Press.

Jones, M. (1991). Gender stereotyping in advertisements. *Teaching of Psychology, 18,* 231–233.

Macrae, C. N., Hewstone, M., & Griffiths, R. J. (1993). Processing load and memory for stereotype-based information. *European Journal of Social Psychology, 23,* 77–87.

Miller, D. T., Taylor, B., & Buck, M. L. (1991). Gender gaps: Who needs to be explained? *Journal of Personality and Social Psychology, 61,* 5–12.

Peirce, K. (1990). A feminist theoretical perspective on the socialization of teenage girls through Seventeen magazine. *Sex Roles, 23,* 491–500.

Sommers-Flanagan, R., Sommers-Flanagan, J., & Davis, B. (1993). What's happening on music television? A gender role content analysis. *Sex Roles, 28,* 745–753.

Tavris, C. (1992). *The mismeasure of woman.* New York: Simon & Schuster.

READING REACTIONS

1. How does Matlin explain our need to stereotype?
2. In what ways does "the media" contribute to gender stereotypes?
3. What examples of gender stereotypes does Matlin mention to support her argument? What sorts of stereotypes do you see in modern ads (think about the earlier discussion in this chapter about Dove, Axe, and the Breast Milk Baby)?
4. What is the danger in grouping genders in two distinct groups? How is this danger further complicated by transgender individuals?
5. Explain, in your own words, the concept of normative male gaze. Is male experience and perspective still considered the norm? Offer examples to support your opinion.
6. At a little more than a decade old, this piece is a bit dated. Do you think the trends mentioned in the article (for example, women are not seen as much in media) still hold true?
7. Because this piece is more than a decade old, do you expect a writer could include this piece as a source in a paper now? What sort of strategies would

the writer need to take up to position this article as important to the current debate?

8. Take a few moments to examine your own gender bias. Do you believe men and women behave differently at work, in class, on a date, online?

Procter & Gamble has used Mr. Clean for decades to brand their product by associating it with masculine strength and an idealized physique (placeholder)

● Doreen Carvajal

Europe Takes Aim at Sexual Stereotyping in Ads

Carvajal is a reporter for *The New York Times* and the *International Herald Tribune.* Her work on international business and finance issues was recognized in 2010 by the University Association for Contemporary European Studies (UACES) annual "Reporting Europe" award committee.

In Madison Avenue's mind's eye, women are still preternaturally obsessed with the cleanliness of their kitchen floors, while men ruminate constantly about which shaving products will render them more attractive to the opposite sex.

The European Parliament has set out to change this. Last week, the legislature voted 504 to 110 to scold advertisers for "sexual stereotyping," adopting a nonbinding report that seeks to prod the industry to change the way it depicts men and women.

The lawmakers' ire has many targets, from a print ad for Dolce & Gabbana (which had a woman in spike heels pinned to the ground and surrounded by sweaty men in tight jeans) to Mr. Clean, the 1950s advertising icon whose muscular physique might imply that only a strong man is powerful enough to tackle dirt.

Clearly, the advertising industry is not quaking in its boots. But the move, however laughable as a gesture of political correctness, may well provoke some debate among agency executives and their clients about the messages they are sending. (That said, the people who approved the gender-stereotype measure are the same ones who suggested that all car advertisements should have warning labels because of the toxic impact of gas fumes.)

Such debate could well lead to legally binding legislation, said Mary Honeyball, a British

Figure 4.11 Procter & Gamble has used Mr. Clean for decades to brand their product by associating it with masculine strength and an idealized physique

lawmaker and a member of the Women's Rights and Gender Equality Committee, which developed the report.

"What I think it might do is encourage the industry in member states of Europe to improve," she said. "The report was passed by a big majority, and so there's obviously recognition that there is a need to look at this. There is unacceptable stereotyping."

The concern, according to the committee report, is that stereotypes in advertising can "straitjacket women, men, girls and boys by restricting individuals to predetermined and artificial roles that are often degrading, humiliating and dumbed-down for both sexes."

The vote by Parliament reflects a growing uneasiness in Europe about how advertisers and big business promote their products. In France, the Senate is considering a proposal—already passed in the National Assembly—to levy fines of up to 45,000 euros, or $64,000, for advertisements that promote or incite anorexia. The European Parliament took note of the issue during its debate last week, calling on advertisers "to consider carefully their use of extremely thin women to advertise products."

Last year, the Spanish government weighed in, demanding that Dolce & Gabbana pull its "fantasy rape" advertisement in a country where headlines about violence against women are all too common. The designers at the fashion house, based in Milan, relented, but not before observing in the Italian press that Spain was "a bit behind the times" and that the ads were artistic in nature. But then Italian lawmakers started to fume about the images, and the ads were also withdrawn in Italy.

With its vote, the European Parliament is raising alarms not only about provocative images, but also about some that consumers might consider benign. Ms. Honeyball's rogues' gallery includes an ad for LG Electronics featuring the muscular backside of a naked man who is facing a washing machine (a spot that won an advertising award in Cannes). But it also includes a gray-suited businessman in a Lufthansa ad, and a Miele campaign that features a woman, potholder in hand, fawning over a cake in an oven.

Malte Lohan, a spokesman for the World Federation of Advertisers, a trade association representing 55 national advertiser associations on five continents, said that his group was wary that the debate "about the alleged role of advertising in gender discrimination keeps coming again and again."

"The essential concern that we have is that it is mixing two different things: gender stereotyping with discrimination and degrading images," Mr. Lohan said. "That's a real problem because stereotypes are not necessarily something that are bad. They can be totally harmless or quite entertaining."

He said the industry supported efforts to eliminate degrading or discriminatory images of women. The association, however, has not taken a position on the debate over extremely thin women. "That's still a fairly recent issue," he said. "Before, advertisers were criticized for causing obesity rates to go up, and that's being turned on its head."

Eva-Britt Svensson, a Swedish member of Parliament and author of the report on advertising images, said that, at this point, legislators were pressing simply for self-regulation among advertisers. But she also suggested that consumers could act.

"If they have more information and awareness about the impact of gender stereotypes," she said, "they can start boycotting products."

READING REACTIONS

1. What issues do you see with governments and courts attempting to police "sexual stereotyping"?

2. What social, cultural, and political values and actions might be impacting advertising's current tendency to, according to the Women's Rights and Gender Equality Committee report, "straitjacket women, men, girls, and boys by restricting individuals to predetermined and artificial roles"?

3. This report talks about the dangers of extremely thin women in ads. Is male body image an issue too? Why or why not?

4. There is a saying about "art imitating life or life imitating art." Which do you see happening here—is advertising dictating what should happen in culture or merely reflecting it? Both? How does this complicate plans to regulate stereotypes in ads?

5. Respond to Malte Lohan's statement that "stereotypes are not necessarily something that are bad."

6. What are our social or cultural associations and values regarding bodies in print and television advertisements? Are these bodies stand-ins for us as consumers or are they products in and of themselves?

7. Do the social and cultural associations and values of new media (like Facebook, wikis, and Pinterest) differ from those of advertising? Is new media changing, reinforcing, or challenging sexual stereotypes? Explain.

● Gail Tom and Anmarie Eves

The Use of Rhetorical Devices in Advertising

Gail Tom is a professor of marketing at California State University, Sacramento. Her work appears in the *Journal of Psychology, Psychology & Marketing*, and *Review of Business*. Coauthor Anmarie Eves was a student at California State University, Sacramento, studying English and advertising at the time this article was published.

The purpose of advertisements is not only to inform but also to persuade. Rhetorical devices, artful deviations that put a twist on the familiar, are frequently found in advertisements. This paper reports on the effectiveness of advertisements that use rhetorical devices compared to advertisements that do not. The findings indicate that advertisements that use rhetorical figures result in superior recall and superior persuasion.

Rhetoric, the discipline of argumentation, is concerned not only with the message but with the determination of the most effective persuasive methods of presentation and frequently incorporates the use of rhetorical figures/devices. A rhetorical device is an artful deviation (Corbett, 1990) and "occurs when an expression deviates from expectation, the expression is not rejected as nonsensical or faulty, the deviation occurs at the level of form rather than content, and the deviation conforms to a template that is invariant across a variety of content and contexts" (McQuarrie and Mick, 1996).

Recognizing that a major goal of advertising is not only to inform, but also to persuade, it is not surprising that advertising is sprinkled with rhetorical devices (Leigh, 1994). For example, the current Benson & Hedges Cigarette campaign employs the rhetorical figure, personification (Pullack, 1997), and was preceded with campaigns employing other rhetorical figures, puns, and resonance. The long-running Absolute Vodka advertising campaigns are well known for their use of rhetorical figures. In a foundation-laying paper, McQuarrie and Mick (1996) offer a taxonomy of rhetorical figures in advertising language to provide an integrative framework for a systematic investigation of the rhetorical structure in advertising language, which heretofore had been piecemeal and isolated (e.g., for rhetorical questions, see Swasy and Much, 1985; for puns, see McQuarrie and Mick, 1992).

Unlike argumentation presentation in other fields which must rely exclusively or heavily on the verbal component, presentations in marketing via its advertising specialty can rely more heavily on the nonverbal components: olfaction, visual, auditory, and tactile. The use of sense/smell strips allow consumers to experience the fragrance of perfumes and colognes; consumers are exposed to pictorial portions of advertisements and packages; computer chips talk and sing to consumers from the printed page; free product samples offer consumers the opportunity to touch and/or taste the product; promotional items serve as tangible reminders of the persuasive communication.

Of these nonverbal components, the visual component is the predominant nonverbal element of presentation in advertisements. The prevalent theoretical approach to the research investigating the pictorial element of advertising has been the copy theory. In copy theory, pictures are conceived as natural, realistic reflections of reality, and elements such as visual viewpoint, focus, graphics, and layout are considered as variables independent of the message. Scott (1994) has noted the shortcomings of copy theory and has suggested that a theory of visual rhetoric be based upon the key premise that "pictures are not merely analogues to visual perception, but symbolic artifacts constructed from the conventions of a particular culture." A theory of visual rhetoric would recognize that pictures are a symbol system employed for the purpose of persuasion. Pictorial elements are altered, combined, arranged, adopt viewpoints, and focus to create artful deviations, characteristic of rhetorical figures. Kaplan's (1992) investigation of the use of visual metaphors in advertisements is one of very few studies representative of research that recognizes the use of rhetorical figures in the pictorial component of advertisements.

Current thinking points to the importance and criticality of taking into account the effects of rhetorical devices in both the verbal and pictorial components of advertisements. Both verbal and visual rhetorical devices employ artful deviations that provide a twist on the familiar. This inherent incongruity of rhetorical devices allows them to carry additional meaning(s) and is the basis of their persuasive impact. It has been suggested that, compared to advertisements that do not use rhetorical figures, advertisements using rhetorical figures may more likely lead to greater attention (Berlyne, 1971), preference, and memorability (McQuarrie and Mick, 1996) and may be instrumental in the formation of brand images (King, 1989).

The principle purpose of this article is to use performance data to compare the effectiveness of advertisements that use rhetorical devices to advertisements that do not use rhetorical devices. In order to be effective, advertisements must, at a minimum, capture sufficient consumer attention to process the information. An additional, more stringent requirement for effectiveness is that advertisements must also be persuasive. A measurement of effectiveness comparing different executions of advertisements for brands within the same product category would perhaps provide a cleaner comparison and provide results less subject to noise and alternative interpretations than comparisons of advertising presentations in different product categories.

Performance data would provide more definitive evidence of advertising effectiveness than current experimental paradigms or descriptive studies. Descriptive studies are limited to information that report on the occurrence of selected variables (e.g., headline placement, frequency of the use of celebrities) in advertisements. Experimental studies have been criticized for their lack of realism. These studies typically require participants to focus attention on the advertisements. It is questionable whether participants would be that attentive to the advertisement under everyday conditions when they are not required to do so. In contrast, the strength of performance data is its grounding to everyday conditions. It reports the effectiveness of the advertisement within the context of the everyday.

The source of the data selected for this study was the sixth, seventh, and eighth editions of *Which Ad Pulled Best* (Burton and Purvis, 1997, 1993, 1991). In each edition, Gallup & Robinson performance scores are provided for each of 40[1] pairs of advertisements. Each pair of advertisements represent brands within the same product category. Gallup & Robinson provides two performance measurements: (1) recall—proved name registration and (2) persuasion—favorable buying attitude. The 40 advertisements selected for each edition of *Which Ad Pulled Best* clearly were not for the purpose of this study. However, this lack of intention can be viewed as a strength of the procurement of an unbiased data set.

METHOD

Each pair of advertisements was classified as using or not using a rhetorical figure. For those pairs of advertisements in which at least one of the advertisements used a rhetorical figure, the advertisement that received the higher performance score for recall and/or persuasion was recorded. The data set provided a total of 120 pairs of (240) advertisements.

An advertisement was classified as using rhetorical figures if either the verbal and/or pictorial elements used rhetorical devices. McQuarrie and Mick's taxonomy for rhetorical figures in advertising language (1996) was used to determine whether or not the verbal component of the advertisement incorporated the use of rhetorical figures. The pictorial component of the advertisement was classified as using rhetorical figure(s) if the picture was not a copy of reality. This included distortions, hyperboles, unrealistic context, or juxtaposition of objects (Kapalan, 1992). Two researchers classified each ad independently. The results indicated 96 percent agreement. Discrepancies were resolved with discussions.

Table 4.1 presents the results for all 120 pairs of advertisements for all three editions of *Which Ad Pulled Best*. **Table 4.2** presents the data for each of the three editions separately.

---

[1]*Each edition of* Which Ad Pulled Best *provides 50 pairs of advertisements, 40 targeted for consumers and 10 targeted for business. Only consumer-targeted advertisements were included in this study.*

Table 4.1 A Comparison of All Pairs of Advertisements

Performance Measurements	Advertisements	
	Use Rhetorical Figures	Do Not Use Rhetorical Figures
Recall	48	21*
Persuasion	40	24**

*chi square = 10.56; df = 1; p = .001.
**chi square = 4.00; df = 1; p = .046.

Table 4.2 A Separate Comparison of the Pairs of Advertisements from Each Edition

Performance Measurements	Advertisements—Edition 6	
	Use Rhetorical Figures	Do Not Use Rhetorical Figures
Recall	15	7*
Persuasion	13	9

*chi square = 2.909; dj = 1, p = .088

Performance Measurements	Advertisements—Edition 7	
	Use Rhetorical Figures	Do Not Use Rhetorical Figures
Recall	16	7*
Persuasion	15	8

*chi square = 3.52, df = l, p = .061

Performance Measurements	Advertisements—Edition 8	
	Use Rhetorical Figures	Do Not Use Rhetorical Figures
Recall	17	7*
Persuasion	12	7

*chi square = 4.17; df = 1; p = .041.

RESULTS

The results revealed that 45 percent (54 of the 120) of the advertisements in this data set use rhetorical figures. The findings for the total data set indicate that advertisements that incorporate rhetorical devices perform better than advertisements that do not for both measurements of recall and persuasion[2]. However, as shown in Table 4.2, when the data set is considered separately for each of the three editions of *Which Ad Pulled Best,* the results are not as strong.

An examination of the results by product type (e.g., high involvement/low involvement; service/goods) did not suggest that the use of rhetorical devices was more effective for any particular product category or that the frequency of usage of rhetorical devices differed by product category.

DISCUSSION

The findings of this study suggest the superior performance effectiveness of advertisements that contain rhetorical figures. Even though the results of this study are clear, given the source of the data set, these findings, although promising, must be taken only as preliminary and suggestive. Future research must be undertaken with different data sets and with different performance measurements (e.g., Starch scores). The exploratory nature of the present study and the data set precluded the value of a formal inquiry for particular product categories and/or particular rhetorical figures. Research that compares the effectiveness of selected rhetorical figures for selected product categories may provide practical benefits and guidelines for practitioners.

The results of this study revealed that in some cases literal presentations were more effective than presentations incorporating rhetorical figures and, in those instances where rhetorical devices were used in both advertisements, the superiority of some rhetorical devices over others. Future research efforts can be directed to determine the theoretical underpinnings for these greater performance effectiveness.

REFERENCES

Berlyne, D. E. *Aesthetics and Psychobiology.* New York: Appleton, 1971.

Burton, P. W., and S. C. Purvis, eds. *Which Ad Pulled Best,* 6th ed. Lincolnwood, IL: NTC Publishing, 1991.

_____, and_____. *Which Ad Pulled Best,* 7th ed. Lincolnwood, IL: NTC Publishing, 1995.

_____, and_____. *Which Ad Pulled Best,* 8th ed. Lincolnwood, IL: NTC Publishing, 1996.

Corbett, E. P. J. *Classical Rhetoric for the Modern Student.* New York: Oxford University Press, 1990.

Kaplan, S. J. "A Conceptual Analysis of Form and Content in Visual Metaphors." *Communications* 13, (1992): 197–209.

---

[2]*In cases where insufficient data precluded the reporting of a persuasion score for an advertisement, the advertisement for which there was sufficient data was classified as superior.*

Leigh, J. H. "The Use of Figures of Speech in Print Ad Headlines." *Journal of Advertising* 23, 2 (1994): 17–34.

McQuarrie, E. F., and D. G. Mick. "Figures of Rhetoric in Advertising Language." *Journal of Consumer Research* 22, 4 (1996): 424–38.

Pullack, J. "Anthropomorphic Cigs Star in Ads for Benson & Hedges." *Advertising Age,* April 14, 1997.

Scott, L. M. "Images in Advertising: The Need for a Theory of Visual Rhetoric." *Journal of Consumer Research* 21, 2 (1994): 252–73.

Swasy, J. L., and J. M. Munch. "Examining the Target of Receiver Elaborations: Rhetorical Question Effects on Source Processing and Persuasion." *Journal of Consumer Research* 11, 4 (1985): 877–86.

READING REACTIONS

1. According to the authors, what do rhetoric and advertising have in common? Think specifically about the end goal of each.

2. Summarize, in your own words, the major findings of this research study.

3. Who is the intended reader for this piece? How can you tell? What are readers "supposed to" do or feel after reading this research?

4. How does the message—the research findings in this case—of this article help shape membership in a community and/or establish common goals and values among readers?

5. Tom and Eves report that "the visual component is the predominant nonverbal element of presentation in advertisements." According to the authors and scholar L. M. Scott (1994), how do pictures work in ads to relay messages?

6. What sort of evidence do the authors use to support their argument regarding the usefulness of rhetorical devices in print advertisements?

7. This piece, written in 1999, discusses some older ad campaigns, including Absolut vodka and Benson & Hedges cigarettes. Find a current advertisement and identify rhetorical devices (for example, personification, hyperbole, visual metaphor) it uses to persuade viewers.

● Michael A. Messner and Jeffrey Montez de Oca

The Male Consumer as Loser: Beer and Liquor Ads in Mega Sports Media Events

Michael A. Messner is a professor of sociology and gender studies at the University of Southern California. His research concerns gender and sports and gender-based violence. He has authored several journal articles and book chapters as well as the 2011 book *King of the Wild Suburb: A Memoir of Fathers, Sons and Guns.* Montez de Oca is an assistant professor of sociology at the University of Colorado at Colorado Springs. His research includes sports, media, and identity and inequality. His work has appeared in *American Studies, Gender & Society,* and *The Journal of Historical Sociology.*

The historical development of modern men's sport has been closely intertwined with the consumption of alcohol and with the financial promotion and sponsorship provided by beer and liquor producers and distributors, as well as pubs and bars (Collins and Vamplew, 2002). The beer and liquor industry plays a key economic role in commercialized college and professional sports (Zimbalist, 1999; Sperber, 2000). Liquor industry advertisements heavily influence the images of masculinity promoted in sports broadcasts and magazines (Wenner, 1991). Alcohol consumption is also often a key aspect of the more dangerous and violent dynamics at the heart of male sport cultures (Curry, 2000; Sabo, Gray, and Moore, 2000). By itself, alcohol does not "cause" men's violence against women or against other men; however, it is commonly one of a cluster of factors that facilitate violence (Koss and Gaines, 1993; Leichliter et al., 1998). In short, beer and liquor are central players in "a high holy trinity of alcohol, sports, and hegemonic masculinity" (Wenner, 1998).

This article examines beer and liquor advertisements in two "mega sports media events" consumed by large numbers of boys and men—the 2002 and 2003 Super Bowls and the 2002 and 2003 *Sports Illustrated* swimsuit issues. Our goal is to illuminate tropes of masculinity that prevail in those ads. We see these ads as establishing a pedagogy of youthful masculinity that does not passively teach male consumers about the qualities of their products so much as it encourages consumers to think of their products as essential to creating a stylish and desirable lifestyle. These ads do more than just dupe consumers into product loyalty; they also work with consumers to construct a consumption-based masculine identity relevant to contemporary social conditions. Drawing on insights from feminist cultural studies (Walters, 1999), we argue that these gendered tropes watched by tens of millions of boys and men offer a window through which we can broaden our understanding of contemporary continuities, shifts, and strains in the social construction of masculinities.

GENDER, MEN'S SPORTS, AND ALCOHOL ADS

Although marketing beer and liquor to men is not new, the imagery that advertisers employ to pitch their product is not static either. Our analysis of past Super Bowls and *Sports Illustrated* beer and liquor ads suggests shifting patterns in the gender themes encoded in the ads. Consistently, over

Michael A. Messner and Jeffrey Montez de Oca, "The Male Consumer as Loser: Beer and Liquor Ads in Mega Sports Media Events," *Signs: Journal of Women in Culture and Society,* 2005, vol. 30, no. 3.

time, the ads attempt not to simply "plug" a particular product but to situate products within a larger historically specific way of life. Beer and liquor advertisers normally do not create product differentiation through typical narratives of crisis and resolution in which the product is the rescuing hero. Instead, they paint a series of images that evoke feelings, moods, and ways of being. In short, beer and liquor advertising engages in "lifestyle branding." Rather than simply attaching a name to a product, the brand emanates from a series of images that construct a plausible and desirable world to consumers. Lifestyle branding—more literary and evocative than simple crisis/resolution narratives—theorizes the social location of target populations and constructs a desiring subject whose consumption patterns can be massaged in specific directions. As we shall see, the subject constructed by the beer and liquor ads that we examined is an overtly gendered subject.

Beer and alcohol advertising construct a "desirable lifestyle" in relation to contemporary social conditions, including shifts and tensions in the broader gender order. Ads from the late 1950s through the late 1960s commonly depicted young or middle-aged white heterosexual couples happily sharing a cold beer in their suburban backyards, in their homes, or in an outdoor space like a park.

In these ads, the beer is commonly displayed in a clear glass, its clean, fresh appearance perhaps intended to counter the reputation of beer as a working-class male drink. Beer in these ads symbolically unites the prosperous and happy postwar middle-class couple. By the mid-1970s, women as wives and partners largely disappeared from beer ads. Instead of showing heterosexual couples drinking in their homes or backyards, these ads began primarily to depict images of men drinking with other men in public spaces. Three studies of beer commercials of the 1970s and 1980s found that most ads pitched beer to men as a pleasurable reward for a hard day's work. These ads told men that "For all you do, this Bud's for you." Women were rarely depicted in these ads, except as occasional background props in male-dominated bars (Postman et al., 1987; Wenner, 1991; Strate, 1992).

The 1950s and 1960s beer ads that depicted happy married suburban couples were part of a moment in gender relations tied to postwar culture and Fordist relations of production. White, middle-class, heterosexual masculinity was defined as synonymous with the male breadwinner, in symmetrical relation to a conception of femininity grounded in the image of the suburban housewife. In the 1970s and early 1980s, the focus on men's laboring bodies, tethered to their public leisure with other men, expressed an almost atavistic view of hegemonic masculinity at a time when women were moving into public life in huge numbers and blue-collar men's jobs were being eliminated by the tens of thousands.

Both the postwar and the postindustrial ads provide a gendered pedagogy for living a masculine lifestyle in a shifting context characterized by uncertainty. In contrast to the depiction of happy white families comfortably living lives of suburban bliss, the postwar era was characterized by anxieties over the possibility of a postwar depression, nuclear annihilation, suburban social dislocation, and disorder from racial and class movements for social justice (Lipsitz, 1981; May, 1988; Spigel, 1992). Similarly, the 1970s and 1980s beer ads came in the wake of the defeat of the United States in the Vietnam War, the 1972 gas crisis, the collapse of Fordism, and the turbulence in gender relations brought on by the women's and gay/lesbian liberation movements. All of these social ruptures contributed to produce an anxious white male subject (Connell, 1995; Lipsitz, 1998). Therefore, there is a sort of crisis/resolution narrative in these beer ads: the "crisis" lies broadly in the construction of white masculinities in the latter half of the twentieth century (Kimmel, 1987), and the resolution lies in the construction of a lifestyle outside of immediate anxieties. The advertisements do not straightforwardly tell consumers to buy; rather, they teach consumers how to live a happy, stress-free life that includes regular (if not heavy) consumption of alcoholic beverages.

The 2002 and 2003 ads that we examine here primarily construct a white male "loser" whose life is apparently separate from paid labor. He hangs out with his male buddies, is self-mocking and ironic about his loser status, and is always at the ready to engage in voyeurism with sexy fantasy women but holds committed relationships and emotional honesty with real women in disdain. To the extent that these themes find resonance with young men of today, it is likely because they speak to basic insecurities that are grounded in a combination of historic shifts: deindustrialization, the declining real value of wages and the male breadwinner role, significant cultural shifts brought about by more than three decades of struggle by feminists and sexual minorities, and challenges to white male supremacy by people of color and by immigrants. This cluster of social changes has destabilized hegemonic masculinity and defines the context of gender relations in which today's young men have grown toward adulthood.

In theorizing how the loser motif in beer and liquor ads constructs a version of young white masculinity, we draw on Mikhail Bakhtin's (1981) concept of the chronotope. This is especially relevant in analyzing how lifestyle branding goes beyond the reiteration of a name to actually creating desirable and believable worlds in which consumers are beckoned to place themselves. The term *chronotope*—literally meaning "time-space"—describes how time and space fuse in literature to create meaningful structures separate from the text and its representations (Bakhtin, 1981). The ads that we looked at consistently construct a leisure-time lifestyle of young men meeting in specific sites of sports and alcohol consumption: bars, television rooms, and stadiums. This meeting motif gives a temporal and spatial plane to male fantasy where desire can be explored and symbolic boundaries can simultaneously be transgressed and reinscribed into the social world.

TWO MEGA SPORTS MEDIA EVENTS

This article brings focus to the commercial center of sports media by examining the gender and sexual imagery encoded in two mega sports media events: the 2002 and 2003 Super Bowls and the 2002 and 2003 *Sports Illustrated* swimsuit issues.[1]

Mega sports media events are mediated cultural rituals (Dayan and Katz, 1988) that differ from everyday sports media events in several key ways: sports media actively build audience anticipation and excitement throughout the year for these single events; the Super Bowl and the swimsuit issue are each preceded by major pre-event promotion and hype—from the television network that will broadcast the Super Bowl to *Sports Illustrated* and myriad other print and electronic media; the Super Bowl and the swimsuit issue are used as marketing tools for selling the more general products of National Football League (NFL) games and *Sports Illustrated* magazine subscriptions; the Super Bowl and the swimsuit issue each generate significant spin-off products (e.g., videos, books, "making of" TV shows, calendars, frequently visited Web pages); the Super Bowl and the swimsuit issue generate significantly larger audiences than does a weekly NFL game or a weekly edition of *Sports Illustrated*; and advertisements are usually created specifically for these mega sports media events and cost more to run than do ads in a weekly NFL game or a weekly edition of *Sports Illustrated*.

To be sure, the Super Bowl and the *Sports Illustrated* swimsuit issue are different in some fundamental ways. First, the Super Bowl is a televised event, while the swimsuit issue is a print event. Second, the Super Bowl is an actual sporting contest, while the swimsuit issue is a departure from *Sports Illustrated*'s normal coverage of sports. However, for our purposes, we see these two events as comparable, partly because they are mega sports media events but also because their ads target young males who consume sports media.

Super Bowl ads

Since its relatively modest start in 1967, the NFL Super Bowl has mushroomed into one of the most expensive and most watched annual media events in the United States, with a growing world audience (Martin and Reeves, 2001), the vast majority of whom are boys and men. Increasingly over the past decade, Super Bowl commercials have been specially created for the event. Newspapers, magazines, television news shows, and Web sites now routinely run pre–Super Bowl stories that focus specifically on the ads, and several media outlets run post–Super Bowl polls to determine which ads were the most and least favorite. Postgame lists of "winners" and "losers" focus as much on the corporate sponsors and their ads as on the two teams that—incidentally?—played a football game between the commercials.

Fifty-five commercials ran during the 2003 Super Bowl (not counting pregame and postgame shows), at an average cost of $2.1 million for each thirty-second ad. Fifteen of these commercials were beer or malt liquor ads. Twelve of these ads were run by Anheuser-Busch, whose ownership of this Super Bowl was underlined at least twenty times throughout the broadcast, when, after commercial breaks, the camera lingered on the stadium scoreboard, atop which was a huge Budweiser sign. On five other occasions, "Bud" graphics appeared on the screen after commercial breaks, as voice-overs reminded viewers that the Super Bowl was "brought to" them by Budweiser. This represented a slight increase in beer advertising since the 2002 Super Bowl, which featured thirteen beer or malt liquor commercials (eleven of them by Anheuser-Busch), at an average cost of $1.9 million per thirty-second ad. In addition to the approximately $31.5 million that the beer companies paid for the 2003 Super Bowl ad slots, they paid millions more creating and testing those commercials with focus groups. There were 137.7 million viewers watching all or part of the 2003 Super Bowl on ABC, and by far the largest demographic group watching was men, aged twenty-five to fifty-five.

Sports Illustrated swimsuit issue ads

Sports Illustrated began in 1964 to publish an annual February issue that featured five or six pages of women modeling swimsuits, embedded in an otherwise normal sixty-four-page magazine (Davis, 1997). This modest format continued until the late 1970s, when the portion of the magazine featuring swimsuit models began gradually to grow. In the 1980s, the swimsuit issue morphed into a special issue in which normal sports coverage gradually disappeared. During this decade, the issue's average length had grown to 173 pages, 20 percent of which were focused on swimsuit models. By the 1990s the swimsuit issue averaged 207 pages in length, 31 percent of which featured swimsuit models. The magazine has continued to grow in recent years. The 2003 issue was 218 pages in length, 59 percent of which featured swimsuit models. The dramatic growth in the size of the swimsuit issue in the 1990s, as well as the dropping of pretense that the swimsuit issue had anything to do with normal "sports journalism," were facilitated by advertising that began cleverly to echo and spoof the often highly sexualized swimsuit imagery in the magazine. By 2000, it was more the rule than the exception when an ad in some way utilized the swimsuit theme. The gender and sexual themes of the swimsuit issue became increasingly seamless, as ads and *Sports Illustrated* text symbiotically echoed and played off of each other. The 2002 swimsuit issue included seven pages of beer ads and seven pages of liquor ads, which cost approximately $230,000 per full page to run. The 2003 swimsuit issue ran the equivalent of sixteen pages of beer ads and thirteen pages of liquor ads. The ad space for the 2003 swimsuit issue sold for $266,000 per full-page color ad.

The millions of dollars that beer and liquor companies spent to develop and buy space for these ads were aimed at the central group that reads the magazine: young and middle-aged males. *Sports Illustrated* estimates the audience size of its weekly magazine at 21.3 million readers, roughly 76 percent of whom are males.[2] Nearly half of the male audience is in the coveted eighteen- to thirty-four-year-old demographic group, and three quarters of the male *Sports Illustrated* audience is between the ages of eighteen and forty-nine. A much larger number of single-copy sales gives the swimsuit issue a much larger audience, conservatively estimated at more than 30 million readers.[3]

The Super Bowl and the *Sports Illustrated* swimsuit issue are arguably the biggest single electronic and print sports media events annually in the United States. Due to their centrality, size, and target audiences, we suggest that mega sports media events such as the Super Bowl and the swimsuit issue offer a magnified view of the dominant gender and sexual imagery emanating from the center of the sports-media-commercial complex. Our concern is not simply to describe the stereotypes of masculinity and femininity in these ads; rather, we use these ads as windows into the ways that cultural capitalism constructs gender relationally, as part of a general lifestyle. In this article, we will employ thick description of ads to illuminate the four main gender relations themes that we saw in the 2002 and 2003 ads, and we will follow with a discussion of the process through which these themes are communicated: erotic and often humorous intertextual referencing. We will end by discussing some of the strains and tensions in the ads' major tropes of masculinity.

LOSERS AND BUDDIES, HOTTIES AND BITCHES

In the 2002 and 2003 beer and liquor ads that we examined, men's work worlds seem mostly to have disappeared. These ads are less about drinking and leisure as a reward for hard work and more about leisure as a lifestyle in and of itself. Men do not work in these ads; they recreate. And women are definitely back in the picture, but not as wives who are partners in building the good domestic life. It is these relations among men as well as relations between men and women that form the four dominant gender themes in the ads we examined. We will introduce these four themes by describing a 2003 Super Bowl commercial for Bud Lite beer.

Two young, somewhat nerdy-looking white guys are at a yoga class, sitting in the back of a room full of sexy young women. The two men have attached prosthetic legs to their bodies so that they can fake the yoga moves. With their bottles of Bud Lite close by, these voyeurs watch in delight as the female yoga teacher instructs the class to "relax and release that negative energy . . . inhale, arch, *thrust* your pelvis to the sky and exhale, *release* into the stretch." As the instructor uses her hands to push down on a woman's upright spread-eagled legs and says "focus, focus, focus," the camera (serving as prosthesis for male spectators at home) cuts back and forth between close-ups of the women's breasts and bottoms, while the two guys gleefully enjoy their beer and their sexual voyeurism. In the final scene the two guys are standing outside the front door of the yoga class, beer bottles in hand, and someone throws their fake legs out the door at them. As they duck to avoid being hit by the legs, one of them comments, "*She's* not very relaxed."

We begin with this ad because it contains, in various degrees, the four dominant gender themes that we found in the mega sports media events ads:

1. Losers: Men are often portrayed as chumps, losers. Masculinity—especially for the lone man—is precarious. Individual men are always on the cusp of being publicly humiliated, either by their own stupidity, by other men, or worse, by a beautiful woman.

2. Buddies: The precariousness of individual men's masculine status is offset by the safety of the male group. The solidity and primacy—and emotional safety—of male friendships are the emotional center of many of these ads.

3. Hotties: When women appear in these ads, it is usually as highly sexualized fantasy objects. These beautiful women serve as potential prizes for men's victories and proper consumption choices. They sometimes serve to validate men's masculinity, but their validating power also holds the potential to humiliate male losers.

4. Bitches: Wives, girlfriends, or other women to whom men are emotionally committed are mostly absent from these ads. However, when they do appear, it is primarily as emotional or sexual blackmailers who threaten to undermine individual men's freedom to enjoy the erotic pleasure at the center of the male group.

To a great extent, these four gender themes are intertwined in the Super Bowl "Yoga Voyeurs" ad. First, the two guys are clearly not good-looking, high-status, muscular icons of masculinity. More likely they are intended to represent the "everyman" with whom many boys and men can identify. Their masquerade as sensitive men allows them to transgress the female space of the yoga class, but they cannot pull the masquerade off and are eventually "outed" as losers and rejected by the sexy women. But even if they realize that they are losers, they do not have to care because they are so happy and secure in their bond with each other. Their friendship bond is cemented in frat-boy-style hijinks that allow them to share close-up voyeurism of sexy women who, we can safely assume, are way out of these men's league. In the end, the women reject the guys as pathetic losers. But the guys do not seem too upset. They have each other and, of course, they have their beers.

Rarely did a single ad in our study contain all four of these themes. But taken together, the ads show enough consistency that we can think of these themes as intertwined threads that together make up the ideological fabric at the center of mega sports media events. Next, we will illustrate how these themes are played out in the 2002 and 2003 ads, before discussing some of the strains and tensions in the ads.

REAL FRIENDS, SCARY WOMEN

Five twenty-something white guys are sitting around a kitchen table playing poker. They are laughing, seemingly having the time of their lives, drinking Jim Beam whiskey. The caption for this ad reflects the lighthearted, youthful mood of the group: "Good Bourbon, ice cubes, and whichever glasses are clean." This ad, which appeared in the 2002 *Sports Illustrated* swimsuit issue, is one in a series of Jim Beam ads that have run for the past few years in *Sports Illustrated* and in other magazines aimed at young men.[4] Running under the umbrella slogan of "Real Friends, Real Bourbon," these Jim Beam ads hail a white, college-age (or young college-educated) crowd of men with the appeal of playful male bonding through alcohol consumption in bars or pool halls. The main theme is the safety and primacy of the male group, but the accompanying written text sometimes suggests the presence of women. In one ad, four young white guys partying up a storm together and posing with arms intertwined are accompanied by the caption, "Unlike your girlfriend, they never ask where this relationship is going." These ads imply that women demand levels of emotional commitment and expression undesirable to men, while life with the boys (and the booze) is exciting, emotionally comfortable, and safe. The comfort that these ads suggest is that bonding and intimacy have clear (though mostly unspoken) boundaries that limit emotional expression in the male group. When drinking with the guys, a man can feel close to his friends, perhaps even drape an arm over a friend's shoulder, embrace him, or tell him that he loves him. But the context of alcohol consumption provides an escape hatch that contains and rationalizes the eruption of physical intimacy.

Although emotional closeness with and commitment to real women apparently are to be avoided, these ads also do suggest a role for women. The one ad in the Jim Beam series that includes an image of a woman depicts only a body part (*Sports Illustrated* ran this one in its 2000 swimsuit issue in 3-D).

Four guys drinking together in a bar are foregrounded by a set of high-heeled legs that appear to be an exotic dancer's. The guys drink, laugh, and seem thoroughly amused with each other. "Our lives would make a great sitcom," the caption reads, and continues, "of course, it would have to run on cable." That the guys largely ignore the dancer affirms the strength and primacy of their bond with one another—they do not need her or any other women, the ad seems to say. On the other hand—and just as in the "Yoga Voyeurs" commercial—the female dancer's sexualizing of the chronotopic space affirms that the bond between the men is safely within the bounds of heterosexuality.*

TENSION, STABILIZATION, AND MASCULINE CONSUMPTION

We argued in our introduction that contemporary social changes have desta-bilized hegemonic masculinity. Examining beer and liquor ads in mega sports media events gives us a window into the ways that commercial forces have seized on these destabilizing tendencies, constructing pedagogical fantasy nar-ratives that aim to appeal to a very large group—eighteen- to thirty-four-year-old men. They do so by appealing to a broad zeitgeist among young (especially white, heterosexual) men that is grounded in widespread tensions in the con-temporary gender order.[6] The sexual and gender themes of the beer and liquor ads that we examine in this article do not stand alone; rather they reflect, and in turn contribute to, broader trends in popular culture and marketing to young white males. Television shows like *The Man Show*, new soft-core porn maga-zines like *Maxim* and *FHM*, and radio talk shows like the syndicated *Tom Leykus Show* share similar themes and are targeted to similar audiences of young males. Indeed, radio talk show hosts like Leykus didactically instruct young men to avoid "girlie" things, to eschew emotional commitment, and to think of women primarily as sexual partners (Messner, 2002, 107–8). The chro-notope of these magazines and television and radio shows constructs young male lifestyles saturated with sexy images of nearly naked, surgically enhanced women; unabashed and unapologetic sexual voyeurism shared by groups of laughing men; and explicit talk of sexual exploits with "hotties" or "jug-gies." A range of consumer products that includes—often centrally, as in *The Man Show*—consumption of beer as part of the young male lifestyle stitches together this erotic bonding among men. Meanwhile, real women are either absent from these media or they are disparaged as gold diggers (yes, this term has been resuscitated) who use sex to get men to spend money on them and trick them into marriage. The domesticated man is viewed as a wimpy victim who has subordinated his own pleasures (and surrendered his paychecks) to a

*The original article includes several images from advertisements and also more extensive textual analysis of a few specific ads. Please see the full article at *www.nku.edu/~lipping/PHE385/16670728.pdf*.

woman. Within this framework, a young man should have sex with as many women as he can while avoiding (or at least delaying) emotional commitments to any one woman. Freedom from emotional commitment grants 100 percent control over disposable income for monadic consumption and care of self. And that is ultimately what these shows are about: constructing a young male consumer characterized by personal and emotional freedom who can attain a hip lifestyle by purchasing an ever-expanding range of automobile-related products, snack foods, clothes, toiletries, and, of course, beer and liquor.

At first glance, these new media aimed at young men seem to resuscitate a 1950s "*Playboy* philosophy" of men's consumption, sexuality, and gender relations (Ehrenreich, 1983). Indeed, these new media strongly reiterate the dichotomous bitch-whore view of women that was such a lynchpin of Hugh Hefner's "philosophy." But today's tropes of masculinity do not simply reiterate the past; rather, they give a postfeminist twist to the *Playboy* philosophy. A half-century ago, Hefner's pitch to men to recapture the indoors by creating (purchasing) one's own erotic "bachelor pad" in which to have sex with women (and then send them home) read as a straightforwardly masculine project. By contrast, today's sexual and gender pitch to young men is delivered with an ironic, self-mocking wink that operates, we think, on two levels. First, it appears to acknowledge that most young men are neither the heroes of the indoors (as Hefner would have it) nor of the outdoors (as the 1970s and 1980s beer ads suggested). Instead, the ads seem to recognize that young white men's unstable status leaves them always on the verge of being revealed as losers. The ads plant seeds of insecurity on this fertile landscape, with the goal of creating a white guy who is a consistent and enthusiastic consumer of alcoholic beverages. The irony works on a second level as well: the throwback sexual and gender imagery—especially the bitch-whore dichotomization of women—is clearly a defensively misogynistic backlash against feminism and women's increasing autonomy and social power. The wink and self-mocking irony allow men to have it both ways: they can engage in humorous misogynist banter and claim simultaneously that it is all in play. They do not take themselves seriously, so anyone who takes their misogyny as anything but boys having good fun just has no sense of humor. The humorous irony works, then, to deflect charges of sexism away from white males, allowing them to define themselves as victims, as members of an endangered species. We suspect, too, that this is a key part of the process that constructs the whiteness in current reconstructions of hegemonic masculinity. As we have suggested, humorous "boys-will-be-boys" misogyny is unlikely to be taken ironically and lightly when delivered by men of color.

The white-guy-as-loser trope, though fairly new to beer and liquor ads, is certainly not new to U.S. media. Part of the irony of this character is not that he is a loser in every sense; rather he signifies the typical everyman who is only a loser in comparison to versions of masculinity more typical to beer and liquor ads past—that is, the rugged guys who regularly get the model-beautiful women. Caught between the excesses of a hypermasculinity that is often discredited and caricatured in popular culture and the increasing empowerment of women, people of color, and homosexuals, while simultaneously being undercut by the postindustrial economy, the "Average Joe" is positioned as the ironic, vulnerable but lovable hero of beer and liquor ads. It is striking that the loser is not, or is rarely, your "José Mediano," especially if we understand the construction as a way to unite diverse eighteen- to thirty-four-year-old men. This is to say that the loser motif constructs the universal subject as implicitly white, and as a reaction against challenges to hegemonic masculinity it represents an ongoing possessive investment in whiteness (Lipsitz, 1998).

Our analysis suggests that the fact that male viewers today are being hailed as losers and are being asked to identify with—even revel in—their loser status has its limits. The beer and liquor industry dangles images of sexy women in front of men's noses. Indeed, the ads imply that men will go out of their way to put themselves in position to be voyeurs, be it with a TV remote control, at a yoga class, in a bar, or on the *Sports Illustrated*/Miller Beer swimsuit photo shoot Web site. But ultimately, men know (and are increasingly being told in the advertisements themselves) that these sexy women are not available to them. Worse, if men get too close to these women, these women will most likely humiliate them. By contrast, real women—women who are not model-beautiful fantasy objects—are likely to attempt to ensnare men into a commitment, push them to have or express feelings that make them uncomfortable, and limit their freedom to have fun watching sports or playing cards or pool with their friends. So, in the end, men have only the safe haven of their male friends and the bottle.

This individual sense of victimization may feed young men's insecurities while giving them convenient scapegoats on which to project anger at their victim status. The cultural construction of white males as losers, then, is tethered to men's anger at and desire for revenge against women. Indeed, we have observed that revenge-against-women themes are evident in some of the most recent beer and liquor ads. And it is here that our analysis comes full circle. For, as we suggested in the introduction, the cultural imagery in ads aimed at young men does not simply come from images "out there." Instead, this imagery is linked to the ways that real people live their lives. It is the task of future research—including audience research—to investigate and flesh out the specific links between young men's consumption of commercial images, their consumption of beer and liquor, their attitudes toward and relationships with women, and their tendencies to drink and engage in violence against women.

REFERENCES

Bakhtin, Mikhail. 1981. "Forms of Time and the Chronotope in the Novel." In *The Dialogic Imagination: Four Essays,* trans. Caryl Emerson and Michael Holmquist, 84–258. Austin: University of Texas Press.

Beneke, Timothy. 1982. *Men on Rape.* New York: St. Martin's.

Collins, Tony, and Wray Vamplew. 2002. *Mud, Sweat, and Beers: A Cultural History of Sport and Alcohol.* New York: Berg.

Connell, R. W. 1995. *Masculinities.* Berkeley: University of California Press.

Curry, Timothy. 2000. "Booze and Bar Fights: A Journey to the Dark Side of College Athletics." In *Masculinities, Gender Relations, and Sport,* ed. Jim McKay, Donald F. Sabo, and Michael A. Messner, 162–75. Thousand Oaks, CA: Sage.

Davis, Laurel L. 1997. *The Swimsuit Issue and Sport: Hegemonic Masculinity in* Sports Illustrated. Albany, NY: SUNY Press.

Dayan, Daniel, and Elihu Katz. 1988. "Articulating Consensus: The Ritual and Rhetoric of Media Events." In *Durkheimian Sociology: Cultural Studies,* ed. Jeffrey C. Alexander, 161–86. Cambridge: Cambridge University Press.

Ehrenreich, Barbara. 1983. *The Hearts of Men: American Dreams and the Flight from Commitment.* New York: Anchor Doubleday.

Ferguson, Ann Arnett. 2000. *Bad Boys: Public Schools in the Making of Black Masculinity.* Ann Arbor: University of Michigan Press.

Goldman, Robert, and Stephen Papson. 1996. *Sign Wars: The Cluttered Landscape of Advertising.* New York: Guilford.

———. 1998. *Nike Culture: The Sign of the Swoosh.* Thousand Oaks, CA: Sage.

Kimmel, Michael S. 1987. "Men's Responses to Feminism at the Turn of the Century." *Gender and Society* 1(3):261–83.

Koss, Mary, and John A. Gaines. 1993. "The Prediction of Sexual Aggression by Alcohol Use, Athletic Participation, and Fraternity Affiliation." *Journal of Interpersonal Violence* 8(1):94–108.

Leichliter, Jami S., Philip W. Meilman, Cheryl A. Presley, and Jeffrey R. Cashin. 1998. "Alcohol Use and Related Consequences among Students with Varying Levels of Involvement in College Athletics." *Journal of American College Health* 46(6):257–62.

Lipsitz, George. 1981. *Class and Culture in Cold War America: "A Rainbow at Midnight."* New York: Praeger.

———. 1998. *The Possessive Investment in Whiteness: How White People Profit from Identity Politics.* Philadelphia: Temple University Press.

Martin, Christopher R., and Jimmie L. Reeves. 2001. "The Whole World Isn't Watching (but We Thought They Were): The Super Bowl and U.S. Solipsism." *Culture, Sport, and Society* 4(2):213–54.

May, Elaine Tyler. 1988. *Homeward Bound: American Families in the Cold War Era.* New York: Basic Books.

Messner, Michael A. 2002. *Taking the Field: Women, Men, and Sports.* Minneapolis: University of Minnesota Press.

O'Donohoe, Stephanie. 1997. "Leaky Boundaries: Intertextuality and Young Adult Experiences of Advertising." In *Buy This Book: Studies in Advertising and Consumption,* ed. Mica Nava, Andrew Blake, Ian McRury, and Barry Richards, 257–75. London: Routledge.

Postman, Neil, Christine Nystrom, Lance Strate, and Charlie Weingartner. 1987. *Myths, Men, and Beer: An Analysis of Beer Commercials on Broadcast Television, 1987.* Washington, DC: AAA Foundation for Traffic Safety.

Sabo, Don, Phil Gray, and Linda Moore. 2000. "Domestic Violence and Televised Athletic Events: 'It's a man thing.'" In *Masculinities, Gender Relations, and Sport,* ed. Jim McKay, Don Sabo, and Michael A. Messner, 127–46. Thousand Oaks, CA: Sage.

Sperber, Murray. 2000. *Beer and Circus: How Big-Time College Sports Is Crippling Undergraduate Education.* New York: Henry Holt.

Spigel, Lynn. 1992. *Make Room for TV: Television and the Family Ideal in Postwar America.* Chicago: University of Chicago Press.

Strate, Lance. 1992. "Beer Commercials: A Manual on Masculinity." In *Men, Masculinity, and the Media,* ed. Steve Craig, 78–92. Newbury Park, CA: Sage.

Walters, Suzanna Danuta. 1999. "Sex, Text, and Context: (In) Between Feminism and Cultural Studies." In *Revisioning Gender,* ed. Myra Marx Ferree, Judith Lorber, and Beth B. Hess, 222–57. Thousand Oaks, CA: Sage.

———. 2001. *All the Rage: The Story of Gay Visibility in America.* Chicago: University of Chicago Press.

Wenner, Lawrence A. 1991. "One Part Alcohol, One Part Sport, One Part Dirt, Stir Gently: Beer Commercials and Television Sports." In *Television Criticism: Approaches and Applications,* ed. Leah R. Vende Berg and Lawrence A. Wenner, 388–407. New York: Longman.

———. 1998. "In Search of the Sports Bar: Masculinity, Alcohol, Sports, and the Mediation of Public Space." In *Sport and Postmodern Times,* ed. Genevieve Rail, 303–32. Albany, NY: SUNY Press.

Zimbalist, Andrew. 1999. *Unpaid Professionals: Commercialism and Conflict in Big-Time College Sports.* Princeton, NJ: Princeton University Press.

READING REACTIONS

1. The subject of the ads studied in the foregoing article is beer and alcohol, but what else, according to the authors, are these ads selling?

2. The second paragraph of this article mentions "tropes of masculinity." First, define *trope.* Then list tropes of masculinity the authors mention as well as others you might notice in advertisements.

3. Understanding context is critical to creating and decoding texts. What role does context—particularly historical and cultural context—play in regard to beer and

alcohol ads aimed at men? Think specifically about the ways the authors see beer ads from the 1950s and 1960s differing from those in the 1970s and 1980s and then those produced in 2002 or later.

4. Messner and Montez de Oca spend a fair amount of their article offering historical background and details on the Super Bowl and the *Sports Illustrated* swimsuit issue. How does this detailed analysis shape the authors' ethos, and how does it situate the argument for readers?

5. The authors offer a detailed breakdown of a Bud Lite commercial set in a yoga studio. Reread the authors' analysis and explain how the authors move beyond summarizing the advertisement to in-depth analysis of how commercial viewers are meant to read and respond to this visual argument.

6. What relationship, according to this study, do white men in these ads have to women?

7. Context is important to advertisements as texts. Under what contexts or conditions did the authors complete this study? Why do you think that might be important?

Natasha Walter

Learn to Love Your Tree, Baby

Natasha Walter is a British writer and feminist scholar. She is the author of *The New Feminism* and *Living Dolls* and is now a columnist for *The Guardian*. She currently writes for *The New Statesman*, *Vogue*, and *The Observer*.

There seem to be moves afoot in the fashion and beauty world to make the industry a little more inclusive and a little more open to all sorts of shapes and sizes and ages of women—and who could argue with that? If you're riding an escalator and you see a poster of a woman with wrinkles, and a caption that says that she can be beautiful, you will probably simply think, yes, it's true, she is rather beautiful. Why don't I see women like her more often in advertisements?

"Ordinary" women respond very well to advertising campaigns that use "ordinary" women. Dove, which is currently running the campaign that showcases plump and wrinkled and freckly women, found that when it used less-than-perfect women for its last advertisements, it became the fastest-growing beauty brand in western Europe. The success isn't at all bizarre. What is bizarre is that the fashion and beauty industry so rarely catches up with the attitudes that most women actually have towards clothes and cosmetics: that they want to use them for enjoyment and pleasure rather than perfection and obsession.

Figure 4.12 Dove brands its product by embracing different sizes, shapes, and ethnicities of women in their campaign for real beauty

So Dove has taken some good, appealing pictures—but oh, if only it didn't take itself so seriously. We all know, and accept, that these pictures are there to sell a product, and to do it as successfully as they can. Look at how Dove itself describes its strategy on its own website: "The Dove campaign . . . builds on women's emotional connection with the brand to bring a completely new and refreshing range of products." Yup, of course: Dove wants to sell us body lotion. So why does it have to co-opt the rhetoric of feminism to do that?

Next to its pretty pictures of Ms Freckly or Ms Plump (I'm sorry, Leah Sheehan and Tabatha Roman, but that is what you are for Dove) are quasi-feminist slogans: "Real beauty comes in many shapes, sizes, colours and ages. It's why we started the campaign for real beauty. And why we hope you'll take part. Join the beauty debate."

Campaign. Take part. Join. Debate. The suggestion is that this is about action, this is about a change in consciousness, this is something that you should do for the sake of other women. When such rhetoric is used as an advertising gimmick to sell more soap, then the rhetoric itself becomes meaningless.

This co-option of feminist language in the service of pure product placement is not new. Virginia Slims started it in 1969, with those "You've come a long way, baby" advertisements, which contrasted the independent 1960s female smoker with a turn of the century woman who had to hide her habit. In the late 1980s, Nike took on similar rhetoric. The tag "Just do it!" together with images of sporty women was a conscious strategy to increase its appeal for young female consumers.

We have become almost inured now to the way that the "new year, new you" articles that pour out of the magazines and newspapers at this time of year rely on similar quasi-feminist rhetoric. Dieting is not about losing weight or attracting men, but about "empowerment" and taking control, finding "confidence," "motivation" and "self-esteem." "I dropped a size and tripled my confidence!" runs a typical headline in this month's *New Woman*. "Now I've got lots more energy and feel far more positive and motivated about everything." The diet book that comes with the magazine exhorts us to: "Imagine losing pounds and jumpstarting your self-esteem."

No wonder advertisers and copywriters are using feminist rhetoric of empowerment and self-esteem in this way, because for a long time some of the west's most prominent feminist writers have talked as if one of the greatest goals is to make women more comfortable in their bodies. This kind of highly personalised feminism is all about the revolution that will happen if you learn to love your stomach.

The American feminist Eve Ensler could very well have been an adviser on the Dove advertisements. In her most recent work, *The Good Body*, she quotes a Masai woman: "Do you say that tree isn't pretty cause it doesn't look like another tree? We're all trees . . . You've got to love your body, Eve. You've got to love your tree. Love your tree."

Learning to love ourselves is a comforting ideal. But where feminism gets effective rather than comforting is where women start talking not just about loving themselves, but also respecting other women, and doing things with them, and working for social change in some area other than your eating habits. Ensler herself may be best known for banging on about the beauty of the vagina or the plump tummy, but in fact she gets most interesting when she starts talking about some of the women she has worked with, from Afghanistan to Kenya, Iraq to Mexico, who are trying to find concrete empowerment through social change in the most taxing circumstances.

The use of feminist rhetoric in the service of pure self-improvement is seen everywhere at the moment, while the feminist movement towards equalising power in the real world still gets a poor press. So don't campaign for real beauty. Instead, we could campaign for real feminism, or, at least, join that debate.

READING REACTIONS

1. Where does the title of this article come from, and what cultural assumptions does it allude to? What is the title's intended impact on the reader?
2. Think about the language used in this article and in the Dove advertising campaign. Based on the article, how would you define "real," "ordinary," and "beautiful"?

3. In what contexts or conditions (historical, political, cultural) was the Dove ad campaign created? Why, in your opinion, was the campaign so popular?

4. Pathos is a key part of the Dove ad campaign. According to the company, "The Dove campaign . . . builds on women's emotional connection with the brand." How, specifically, do you see the creators of this campaign appealing to pathos?

5. Walter argues that Dove has wrongly co-opted "the rhetoric of feminism." First, how do you define the rhetoric of feminism? What does it value? What cultural assumptions and associations are tied to the word "feminism"? Next, is it appropriate for Dove to use this language?

6. In describing the campaign, Walter renames the women in the ads "Ms Freckly" and "Ms Plump." What is the rhetorical goal of this strategy? What point is the author making?

7. Does this advertising campaign encourage social action? What kind? How? Does the article itself encourage any sort of action?

Julie Bosman

How to Sell Body Sprays to Teenagers? Hint: It's Not Just Cleanliness

Julie Bosman has been a *New York Times* reporter since 2002 and covers a variety of topics, from education to politics to advertising and new media trends. A graduate of the University of Wisconsin, her work has appeared in *The New Republic, The Wall Street Journal,* and *Slate.*

Advertisers long ago mastered the trick of playing on teenage insecurity. For years, they hawked acne products like Oxy and Clearasil with ubiquitous ads in print and on television, convincing teenagers that clearing their skin would improve their social status.

Now, the acne parade is giving way to a new marketing effort tackling another teenage fear: sweat. Body sprays and deodorants are being aimed at teenage boys and girls with a new zeal, from the Axe line by Unilever to Tag from Gillette and Secret Body Spray from Procter & Gamble. The body sprays Tag and Axe have taken a nearly identical selling approach, telling teenage boys that using the products will make them irresistible to the opposite sex.

In one Tag ad, created by Arnold Worldwide in Boston, several girls pursue a teenage boy who is wearing the body spray, chasing him onto the top of a bus kiosk, where they try to tear off his clothing. The ad reads: "The makers of new Tag body spray cannot be held responsible for the floods of overeager ladies." Even the names of scents are suggestive—body sprays come in Lucky Day, First Move, Midnight or After Hours.

"The real drive in the ads is what guys want, which is to get the girl," said Kara Salzillo, a spokeswoman for Tag, which introduced its body sprays earlier this year. "That's all it's about at the end of the day. It's all about taking your game up a notch."

"There are universal truths about teenage boys," said Pete Favat, the executive creative director and managing partner at Arnold, part of Havas. "They have the need to rebel, the need to fit into a particular group, the need to take risks. This product is designed to give them a little boost and a little confidence in that area."

The ads are very similar to those from the campaign for Axe body sprays, which Unilever introduced in the United States three years ago with the slogan "How Dirty Boys Get Clean." (The product was created in France in 1983 and is sold as Lynx in Britain, Ireland and Australia.)

The campaign, created by Bartle Bogle Hegarty of New York, has a simple theme: Use Axe body sprays, and women will pursue you. One ad features a single shower stall with a sign on the wall reading, "Occupancy by more than five persons is unlawful." The product Web site, www.theaxeeffect.com, coyly promises: "The Axe effect feels so good. And there are so many ways to do it."

Kevin George, the marketing director for Unilever deodorants, said the "mating game" concept was intended to attach an emotional element to a purely functional product.

"We kind of turned the category on its head," he said. "It used to be about the absence of negatives—not smelling bad."

Sales of teenage grooming products, particularly for male consumers, are more robust than ever. According to a study by Media Research Inc., the grooming category for 18- to 24-year-old men grew 38 percent, to more than $143 million, in 2004, while the body spray category grew 62 percent from August 2004 to August 2005.

Sales of Axe have increased 27 percent in the last year, while Tag's sales have soared to more than $12.6 million since its introduction earlier this year, according to the latest sales figures from Information Resources Inc., a market research firm in Chicago.

Procter & Gamble's Secret brand is taking on the female portion of the market with its four body sprays, which are intended to act more as perfume than deodorant. The company has done very little traditional advertising, focusing more on a partnership with MySpace.com, a social network that is used by 33 million young people, and is sponsoring the world tour of the recording artist Rihanna.

"We've taken a necessary product and turned it into something more beauty-oriented," said Michelle Vaeth, a spokeswoman for Procter & Gamble.

Even teenage boys are more grooming-obsessed than their parents' generation, partly because they're influenced by the growing number of men's magazines advertising male-oriented beauty products, Ms. Salzillo, of Tag, said.

"Grooming to them is not just about a bar of soap," she said. "They're constantly looking for new products to keep in their medicine cabinets."

As beer companies have demonstrated in the past with their brew-and-babes television commercials, effectively targeting young men often results in alienating women—and creating ads that can easily be perceived as sexist. Mr. George said he hoped that perception was debunked by the exaggerated nature of the Axe ads.

"Everything that we do, we test with both moms and young women," Mr. George said. "We want to make sure that people know it's an over-the-top, tongue-in-cheek take on the mating game. There's hyperbole in everything we do."

"It is capital-D dude humor," said Deborah Morrison, an advertising professor at the University of Oregon, who also is the mother of three boys. "I tend to think it's frivolous. But I have feminist friends whose hair curls when they see it."

READING REACTIONS

1. What rhetorical techniques and appeals do the Axe and Tag body spray producers use to sell their product?

2. Considering this article—and the images in this chapter as well as online ads for these products—what image of women do these ads sell?

3. Would such advertising texts appeal to diverse groups or interests (including different ethnicities, genders, sexual orientations, and ages)? Why or why not?

4. The article reports a 27 percent increase in Axe sales in 2005, based in large part on the success of the television and Internet commercial campaign targeting young men. Procter & Gamble's Secret, however, chose to sell a similar product to young women by focusing on social networking sites rather than traditional media. Why the difference in media? What social or cultural associations or values does social media have regarding gender specifically?

5. These body spray makers are said to be selling boys products that "will make them irresistible to the opposite sex." Is this the same as selling girls products that will make them beautiful? Is one an explicit message and one an implicit message? Explain.

6. What are the social contexts under which this advertising message is created? Think about Deborah Morrison's mention of her "feminist friends"

and Kevin George's insistence that the ads are "over-the-top, tongue-in-cheek." What do these say about teenage sexuality and gender representations specifically?

7. These ads, like many media products overtly referencing gender, are controversial. How does Bosman discuss this issue and strive for balance in her argument? Is she successful?

○ Mandy Van Deven

On the Map: Breastfeeding Is Best for Baby . . . But for Babydolls?

Van Deven is a writer, activist, and coauthor of *Hey, Shorty!: A Guide to Combating Sexual Harassment and Violence in Schools and on the Streets.* She is an editorial fellow at *Salon.com* and guest edited Issue 8.3 of *The Scholar & Feminist Online,* titled "Polyphonic Feminisms: Acting in Concert."

I find the controversy in recent years surrounding public breastfeeding in the United States to be indicative of American over-saturation of the male view of breasts as a sexual object instead of something that serves the function of nurturing a child. Despite breast milk being the healthiest (and cheapest!) way to feed a baby while providing numerous short- and long-term benefits for the child (better immune system, higher intelligence, less likelihood of developing allergic diseases) and mother (reduction of uterine bleeding, natural postpartum contraception, reduced risk of several cancers and heart disease), many Americans still can't get past the part of the medium of delivery being a pair of engorged tits.

In the mid-1950s, breastfeeding in the US dropped to nearly 20% and a group of concerned women stepped up to bat for the benefits of breastmilk; that group was La Leche League. These days that rate has nearly flipped with three-quarters of American women initiating breastfeeding at birth, but this number slowly declines to just 25% a year after the child's birth. Evidence that we might not have come as far as we think.

Perhaps it's this equating of the breast as a solely sexual object that has gotten Spanish dollmaker Berjuan's Bebé Glotón (Baby Glutton) so much American media attention over the past few days. Despite the doll not being sold in the States (yet), the US media has run 165 articles compared to only 14 in Spain, which tells me this controversy is more about American culture than it is about consumerism.

Two somewhat conflicting feminist arguments can be made about the doll: 1) it promotes little girls playing the role of "mommy" for a newborn baby and reinforces motherhood as expected and ideal and 2) it reinforces breastfeeding as a natural element of child rearing, decreasing the culture of shame surrounding this women's issue.

Though some have raised these issues, these aren't the arguments several journalists and television personalities are making against the Bebé.

On the *Today Show*, Hoda Kotb and Kathie Lee Gifford exchanged comments of incredulity: "Why would you want a suckling doll for an 8-year-old?" asks Kotb. "It's got a little creep factor," says Gifford.

NJ.com's Eric Ruhalter was made to apologize for his comparisons of Bebé Glotón to an alcoholic doll, one that has erectile dysfunction, or a doll that is the victim of prison rape.

And in Fox News' typical outrageous style, the network suggests BebéGlotón "may even promote early pregnancy" by "speed[ing] up maternal urges in the little girls who play it." Their health editor goes so far as to compare playing with the doll to "introducing sex education in first grade" and says "it could inadvertently lead little girls to become traumatized."

Am I the only one who thinks it's unbelievable that Ruhalter's article made it past his editor? And I dunno about you, but the idea of girls being traumatized by a breastfeeding doll seems more than a little extreme. (Berjuan did consult with psychologists and teachers in developing the toy.) The bulk of the objections seem to revolve around BebéGlotón not being age-appropriate, but this completely disregards the difference between adults' and children's sexual comprehension. There are also few indications given as to *why* people believe the doll may not be age-appropriate (save for Fox's ridiculous exaggeration) leaving much to be desired in the way of explanation; the statement is simply taken as "the truth"—and that's that.

But *that*, quite frankly, isn't good enough. It's irresponsible journalism to present something as "fact" having no evidence except opinion to back it up. This is especially conspicuous when considering the implications these types of stories have in furthering the notion that breastfeeding is a sexual act, particularly when the faux-feeder is a five-year-old girl. You see, the US media can't talk about what is *really* bothering them because then they'd have to admit that our culture sexualizes children. And if they admit that's the case, then they're slipping down a slope they don't want to be on. Because that slope is the staunchly intellectual property of feminism.

So instead of engaging in an active debate, these media folks continue to stick to the status quo: Bratz in fishnets, short skirts, and stilettos are okay for little girls to play with because that's just make believe, but a breastfeeding doll isn't good for them because that's too "adult." I like that BebéGlotón is encouraging some Americans to take an introspective look at their hangups about breasts and sexuality, but I can't say I'm enamored with our shoddy media analysis.

READING REACTIONS

1. Consider the author's tone in this online article. Comment specifically on certain language (for example, "engorged tits") and emotional speech Van Deven uses. Who is her audience, and what is the intended impact on them? What are readers "supposed to do"?

2. What evidence does the author offer that controversy regarding breastfeeding is an American cultural phenomenon?

3. What is Van Deven's overall argument? What do you think she wants readers to learn?

4. What social or cultural associations or values are linked to breastfeeding in general? How does this impact the Breast Milk Baby and similar toys?

5. Does Van Deven's writing seem neutral, or does it evidence her own bias in this article? Offer examples to support your opinion.

6. What is the relationship between image (the print and video ads of young girls playing with the Breast Milk Baby) and the content (the potential sexualizing of young girls, the social pressure for "mothering" to be done a certain way, and so on) of this controversy? How might such images be important to making the point that playing with a breastfeeding doll is either natural or not natural?

Additional Writing and Composing Activities

1. **Short Written Argument.** Choose a magazine or genre of magazine (parenting, fashion, auto) and review two editions of the magazine(s) from three different decades (1950s, 1980s, current time). Focus on advertising and the role of gender in print ads in each edition. What trends do you see? Do you notice differences in ways men and women are depicted? Are men and women depicted selling the same products or different ones? Do you notice any gendered language (for example, *pretty*, *sweet*, *strong*, *tough*)? Do those depictions and distinctions change or lessen over time?

   Use your list of observations to begin crafting a thesis statement for a short written argument about your topic. Some sample thesis statements might include the following:

   - Despite the shifting roles of women in society, food advertisements in *Parents Magazine* spanning three decades continue to depict women as the main food preparers for families.
   - A study of car advertisements reveals a shift in representations of masculinity from the 1950s performance of doing manly things to the current era's fascination with looking manly.

   Incorporate specific details from your observations, along with concepts from this chapter, to build your argument.

2. **Visual analysis of a Facebook profile.** Gender is foregrounded the moment you sign up for a profile and are asked to identify as male or female and then to include your relationship status. Do men and women use Facebook differently? Do women use Facebook more often for business or professional contacts than men? Do men post more photo albums? Are there differences in status-update styles, types of photos posted, or amount and type of personal information disclosed? What about other genders? Is gender a useful distinction on Facebook? Is gender a useful distinction in new media spaces? What other distinctions might be more pertinent (for example, age, socioeconomic status, race, access level)?

3. **Flyer.** Using only photos stored for you in a classroom folder or using only photos on your official university website, work in groups of three or four to create a flyer. Your group can decide on the specific argument, audience, and purpose of the flyer, but you may use only the images available to or agreed upon by the entire class. The goal of this activity is to think of photography and visual arrangement as composition and to consider the nearly endless options for visual design based on things like arrangement, color, tone, point of view, and the other options noted earlier in this chapter as strategies for decoding visuals. Share your final flyers with the rest of the class and be prepared to discuss the following:

   - What sorts of decisions did your group make about images?
   - Did alphabetic text or image take precedence? Why?
   - Who do you envision as your audience? What is the intended impact on viewers? What are they "supposed to do"?
   - What are the flyer's social or cultural associations or values?

Online Resources

Resources available through the English CourseMate for this text include the following:

Websites:

The Gender Ads Project
Ad Busters Magazine
Axe Body Spray ads
Dove Campaign for Real Beauty website

Videos:

Dove. "Evolution."
"Breastfeeding Dolls: Too Much, Too Soon?"
   Good Morning America.
Jean Kilbourne. "Killing Us Softly."
Gunther Kress. "What Is Multimodality?"

Blogs:

Lisa Wade and Gwen Sharp. "Sociological
   Images."

Podcasts:

Brad Forsythe and Ray Shilens. "The
   Advertising Show."

Online Articles:

Ian O'Saben. "Visual Rhetoric Examples."
Monica Brasted. "Care Bears vs. Tranformers:
   Gender Stereotypes in Advertisements."

Gaming Worlds

Playing a video game used to require the purchase of the latest console and most popular game titles, but now video games are everywhere.

From *Bejeweled Blitz* on Facebook to preloaded games on most cell phones and even video game companions on movie DVDs like *Harry Potter*, it seems video games surround us and that though many of us might not consider ourselves "gamers," perhaps we should. At the very least, marketers do. According to the Entertainment Software Association, 72 percent of American households play computer and video games. And these games aren't just for kids—82 percent of gamers are eighteen years of age or older, and adult women now account for more of the gaming population than teenage boys. What is it about gaming worlds and lives that are so appealing to us? Is it the promise of fantasy? Of escape? Or is it simply too tempting to live another life where all things are possible,

Figure 5.1 Girls playing a handheld video game

including flying from island to island in *Second Life*, quarterbacking an NFL game in *Madden NFL*, or battling aliens on the twenty-sixth-century *Halo* landscape.

Perhaps at the heart of our fascination with gaming is the ability to control our identities. Studies show that many of us go online to re-create rather than escape our offline lives. Consider, the Mii characters populating the Wii universe. With thousands of options for height, hair, and eye color, and the ability to add glasses and beards and even change face shape, Mii designers frequently choose to use the technology to assemble an approximation of their offline looks. For many of us, there seems a joy and power in re-creating—through an avatar—our identity. Understanding how we create identities in game, why we game, and how we learn the rules of gaming worlds can shed light on ways we construct ourselves as communicators.

TECHNOLOGIES Images of superheroes like Batman, Spiderman, and the Avengers have flickered on the silver screen for generations, but what would it mean to step into those tights and become a hero yourself? At the Hero Factory (http://cpbherofactory.com), users can design a custom superhero of their own.

Go to the Hero Factory and create your own superhero. As you move through the design options, pay special attention to the role of symbolism and colors and the ways a body can be designed or dressed.

Once you create your hero, answer the following:

- Is the hero you created a "good guy" or a "bad guy"? What types of strategies, such as color, size, and symbols, help create your overall persuasive point regarding your avatar's personality?

- What social or cultural associations or values does your design allude to?

- What is the intended impact of your hero's design on the viewer? What is the viewer "supposed to feel"—safe, scared, threatened?

Being You—or Someone Else—in a Gaming World

The first step in entering a gaming world is to create or select a symbol to represent you in game. Such symbolic images (as discussed in the previous chapter) offer players a way not only to interact with virtual spaces and other players, but also to in some way be embodied in an online space. *Embodiment* refers to the ways our physical (or virtual) bodies shape our minds and actions. Sherry Turkle, who researches and writes on the topic of living in online spaces, discusses ways embodying online bodies and identities allows for identity exploration and the ability to "try on" new roles and personas. (For an essay by Turkle on this topic, see Chapter 7.) Building or "putting on" an avatar offers access to new virtual worlds and also allows reflection on and critique of who we are offline. An avatar is an interactive, social representation of a gamer that reflects both the rules and the social norms of the gaming world and also at least something of the user who controls the avatar. An avatar forces a fragmented yet focused identity that is created and performed with a specific goal in mind.

How is using an avatar for a game different from crafting online identities outside of gaming (through social networking profiles or online dating, for example)? In gaming worlds, there is no expectation of truth—although truth or at least an attempted mirror of reality is sometimes the goal for avatar creators. Instead, the ability to pass and perform as an insider in a crafted community is key.

Worlds of Created Realities

Though avatar creators often have all kinds of freedom when it comes to designing players, gamers are always constrained by the media itself as well as by the expectations of the gaming community. Gaming worlds, though entirely crafted, are bound to their own realities and rules. Though these realities resemble, to varying degrees, the realities of our offline world—with the same possibility for kindness and abuse—gaming worlds become their own sorts of subcultures with very specific social norms.

Akin to the concept of discourse communities (discussed in depth in Chapter 7), gaming worlds utilize specific language, visual markers, activities, and other communication devices to bind the community together and to help both insiders and outsiders understand the society's values and goals. Social norms, then, may seem even more pronounced in created societies. While norms and rules seem to evolve naturally in offline spaces, game designers—and sometimes players—purposefully design codes of conduct and ways to succeed in gaming worlds. Exploring these created gaming worlds may then provide opportunities to critique and question the ways social norms develop organically in our offline worlds.

Few created online worlds offer such a clear tension between our lived worlds and created worlds as *Second Life*. Launched in 2003, *Second Life*'s popularity is declining, but it persists as a virtual space for socializing, education, and business. Hard numbers for active *Second Life* players—called *residents*—are hard to come by, but millions of accounts are registered, and tens of thousands of residents are online together at any given time in the virtual world. According to the introduction video on the *Second Life* home page, players are invited to experience this world as "a place to connect, a place to shop, a place to work, a place to love, a place to explore, a place to be different." While things like flying, stepping into a person-size unicorn avatar identity, and engaging in cybersex with strangers certainly suggests this as a place all about fantasy and escape, many more everyday activities also occupy *Second Life* residents. People sell wares, attend college classes, and purchase real estate. In this way, *Second Life* is said to be a place "to be yourself. Free yourself. . . . Love your life."

This blurring of the surreal and the ordinary is what separates *Second Life* from more traditional gaming worlds. Many games, like *Second Life*, are categorized as massive multiplayer online (MMO) games, but most others have clear missions and goals. *World of Warcraft* (*WoW*), for example, focuses on clan building and resource gathering. *Halo*'s agenda is war against enemies of humanity, wherein players are first-person shooters. *Second Life*, then, is unique in its lack of preset goals. There is no bad guy to kill, no princess to save. Instead, the community of players defines what will happen in the space based on relationships among avatars as well as the influence of the offline and online environments.

Was it this ability to "live" a whole second life online—one complete with sex, travel, business, and even crime—that eventually led to the decline of

---

COMMUNITIES   Help a video game character join a new mediated world and live a new online life. For example, design a Facebook profile or page for Mario from *Mario Kart* or another favorite video game character, or create a Last.fm profile for an elf in *WoW*. How will you fill in the information about your character beyond the game? What context clues will help you flesh out your character profile?

Second Life? What do we want from a video game world and identity? Is it enough to be someone else, or do we want to simply re-create ourselves in pixilated form? Do we want both?

Gaming Worlds Are Real Worlds

Despite the promise of escape and adventure, virtual worlds remain governed by laws and values just like offline worlds. In a world where one can literally "be" anyone or anything, many of the problems of society seem to follow us to the console. Writing on gaming—called *new games journalism*—is filled with discussions of violence, rape, and racism in gaming worlds.

Consider the recent controversy when a gamer in *Space Quest IV* spoke out after another player was labeled "sicko" for cross-dressing in game. As Jim Sterling reported on his blog, *Destructoid*, the gamer was quickly reproached by other players for being offended by what he and others might consider homophobic hate speech. Many who responded felt that actions in the game should not be held to the standards of conduct of our offline worlds. Is everything done in a gaming world excusable, or are some things out of bounds? How tightly are we bound to offline scripts of behavior in online worlds?

Similarly, gaming journalist Ian Shanahan writes about his experience being called racial slurs while playing *Jedi Knight II*. The slurs were coupled with in-game niceties of bowing that the other player deployed to get the drop on Shanahan. Though his opponent technically broke no game rules, Shanahan explains the issue: "It's not just a trivial game to be played in an idle moment, this is a genuine battle of good versus evil. It has nothing to do with Star Wars or Jedi Knights or any of the fluff that surrounds the game's mechanics. I played by the 'rules' and he didn't, that makes me the 'good' guy and him the 'baddie'" (from Ian Shanahan, "Bow nigger." *always_black.com*.). So even in the absence of laws or those that might enforce the laws in these created and often highly malleable worlds, there are codes of conduct and notions of right and wrong that players are expected to abide by.

Though it is tempting to dismiss actions on our computer screens and gaming consoles, much of who we are as individuals and societies is reflected in the games we play and populate. Although putting on an avatar identity is "playing" in some ways, how does the avatar identity relate to other identities we put on in our offline lives? Consider philosopher and theorist Judith Butler's writings on gender as performance. Those who study gender often draw distinctions between the biological (a person's sex) and the social (our actions and the ways they are linked to masculinity and femininity) aspects of

COMMUNITIES Purchasing new clothes, getting a tattoo or piercing, and even joining the gym are attempts at modifying our material bodies. What does body modification look like in gaming worlds? Log on to *Second Life* and design an avatar that is like you but is in at least one way modified. Consider altering an obvious identity marker—like age, race, or sex—or something subtler. As you create, note what options the templates give you and what alterations you make on your own. Then answer the following:

- **How did it feel** to perform an identity that is at least partially different from your own?

- **What is the intended** impact on viewers who see your avatar? What are they "supposed to do"?

- **How does the message**—in the form of your avatar—help shape membership within the *Second Life* community? How does it help create common goals and values?

gender. For example, we call a baby a boy because of his chromosomes or the way his body looks, but we dress him in blue because this is an action society often expects from new parents of male children. Butler goes even further to define gender neither as simply biology or social creation but rather as a set of actions and strategies deployed in specific ways with specific audiences and purposes in mind.

Gender, then, can be seen as ways to "play" life, to gain status, power, and acceptance in society just as a gamer might adopt strategies and tactics to win a battle or complete an online mission. Further, gender performances can be seen as acknowledgement of the norms and expectations society places on biologically sexed bodies. Why are girls expected to like pink bows and tiaras while boys gravitate to camouflage and toy guns? For Butler and other scholars, these seeming gender differences are not biological imperatives but rather the recognition and acceptance of cultural scripts through which we gain or are denied power in society. Are these scripts different when we are acting as an elf or an animal? Do scripts for things like gender and race and sexuality change when we are able to more completely craft the bodies we perform within? The cross-dressing example suggests that we may resist those scripts in gaming worlds, but not without consequences.

Technological Beginnings: Observing *Second Life*

The popularity of *Second Life* has waned in recent years, but it is still an important space to consider in critiquing the similarities and differences between virtual gaming worlds and our offline world. Spend fifteen to twenty minutes in *Second Life* taking notes on what you observe about the space, about ways others act, about what users and the technology seem to value.

Consider your observations in light of the readings in this chapter. Working in groups of two or three, pair one of the readings with appropriate observations to create a research question relating to *Second Life*. For example, by focusing on Ouyang Dan's piece "The Games We Play: The Whitewashing of Video Games" and your own experience interacting with other *Second Life* residents, your group might come up with one of the following research questions:

- How is the *Second Life* population's racial makeup similar to or different from that of the United States? What accounts for this? Is it, for example, related to access to technology or target audience?

- Often individuals of different races are geographically segregated from one another. Does this happen in *Second Life*?

- Does *Second Life* offer more or less freedom of racial identification than other measures in our offline world? (Think specifically of controversy surrounding the U.S. Census race categories.)

Repeat the preceding process using at least three different readings. Come up with a total of five to ten possible research questions to share with the class. Use one of these questions as a place to start your research about *Second Life* or another gaming world.

Learning the Rules of Created Worlds

Learning the rules for our offline world seems fairly intuitive. You learn what you need to know from parents, friends, teachers, and bosses. But how do players learn the rules of virtual worlds? Learning to navigate gaming worlds is actually similar to successfully moving through offline discourse communities. A *discourse community* is a group or community with shared goals that uses language to reach those goals. Such groups may be professional, like doctors who use specialized terms or acronyms, or personal, like *Hunger Games* fan groups who use shorthand slang and images. Discourse communities often share *commonplaces*—words, images, symbols, and other signifiers that quickly communicate the community's values and goals.

When players sign in to a new game or world, they probably spend at least a little time as a "noob," or newbie. Most gaming worlds—maybe particularly those steeped in competition or battle like *Halo* or *Call of Duty*—value expertise and skills that can be gained only through exposure to the game world. Through experience, players internalize language, rhetorical strategies, values, goals, and rules for the game. As we carefully consider these discourse community markers in a handful of games, we gain critical awareness of not only gaming technologies but also other technologies linked to identity creation. Also, skills learned in gaming communities help us analyze and understand other discourse communities we write in and for.

A key to understanding and eventually joining a discourse community—including a gaming world—starts in deciphering the unique language or jargon used in that community. Specialized language is utilized for a variety of reasons: to express what is unique to the community, for ease or speed of communication, to bind community members to one another through a shared vocabulary, and to keep others out. Specialized language within a community is not restricted to online spaces, but the shift to a virtual world may bring more complex and nuanced language use. Consider the role-play game *Star Wars: The Old Republic*. The game is located within the fictional *Star Wars* universe most of us came to know in the original 1970s trilogy and the prequels released beginning in 1999, but familiarity with the characters and plotlines from Hollywood hardly prepares you to be a competent Jedi knight, Imperial agent, or Sith warrior in the game universe. Terms like "the Force," "the Republic," and "sorcerer" have carryover meanings from the movie, but players need to know these and countless other terms simply to communicate with others and also to identify themselves as part of the Dark Side or not.

Beyond actual word choice is a world of rhetorical strategies, including everything from dress to body movements and location within virtual worlds. Just like offline communication, much of what we say does not come out of our mouths or through the words we type. In the *Star Wars: The Old Republic* game, for example, bowing to other players can be an act of respect or one of submission. Understanding the context of the communicative act is key when deciding how one's avatar should proceed. Bodily tactics are clearly important to combat-simulation games like *Bioshock* and *Call of Duty*. In *Bioshock*, players are transported to an alternate 1960 and are transformed into Jack, a plane crash survivor who must explore an underwater city and survive attacks by mutants. Being stealthy and silent is not only a survival tactic; it also speaks of a player's awareness of danger and an internalization of what the game values—staying alive.

The ways players communicate with words and other means reveals lots not only about the messages being sent and received but also about the values and goals of the gaming community. Not every game is won by defeating an opponent or finding something lost. Some games don't seem winnable at all. Consider *The Sims* game series. While it is possible to get and give stuff and to live and to kill (usually by withholding food or something else an avatar needs), the main goal of the game seems to be to experience the virtual world. This less–clearly defined goal makes *The Sims* a space where players largely decide for themselves what they value. Still the game itself values mediated living and the ability to control one's own avatar and the avatars of others.

Other games, known as *exergames* (see **Figure 5.2**), have direct value to one's unmediated, offline life. The *Just Dance* series seems to value movement, nostalgia evoked by classic songs, and fun, as highlighted by vibrant colors and irreverent graphics. The goal of the game is to counter the common belief that video games lead to inactivity and sedentary lifestyles. The goals and values of this game are therefore united. They are written into the way the game

Figure 5.2 Wii Fit is an example of an exergame

technology works and into the visual representations of faceless avatars that players are invited to inhabit and control with their own bodies.

While goals and values are often embedded—and therefore only implied—in a game's very design, sometimes the actual rules of a game are spelled out fairly explicitly. Some games are highly organized with clear rules. In *Portal 2*, a first-person puzzle platform game, players solve problems in order to maneuver through the Aperture Science Facility. This virtual world's specialized rules include an avatar's ability to fall onto solid surfaces with no ramifications while falling into a pit or toxic liquid will lead to the avatar's demise. Players learn rules through demos, by watching other players, and through trial and error. Other games, like *Skyrim*, offer nonlinear play with freedom for players to explore, accept missions, and join factions of other players. The latest installment in *The Elder Scrolls* series offers lots of freedom in play, but players still must act in certain ways to advance in the game. Finally, a game like *Angry Birds* appears to have few rules: you draw back, launch a bird into the sky, and hope to knock things down. Players are governed only by rules of gravity and math as they estimate the correct trajectory and distance.

One of the best ways to learn about a community is to live in it. Consider immersion programs in foreign countries. Being forced to interact with others in a new place, to speak another language, and to grapple with unfamiliar customs often leads to richer experiences than might be available in a language or history classroom. Many educators have recognized this potential in all kinds of online worlds, and games are frequently used as teaching tools. The question remains though, how does a technological tool like a Microsoft PowerPoint slideshow of images from the Smithsonian National Museum of Natural History differ from a virtual tour of the museum (available through the English CourseMate for this text)? Is the tour a virtual world or simply an interactive video? Can a world exist without true interaction with other players or avatars? Despite being often dismissed as overly time consuming, violent, or impractical, gaming worlds hold potential for problem solving, intellectual and bodily engagement, and, when other players are present, interaction with new people and ideas.

What These Worlds Can Teach Us as Writers

Gaming worlds also have a great deal to teach us about writing and persuasion. Scholar James Paul Gee is well known for showing parents and educators ways video games can actually be useful in schools and as personal learning activities outside of school. His *What Video Games Have to Teach Us about Learning and Literacy* offers thirty-six learning principles taken directly from video games. For writers, video games offer new insights into audience awareness, communication motivated by specific goals, concepts of success when it comes to writing, and the importance of drafting.

Writing for and through these sorts of technologies requires an awareness of who populates the space and why, just as specific written genres—sports magazines, Hemingway novels, *The Hunger Games* trilogy—tell us and require us to know something about the audience reading them.

How do you determine the needs and characteristics of an audience for a video game? After all, there are as many gaming worlds to visit as there are types of gamers. You can look at characteristics like ease of entrance to the gaming world, technical skills needed to maneuver in the game, and the look of the space to determine whom the game is intended for. For example, casual gamers need only commit a couple of minutes and almost no skill to a game of *Fruit Ninja*, while serious gamers spend hundreds of hours in *WoW* transforming themselves into blood elves or dwarves that join guilds, learn skills, complete missions, and gain powers. The audiences for these two games are very different, meaning they have different wants and expectations.

Even game consoles themselves target different audiences. Wii is branded as a family system while Xbox is marketed to "real" gamers. Most technologies reveal something about the people who use them: Twitter users value speed, bloggers value connection, Garmin owners lack a sense of direction or are comforted by extra information while they travel.

Technologies also reveal different communication goals. If we return to the *WoW* example, we find many reasons players communicate—to gain trust and build alliances, to build player ethos, to intimidate, to win. These goals differ from purely player-to-game interactions such as keystrokes or the movement of a controller.

Communication goals reveal much about the games we play. We should also keep them in mind when composing *outside* of gaming worlds. How do goals for a text to a girlfriend or boyfriend compare with goals for an email to your professor? Correctly identifying communication goals helps you choose the words, tone, and structure of a text just as it helps avatars choose words and actions in gaming worlds.

For many games, the communication goal is simply winning. But winning doesn't look the same in all games. It can be surviving a firefight with your enemy, beating your own personal best score in *Angry Birds*, or a few hours well spent as a talking dog or elf. What does winning look like in writing? For a writer, success can most often be described as persuasion. Whether we seek to change a reader's mind, urge her to action, inform him of new information, or summarize key data, we always seek to persuade readers to believe what we are writing. We use proof, effective arrangement, appropriate style, and other rhetorical strategies to persuade audiences to accept us as credible authors (that is, to build ethos) and to accept the appeals we make—be they logical or emotional—to build our case. We might persuade them to "see" a place we create for a piece of fiction, to vote for the candidate we endorse, or to believe we understand a concept as evidenced by a well-researched essay. In writing, winning means using all available means to reach our audience and share with them our vision.

Learning to successfully wield rhetorical tools doesn't come easily or quickly. Neither does learning your way around a new gaming world. Imagine moving to a new city. How do you learn the best restaurants, the shortest way to the mall, and the spots to avoid after dark? Maps and recommendations from locals help, but you can't really get a feel for a city until you spend time in it. Experience and practice are the surest ways to succeed in a video game too. Hours of play, discovering cheat codes, and testing out new strategies in games are akin to the drafting process in composition. No piece of writing is ever polished in the first draft, just as no game should be beatable on the first try. Just as gamers frequently put in hours to improve scores and "level up," writers must expect to produce multiple drafts and assignments or literacy acts to "level up" in their composition skills.

Readings

Gaming worlds vary as much as the players who populate them. Whether channeling their inner star in *Rock Band* or fighting for survival in *Assassin's Creed*, players are drawn to specific virtual worlds for specific reasons. By focusing on a sampling of the issues gamers face, we gain critical awareness of the virtual worlds we inhabit. For those new to gaming, excerpts from Mark Stephen Meadows's text, *I, Avatar*, explain how *Second Life* works and also shed light on the draw of the virtual world. *A Declaration of the Rights of Avatars*, by Raph Koster, goes further to establish not only the rights of gamers but more specifically of avatars. Daniel Sieberg asks us to broaden our definition of *avatar* beyond exclusively pixelated images of bodies to include textual representations like Twitter feeds. Ouyang Dan offers concerns about "The Whitewashing of Video Games" as she draws attention to the need for more multicultural and gender-aware character representations. Finally, *Wired Magazine*'s Julian Dibbell explores the possibility of gaming worlds without rules in his portrait of *griefers*—players who reject any social contracts of gaming communities in favor of pranks and chaos.

● Mark Stephen Meadows

"Rituals and Archetypes" and "Why," excerpts from *I, Avatar: The Culture and Consequences of Having a Second Life*

> With work including writing, illustration, and software design, American author Mark Stephen Meadows has written several books, including *I, Avatar* and *Pause and Effect*. His work combines reflection on personal experiences in digital spaces with observations of community norms and expectations. Meadows completed his BA at St. John's College in Santa Fe, New Mexico.

RITUALS AND ARCHETYPES

People put on masks of ritual and role and build new kinds of culture. A culture, like a city-state, is a group identity that sometimes needs to be defended. But the definition of that culture, like that of any city-state, happens not only outside the walls but inside them as well.

Though the wars were fought at the boundaries of group identity, those avatars within the borders of the culture seemed to get along quite well. They had strong bonds, solid rituals, a diverse range of roles, and a clear sense of why they were there. Within their culture, the members heartily agreed with one another about who they were and how to stay that way. These agreements had to do with behavior, and they appeared in many forms. Some of the agreements were clear and evident, such as how avatars should dress and behave. On all Gorean islands that I know of, for example, it was explicitly forbidden to look anything other than a human from pre-Renaissance Europe. The avatar needed to not only look human, it needed to be dressed in typical sword-and-sorcery leather or lace. Welcome signs told you this, and explained other rules, when you teleported in to any of the Gorean Islands.

The fact that all the "guys" dressed in medieval leather and all the "girls" dressed in saucy see-throughs was easy to pick up on when you entered the space, even without signs. It was strictly forbidden to look like a Furry (or a robot, or a spaceman, or whatever). The agreements of this culture also demanded that the members speak and even move in certain ways. Flying, for example, was not allowed on Gorean islands. The agreements were there for the members of the group to recognize the kind of behavior that was allowed, and what ideas, words, actions, and interactions were and were not part of their emerging culture. These agreements on what kind of behavior was appropriate bordered on a kind of morality. The rituals were built out of rules and roles.

Some of these agreements (such as dress code) were evident and simple. Others, however, were subtle and quite complicated. An example is the Gorean wedding. In Second Life, weddings (and divorces, for that matter) are commonplace and happen at a much faster rate than in the real world. People may be married only for a few weeks. A Gorean wedding, or Free Companion Ceremony, was like a real-world wedding in that there were fancy clothes, and an officiating person, and a church of sorts, and people sat in rows to watch. But a Gorean wedding would only officially last for a real-life year and was also a bit different than a standard wedding. They had their own clothes, of course, and used certain music. It was all a bit medieval: The food was typically turkey legs and whole pigs with apples in their mouths. Not the sort of food that is commonly served at a Western wedding anymore. These Gorean role players refined the words of the wedding to their own culture, and they had special dances that were, I understand, very, very specific. A dance was an animation that someone else made, so the avatar couldn't mess up the move. These things are all rituals that helped to define the culture they had invented.

Mark Stephen Meadows, "Rituals and Archetypes," and "Why," in *I, Avatar: The Culture and Consequences of Having A Second Life, 1st Edition*. Pearson Education, Inc., 2008, pp. 44–46, 82–87. Copyright © 2008 by Pearson Education, Inc. All rights reserved. Reprinted by permission of Pearson Education, Inc., Upper Saddle River, NJ.

My introduction to both Gor and Fur was via ritual. My introduction to Gor was the ritual of Montserrat-Carmen on her knees, asking for forgiveness from Tarl in the forest. My introduction to Fur was also in a forest, but it was a crazed monkey chase scene that took place up in the branches and was similar to a game of tag. These two rituals were each definitions, to some degree, of these respective cultures. In Gor the hierarchically driven interaction between members (and what level an individual could climb to), determined the underpinnings of the society. Among the Furs, the more free-form kind of play and less structured form of interaction was emblematic of that culture.

This kind of thing is just what people do, whether we drive avatars or not. People perform these kinds of little agreements all the time, regardless of age, location, gender, or social context. Consider the handshake. Here in Los Angeles, I've seen kids on the street shake hands, point their thumbs in the air, and bump fists. In Paris I've seen kids of the same age shake hands, slap their hand to their own chest, and then touch elbows. It is a physical way of interacting to say, "We are part of the same group, and we both know it, and we can prove it in our interactions." Avatars represent their users in exactly the same way. It's a basic and integral interaction that represents the user and their cultural role.

Just as rituals help define culture, avatar rituals help define avatar cultures. The analogy to shaking hands might be a word that is typed (such as "Tal") or an animation that is initiated (such as a hug). But the rituals are more important in virtual worlds than in the real world. In a virtual world we don't have some of the same degree of complexity or fidelity of the senses. Given the technology that virtual worlds use, subtleties in human behavior are lost (or translated to other subtleties). And so avatars have to make up for it in other ways, usually by one of these greeting rituals, though it can happen in other situations, depending on what the group likes and invents. That is how the behavior of avatars helps to create rituals.

Archetypes, too, are created by behavior, as well as appearance. The Hero and the Guide are two common archetypes found in literature and movies, and it's pretty easy to tell them apart because they neither look nor act alike. For example, Luke Skywalker (the Hero) doesn't look like Obi-Wan Kenobi (the Guide), and Luke doesn't act like Obi-Wan, either. Their appearance and behavior define them as different archetypes. They are personalities and identities we can point to and identify as archetypes because of their behavior. Avatar designs, both visually and in terms of how they behave, tend to orbit archetypes of one sort or another. The Hero, the Baby, the Guide, the Child, the Sage, and so on.

Avatars represent an archetype of a very personal sort, and these archetypes are linked to the rituals that avatar groups build. The cultural rituals of

Gor, Fur, and the other cultures I came across were dominated by archetypal avatars. In a virtual world, the only things we can exchange are symbols. These symbols, whether they are interactions and rituals or actions and archetypes, become the community's defining text.

Because an archetype has to do with personality and behavior, and because rituals contain behaviors and require specific sorts of personalities, rituals give archetypes meaning and expression, and vice-versa. The visual representation that a person chooses for their avatar has something to do with their role in the society. This is part of what archetype means. That day in the glade, I saw this Conan the Barbarian slave master named Tarl. The visual barbarian archetype mapped well to the behavioral ritual of the slave master. Tarl looked like someone that would dominate and rule in a very physical way. Of course, this avatar was no more "physically" powerful than was Carmen's—neither of them was physical at all, of course—but by appearing that way, by presenting the visual symbols of physical power, it was easier for both of them to accept the ritual. It would be hard to do otherwise. With names like Tarl and Montserrat, I would have a hard time imagining these two doing anything else. The barbarian and the trampled princess were deep in their roles, and I certainly didn't expect either of them to begin discussing something out-of-role, such as homosexual anonymity or automotive repair.

Dress, body shape, action, interaction, words, and all other symbols and elements of their roles and rules were strictly pre-determined boundaries, and it is within these boundaries that most avatars live. In Second Life, archetypes are defined by the people driving the avatars. In World of Warcraft the archetypes and rituals are more defined by the designers of the system. In Eve Online, the avatars are spaceships. But regardless of the system, it is within that cultural set of archetypes and rituals that the avatar lives.

Avatar rituals encourage archetypes, and archetypes encourage rituals, and with these instruments in each hand the avatar plays the songs of personality and narrative.

WHY?

My second life was much like my first, only accelerated, smaller, and more dramatic. People married, money moved, wars began, kingdoms crumbled. Noses and lips and hair and clothes shifted like tiny weather systems, raining images and emotions onto the computer screens of people around the world. Little programs that animated your avatar to kiss another avatar were handed around during Valentine's Day, along with perfume and embarrassment and gossip and more romance. Mood swings and conversation shifts and grand promises and tiny lies. Leather and lace and flowers and swords decorated this Harlequin Romance world, this world of social exchange.

A day in Second Life lasts for four hours. These thin, short days flickered by like a movie, whirring and chattering with the events in this faraway place that had colonized my skull. The sun spun around me as I went through 24-hour cycles in the real world that were punctuated only by biobreaks. Sometimes I completely lost track of what time it was, as the Second Life day dictated my rhythm more than the real days. I continued to dive deep, Carmen was always a few levels deeper, and as we swam it became darker and colder and stranger.

Eventually, my health deteriorating, I was confronted with a decision: Which world did I prefer?

It's a potentially dangerous decision, and many arguments warn against, shall we say, *going native*. Avatars present a danger of isolation from not only the real world, but from ourselves. If an avatar is used too much, it can remove us from our real-world society. We lose touch with reality. The Stanford Institute for the Quantitative Study of Society points out that with only five hours per week of Internet use, 15 percent of people interviewed reported a decrease in real-life social activities. They spent, for example, 25 percent less time talking on the phone to friends and family. Many American adults spend more time than that—an average of more than seven hours a week—playing games, and kids twice that much. This seems like a good reason to start looking more closely at what is going on.

Most of us have had the experience of trying to talk to someone while they're more engaged with their avatar, or zippered down into their fantasy world or game and reluctant to come out. Kids yell, "Be right there, Mom!" as they furiously pump the console to get leveled up before unplugging. Adults mumble half-replies to their kids as they coordinate their guild for the next raid. Roommates refuse to answer the phone. Friends don't IM back as quickly as they used to. People simply get lost in their avatar.

When we make an avatar, we invent a personality. In some cases, it may be the same personality, or a similar one, that we spend most of our days being. But often the alternative personality—the personality of the avatar—can become quite powerful. Part of the danger lies in how we control our avatar and how our avatar controls us. As people become more involved in the roles and rules of their avatar, they can also lose control of their alternative personality they have invented for that system. The alternative personality can become predominant and begin to take over the primary, daily one. This is the situation that most concerns parents. When they see their kid playing hours upon hours of World of Warcraft or Second Life or Lineage or Webkinz, they become concerned that their child will lose touch with the real-world society that is more important. People sometimes prefer their avatar personas to their "real" ones.

Your role as an avatar can take control of your life as a person. This was true long before online games and avatars. The classic example is the corporate executive who comes home and treats his children like employees. Or the marine who comes home and treats his family like recruits. The role has overcome the person and the context in which a person moves.

Losing control of one's life as a person, and therefore losing control of an alter-ego, can endanger others. One day in 2006, several Second Life avatars were having a roll in the virtual hay. A pretty normal day in Second Life—but when it was noticed that a few of them had been designed to look like pre-pubescents, many an eyebrow was raised. Avatars pretending to have sex with kids? Was this pedophilia? It wasn't clear. After all, an avatar that looks like an old woman may be driven by a young boy, and vice versa. The Second Life Teen Grid had been opened up for those under eighteen, so it was assumed the coast was clear enough and adult play could be allowed in the adult grid.

Emily Semaphore, one of the owners of Jailbait, an age-play region in Second Life, was quoted by the *Second Life Herald* as saying, "Being able to 'play' a kid in a 'safe' environment can be very healing for many people." Child-pornogaphy prosecutors in the Netherlands disagreed and brought the case to court. It was later dropped because "the children avatars were not 'realistic enough.'" But this debate, as well as pressure from groups such as Familles de France, eventually contributed to Linden Lab hiring a company named Integrity-Aristotle to oversee identity verification in Second Life. Linden Lab made it clear that it would do nothing with the personal data, but Integrity-Aristotle made no such claim. The end result was the beginning of a kind of driver's license. Avatars needed authentic identities that could be traced to a real human. People were furious about this enforced identity tracking, as well as with the company chosen to do it. They wanted their avatar to remain separate from their real identity, or at least to be able to decide themselves whether to be officially connected to them. Some users left. And although this "driver's license" reduced the ability to keep a psychological division and allowed for prosecution of the rampant alter-ego's owner, it could really do nothing to address the situation's cause. After all, what could Linden Lab do? Ban child avatars from the adult grid? What, then, would happen to the Harry Potter Fan Club?

Other anti-avatar arguments include the anti-social ones, which claim that spending social time online is less valuable and valid than spending time with people in the real world. People, and kids in particular, become shut-ins, pale, maggoty versions of their former selves. By spending too much time online they avoid spending time with anyone different from themselves. They start to lose their ability to interpret signs such as body language and intonation—important social signals that allow navigation through real, human society. They start to smell, and their hair becomes messy. They turn geeky and lose any social skills they may have had.

There are the arguments that claim video games are violent media that lead to violent behavior, and that exposure to violent media creates violent people. Parents cry danger, teachers see distraction, ministers warn of devil worship, and politicians makes speeches about corruption of the young. There's not much new about this argument. Parents, politicians, and pedagogues have always been afraid for our safety, and they have always made the same objections about each medium.

What horror!

Some find avatars to be gateways, into a kind of hell. The avatar user becomes a schizophrenic personality, a hyper-violent, hyper-sexual, child-molesting psychopath, an outsider squinting out at the world, trapped inside an unhealthy body, abusing others, ultimately alone and unable to determine what is important.

Would I become this person if I continued to spend the majority of my waking hours in a geeky little fictional world inhabited by dressed-up strangers driving around in weird doll-machines? Would I continue to let my own life fall to the side and slide away? These are not uncommon questions. Millions have to make the same decisions every day. I considered these questions thoroughly, slipped on my mask, and dove back in.

But why?

The more than 50 million people who choose to spend time as their avatars in virtual worlds probably think about such questions, or at least some of them do. Which gives us many millions of different answers.

For me, it's what I do. I travel, I paint, and I write. So I went back because flying around in a visual world of symbols and social interaction is where I live, what I live to build, and where I love to live. For me it was just a sensible decision. After all, I prefer to live the way I want as much as I can. Where I can fly. Where there is no such thing as scarcity or tragedy. Where I can stretch out my hand and create carpets, trees, castles, and mountains. Where—most of all—I can easily make smiles on the screen-lit faces of my far-flung friends as we dwell, laughing together, in the same dream. That is beautiful. That is a blending of the things in my life that I love most. I'm lucky I can experience this kind of travel.

Different people, of course, have different motivations, and patterns have been noted. Richard Bartle is an internationally recognized authority on virtual worlds, a pioneer of the MMORPG industry, and co-creator of the first text-based virtual world, MUD, back in 1979. He divides user motivations into four primary categories: the Explorers, the Socializers, the Achievers, and the Controllers. Explorers like to uncover beauty and show it to others. Socializers like to form groups, build social infrastructure, and throw parties. Achievers enhance the abilities of their avatars, increasing their power, wealth, and reputation, gaining social respect while doing it. Controllers are there to dominate, compete, and defeat. But whatever people use their avatars for, the avatars allow them to become more like what they want to be.

For some users, virtual worlds provide an alternative, online social life and actually provide access to more social living in real life. In August 2007, in the U.S. journal *CyberPsychology and Behavior*, researchers at Nottingham Trent University published a study called, "Social Interactions in Massively Multiplayer Online Role-Playing Gamers." Of the 1,000 gamers they interviewed, three quarters had made good friends online, half had met in real-life situations, a third had found themselves attracted to another gamer, and a tenth of them had developed physical relationships. So, it's not just that spending time as your avatar allows you to make new friends online; it opens the door for more social interaction in the real world.

Some would argue that sports are challenging and social and that playing them allows you to be competent and self-confident. When I was growing up, playing a lot of video games, adults often told me I should go out and play more sports. American football was the popular recommendation. But which, really, is more violent? Shooting pixels on a screen or breaking real bones on a football field from some kid jumping on your back because his dad's screaming from the bleachers?

Which really allows for increased social interaction? Which initiates group problem-solving and collaborative thinking?

Many spend time as their avatar not because they are addicted to a new thrill but because they are satisfying an old need. World of Warcraft, Second Life, and other role-playing games are engaging because they serve the primary human drives of socializing and being competent at a skill set. This has been confirmed by several researchers over the years. In 2006, the University of Rochester (N.Y.) and researchers at Immersyve Inc. interviewed 1,000 gamers in various MMOs. According to Richard Ryan, a motivational psychologist at the University, ". . . the psychological 'pull' of games is largely due to their capacity to engender feelings of autonomy, competence, and relatedness."

When someone slips into an avatar, they slip into the ability to be competent, to be who they want, and to spend time with a community that they choose. Being able to do all three things at once is a rare experience for many people—perhaps because of appearance, gender, race, sexuality, age, or simply the fact that they want more friends of different sorts, or more enemies, or for any of a million different reasons and justifications. For example, one wheelchair-bound 19-year-old man says, "I really love gaming. I love gaming because I can't really do what other people do because of my own problems as you see. But in games, I am just like everybody else, it's like I live my life there, and I'm not different, and I like that."

Everyone experiences some discomfort among their fellow humans; everyone has some way in which they would like a fantasy, or an improvement, or even just a break. Everyone is, on some level, fighting a great battle, and everyone finds life a bit difficult at times. Avatars can give us an alternative, a break from daily hardships, and a space to practice for another try.

The first avatars and indeed the first large-scale virtual environment built for multi-user operation were built for this very reason. Chip Morningstar and F. Randall Farmer developed Lucasfilm's Habitat specifically so that hospitalized children could have an alternative, and a break from a limbo life in a hospital bed. The system, built on Commodore 64s, gave the kids a chance to go on quests together when they couldn't even get out of a hospital bed. Morningstar adopted the term "avatar" from Hindu mythology to describe the graphical representation of a user. This happened in California, in 1985.

The avatar is a Californian invention that uses computer software. It is a technological, automated American Dream. This is important for understanding why people use avatars.

The "American Dream" tells as that we can become who we want, and we can profit by doing so. It is the dream of independence and success and that core ability to make yourself into who and what you want. During the population explosion of Los Angeles, in 1931, James Adams published a book titled *The Epic of America* and in it he describes The American Dream as, "that dream of a land in which life should be better and richer and fuller for every man, with opportunity for each according to his ability or achievement." This dream of profit and social mobility via industry wasn't, nor is it now, particularly *American*. The immigrants to L.A. were pre-industrial nomads, rootless and willing to give up their homes, friends, and families back East or in Europe in exchange for a promise of a world they could build themselves. It was a "My land, my imagination" mentality. These were people who didn't fit within a community of strict rules, who didn't recognize themselves as members of that community and because they were nomadic they were also community builders. So they built a new kind of community that allowed them to be freer, and more recognized as individuals with less social pressure. They packed their bags, walked away from their past, and started on an ambitious and strange project that we now call Los Angeles.

The same thing has happened in Second Life. These two sets of immigrants were not only demographically similar, as I've pointed out, but they were also moved by many of the same motivations as immigrants to Second Life and other virtual worlds. In 2007, I surveyed, either via form or interview, more than 300 virtual-world residents. Some interviews were with the ten percent who had been spending about as much time in-world as a full-time job. What I found made a kind of grim sense: These people had assembled their own synthetic communities because they had none on hand in the real world. Most of them came from small families, had no siblings, came from small communities, traveled a great deal. Eighty percent of these users lived in cities more than 100 miles from where they were born. More than a third moved to a new city every four years. About a third were Asian, a little over half were male, and all had a desire to leave a system they disliked. Avatars had allowed them to create their own community.

Avatars also give these same people an opportunity to explore a place that is safer than what the modern world seems to afford. If I believe the media I notice around me, the world seems to be getting a lot more dangerous. Compared to a decade ago the danger level in the United States is probably not higher, but the fear level certainly is. Parents are less inclined to let their children play alone in the streets. Governments are less inclined to advise their citizens to travel abroad. Gangs roam in front of your home, terrorists lurk in your neighborhood alley, danger supposedly hides under every bridge. Living in Los Angeles, I hear an awful lot of noise about how dangerous it is outside. Newspapers, radios, televisions, and airport ceiling-robots scream about the dangers nearby. We are pushed by our media to risk less. We are told by our police force to avoid strangers. We are told to be afraid. We are told to stay at home. And so we go into the virtual world. Avatars offer an alternative to the "American Dream" of decentralized cities full of anonymous faces, depersonalized living, mass media, and fear.

Avatars, self-assembled constellations of the individual and the community, allow a way to return to something that is central to the human experience. They bring us back to a smaller society of people whom we know and care about and trust.

Ironically, avatars offer a return to pre-industrial, pre-automated societies; to small groups of families and friends that once existed only in villages.

As my friend, the novelist William Kowalski, writes: "Is this an attempt for us to get back to the life that really matters—the symbolic life? Is this our weird American version of waking up and saying that the world we actually live in, the world we've created for ourselves—strip malls, pollution, racism, meaningless jobs—is absolute bullshit, and not worth living?"

Carmen's take on it is similar: "One of the things that fuels synthetic worlds is that the society we live in is so rigid and the roles are so over-determined, yet none of them works. People are rebuilding western society inside these worlds, just as they did in the Renaissance."

Simply put, avatars fill in the social blanks of contemporary society and in doing so, if used too much, offer real dangers.

People get more and more deeply involved, passing more and more heart-beats, exploring broader landscapes with their avatars, playing these "games" and letting what may be unsatisfying or potentially unconnected lives—their first lives—fade and fall to the side in favor of something that often feels like a cross between a movie and a dream, perhaps because their real lives are nightmares. It only makes sense that another life offering greater engagement might start to compete with one that, for many people, is not what they'd hoped. They have another option.

Virtual worlds are the American Dream, second edition—a response to the American Dream, first edition.

READING REACTIONS

1. What dangers does Meadows discuss regarding the use of avatars?

2. Consider the discussion of pedophilia on *Second Life*. Are some things taboo online? Should people be held accountable for wrongdoing online? Are these "real" crimes, or are they so mediated by technology as to be meaningless?

3. Some consider time spent building relationships online as "less valuable and valid than spending time with people in the real world." Consider the role online spaces play in your personal relationships. Do you agree or disagree with this statement?

4. Meadows offers many reasons for rituals in *Second Life*, including to help build group identity. What roles do you think rituals play in *Second Life*? Think of another online community like Facebook or *Halo*, and list some rituals you see community members participating in. Why do they do so?

5. Consider the first line of Meadows's "Why?" section: "My second life was much like my first, only accelerated, smaller, and more dramatic." What impact does this have on the reader? How does this statement affect author ethos?

6. The author seems to know that he has an uphill battle in explaining the virtual *Second Life* world to some readers. What strategies does he use to build his case for the usefulness of rituals and archetypes that might at first glance seem silly or meaningless?

● Raph Koster

A Declaration of the Rights of Avatars

Raph Koster is a game designer living in San Diego, California. In addition to creating virtual worlds, Koster also writes about gameplay, avatars, and players' rights. Koster received his Master of Fine Arts degree from the University of Alabama.

When a time comes that new modes and venues exist for communities, and said modes are different enough from the existing ones that [the] question arises as to the applicability of past custom and law, and when said venues have become a forum for interaction and society for the general public regardless of the intent of the creators of said venue, and at a time when said communities and spaces are rising in popularity and are now widely exploited for commercial gain, it behooves those involved in said communities and venues to affirm and declare the inalienable rights of the members of said communities. Therefore herein have been set forth those rights which are inalienable rights of the inhabitants of virtual spaces of all sorts, in their form henceforth referred to as avatars, in order that this declaration may continually remind those who hold power over virtual spaces and the avatars contained therein of their duties and responsibilities; in order that the forms of administration of a virtual space may be at any time compared to that of other virtual spaces; and in order that the grievances of players may hereafter be judged against the explicit rights set forth, to better govern the virtual space and improve the general welfare and happiness of all.

Therefore this document holds the following truths to be self-evident: That avatars are the manifestation of actual people in an online medium, and that their utterances, actions, thoughts, and emotions should be considered to be as valid as the utterances, actions, thoughts, and emotions of people in any other forum, venue, location, or space. That the well-established rights of man approved by the National Assembly of France on August 26th of 1789 do therefore apply to avatars in full measure saving only the aspects of said rights that do not pertain in a virtual space or which must be abrogated in order to ensure the continued existence of the space in question. That by the act of affirming membership in the community within the virtual space, the avatars form a social contract with the community, forming a populace which may and must self-affirm and self-impose rights and concomitant restrictions upon their behavior. That the nature of virtual spaces is such that there must, by physical law, always be a higher power or administrator who maintains the space and has complete power over all participants, but who is undeniably part of the community formed within the space and who must therefore take action in accord with that which benefits the space as well as the participants, and who therefore also has the rights of avatars and may have other rights as well. That the ease of moving between virtual spaces and the potential transience of the community do not limit or reduce the level of emotional and social involvement that avatars may have with the community, and that therefore the ease of moving between virtual spaces and the potential transience of the community do not in any way limit, curtail, or remove these rights from avatars on the alleged grounds that avatars can always simply leave.

Articles:

1. Avatars are created free and equal in rights. Special powers or privileges shall be founded solely on the common good, and not based on whim, favoritism, nepotism, or the caprice of those who hold power. Those who act as ordinary avatars within the space shall all have only the rights of normal avatars.

2. The aim of virtual communities is the common good of its citizenry, from which arise the rights of avatars. Foremost among these rights is the right to be treated as people and not as disembodied, meaningless, soulless puppets. Inherent in this right are therefore the natural and inalienable rights of man. These rights are liberty, property, security, and resistance to oppression.

3. The principle of all sovereignty in a virtual space resides in the inalterable fact that somewhere there resides an individual who controls the hardware on which the virtual space is running, and the software with which it is created, and the database which makes up its existence. However, the body populace has the right to know and demand the enforcement of the standards by which this individual uses this power over the community, as authority must proceed from the community; a community that does not know the standards by which the administrators use their power is a community which permits its administrators to have no standards, and is therefore a community abetting in tyranny.

4. Liberty consists of the freedom to do anything which injures no one else including the weal of the community as a whole and as an entity instantiated on hardware and by software; the exercise of the natural rights of avatars are therefore limited solely by the rights of other avatars sharing the same space and participating in the same community. These limits can only be determined by a clear code of conduct.

5. The code of conduct can only prohibit those actions and utterances that are hurtful to society, inclusive of the harm that may be done

to the fabric of the virtual space via hurt done to the hardware, software, or data; and likewise inclusive of the harm that may be done to the individual who maintains said hardware, software, or data, in that harm done to this individual may result in direct harm done to the community.

6. The code of conduct is the expression of the general will of the community and the will of the individual who maintains the hardware and software that makes up the virtual space. Every member of the community has the right to contribute either directly or via representatives in the shaping of the code of conduct as the culture of the virtual space evolves, particularly as it evolves in directions that the administrator did not predict; the ultimate right of the administrator to shape and define the code of conduct shall not be abrogated, but it is clear that the administrator therefore has the duty and responsibility to work with the community to arrive at a code of conduct that is shaped by the input of the community. As a member of the community himself, the administrator would be damaging the community itself if he failed in this responsibility, for abrogation of this right of avatars could result in the loss of population and therefore damage to the common weal.

7. No avatar shall be accused, muzzled, toaded, jailed, banned, or otherwise punished except in the cases and according to the forms prescribed by the code of conduct. Any one soliciting, transmitting, executing, or causing to be executed, any arbitrary order, shall be punished, even if said individual is one who has been granted special powers or privileges within the virtual space. But any avatar summoned or arrested in virtue of the code of conduct shall submit without delay, as resistance constitutes an offense.

8. The code of conduct shall provide for such punishments only as are strictly and obviously necessary, and no one shall suffer punishment except it be legally inflicted according to the provisions of a code of conduct promulgated before the commission of the offense; save in the case where the offense endangered the continued existence of the virtual space by attacking the hardware or software that provide the physical existence of the space.

9. As all avatars are held innocent until they shall have been declared guilty, if detainment, temporary banning, jailing, gluing, freezing, or toading shall be deemed indispensable, all harshness not essential to the securing of the prisoner's person shall be severely repressed by the code of conduct.

10. No one shall be disquieted on account of his opinions, provided their manifestation does not disturb the public order established by the code of conduct.

11. The free communication of ideas and opinions is one of the most precious of the rights of man. Every avatar may, accordingly, speak, write, chat, post, and print with freedom, but shall be responsible for such abuses of this freedom as shall be defined by the code of conduct, most particularly the abuse of affecting the performance of the space or the performance of a given avatar's representation of the space.

12. The security of the rights of avatars requires the existence of avatars with special powers and privileges, who are empowered to enforce the provisions of the code of conduct. These powers and privileges are therefore granted for the good of all and not for the personal advantage of those to whom they shall be entrusted. These powers and privileges are also therefore not an entitlement, and can and should be removed in any instance where they are no longer used for the good of all, even if the offense is merely inactivity.

13. A common contribution may, at the discretion of the individual who maintains the hardware, the software, and the data that make up the virtual space, be required in order to maintain the existence of avatars who enforce the code of conduct and to maintain the hardware and the software and the continued existence of the virtual space. Avatars have the right to know the nature and amount of the contribution in advance, and said required contribution should be equitably distributed among all the citizens without regard to their social position; special rights and privileges shall never pertain to the avatar who contributes more except insofar as the special powers and privileges require greater resources from the hardware, software, or data store, and would not be possible save for the resources obtainable with the contribution; and as long as any and all avatars are able to make this contribution and therefore gain the powers and privileges if they so choose; nor shall any articles of this declaration be contingent upon a contribution being made.

14. The community has the right to require of every administrator or individual with special powers and privileges granted for the purpose of administration, an account of his administration.

15. A virtual community in which the observance of the code of conduct is not assured and universal, nor the separation of powers defined, has no constitution at all.

16. Since property is an inviolable and sacred right, and the virtual equivalent is integrity and persistence of data, no one shall be deprived thereof except where public necessity, legally determined per the code of conduct, shall clearly demand it, and then only on condition that the avatar shall have been previously and equitably indemnified, saving only cases wherein the continued existence of the space is jeopardized by the existence or integrity of said data.

17. The administrators of the virtual space shall not abridge the freedom of assembly, save to preserve the performance and continued viability of the virtual space.

18. Avatars have the right to be secure in their persons, communications, designated private spaces, and effects, against unreasonable snooping, eavesdropping, searching and seizures, no activity pertaining thereto shall be undertaken by administrators save with probable cause supported by affirmation, particularly describing the goal of said investigations.

19. The enumeration in this document of rights shall not be construed to deny or disparage others retained by avatars.

—January 26, 2000

READING REACTIONS

1. According to Koster, "avatars are the manifestations of actual people in an online medium." Do you agree? Do avatars differ from property? If so, how?

2. What sorts of rights does this document propose are owed to avatars? How do these compare to the rights of citizens in this country? What are the biggest differences and the most striking similarities?

3. Consider the second article's statement that avatars have the "right to be treated as people and not as disembodied, meaningless, soulless puppets." How does the author build this case? Do you agree? Why or why not?

4. Do you see avatars you have created or embodied (for class in *Second Life*, in your favorite video game, or even as an online placeholder) as their own entity, as an extension of you, as property, or as some combination of those? Offer examples from your own experience to support your argument.

5. This declaration of rights was written specifically in reference to *Second Life* residents. Do these rights apply to avatars in other gaming worlds? Why or why not?

6. Describe the author's tone in this piece. How does it impact his ethos? Can you locate examples of claims to pathos and logos?

7. How does this piece work rhetorically? What other famous writing and genre is it based on? Look for specific phrases as examples of ways Koster is taking on the voice and style of a famous text.

● Daniel Sieberg

Is Your Avatar Giving You an Identity Crisis?

Emmy-nominated Daniel Sieberg is a former CBS News science and technology correspondent and current host of *Tech This Out!* on ABC News. He contributes science and technology stories to shows like *Nightline* and *Good Morning America*. His written work has appeared on the *Huffington Post, Details,* and Salon.com. He is also the author of *The Digital Diet: A Four-Step Plan to Break Your Tech Addiction and Regain Balance in Your Life.*

How do you see yourself? No, really. We each have shortcomings and body hangups and things we'd like to exchange for a newer model. And most of the time we'd prefer not to expose our naked physical selves to the world. But what about digging below the surface like examining your intellect or your emotions or your accomplishments. How do you look now? Happy with the way things are going? Undoubtedly we're all a work in progress. But we're probably much more acutely aware of how we look in a mirror than how we appear to the outside world. Or put another way, we may be in denial over our inner faults and more plugged in to the "first impressions" of appearance. We just sort of are who we are, and that's that, right?

OK, enough psycho-babble. The point is to lead in to how we view our online selves. By that I mean the fine-tuning we do to portray our lives to those who might "know" us on social networks. In essence: our avatars.

Let's start with those 140 characters. When Twitter hit the scene in a big way last year it asked users a simple question: "What's happening?" There were the early adopters who enjoyed telling people they were ironing their socks or rearranging their paper clip collection. And we made fun of them. We yelled a collective: "Who cares??" Then more and more people (myself included) got enamored with the idea of having "followers" and telling those followers exactly what we thought about some product or where we were going or how we were so incredibly bummed out that Paula Abdul wouldn't be a judge on American Idol anymore. (Breathe, Daniel, I'm sure Ellen DeGeneres will be fine.)

But suddenly we started defining ourselves by the number of followers we had and clamored for more. Gaining a follower for me would be exciting. What will this person think of me? Who are they exactly? But I got sucked in to the trap of wanting that number to go up and not really considering the actual connections being made (or not). If you have a Twitter account then I bet you know exactly how many followers you have within a small margin. But what do you really know about any of them? And the more people who "listened" to us the more excited we got. Except that it doesn't seem to me like many people are actually hearing anything. Sure, we clicked on links and made occasional comments. But for many users it quickly turned into a competition—who could Tweet the wittiest comment about Tiger Woods? Who would be first to tell their followers that Michael Jackson was dead? Who was having the MOST AWESOME FABULOUS FUN TIME AT SOME EXOTIC LOCATION??

Look, I don't mean to make it sound like we shouldn't share our lives with people we care about or vice versa. Remember, I'm not anti-communication. I'm seeking the exact opposite—meaningful communication and making technology work the right way for your life. It's all relative. But at some point many people get carried away with sites like Twitter and perhaps more concerned about how their fellow followers viewed their feed (aka personal story) as opposed to their real and actual and present life. And maybe the definition of the two began to blur. It certainly did in my case. I can remember getting a bit anxious about what to post. I felt the need to be funny but still professional. That often ended up being boring and no one wants to follow a dud. So what would I say? Sometimes it was easy and obvious when I was working on something interesting but other times it was just a chore.

When I'd broadcast what I was working on or where I was going, I'd get this tinge of guilt like I shouldn't be bragging about myself. But I didn't listen to that voice and soldiered on with my Tweets. I kept imagining my followers (866 of them, you'll recall) reading about me and therefore wanted to put my best binary face forward. But that's not real. What was anyone learning and what did they want to know? It began to become more difficult. Over time I felt like I was just a shill for my job. I felt compelled to "put myself out there." Is that what people wanted to hear?

Sure, I'd also link to other science or technology stories and some followers appreciated that connection. I have no problem with that. But at some point even that felt unfulfilling for me. I did enjoy reading some Twitter feeds and news sites can work like a wire service on it, which is clearly useful. But I fell into a constant state of buffering all that data. Buffering. Buffering. That's when the digital diet kicked in.

How then do we make sense of all the noise? There are tools built in to the software that actually allow controls or you could always trust someone else with your password and use it sparingly. This is from Twitter's site in answer to a FAQ about whether it's all just to much information.

"The result of using Twitter to stay connected with friends, relatives, and coworkers is that you have a sense of what folks are up to but you are not expected to respond to any updates unless you want to. This means you can step in and out of the flow of information as it suits you and it never queues up with increasing demand of your attention. Additionally, users are very much in control of whose updates they receive, when they receive them, and on what device. For example, we provide settings for scheduling Twitter to automatically turn off at dinnertime and users can switch off Twitter updates at any point. Simply put, Twitter is what you make of it—receive a lot of information about your friends, or just a tiny bit. It's up to them."

Come on—how many people do you know who minimize the frequency of their Twitter updates? Quite the contrary. It's a nice idea but we seem to crave the attention and the opportunity that brevity coupled with broadcasting provide. Our ego gets a boost. And it all adds more bricks to our virtual foundation. Or more building blocks to our avatars. Each Tweet is like a tiny chapter of our online self. It becomes a chronology, a public diary, and a road map for who we (virtually) are.

For me, the idea of taking away that foundation felt like I wasn't moving forward. Deep down I feared that my avatar would die. I was ultimately spending more time worrying about which Twitter update best encapsulated my mood or my adventures or my SELF. And I was sacrificing part of my real self for my avatar. When I realized that—well, the first step is to realize that you have a problem. And here I am. Again, I want to reiterate that of course not everyone gets so caught up with social networks but just remember there is a pause button. It's always there.

Of course, you could argue that blogs aren't much different because it's "all about me" and just more spouting of opinion. Perhaps. But there is arguably more introspection when it comes to blogs and less of a need to have "followers."

Some blogs get written without many (if any) people reading a single word. Nonetheless they can be a productive exercise. It seems to me that many people drifted away from blogs when a numeric value could be attached to your readers (e.g. followers or friends)—translating into a direct reference to your "audience" and people who perceived you in some way. Maybe instead of imagining yourself or your "followers" as people summed up in 140 characters, remember the last time you had coffee with them or watched a movie together or shared a laugh. And if you've never experienced those real-life activities with most of your followers, and you see signs that segments of your personal life isn't as fulfilling, then it may be time to ask if your avatar is giving you an identity crisis. In any case, before I turn the page for this posting, I would actually like to apologize to bloggers everywhere.

In my original posting about my "disconnect" I asked whatever happened to blogs. Well, here's one of the best responses from someone who goes by "Element22".

"They're alive and well within a strong community of independent writers who value the spoken and written form of communication."

Amen.

Next time: my Facebook self-portrait. Until then, stay connected.

1. At first glance it may seem that a reading on Twitter belongs in the "Social Networks" chapter, but here Sieberg categorizes a Twitter account as an avatar. If a Twitterfeed is an avatar, is Twitter a game? How do you define *game*?

2. Sieberg talks at length about his desire to put his "best binary face forward" by tweeting the right sorts of things. Based on his discussion, what do you think the Twitter community values? What are the goals of those in the Twittersphere?

3. On Twitter, users often define themselves by number of followers. How might one define herself in a more traditional game? By wins or losses? By appearance? By powers? Choose a gaming world as an example and list ways players define themselves in that space.

4. The author tells us that people use Twitter so they can "step in and out of the flow of information" and stay updated on the lives of others. If you are a gamer, why do you play games? If you are not a gamer, why do you think others spend so much time in gaming worlds?

5. Toward the end of his column, the author admits that he "was sacrificing part of [his] real self for [his] avatar." What sorts of things was he sacrificing? What sorts of things might one sacrifice for an avatar in a gaming world more like *WoW* or *Halo*?

6. Sieberg starts many of his paragraphs with fairly informal language like *come on*, *look*, and *sure*. Why do you think the author adopts this conversational tone? What does it tell you about the author's intended audience and purpose?

7. At the end of this post, the author offers an apology to bloggers. What sort of rhetorical strategy is this an example of, and what do you think the author wishes to gain from this?

Ouyang Dan

The Games We Play: The Whitewashing of Video Games

Ouyang Dan is a freelance writer and frequent blogger for *Bitch.com*, *Random Babble. com*, and *FWD/Forward*. An avid gamer, Dan writes frequently on gender, race, and other identity markers related to gaming. She is a U.S. Navy veteran and now lives in Korea.

Many game designers and developers deliver games that meet the minimal requirements to make me happy, but there are certain game delivery elements that always ruin it for me. The lack of diversity in many games is one of these, and I often see it when I walk down the store aisle or rummage through my collection.

Some companies actually attempt to put out games with decent diversity, and succeed to varying degrees. Ubisoft's *Assassin's Creed*, ASII, and *Assassin's Creed: Brotherhood* were created by teams made up of multi-ethnic, multi-cultural, sensitivity-trained personnel. Sure, it would have been fun to be able to create my own avatar or have some kind of gender selection, but there I go complaining again. Odd to me, though, that Altaïr Ibn-La'Ahad, the main character of a game set in The Holy Land during the Third Crusade, is as white as his bedsheet armor. I understand that people from that region can vary in shade, and that non-white people don't look any certain way, but it would be nice if game companies took a slight effort, occasionally, to make PCs darker in order to represent the rest of us. Yes, yes, the Animus. Yes, yes, Desmond. If you are going to try to stretch my imagination, I think that stretching it and introducing something fresh, like actual representations that more non-white people can relate to, might be more compelling.

Yikes! You might think I didn't like the games! Actually, *Assassin's Creed* was the first XBox 360 game that didn't make me want to throw the control. *Right away.* Though, it did sit in the freezer for a while.

The same thing happened with *Prince of Persia*. The game series features a very fair-skinned and light-eyed hero (as did the eponymous movie starring Jake Gyllenhaal). While I understand, once again, that people living in the region where this game is set can range from darker skinned to light skin and have varying eye colors, the trend in video games to churn out light-skinned male hero after light-skinned male hero leaves me desiring a hero with non-white features, especially if we aren't going to be creating our own avatars.

Dragon Age 2 released its anxiously awaited demo the last week of February, and we will see if it lives up to its "Best RPG of 2009" predecessor, which stands as one of my favorites still, and first game I have beaten before my partner. The demo contained some amazing improvements on *Dragon Age: Origins*, while not surpassing it in every way or living up to every expectation I had. One being that BioWare has a good reputation for character creation and also NPC diversity (though not perfect). So, why is it that when the promos for the game were released, a character known to be of a non-white ethnicity turned out to be paper white? Isabela is a party member of your PC, and is a Captain Jack Sparrow-esque pirate who was bleached out when EA released the promo stills and trailer for the game [Trigger Warning for violence].

Resident Evil 5 released a Gold Edition of their already controversial game. The original cover for 360 featured Chris Redfield and Sheva Alomar, with Sheva's race and ethnicity listed at the RE5 wiki as African. When the Gold

Edition was released, Capcom changed the cover to feature series darling Jill Valentine and Chris Redfield, respectively, with this iteration's Jill being very fair and blond. And decked out in a very fetching battle suit. Jill was added as a playable character as downloadable content for the game, and only after achieving a certain point in the campaign with Sheva, who is a playable character throughout the entirety of the game, and actually has to help you rescue Jill (without going into too many spoilers). Wiping Sheva from the cover felt, um, awful. Sure, Jill has long been part of the franchise, but she wasn't this game's hero. She wasn't part of the team meant to come in and win against Albert Wesker once and for all.

When non-white people and people of color aren't represented in games, I wonder what conclusion is meant to be drawn. An easy message to glean from whitewashing of this type is that major companies don't believe that non-white folks are interested in playing games. I wonder if another message could be that gaming companies believe that they do not exist, or that they exist only to act as support staff or as enemies to a PC. It certainly doesn't mean that we stop enjoying the games that are offered to us, but seeing a body on the screen that represents or reflects our own certainly can enhance the enjoyable experience. I know it seems like a "little" thing, but all of these "little" things keep piling up, don't they?

READING REACTIONS

1. The author of this blog post focuses on disparities in multicultural and gender representations in video games. Why, according to the author, should game manufacturers care about this issue? What does a lack of diverse avatar representations mean to players?

2. To whom is the author referring when she bemoans the game industry's failure "to represent the rest of us"?

3. Dan states that "seeing a body on the screen that represents or reflects our own certainly can enhance the enjoyable experience" of gaming. How are visual representations and embodiment connected?

4. The author refers a few times to the option of designing one's avatar. Consider avatars you have played as or with. Do you prefer characters you create or characters you are given? Why?

5. What sorts of training should game designers have to address the issues Dan identifies?

6. Dan frequently uses phrases like "the rest of us" and "we." How does this strategy impact the author's tone and ethos?

7. What does the writer's frequent use of jargon and abbreviations like PC and NPC suggest about the audience for this blog and the goal of this piece?

● Julian Dibbell

Griefer Madness

Julian Dibbell is an American author and technology journalist writing on a range of topics, including "A Rape in Cyberspace," the evolution of online gaming worlds, social media, and cultural, political, and philosophical questions related to such technologies. He is a contributing editor for *Wired Magazine* and a nonresident fellow of the Center for Internet and Society at Stanford Law School.

The Albion Park section of Second Life is generally a quiet place, a haven of whispering fir trees and babbling brooks set aside for those who "need to be alone to think, or want to chat privately." But shortly after 5 pm Eastern time on November 16, an avatar appeared in the 3-D-graphical skies above this online sanctuary and proceeded to unleash a mass of undiluted digital jack-assery. The avatar, whom witnesses would describe as an African-American male clad head to toe in gleaming red battle armor, detonated a device that instantly filled the air with 30-foot-wide tumbling blue cubes and gaping cartoon mouths. For several minutes the freakish objects rained down, immobilizing nearby players with code that forced them to either log off or watch their avatars endlessly text-shout Arnold Schwarzenegger's "Get to the choppaaaaaaa!" tagline from *Predator*.

The incident, it turns out, was not an isolated one. The same scene, with minor variations, was unfolding simultaneously throughout the virtual geography of Second Life. Some cubes were adorned on every side with the infamous, soul-searing "goatse" image; others were covered with the grinning face of Bill Cosby proffering a Pudding Pop.

Soon after the attacks began, the governance team at San Francisco-based Linden Lab, the company that runs Second Life, identified the vandals and suspended their accounts. In the popular NorthStar hangout, players located the offending avatars and fired auto-cagers, which wrapped the attackers' heads in big metallic boxes. And at the Gorean city of Rovere—a Second Life island given over to a peculiarly hardcore genre of fantasy role-play gaming—a player named Chixxa Lusch straddled his giant eagle mount and flew up to confront the invaders avatar-to-avatar as they hovered high above his lovingly re-created medieval village, blanketing it with bouncing 10-foot high Super Mario figures.

"Give us a break you fucks," typed Chixxa Lusch, and when it became clear that they had no such intention, he added their names to the island's list of banned avatars and watched them disappear.

"Wankers," he added, descending into the mess of Super Marios they'd left behind for him to clear.

Bans and cages and account blocks could only slow the attackers, not stop them. The raiders, constantly creating new accounts, moved from one location to another throughout the night until, by way of a finale, they simultaneously crashed many of the servers that run Second Life. And by that time, there was not the slightest mystery in anyone's minds who these particular wankers were: The Patriotic Nigras had struck again.

The Patriotic Nigras consist of some 150 shadowy individuals who, in the words of their official slogan, have been "ruining your Second Life since 2006." Before that, many of them were doing their best to ruin Habbo Hotel, a Finland-based virtual world for teens inhabited by millions of squat avatars reminiscent of Fisher-Price's Little People toys. That's when the PNs adopted their signature dark-skinned avatar with outsize Afro and Armani suit.

Though real-life details are difficult to come by, it's clear that few, if any, PNs are in fact African-American. But their blackface shenanigans, they say, aren't racist in any heartfelt sense. "Yeah, the thing about the racist thing," says ^ban^, leader of the Patriotic Nigras, "is . . . it's all just a joke." It's only one element, he insists, in an arsenal of PN techniques designed to push users past the brink of moral outrage toward that rare moment—at once humiliating and enlightening—when they find themselves crying over a computer game. Getting that response is what it's all about, the Nigras say.

"We do it for the lulz," ^ban^ says—for laughs. Asked how some people can find their greatest amusement in pissing off others, ^ban^ gives the question a moment's thought: "Most of us," he says finally, with a wry chuckle, "are psychotic."

Pwnage, zerging, phat lewts—online gaming has birthed a rich lexicon. But none, perhaps, deserves our attention as much as the notion of the griefer. Broadly speaking, a griefer is an online version of the spoilsport—someone who takes pleasure in shattering the world of play itself. Not that griefers don't like online games. It's just that what they most enjoy about those games is making other players not enjoy them. They are corpse campers, noob baiters, kill stealers, ninja looters. Their work is complete when the victims log off in a huff.

Griefing, as a term, dates to the late 1990s, when it was used to describe the willfully antisocial behaviors seen in early massively multiplayer games like *Ultima Online* and first-person shooters like *Counter-Strike* (fragging your own teammates, for instance, or repeatedly killing a player many levels below you). But even before it had a name, grieferlike behavior was familiar in prehistoric text-based virtual worlds like LambdaMOO, where joyriding invaders visited "virtual rape" and similar offenses on the local populace.

While ^ban^ and his pals stand squarely in this tradition, they also stand for something new: the rise of organized griefing, grounded in online message-board communities and thick with in-jokes, code words, taboos, and an increasingly articulate sense of purpose. No longer just an isolated pathology, griefing has developed a full-fledged culture.

This particular culture's roots can be traced to a semi-mythic place of origin: the members-only message forums of Something Awful, an online humor site dedicated to a brand of scorching irreverence and gross-out wit that, in its eight years of existence, has attracted a fanatical and almost all-male following. Strictly governed by its founder, Rich "Lowtax" Kyanka, the site boasts more than 100,000 registered Goons (as members proudly call themselves) and has spawned a small diaspora of spinoff sites. Most noticeable is the anime fan community 4chan, with its notorious /b/ forum and communities of "/b/tards." Flowing from this vast ecosystem are some of the Web's most infectious memes and catchphrases ("all your base are belong to us" was popularized by Something Awful, for example; 4chan gave us lolcats) and online gaming's most exasperating wiseasses.

Not all the message boards celebrate the griefers in their midst: Kyanka finds griefing lame, as do many Goons and /b/tards. Nor do the griefers themselves all get along. Patriotic Nigras, /b/tards all, look on the somewhat better-behaved Goon community—in particular the W-Hats, a Second Life group open only to registered Something Awful members—as a bunch of uptight sellouts. The W-Hats disavow any affiliation with the "immature" and "uncreative" Nigras other than to ruefully acknowledge them as "sort of our retarded children."

If there's one thing, though, that all these factions seem to agree on, it's the philosophy summed up in a regularly invoked catchphrase: "The Internet is serious business."

Look it up in the Encyclopedia Dramatica (a wikified lexicon of all things /b/) and you'll find it defined as: "a phrase used to remind [the reader] that being mocked on the Internets is, in fact, the end of the world." In short, "the Internet is serious business" means exactly the opposite of what it says. It encodes two truths held as self-evident by Goons and /b/tards alike—that nothing on the Internet is so serious it can't be laughed at, and that nothing is so laughable as people who think otherwise.

To see the philosophy in action, skim the pages of Something Awful or Encyclopedia Dramatica, where it seems every pocket of the Web harbors objects of ridicule. Vampire goths with MySpace pages, white supremacist bloggers, self-diagnosed Asperger's sufferers coming out to share their struggles with the online world—all these and many others have been found guilty of taking themselves seriously and condemned to crude but hilarious derision.

You might think that the realm of online games would be exempt from the scorn of Goons and /b/tards. How seriously can anyone take a game, after all? And yet, if you've ever felt your cheeks flush with anger and humiliation when some 14-year-old Night Elf in virtual leather tights kicks your ass, then you know that games are the place where online seriousness and online ridiculousness converge most intensely. And it's this fact that truly sets the griefer apart from the mere spoilsport. Amid the complex alchemy of seriousness and play that makes online games so uniquely compelling, the griefer is the one player whose fun depends on finding that elusive edge where online levity starts to take on real-life weight—and the fight against serious business has finally made it seem as though griefers' fun might have something like a point. History has forgotten the name of the Something Awful Goon who first laid eyes on Second Life, but his initial reaction was undoubtedly along the lines of "Bingo."

It was mid-2004, and Goons were already an organized presence in online games, making a name for themselves as formidable players as well as flamboyantly creative griefers. The Goon Squad guilds in games like *Dark Age of Camelot* and *Star Wars: Galaxies* had been active for several years. In *World of Warcraft*, the legendary Goons of the Mal'ganis server had figured out a way to slay the revered nonplayer character that rules their in-game faction—an achievement tantamount to killing your own team mascot.

But Second Life represented a new frontier in troublemaking potential. It was serious business run amok. Here was an entire population of players that insisted Second Life was not a game—and a developer that encouraged them to believe it, facilitating the exchange of in-game Linden dollars for real money and inviting corporations to market virtual versions of their actual products.

And better still, here was a game that had somehow become the Internet's top destination for a specimen of online weirdo the Goons had long ago adopted as their favorite target: the Furries, with their dedication to role-playing the lives—and sex lives—of cuddly anthropomorphic woodland creatures.

Thus began the Second Life Goon tradition of jaw-droppingly offensive theme lands. This has included the re-creation of the burning Twin Towers (tiny falling bodies included) and a truly icky murdered-hooker crime scene (in which a hermaphrodite Furry prostitute lay naked, violated, and disemboweled on a four-poster bed, while an assortment of coded-in options gave the visitor chances for further violation). But the first and perhaps most expertly engineered of these provocations was Tacowood—a parody of the Furry region known as Luskwood. In Tacowood, rainbow-dappled woodlands have been overrun by the bulldozers and chain saws of a genocidal "defurrestation" campaign and populated with the corpses of formerly adorable cartoon animal folk now variously beheaded, mutilated, and nailed to crosses.

As the media hype around Second Life grew, the Goons began to aim at bigger targets. When a virtual campaign headquarters for presidential candidate John Edwards was erected, a parody site and scatological vandalism followed. When SL real estate magnate Anshe Chung announced she had accumulated more than $1 million in virtual assets and got her avatar's picture splashed across the cover of *BusinessWeek*, the stage was set for a Second Life goondom's spotlight moment: the interruption of a CNET interview with Chung by a procession of floating phalluses that danced out of thin air and across the stage.

People laughed at those attacks, but for Prokofy Neva, another well-known Second Life real estate entrepreneur, no amount of humor or creativity can excuse what she sees as "terrorism." Prokofy (Catherine Fitzpatrick in real life, a Manhattan resident, mother of two, and Russian translator and human-rights worker by trade) earns a modest but bankable income renting out her Second Life properties, and griefing attacks aimed at her, she says, have rattled some tenants enough to make them cancel their leases. Which is why her response to those who defend her griefers as anything but glorified criminals is blunt: "Fuck, this is a denial-of-service attack . . . it's anti-civilization . . . it's wrong . . . it costs me hundreds of US dollars."

Of course, this attitude delights the terrorists in question, and they've made Prokofy a favorite target. The 51-year-old Fitzpatrick's avatar is male, but Goons got ahold of a photo of her, and great sport has been made of it ever since. One build featured a giant Easter Island head of Fitzpatrick spitting out screenshots of her blog. Another time, Prokofy teleported into one of her rental areas and had the "very creepy" experience of seeing her own face looking straight down from a giant airborne image overhead.

Still, even the fiercest of Prokofy's antagonists recognize her central point: Once real money is at stake, "serious business" starts to look a lot like, well, serious business, and messing with it starts to take on buzz-killing legal implications. Pressed as to the legality of their griefing, PNs are quick to cite the distinction made in Second Life's own terms of service between real money and the "fictional currency" that circulates in-game. As ^ban^ puts it, "This is our razor-thin disclaimer which protects us in real-life" from what /b/tards refer to as "a ride in the FBI party van."

Real money isn't always enough to give a griefer pause, however. Sometimes, in fact, it's just a handy way of measuring exactly how serious the griefers' game can get.

Consider the case of the Avatar class Titan, flown by the Band of Brothers Guild in the massively multiplayer deep-space EVE Online. The vessel was far bigger and far deadlier than any other in the game. Kilometers in length and well over a million metric tons unloaded, it had never once been destroyed in combat. Only a handful of player alliances had ever acquired a Titan, and this one, in particular, had cost the players who bankrolled it in-game resources worth more than $10,000.

So, naturally, Commander Sesfan Qu'lah, chief executive of the GoonFleet Corporation and leader of the greater GoonSwarm Alliance—better known outside EVE as Isaiah Houston, senior and medieval-history major at Penn State University—led a Something Awful invasion force to attack and destroy it.

"EVE was designed to be a cold, hard, unforgiving world," explains EVE producer Sígurlina Ingvarsdóttir. It's this attitude that has made EVE uniquely congenial for Goons.

"The ability to inflict that huge amount of actual, real-life damage on someone is amazingly satisfying" says Houston. "The way that you win in EVE is you basically make life so miserable for someone else that they actually quit the game and don't come back."

And the only way to make someone that miserable is to destroy whatever virtual thing they've sunk the most real time, real money, and, above all, real emotion into. Find the player who's flying the biggest, baddest spaceship and paid for it with the proceeds of hundreds of hours mining asteroids, then blow that spaceship up. "That's his life investment right there," Houston says.

The Goons, on the other hand, fly cheap little frigates into battle, get blown up, go grab another ship, and jump back into the fight. Their motto: "We choke the guns of our enemies with our corpses." Some other players consider the tactic a less-than-sporting end run around a fair fight, still others call it an outright technical exploit, designed to lag the server so the enemy can't move in reinforcements.

Either way, it works, and the success just adds force to GoonFleet's true secret weapon: morale. "EVE is the only game I can think of in which morale is an actual quantifiable source of success," Houston says. "It's impossible to make another person stop playing or quit the game unless their spirit is, you know, crushed." And what makes the Goons' spirit ultimately uncrushable is knowing, in the end, that they're actually playing a different game altogether. As one GoonFleet member's online profile declared, "You may be playing EVE Online, but be warned: We are playing Something Awful."

The Internet is serious business, all right. And of all the ironies inherent in that axiom, perhaps the richest is the fate of the arch-Goon himself, Rich Kyanka. He started Something Awful for laughs in 1999, when he began regularly spotlighting an "Awful Link of the Day." He depends on revenue from SA to sustain not just himself but his pregnant wife, their 2-year-old daughter, two dogs, a cat, and the mortgage on a five-bedroom suburban mini-manor in Missouri. His foothold in the upper middle class rests entirely on the enduring comic appeal of goofy Internet crap.

Sitting in his comfortable basement office at the heart of the Something Awful empire, surrounded by more monitors than the job could possibly require and a growing collection of arch pop-surrealist paintings, Kyanka recounts some of the more memorable moments. Among them: numerous cease-and-desist letters from targets of SA's ridicule, threats of impending bodily harm from a growing community of rage-aholics permabanned from the SA forums, and actual bodily harm from B-movie director Uwe Boll. A onetime amateur boxer, Boll publicly challenged his online critics to a day of one-on-one real-world fights and then pummeled all who showed up, Kyanka among them. (See "Raging Boll," issue 14.12.)

Given that track record, you might think that a family man and sole breadwinner like Kyanka would be looking into another line of work by now. But he's still at it, proudly. "My whole mindset is, there are terrible things on the Internet: Can I write about them and transform them into something humorous?"

But ultimately, Kyanka's persistence is a testament to just how seriously he refuses to take the Internet seriously. Consider: When comments on the Web site of popular tech blogger Kathy Sierra escalated from anonymous vitriol to anonymous death threats last March, it sparked a story that inspired weeks of soul-searching and calls for uniform standards of behavior among bloggers and their communities. In response, Kyanka wrote a Something Awful column, which began with the question: "Can somebody please explain to me how is this news?"

Kyanka went on to review the long and bloodless history of death threats among Internet commenters, then revealed his own impressive credentials as a target: "I've been getting death threats for years now. I'm the king of online dying," he wrote. "Furries hate me, Juggalos hate me, script kiddies hate me, people banned from our forums hate me, people not banned from our forums hate me, people who hate people banned from our forums hate me . . . everybody hates me."

So far, so flip. But almost as an afterthought, Kyanka appended the text of a death threat sent from a banned ex-Goon, aimed not at him but at his infant daughter: "Collateral damage. Remember those words when I kick in your door, duct tape Lauren Seoul's mouth, fuck her in the ass, and toss her over a bridge."

Next to that text, Kyanka posted a photo of himself holding the smiling little girl. His evident confidence in his own safety, and that of the child in his arms, was strangely moving—in an unnerving sort of way.

Moving, and maybe even illuminating. In the end, no matter what they say, life on the Internet really is a serious business. It matters. But the tricky thing is that it matters above all because it mostly doesn't—because it conjures bits of serious human connection from an oceanic flow of words, pictures, videoclips, and other weightless shadows of what's real. The challenge is sorting out the consequential from the not-so-much. And, if Rich Kyanka's steely equanimity is any example, the antics of the Goons and /b/tards might actually sharpen our ability to make that distinction. To those who think the griefers' handiwork is simply inexcusable: Well, being inexcusable is, after all, the griefers' job. Ours is to figure out that caring too much only gives them more of the one thing they crave: the lulz.

READING REACTIONS

1. This article explores what Dibbell terms "digital jackassery". How would you define "griefing"? What role does it play in virtual gaming worlds? What role should it play?

2. The article profiles a particularly active griefer group known as the Patriotic Nigras. According to the author, none or nearly none of the members are actually African-American despite the clear racial implications of the group's name. In a virtual space where players can choose and create names and appearance, is it OK for these group members to use this name? Why or why not?

3. This reading explores the concepts of "griefing," "virtual rape," and the connection between players' offline lives and online avatars. Given these concepts, what are and should be the consequences of "willfully antisocial behaviors"?

4. Consider these lines from "Griefer Madness": "nothing on the Internet is so serious it can't be laughed at, and . . . nothing is so laughable as people who think otherwise." Do you agree? Why or why not?

5. Is taking over another player's avatar in a game the same as taking over a Facebook account? Why or why not?

6. Despite griefers' presence in many gaming worlds, Dibbell presents them as their own discourse community. What sort of specific examples does he offer to back up this argument?

7. What do you make of the author's tone in this article? Is Dibbell attempting neutrality, or is his article biased toward a particular group or way of life? Find instances where the author succeeds or fails to address counterarguments and a balance of sources.

Making word clouds of personal writing can be a fun way to experiment with non–image based avatars. A word cloud created by collecting a year's worth of Twitter or Facebook updates, for example, might allow users to track trends in their personal lives. Word clouds may also be useful in your academic life.

Consider pasting some of your own text or part of an article into a word cloud generator like Wordle.net or Tagcrowd.com to identify possible themes in the writing. Using such programs you can see what words are used most often in whatever piece of writing you are analyzing. Consider **Figure 5.4**, a Wordle depicting the most common words in the U.S. Constitution. How might word cloud software help you brainstorm possible research topics or start crafting thesis statements? Consider visiting a video game blog or forum. Pasting in a day's worth of posts on a particular topic or game space might help you begin to see themes or topics important to players in those gaming worlds and therefore possible starting places for your own scholarly critical examination of such a world.

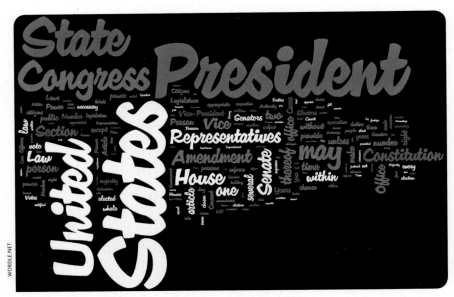

WORDLE.NET

Figure 5.4 US Constitution Wordle

Additional Writing and Composing Activities

SCHOLARLY ARTICLE REVIEW

The article review is intended to offer practice choosing and critiquing scholarship related to the field of new media and identity performance and construction. By carefully analyzing a published scholarly article (from a traditional academic journal, a peer-reviewed online journal, an edited collection, another scholarly publication), you will gain insight into the conventions of this genre as well as a better understanding of the scholarly conversation in the field.

First, choose an article to critically analyze. A good place to start looking for credible scholarly articles is a search engine at your school library—like Ebscohost, Lexis-Nexis, or Academic Search Premier. You may also want to check out some scholarly journals that focus on new media, such as *New Media and Society*, *Games Studies*, or *First Monday*. Write a review, paying special attention to the author's ethos, the use of appeals to logic and emotion, overall structure and clarity of the piece, and how the article contributes (or fails to contribute) to the scholarly discussion in the field. Tip: a clear, focused thesis statement is key to this assignment. You will want to make a judgment about the scholarship you are reviewing (It is useful because . . . , This piece fails because . . . , This scholarship reveals something new about . . .).

MEDIUM ANALYSIS

No game is neutral. Even the most mundane plotlines—like virtual farming or knocking over things with tiny cartoon birds—have clear values, linguistic and visual rhetorics, and rules of conduct. For this project you will critically analyze a specific new media world and related scholarship, along with your own observations of the world, to attend to the visual, linguistic, and discourse community conventions of that gaming world.

For this assignment, critically analyze a technology (for example, an online game, a gaming app, an online society like *Second Life*, or a software application related to gaming worlds). Pay special attention to the shared goals and purposes of people who use such technologies as well as to the language and communication conventions. Pay careful attention to the ways users craft identities through such technologies and ways such technologies shape identity. Keep in mind that it is not enough to summarize what you see in the virtual world. You need to make an argument about the virtual world you analyze.

Online Resources

Resources available through the English CourseMate for this text include the following:

Websites

Linden Research, Inc. *Second Life* Welcome page. "What Is Second Life?"

Clive Thompson. "Scientists Remount Milgram 'Shock' Experiment Using 3D Avatars."

Official *Halo Wars* Community Site

Blogs

Ars Technica Blog: Opposable Thumbs/ Gaming & Entertainment section

Jesper Juul. The Ludologist.

The Guardian. "Games Blog."

Henry Jenkins (author of *Convergence Culture*). "Confessions of an Aca-Fan: The Official Weblog of Henry Jenkins."

Game

Juliet Davis. *Polystyrene Dream.*

Virtual Spaces

Panoramic Virtual Tour. Smithsonian National Museum of Natural History

Journals and Resources

Games Studies

Eludamos

The Digital Games Research Association Homepage

Online Articles

Clive Thompson. "Me and My Big Dwarf Nose: A *Wired News* Column on Race in Online Games," *Collision Detection blog.*

Harold Goldberg. "How Video Games Have Shifted the Culture."

Community Engagement and Relations

Figure 6.1 Political science students paint church for service learning project

C. PAPPAS

Have you ever participated in a service project? You might have volunteered with a local community group like Big Brothers and Big Sisters, done a clean-up project for your city, or even completed mandatory volunteer hours to meet obligations for work or school. Many workplaces have a "day of service" to the community. High schools often require a certain amount of volunteer hours. Universities might set up "service-learning" opportunities, in which students serve a community or organization while learning a skill, usually pertinent to course material.

225

Each of these activities may build what scholar Robert Putnam, author of *Bowling Alone*, refers to as *social capital*: "By analogy with notions of physical capital and human capital—tools and training that enhance individual productivity—'social capital' refers to features of social organization such as networks, norms, and social trust that facilitate coordination and cooperation for mutual benefit." In other words, social capital is what allows us to rely on our neighbors and community members, and it therefore has great value.

Community Literacy

We can use the definitions of literacy (critical, media, information, visual, oral, cultural) from other chapters in this textbook to arrive at a sense of what it means to have community literacy. To be literate in community practices, to critically understand the different cultures, ethnicities, and diverse living situations of your community, you must make meaning of your environment by getting involved. Many people do this through activities like volunteering, which helps them decode the multicultural practices in their community. If we aren't able to "read" the people in our community, how are we to help those in need or critically determine the best practices for our cities? What difference can improved social capital mean to a community? What

> **CULTURES** What might a group of people, such as the political science students shown in **Figure 6.1**, learn from painting the exterior of a church in an impoverished neighborhood? How might this activity help people learn about the constituents of the church, the neighborhood, or even political science or teamwork?

> **TECHNOLOGIES** Visit the English CourseMate for this text for a tutorial on accessing the most recent census data for your community. What information about your state, county, or city surprises you? Are the poverty rates high or low? Are the ethnic and racial numbers what you expected?

role can a diverse group of people or volunteers play in your community or on your campus?

Global Literacy

Whereas people might seek community literacy by engaging with their local communities, many people serve in other countries to express their *global* citizenship and increase their cultural literacy. Many believe that visiting other countries and building houses or schools shows the people of those countries that U.S. values and our citizenship practices extend to other countries because we are all citizens of the globe. To be successful, however, such

COMMUNITIES Analyze **Figure 6.2.** What can you assume about the organization portrayed in the image? How does the image enhance the accompanying textual information? How does the image reflect the mission of the organization? Can you predict what standard colors or logos the organization might use?

Research your own community to find an organization that serves globally and that you are interested in joining or helping. What services does it provide? How does it choose its constituents? What is its mission? What kind of help does it need? What skills can you offer?

Figure 6.2 Habitat for Humanity International website

projects (especially those outside the United States) must account for the community practices, rules, values, and goals.

How can we learn the practices and values of cultures and communities across the globe? We must take time to critically analyze how the culture distributes social, political, and economic power and trace the history of inequities and the current inequities that affect those communities. We must learn about the diversity of the people of the globe, about differences in gender, religion and ethnicity, and so on. We must connect with ourselves and understand our own position within the larger systems of global privilege. To be globally literate or a global citizen is to want to share your culture and reciprocate by learning about other cultures. It is to want to understand the physical and cultural borders of, and to commit to, critical awareness of those differences. Once you educate yourself about a community different from your own, you'll develop an understanding of the importance of your obligation to respond to and respect the differing needs of the greater community of humans and the globe.

Think about the work our military does globally. Many Americans, even those against the war in Iraq, are happy to see our military rebuilding schools and facilitating leadership programs so our countries can work together in the future to make world relations more manageable for all of us. Building relations globally, even at the level of the everyday citizen, helps us engage in practices that make our cultures understand each other at a more personal level. The hope is that this understanding and engagement will build global literacy and citizenship.

Defining Valuable Community Service

Emma Zink of *The Daily Utah Chronicle* argues that self-interest is often students' main motivation in service learning projects. In her article "An Outsider's Mentality: Community Projects Scream for Engaged Volunteers," she explains that most students expect service to help shape their image on a resume and to make them feel good about being a good citizen, but what they often don't consider is whether or not the community members are empowered to effect change themselves through participation in such a program. Zink would argue that meaningful service happens when the change comes from within the community, not from outside volunteers.[1]

Another definition of meaningful community service is implied in **Figure 6.3**, also available through the English CourseMate for this text.

Writing a definition essay or using a definition in an essay is a common practice in college writing. Often, instructors use the terms *denotation* and *connotation* when discussing use of definitions in essays. *Denotations* are what you might find if you look up a term in a dictionary or even on Wikipedia.

Figure 6.3 Thin vs. Thick Service

Denotation is usually pretty clear-cut. *Connotation* is much more variable and has to do with a term's common associations. For instance, the denotative meanings of the words "home" and "house" are similar, but the connotative meanings are more complex. The word "home" connotes something more personal. The same goes for "stomach" and "belly." Both refer to the same part of the body, but "belly" often has a negative connotation.

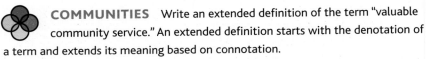

CULTURES   Analyze Figure 6.3. What definitions does the author imply for "thick" and "thin"? What is the difference between meaningful and meaningless "service"? What might your community define as meaningful service? How could you make the current service projects in your life less disruptive and more genuine? What does this image try to say about the importance of community literacy? How does the artist's use of sarcasm foster her argument?

COMMUNITIES   Write an extended definition of the term "valuable community service." An extended definition starts with the denotation of a term and extends its meaning based on connotation.

For instance, "house" and "home" are similarly defined. Both are a place or structure in which a person or group of people live. However, in the case of "home," the connotation extends to something more personal or shared with someone. When I ask my brother if he is going "home," he knows I mean our parents' house because we share a past in that structure. However, when I ask the same question of my spouse, he knows I mean our house. Therefore, the relationship you have with someone, as well as what the structure means to both of you personally, affects the connotation of the word "home" and affects how "house" and "home" are used in conversation and by definition.

For this assignment, try some of the following techniques to develop the connotation of "valuable community service": indicate how the term relates to a literacy practice, compare and/or contrast the term to "volunteering," give an example, use a metaphor, discuss cause and effect, or use negation (explain what the term is *not*). Most importantly, consider your audience so you connect with them.

It's perfectly appropriate to support your definition by using some of the readings presented later in this chapter. Just be sure to document the sources you use both within your essay (this is often called internal documentation or parenthetical documentation) and on a works cited page or bibliography at the end of your essay. Remember: research is supposed to *enhance* your own commentary and ideas, not overwhelm them.

Readings

The readings for this chapter include articles that feature definitions, proclamations, or missions, and ideas for how to incorporate valuable service and community engagement into a classroom or an individual's life. "What Is Service Learning?" offers a definition of service learning and explains why service is vital to the success of a community. President Barack Obama's proclamation names September 11th as a Patriot Day and National Day of Service and Remembrance. He asks Americans to participate in community service to honor those who died serving their country on that day. In "How Higher Education Is Integrating Diversity and Service Learning: Findings from Four Case Studies," Vogelgesang defines service learning but also discusses its connections to diversity studies and multicultural education.

The National Service-Learning Clearinghouse Disaster Services website not only stipulates its objectives but also provides several links (see the English CourseMate for this text) to guides, strategic plans, and preparation and relief services appropriate to service learning activities. Robert Putnam's article "The Prosperous Community: Social Capital and Public Life" details the importance of social capital in the success of a community. He claims that "If we want prosperity, we might begin by working to restore the fabric of community."

COMMUNITIES   Find out more about an organization you belong to. What documents does it require to function and be officially recognized by your university or the parent organization? Usually, the organization's sponsor or the university student activities office or student issues office keeps copies of these documents. Does your organization meet all the current requirements? Do you think the mission or bylaws or any other document needs to be updated or added to the required documents? Even if documents aren't required or don't need to be updated, what revisions would you make? If you make a revision, consider including a clause about community relations, diversity, and multiculturalism that incorporates the direct constituents of the group and the community.

What Is Service Learning?

Learn and Serve America is a program associated with the Corporation for National and Community Service (http://www.nationalservice.gov) that "enables over one million students to make meaningful contributions to their community while building their academic and civic skills." By involving students in service learning early, the organization hopes to encourage them to serve throughout their lives. The following reading is posted on the Learn and Serve America website.

Service-learning offers a unique opportunity for America's young people—from kindergarten to college students—to get involved with their communities in a tangible way by integrating service projects with classroom learning. Service-learning engages students in the educational process, using what they learn in the classroom to solve real-life problems. Students not only learn about democracy and citizenship, they become actively contributing citizens and community members through the service they perform.

Service-learning can be applied across all subjects and grade levels; it can involve a single student or group of students, a classroom or an entire school. Students build character and become active participants as they work with others in their school and community to create service projects in areas like education, public safety, and the environment.

WHY IS SERVICE-LEARNING IMPORTANT?

A national study of Learn and Serve America programs suggests that effective service-learning programs improve grades, increase attendance in school, and develop students' personal and social responsibility. A growing body of research recognizes service-learning as an effective strategy to help students by:

• Promoting learning through active participation in service experiences;

• Providing structured time for students to reflect by thinking, discussing and writing about their service experience;

• Providing an opportunity for students to use skills and knowledge in real-life situations;

• Extending learning beyond the classroom and into the community; and

• Fostering a sense of caring for others.

Service-learning also strengthens both education and local communities by:

• Building effective collaborative partnerships between schools or colleges and other institutions and organizations.

Learn and Serve America, "What Is Service-Learning?" *http://www.learnandserve.gov.*

- Engaging parents and other adults in supporting student learning.
- Meeting community needs through the service projects conducted.
- Providing engaging and productive opportunities for young people to work with others in their community.

READING REACTIONS

1. According to this site, what role can service play in the classroom?
2. What does the site argue about the benefits of service? According to this site, how does service help citizens think critically?
3. What arguments do you agree or disagree with? Why?
4. How might any of the listed objectives be used in your classroom or align with the subject matter in your course?
5. How might writing a reflection about community service help students understand their contribution to the community?

● Barack Obama

Presidential Proclamation. "Patriot Day and National Day of Service and Remembrance."

President Barack Obama's proclamation for a National Day of Service was meant to change the commemoration of September 11th from one of tragedy and loss to one of patriotism and service. In this way, President Obama attempted to shift the definition of *patriotism* from simple honor and pride in the United States to include service, unity, and goodwill to all citizens.

In the aftermath of the terrorist attacks of September 11, 2001, the American people demonstrated that in times of hardship, the values that define us do not simply endure—they are stronger than ever. As a Nation, we responded to unthinkable tragedy with an outpouring of service and goodwill. On that dark day, first responders rushed into a burning Pentagon and climbed the stairs of smoking towers on the verge of collapse, while citizens risked their own health and safety to prevent further heartbreak and destruction. As Americans, we came together to help our country recover and rebuild.

Figure 6.4 President Obama serves food at S.O.M.E.

Barack Obama, "Patriot Day and National Day of Service and Remembrance," September 9, 2011.

Today, we pay tribute to the selfless heroes and innocent victims of September 11, 2001, and we reaffirm the spirit of patriotism, service, and unity that we felt in the days and months that followed. By volunteering our time and unique skills, we can enrich communities across our country, and together, we can strengthen our Nation to meet the challenges of the 21st century.

In the days to come, I ask all Americans to join together in serving their communities and neighborhoods in honor of the victims of the September 11 attacks. Today and throughout the year, scores of Americans answer the call to make service a way of life—from helping the homeless to teaching underserved students to bringing relief to disaster zones. I encourage all Americans to visit Serve.gov, or Servir.gov for Spanish speakers, to learn more about service opportunities across our country.

As we join in serving causes greater than ourselves and honoring those we lost, we are reminded of the ways that the victims of 9/11 live on—in the people they loved, the lives they touched, and the courageous acts they inspired. On Patriot Day and National Day of Service and Remembrance, we pledge to carry on their legacy of courage and compassion, and to move forward together as one people.

By a joint resolution approved December 18, 2001 (Public Law 107-89), the Congress has designated September 11 of each year as "Patriot Day," and by Public Law 111-13, approved April 21, 2009, the Congress has requested the observance of September 11 as an annually recognized "National Day of Service and Remembrance."

NOW, THEREFORE, I, BARACK OBAMA, President of the United States of America, do hereby proclaim September 11, 2011, as Patriot Day and National Day of Service and Remembrance. I call upon all departments, agencies, and instrumentalities of the United States to display the flag of the United States at half-staff on Patriot Day and National Day of Service and Remembrance in honor of the individuals who lost their lives on September 11, 2001. I invite the Governors of the United States and the Commonwealth of Puerto Rico and interested organizations and individuals to join in this observance. I call upon the people of the United States to participate in community service in honor of those our Nation lost, to observe this day with appropriate ceremonies and activities, including remembrance services, and to observe a moment of silence beginning at 8:46 a.m. Eastern Daylight Time to honor the innocent victims who perished as a result of the terrorist attacks of September 11, 2001.

IN WITNESS WHEREOF, I have hereunto set my hand this ninth day of September, in the year of our Lord two thousand eleven, and of the Independence of the United States of America the two hundred and thirty-sixth.

1. What types of activities does the president suggest for this day?
2. What does the president hope to accomplish by making an official proclamation?
3. What does the president argue and/or define in his proclamation?
4. What does it mean to "make service a way of life"?
5. What does the president mean by "serving causes greater than ourselves"? What types of opportunities in your community might constitute the kind of service the president refers to?
6. In the proclamation, the president says, "I encourage all Americans to visit Serve. gov, or Servir.gov for Spanish speakers, to learn more about service opportunities across our country." This is an obvious rhetorical move to include diverse ethnic groups and multicultural communities in the Day of Service. Why is this included? What does this say about President Obama's stake in community relations?
7. How might your class serve a greater cause but still stay within the learning objectives of the course? Draft a petition for a proclamation for a Day of Service for the university to consider.

Lori J. Vogelgesang, M. Drummond, S.K. Gilmartin

How Higher Education Is Integrating Diversity and Service Learning: Findings from Four Case Studies

This article is prefaced by directors of the California Campus Compact, an organization that focuses on service learning in higher education. In this study, the authors claim that service learning practices continue to benefit the community even after the required service is completed. Additionally, the study shows that service also engages students as responsible community members and that recruiting university members of color helps facilitate community dialogue.

PREFACE

As California struggles to address the complex issues of diversity in this state—race, economics, gender, religion, and sexual orientation, to name a few—it is critical that the education system in the state prepare students to be conscientious, aware, and engaged citizens. In recent years, both service-learning and multicultural education have been seen as effective ways to

Lori J. Vogelgesang, M. Drummond, S.K. Gilmartin, "How Higher Education is Integrating Diversity and Service Learning: Findings from Four Case Studies," San Francisco: CA, *Campus Compact 2003.* Copyright © 2003 by CA Campus Compact. All rights reserved. Reproduced by permission.

achieve this goal. While many have noted the strong link between the two fields, rarely have academicians and practitioners in either field focused on establishing strong collaborative partnerships between the two.

It is important to note that in implementing service learning, diversity exists "within and between higher education cultures and grassroots community cultures" (Langseth, 2000 p. 252). Service-learning programs operate within complex, diverse environments. This is the underlying assumption in the importance of addressing the connections between service learning and diversity. Students matriculate to colleges from all over the state and nation, increasing the likelihood that the student body population may be quite different from the communities these institutions work with. This makes exploring the issue of diversity between campus and community even more relevant and important (Cone, 2001).

With funding from The James Irvine Foundation, California Campus Compact (CACC) designed the Community/University Initiative on Diversity, Equity, and Service (IDEAS) program, focusing on the integration of diversity and service learning in higher education. The goal of this program was to encourage collaborative efforts between and across institutions around diversity and service learning. Through this goal we hoped to: 1) build the capacity of the independent sector of California higher education to increase focus on and integration of diversity and service-learning education, and 2) prepare all students for participation and leadership in a diverse society.

One major component of this project was a research study designed to examine issues of collaboration and how service learning and diversity work might be more closely connected from an institutional perspective. Although this research project concentrated on four independent colleges and universities in California, we believe that the information gleaned from this study will be informative for a variety of institutions.

Elaine K. Ikeda, Ph.D.
Executive Director
California Campus Compact

Joy Bianchi Brown, M.Ed.
Associate Director
California Campus Compact

SECTION ONE: BACKGROUND OF THE STUDY

Defining Service Learning and Diversity for this Study

For the purposes of this study, we let participants use the vocabulary they were most comfortable with around these issues; we didn't ask them to define terms. As we report the findings, though, it is necessary to balance the use of different terms with writing that is clear and somewhat consistent. So we spend just a moment here to address this particular language issue.

A good deal of the work around diversity issues on campus is understood in the context of multicultural education, and offices of multicultural education are commonly the administrative home for diversity programs. Although the word "diversity" and "multiculturalism" are not synonymous, they are used somewhat interchangeably when discussing learning outcomes and campus climate. Similarly, we use them in this report in interchangeable contexts.

The term "service learning" likewise holds different meanings for people, and some resist even using the word "service." Some would prefer the term "community-based learning," others argue for a broader language such as "civic engagement." Here we mostly use the term "service learning" and are referring to course-based community work done by students. Clearly, the principles, supports, and challenges to this work are applicable to broader work as well, and we want to focus on these broader issues.

History of Service Learning and Multicultural Education Movements

Both the service learning and diversity movements challenge the traditional curriculum and way of doing things in higher education. In other words, both are potentially transformative approaches because they call for radical change in the way we think about learning and teaching. It is apparent that both service learning and multiculturalism are often marginalized on campus. However, there are some differences in how this marginalization gets enacted, and a brief look at the history of these movements can help us understand why.

Multiculturalism emerges from the civil rights movement of the 1960s (O'Grady, 2001); service learning, by comparison, draws from the work of Dewey, experiential education and community action programs of the 1960s and 1970s (Stanton, Giles & Cruz, 1999). Neither movement is monolithic, but both have at least some roots in social justice issues. Indeed, as is discussed in this report, social justice concerns can be the focus of work when diversity and service learning efforts are coordinated. Certainly among service-learning practitioners, there is not general agreement on social justice as the primary outcome of the practice. There is much evidence that other outcomes (enhanced learning for students, for instance) have been the aim of mainstream practitioners. Likewise, some proponents of diversity work focus on the ways in which diversity enhances learning for all students, while others place more emphasis on social justice issues of inequity in educational access and outcomes for different groups.

Although both movements have roots in the social movements of the 1960s and 1970s, service learning enjoys a great deal of visible federal support—both financial and verbal—and has grown dramatically in the last decade. By contrast, notes O'Grady, multicultural education with its focus on oppression has received less support and has been viewed by many as "too radical or as divisive" (2001, p. 13). This reality has implications for collaborations between the two fields, and some of this study's findings can be better understood in light of this history.

Theoretical Framework

The literature on intersections between multiculturalism and service learning discusses how both can enhance student learning and contribute to a greater social good. The focus is on student learning, in the context of supporting students' intellectual and social development as they engage in service learning—both the classroom and the community elements. Understanding the pedagogical implications of this work is essential, but what is missing is the organizational perspective on how one integrates the two bodies of work administratively. This study and the larger IDEAS project are designed to explore issues of how service learning and diversity work might be more closely connected from an institutional perspective. Thus, in collecting data for these case studies, we sought to carefully hear and understand how organizational factors such as the leadership, the academic culture, and institutional values work to shape the environment in which both diversity and service-learning work happens. We also heard about the ways in which external forces (e.g. funding) play a catalytic role in these collaborations.

Methodology

In order to frame the issues from an organizational perspective, we employ a case study method of inquiry. In November and December of 2001, we visited four independent institutions in California, gathering documentation and interviewing faculty, administrators, and students who were engaged in the work of service learning, multicultural education, or both. Three of the universities are Catholic institutions, and the fourth is not religiously affiliated. All are located in racially, socioeconomically and otherwise diverse urban communities. For the purposes of masking specific institutional identities, we refer to all institutions as universities.

SECTION TWO: FINDINGS FROM THE CASE STUDIES

As might be expected, we heard faculty and staff discuss some issues that appeared to be common across all four institutions. These issues have to do with challenges facing those attempting to facilitate organizational change in general such as resistance to change and limited resources. Other issues raised more narrowly address the fields of service and diversity, such as language and politics around the appropriateness and efficacy of investing in such efforts in higher education. But we also heard numerous examples of collaborations and barriers to collaborations that seem to be a result of the specific institutional culture or individuals on a particular campus. After examining organizational factors in general, we present some promising practices that emerged from one or more institutions visited.

Clearly, combining service and diversity work happens outside of collaborations between the offices that coordinate such work. This common-sense observation was confirmed by our site visits. For instance, one service-learning center has always had a social justice focus, and included training and other reflections that incorporate issues of diversity, but this work hasn't historically involved the diversity office on that campus. Similarly, a good number of faculty we spoke with either are or were incorporating service and diversity into their courses without direct support from either office. One might legitimately ask if there is indeed any unique benefit to strengthening collaborations at the organizational level between service learning and diversity. This study examines the relationship between these informal means of incorporating diversity and service learning and the more formal organizational collaborations between offices.

In this section, we examine diversity and service work on these four campuses from several perspectives of the educational organization, including institutional mission, leadership, academic culture, and structural organization. We then discuss findings around issues of collaborations and partnerships, external funding, and assessment before presenting some promising practices.

Institutional Mission

In general, the missions of all four institutions support engaging in both diversity and community-based work. This was framed as working for a socially just world, cultivating responsible citizens, or educating students to provide leadership in a more interdependent world. At one institution the mission statement was revised right before we visited. The changes in mission statement were crafted under the direction of a new president. The new mission statement notes that the university aims to be a "diverse, socially responsible learning community of high quality scholarship and academic rigor . . ." The same statement includes the university value: "a culture of service that respects and promotes the dignity of every person." It would be interesting to visit this school again in five years to see if staff, students and faculty find that changes in the mission and values statements lead to stronger support for work that integrates diversity and service.

In comparison, another institution's mission statement does not address diversity and curricular service so directly. Indeed, one person noted that the (recently revised) mission statement of the university actually does not employ vocabulary that supports the notion of community work for social justice. Nonetheless, notes the participant, faculty engaged in community-based work seem to assume the mission includes a social justice goal, because it is a Catholic institution and social justice is part of that church's teachings. Zlotkowski reminds us that successful (service-learning) programs "draw upon the institution's own understanding of its fundamental mission" (1998; p. 9). In this case, then, faculty understanding of the fundamental mission appeared to go beyond the actual words written in the mission.

Leadership

At all four universities, we heard administrators and faculty members discuss the critical role that support from top leadership has played in the success they have experienced. Whether this support came in the form of verbal recognition, financial support for grant initiatives as the grant closed out, or a president or provost really being a source of inspiration and passion for these efforts, participants in this study articulated the importance of the institution's formal leadership in making a place for their work in the surrounding community.

Where there are separate offices for service learning and diversity, the importance of support from "the top" was expressed more directly by those in service learning than by those doing diversity work. It is not so much that the latter group experienced less support (though some did). Rather, they tempered their remarks with comments about how much work still remains to be done, and how very difficult it is for the campus community to have open dialogue—much less visible action—around diversity initiatives. As one participant wryly remarked about the campus, "Diversity is separate from everything." This supports O'Grady's (2001) observation that diversity issues may be more contested and thus more politically sensitive than are those around service learning.

Although there was widespread agreement that more needs to be done, there were also examples where the institutional leaders strived to incorporate diversity into not only service experiences, but to make diversity meaningful across the curriculum and indeed the institution. At one institution this was done in part through revising the mission statement. At another there was a strategic reorganization of the institution to align itself with the institutional values. Here the service-learning and diversity offices both fall under the supervision of a high ranking academic administrator who has inspired and supported the staff in both offices, and been a critical force in increasing the number of faculty members who include a community-based opportunity for students in their classes.

One participant in the study noted that there is a certain "plateau" that has been reached at the institution; the diversity initiatives so far are seen as successful, but deeper cultural change is not something that university administrators have been trained to lead. Since there was widespread agreement on the importance of top administrators supporting this work, this observation raises some important issues about the possibilities for further cultural changes at the university. How do proponents of these change efforts push the boundaries of institutional culture when leaders do not have the skills to facilitate these difficult discussions and indeed, institutional "soul-searching"? Is there a fundamental difference when the change effort is conceived of by "the middle"— the service-learning director or diversity director or both—and supported by top administrators versus a top administrator (e.g. provost or president) envisioning the change and moving the institution in that direction?

Framing Diversity and Service Learning Around Forming Community Partnerships

Several institutions' service-learning centers combine diversity and service learning by framing their work around campus and/or community partnerships. We only saw one diversity office framing its vision around partnerships, although at an additional institution the diversity office provided a framework for cultural competency that the service-learning office employs. We describe the service-learning partnerships first, followed by the approach of the diversity office.

There is, in several cases, a core set of community partners with whom the service-learning office has formed partnerships. These offices have a group of community representatives who function as part of an advisory board, and this is part of a commitment to long-term partnerships with these agencies. In this way, according to administrators, the relationships formed between the institution and the community move in the direction of being more authentically reciprocal. At the same time, moreover, the community partners are committed to working with the university to see that issues of diversity are addressed in appropriate ways, through giving feedback on course materials, providing orientations or training, or working with the service-learning center to make long-term plans.

One service-learning office identified the neighborhood adjacent to the campus as a place where the institution should have a visible presence. By having clear goals of cultivating the relationships here, the office has created a "niche" and is able to speak clearly to what is working and what the goals for the future of the partnership are. The community task force, initiated by some external funding several years ago, continues to be a critical part of planning. At another institution the geographic area served is more broadly defined, but the service-learning office maintains a set of core partnerships that reflect long-term commitments. In both cases, though, community representatives play important roles in decision-making by the service-learning office.

In contrast, another institution has a structure much more typical in higher education. The service-learning officer here serves more as a broker of information for faculty and students, as well as the coordinating body for faculty workshops. The language here, then, appears to be based on providing resources to faculty and students to enhance their work.

Typically the diversity office work was focused on recruiting and supporting students and faculty of color, and facilitating campus dialogues around diversity issues. We only saw one case where the diversity office included community service in its vision statements. Here there was a formal connection to the service-learning office and community as partners in addressing issues of multiculturalism. One of the functions of the partnership is to disperse grant monies associated with a campus-wide initiative to enhance multiculturalism. The self-evaluation of this model was positive, but there is concern expressed that the committee is viewed by the campus community primarily as a source of funding for programs. Nonetheless, this is an example of a diversity office creating an organizational link to a service-learning office.

External Funding

External funding has served an important role in the work of several of the universities we visited. We heard mixed reviews of whether programs started with grant money were subsequently institutionalized by the university, but this appeared to be happening at least some of the time. Not surprisingly these participants talked about James Irvine Foundation grants, but other sources were mentioned as well, especially by staff in service-learning offices. James Irvine Foundation grants targeting diversity initiatives provided opportunities for collaboration between community-based work and diversity work on several campuses. In turn, these collaborations have provided some models for how diversity and service work might be combined. Ultimately, focusing on the institution as community citizen, or approaching community involvement from a social justice perspective appear to be strong models for sustaining relationships between diversity work and service work.

One aspect of external funding that appears to be important is when a foundation is willing to fund successive efforts at the same institution, and fund the institution generously enough to put in place a position or some substantial programs that can make a noticeable impact. Several programs are funded by generous endowments, allowing the offices to make long-term plans and commitments. Although no one indicated they felt they had "enough" money to do the work they wanted to do, offices that were now institutionally funded or secured by an endowment didn't express the uncertainty of even being around, much less worrying about specific programs.

Funding successive efforts, as the James Irvine Foundation has done, also seemed to be effective in that it allowed for a learning curve at the institutional level. The second or third grants that institutions are implementing have characteristics of working on institutional change. At one university, for instance, the process of writing the proposal to the James Irvine Foundation changed dramatically after the first grant, and several people we spoke with noted it went from a rather "patchwork" approach of funding a variety of institutional programs to a clear plan of how each initiative proposed across campus fit with an overall goal. The subsequent funding, then, enabled the university to reflect on what worked and where the institution was headed, and then to get funding to implement the next steps.

One person we spoke with raised some interesting questions about the "agenda" that gets defined by the funding agency. To what extent, he wondered, does the money drive how the institution defines these partnerships, defines diversity? Is it just racial/ethnic diversity? Or is there space for broader conceptualizations and programs to meet a variety of needs? Interestingly, the offices of diversity tend to be defined around creating inclusive climates on campus, but much of their work can be around recruiting and supporting non-white faculty and students. In this case diversity gets defined narrowly. But from a curricular perspective, a number of faculty and administrators noted the impossibility of untangling one aspect from the complexity of the whole person.

Assessment of Diversity and Service Work

There was no one we spoke with who appeared satisfied with the amount and quality of assessment efforts regarding student learning or the programs. Discussing assessment brings up numerous issues. It highlights the lack of consensus around what "diversity" and "service" mean and whether they are appropriate terms. In other words, how do you decide what to measure? It also highlights the ways in which education is contested in general by asking such questions as: What should students be learning? How should they be learning (what methods work best)? What is the role of education in social change? The participants in this study were passionate and eloquent when discussing their hopes for education as a vehicle for social change and why they do what they do. They know these viewpoints are not mainstream faculty perspectives, and that the majority of their colleagues do not engage in their approach to learning.

One faculty member we spoke with also explored the dilemma of the risk faculty take to teach a course dealing with service and diversity, when faculty rewards are based on evaluation of their teaching. How can an institution make it safe to try this sometimes difficult approach? What happens when a faculty member tries something and it doesn't work so well?

Assessment of a partnership—from an organizational perspective—was apparent only in one case where an external source was funding the work of the diversity office. Here the diversity office undertook some partnership evaluation, albeit fairly informal, and reported findings as part of the grant report.

Discussions on assessment also bring up issues of funding and institutional support. It is expensive and time consuming to do assessment well, and these programs struggle with the issue. Several people told us that assessment was what needed most attention, in large part to document the efficacy of these marginalized ways of teaching.

Promising Practices

In this section we summarize some of the practices we heard about that have the potential to be models for other institutions engaged in integrating diversity work with service learning. Each institution we visited has some promising practices which are a function of that individual institution, but also have elements that might be translated to other institutions:

- Use community-centered partnership language to pull in a multicultural perspective more readily. When the partnership is the focus, it's easier to "make sense of" the necessity of understanding community needs, which must address socioeconomic and cultural differences.

- Work to ensure that offices doing diversity and service-learning work report to (the same) high ranking academic officers, centering the collaborations around enhancing diversity and service learning in the curriculum and deepening faculty commitment to this issue.

- Create a structure that brings together the offices of diversity and service learning. A formal partnership to accomplish certain goals can strengthen collaborative efforts and serve to define collaborations.

- Develop a diversity office that has a broad mandate to influence curricular aspects of diversity—broadly defined—as well as the structural aspects such as recruitment and retention of students and faculty of color.

- Connect the work of both offices closely and clearly with the institutional mission. This is necessary but not sufficient, as it appears that the role of support from top administrators is also critical. However, support can come most strongly from the top when initiatives are clearly seen as doing the work the university sees as core to its mission.

A Few Remaining Questions

A focus on community partnerships can provide a vehicle for integrating diversity and service, but such a focus did not guarantee that the office for diversity/multicultural issues was directly engaged in the partnership. An issue worth examining in light of community partnerships, information brokering, and all functions of a service-learning office is the implication that efforts at integrating service and diversity have for the organization. To what extent is it beneficial or necessary for organizational structures (i.e. diversity and service-learning offices) to collaborate? Could the objective of integrating multicultural perspectives in a service-learning experience be accomplished without the support of the office that coordinates diversity efforts? These issues will need to be addressed as institutional representatives tackle them on each campus.

The case studies shed light on a variety of ways in which higher education institutions are trying to understand how to be responsible community members. The diverse organizational arrangements and histories mean different challenges and opportunities for collaboration, and differences in the goals and perspectives of the service-learning and diversity offices. Issues of language and the extent to which the work of the offices is seen as too "political" or too "radical" vary, depending on the programs and also on the institutional culture. The collaborations between offices (where separate offices exist) often depend on individuals and, to a certain extent, leadership, as organizational structures in place might actually support or work against strong collaborations. External funding can play a catalyst role in developing such relationships as well as provide an opportunity to try new ideas. It does appear that when faculty and administrators can focus their work around issues of social justice, community engagement and community partnerships, the language they embrace seems to support the development of opportunities for enhanced collaboration.

Faculty and staff at the sites we visited were committed to this kind of work. This commitment will have to be translated to an organizational commitment to service and diversity as integral components of student learning. Without such an institutional commitment, efforts to integrate diversity and service learning will depend on who is interested in the issue at that moment. Mission statements are an important anchor for this work, but including such goals in the mission statement is no guarantee that support will be provided to fund such efforts.

SECTION FOUR: REFERENCES

Cone, R. (2001). Personal communication.

Langseth, M. (2000). *Maximizing impact, minimizing harm: Why service-learning must more fully integrate multicultural education.* In C.R. O'Grady (Ed.), *Integrating service learning and multicultural education in colleges and universities.* Mahwah, NJ: Lawrence Erlbaum Associates.

O'Grady, C. R. (2000). *Integrating service learning and multicultural education in colleges and universities.* Lawrence Erlbaum Associates, Inc.

Stanton, T. K., Giles, D. G., & Cruz, N. (1999). *Service learning: a movement's pioneers reflect on its origins, practice and future.* San Francisco: Jossey-Bass.

Zlotkowski, E. (Ed.) (1998). *Successful service-learning programs: New models of excellence for higher education.* Bolton, MA: Anker Publishing Co.

READING REACTIONS

1. Vogelgesang's research shows that strong ties to community are most likely to form when the service-learning organization makes long-term relationships with the community constituents. Why do you think this is true? How do long-term relationships benefit both the community and the school?

2. What types of connections did Vogelgesang find between service learning and culture studies, diversity studies, and/or multicultural education?

3. How does Vogelgesang's research redefine service learning?

4. What connections did Vogelgesang's research make between valuable service-learning projects and course objectives? Did funding play any role? Why?

5. According to Vogelgesang, what was the role of social justice in service-learning projects?

6. How does Vogelgesang's article relate to other readings in this chapter in terms of meaningful service-learning projects?

Disaster Services, National Service-Learning Clearinghouse

The Corporation for National and Community Service calls itself "America's Most Comprehensive Service-Learning Resource." The following text is its clearinghouse's strategic plan for service learning. Seeing a strategic-plan model can help you make decisions on how to build your own model, what to include, and what to value.

On February 8, 2011, the Board of Directors of the Corporation for National and Community Service (CNCS) unanimously approved the agency's 2011–2015 Strategic Plan. The Strategic Plan provides a roadmap for using national service to address critical challenges facing our communities and our nation.

The plan recognizes that national service will have its greatest impact if we target resources on a core set of critical problems and carefully measure our progress.

The Strategic Plan outlines the Corporation's strategy for addressing the six focus areas previously identified in the Serve America Act: disaster services, economic opportunity, education, environmental stewardship, healthy futures, and veterans and military families.

To ensure that CNCS programs support interventions that deliver results aligned with the objectives and strategies developed for each focus area, CNCS created Strategy Charts for each focus area. Based on these objectives and strategies, NSLC has gathered resources to help service-learning programs achieve the greatest impact in each of the six focus areas:

- Education

  Within the focus area of education, the Corporation's goal is to provide, support and/or facilitate access to services and resources that contribute to improved educational outcomes for economically disadvantaged people, especially children. CNCS will, throughout its activities, focus on the use of evidence-based and promising practices and will collaborate with other agencies, such as the U.S. Department of Education, the U.S. Department of Labor, and the White House Office of Faith-based Initiatives. Priority in funding new grants will be given to applicants that provide evidence on the effectiveness of their programs.

- Veterans and Military Families

  Within the focus area of veterans and military families, the Corporation's goal is to demonstrate over the next five years, the potential for CNCS-supported, national service interventions to 1) positively impact the quality of life of veterans and 2) improve military family strength.

- Disaster Services

  Within the focus area of disaster services, the Corporation's goal is to build the capacity of national service network organizations to help their states and localities prepare, respond, recover and mitigate disasters and increase community resiliency.

- Economic Opportunity

  Within the focus area of economic opportunity, the Corporation's goal is to provide, support and/or facilitate access to services and resources that contribute to the improved economic well-being and security of economically disadvantaged persons.

"Corporation for National and Community Service 2011–2015 Strategic Plan Focus Areas"
http://www.servicelearning.org/topic/theory-practice/2011-2015-strategic-plan-focus-areas

- Environmental Stewardship

  Within the focus area of environmental stewardship, the Corporation's goal is to provide direct services that contribute to increased energy and water efficiency, renewable energy use, or improving at-risk ecosystems, and support increased citizen behavioral change leading to increased efficiency, renewable energy use, and ecosystem improvements particularly for economically disadvantaged households and economically disadvantaged communities.

- Healthy Futures

  Within the focus area of healthy futures, the Corporation's goal is to provide direct services that enable seniors to remain in their own homes with the same or improved quality of life for as long as possible; improve access to primary and preventive health care; and increase physical activity and improve nutrition in youth with the purpose of reducing childhood obesity.

READING REACTIONS

1. According to the Corporation for National and Community Service, "The Strategic Plan outlines the Corporation's strategy for addressing the six focus areas previously identified in the Serve America Act: disaster services, economic opportunity, education, environmental stewardship, healthy futures, and veterans and military families." Which of these focus areas resonates the most with you as a student? Why? Which area might fit best with the curriculum and objectives of your course?

2. Which of the six focus areas seems to best correlate with community relations? Why?

3. The strategic plan specifically names veterans and military families as groups of focus. Why do you think the plan does not directly mention ethnicity or other diversity issues as areas of focus?

4. In the Education focus area, "economically disadvantaged" people are mentioned. What are the implications of categorizing these particular groups of people as disadvantaged?

5. Imagine you wanted to start an organization on campus that focused on community relations. In your strategic plan, what would you include as focus areas? Design a chart that indicates the relationships among your focus areas.

6. Visit the National Service-Learning Clearinghouse website at http://www.servicelearning.org. Search the site for information that relates to your course that would help with community relations.

● Robert Putnam

The Prosperous Community: Social Capital and Public Life

Robert Putnam is a professor of political policy at Harvard University. He often writes about communities, their ethnicities, and the relationship of those cultural aspects with trust. His influential and controversial book *Bowling Alone: The Collapse and Revival of American Community* was published in 2000, and he has coauthored two books since then. Putnam is the recipient of several distinguished awards, including the Johan Skytte Prize for outstanding contributions to political science.

If we want prosperity, we might begin by working to restore the fabric of community.

> Your corn is ripe today; mine will be so tomorrow. 'Tis profitable for us both, that I should labour with you today, and that you should aid me tomorrow. I have no kindness for you, and know you have as little for me. I will *not*, therefore, take any pains upon your account; and should I labour with you upon my own account, in expectation of a return, I know I should be disappointed, and that I should in vain depend upon your gratitude. Here then I leave you to labour alone; You treat me in the same manner. The seasons change; and both of us lose our harvests for want of mutual confidence and security.
>
> —David Hume

The predicament of the farmers in Hume's parable is all too familiar in communities and nations around the world:

- Parents in communities everywhere want better educational opportunities for their children, but collaborative efforts to improve public schools falter.

- Residents of American ghettos share an interest in safer streets, but collective action to control crime fails.

- Poor farmers in the Third World need more effective irrigation and marketing schemes, but cooperation to these ends proves fragile.

- Global warming threatens livelihoods from Manhattan to Mauritius, but joint action to forestall this shared risk founders.

Failure to cooperate for mutual benefit does not necessarily signal ignorance or irrationality or even malevolence, as philosophers since Hobbes have underscored. Hume's farmers were not dumb, or crazy, or evil; they were trapped. Social scientists have lately analyzed this fundamental predicament in a variety of guises: the tragedy of the commons; the logic of collective action; public goods; the prisoners' dilemma. In all these situations, as in Hume's rustic anecdote, everyone would be better off if everyone could cooperate. In the absence of coordination and credible mutual commitment, however, everyone defects, ruefully but rationally, confirming one another's melancholy expectations.

How can such dilemmas of collective action be overcome, short of creating some Hobbesian Leviathan? Social scientists in several disciplines have recently suggested a novel diagnosis of this problem, a diagnosis resting on the concept of *social capital*. By analogy with notions of physical capital and human capital—tools and training that enhance individual productivity—"social capital" refers to features of social organization, such as networks, norms, and trust, that facilitate coordination and cooperation for mutual benefit. Social capital enhances the benefits of investment in physical and human capital.

Working together is easier in a community blessed with a substantial stock of social capital. This insight turns out to have powerful practical implications for many issues on the American national agenda—for how we might overcome the poverty and violence of South Central Los Angeles, or revitalize industry in the Rust Belt, or nurture the fledgling democracies of the former Soviet empire and the erstwhile Third World. Before spelling out these implications, however, let me illustrate the importance of social capital by recounting an investigation that several colleagues and I have conducted over the last two decades on the seemingly arcane subject of regional government in Italy.

LESSONS FROM AN ITALIAN EXPERIMENT

Beginning in 1970, Italians established a nationwide set of potentially powerful regional governments. These 20 new institutions were virtually identical in form, but the social, economic, political, and cultural contexts in which they were implanted differed dramatically, ranging from the preindustrial to the postindustrial, from the devoutly Catholic to the ardently Communist, from the inertly feudal to the frenetically modern. Just as a botanist might investigate plant development by measuring the growth of genetically identical seeds sown in different plots, we sought to understand government performance by studying how these new institutions evolved in their diverse settings.

As we expected, some of the new governments proved to be dismal failures—inefficient, lethargic, and corrupt. Others have been remarkably successful, however, creating innovative day care programs and job-training centers, promoting investment and economic development, pioneering environmental standards and family clinics—managing the public's business efficiently and satisfying their constituents.

What could account for these stark differences in quality of government? Some seemingly obvious answers turned out to be irrelevant. Government organization is too similar from region to region for that to explain the contrasts in performance. Party politics or ideology makes little difference. Affluence and prosperity have no direct effect. Social stability or political harmony or population movements are not the key. None of these factors is correlated with good government as we had anticipated. Instead, the best predictor is one that Alexis de Tocqueville might have expected. Strong traditions of civic engagement—voter turnout, newspaper readership, membership in choral societies and literary circles, Lions Clubs, and soccer clubs—are the hallmarks of a successful region.

Some regions of Italy, such as Emilia-Romagna and Tuscany, have many active community organizations. Citizens in these regions are engaged by public issues, not by patronage. They trust one another to act fairly and obey the law. Leaders in these communities are relatively honest and committed to equality. Social and political networks are organized horizontally, not hierarchically. These "civic communities" value solidarity, civic participation, and integrity. And here democracy works.

At the other pole are "uncivic" regions, like Calabria and Sicily, aptly characterized by the French term *incivisme*. The very concept of citizenship is stunted there. Engagement in social and cultural associations is meager. From the point of view of the inhabitants, public affairs is somebody else's business—*i notabili*, "the bosses," "the politicians"—but not theirs. Laws, almost everyone agrees, are made to be broken, but fearing others' lawlessness, everyone demands sterner discipline. Trapped in these interlocking vicious circles, nearly everyone feels powerless, exploited, and unhappy. It is hardly surprising that representative government here is less effective than in more civic communities.

The historical roots of the civic community are astonishingly deep. Enduring traditions of civic involvement and social solidarity can be traced back nearly a millennium to the eleventh century, when communal republics were established in places like Florence, Bologna, and Genoa, exactly the communities that today enjoy civic engagement and successful government. At the core of this civic heritage are rich networks of organized reciprocity and civic solidarity—guilds, religious fraternities, and tower societies for self-defense in the medieval communes; cooperatives, mutual aid societies, neighborhood associations, and choral societies in the twentieth century.

These communities did not become civic simply because they were rich. The historical record strongly suggests precisely the opposite: They have become rich because they were civic. The social capital embodied in norms and networks of civic engagement seems to be a precondition for economic development, as well as for effective government. Development economists take note: Civics matters.

How does social capital undergird good government and economic progress? First, networks of civic engagement foster sturdy norms of generalized reciprocity: I'll do this for you now, in the expectation that down the road you or someone else will return the favor. "Social capital is akin to what Tom Wolfe called the 'favor bank' in his novel, *The Bonfire of the Vanities*," notes economist Robert Frank. A society that relies on generalized reciprocity is more efficient than a distrustful society, for the same reason that money is more efficient than barter. Trust lubricates social life.

Networks of civic engagement also facilitate coordination and communication and amplify information about the trustworthiness of other individuals. Students of prisoners' dilemmas and related games report that cooperation is most easily sustained through repeat play. When economic and political dealing is embedded in dense networks of social interaction, incentives for opportunism and malfeasance are reduced. This is why the diamond trade, with its extreme possibilities for fraud, is concentrated within close-knit ethnic enclaves. Dense social ties facilitate gossip and other valuable ways of cultivating reputation—an essential foundation for trust in a complex society.

Finally, networks of civic engagement embody past success at collaboration, which can serve as a cultural template for future collaboration. The civic traditions of north-central Italy provide a historical repertoire of forms of cooperation that, having proved their worth in the past, are available to citizens for addressing new problems of collective action.

Sociologist James Coleman concludes, "Like other forms of capital, social capital is productive, making possible the achievement of certain ends that would not be attainable in its absence. . . . In a farming community . . . where one farmer got his hay baled by another and where farm tools are extensively borrowed and lent, the social capital allows each farmer to get his work done with less physical capital in the form of tools and equipment." Social capital, in short, enables Hume's farmers to surmount their dilemma of collective action.

Stocks of social capital, such as trust, norms, and networks, tend to be self-reinforcing and cumulative. Successful collaboration in one endeavor builds connections and trust—social assets that facilitate future collaboration in other, unrelated tasks. As with conventional capital, those who have social capital tend to accumulate more—them as has, gets. Social capital is what the social philosopher Albert O. Hirschman calls a "moral resource," that is, a resource whose supply increases rather than decreases through use and which (unlike physical capital) becomes depleted if *not* used.

Unlike conventional capital, social capital is a "public good," that is, it is not the private property of those who benefit from it. Like other public goods, from clean air to safe streets, social capital tends to be under-provided by private agents. This means that social capital must often be a by-product of other social activities. Social capital typically consists in ties, norms, and trust transferable from one social setting to another. Members of Florentine choral societies participate because they like to sing, not because their participation strengthens the Tuscan social fabric. But it does.

SOCIAL CAPITAL AND AMERICA'S ILLS

Fifty-one deaths and $1 billion dollars in property damage in Los Angeles last year put urban decay back on the American agenda. Yet if the ills are clear, the prescription is not. Even those most sympathetic to the plight of America's ghettos are not persuaded that simply reviving the social programs dismantled in the last decade or so will solve the problems. The erosion of social capital is an essential and under-appreciated part of the diagnosis.

Although most poor Americans do not reside in the inner city, there is something qualitatively different about the social and economic isolation experienced by the chronically poor blacks and Latinos who do. Joblessness, inadequate education, and poor health clearly truncate the opportunities of ghetto residents. Yet so do profound deficiencies in social capital.

Part of the problem facing blacks and Latinos in the inner city is that they lack "connections" in the most literal sense. Job-seekers in the ghetto have little access, for example, to conventional job referral networks. Labor economists Anne Case and Lawrence Katz have shown that, regardless of race, inner-city youth living in neighborhoods blessed with high levels of civic engagement are more likely to finish school, have a job, and avoid drugs and crime, controlling for the individual characteristics of the youth. That is, of two identical youths, the one unfortunate enough to live in a neighborhood whose social capital has eroded is more likely to end up hooked, booked, or dead. Several researchers seem to have found similar neighborhood effects on the incidence of teen pregnancy, among both blacks and whites, again controlling for personal characteristics. Where you live and whom you know— the social capital you can draw on—helps to define who you are and thus to determine your fate.

Racial and class inequalities in access to social capital, if properly measured, may be as great as inequalities in financial and human capital, and no less portentous. Economist Glenn Loury has used the term "social capital" to capture the fundamental fact that racial segregation, coupled with socially inherited differences in community networks and norms, means that individually targeted "equal opportunity" policies may not eliminate racial inequality, even in the long run. Research suggests that the life chances of today's generation depend not only on their parents' social resources, but also on the social resources of their parents' ethnic group. Even workplace integration and upward mobility by successful members of minority groups cannot overcome these persistent effects of inequalities in social capital. William Julius Wilson has described in tragic detail how the exodus of middle-class and working-class families from the ghetto has eroded the social capital available to those left behind. The settlement houses that nurtured sewing clubs and civic activism a century ago, embodying community as much as charity, are now mostly derelict.

It would be a dreadful mistake, of course, to overlook the repositories of social capital within America's minority communities. The neighborhood restaurant eponymously portrayed in Mitchell Duneier's recent *Slim's Table*, for example, nurtures fellowship and intercourse that enable blacks (and whites) in Chicago's South Side to sustain a modicum of collective life. Historically, the black church has been the most bounteous treasure-house of social capital for African Americans. The church provided the organizational infrastructure for political mobilization in the civil rights movement. Recent work on American political participation by political scientist Sidney Verba and his colleagues shows that the church is a uniquely powerful resource for political engagement among blacks—an arena in which to learn about public affairs and hone political skills and make connections.

In tackling the ills of America's cities, investments in physical capital, financial capital, human capital, and social capital are complementary, not competing alternatives. Investments in jobs and education, for example, will be more effective if they are coupled with reinvigoration of community associations.

Some churches provide job banks and serve as informal credit bureaus, for example, using their reputational capital to vouch for members who may be ex-convicts, former drug addicts, or high school dropouts. In such cases the church does not merely provide referral networks. More fundamentally, wary employers and financial institutions bank on the church's ability to identify parishioners whose formal credentials understate their reliability. At the same time, because these parishioners value their standing in the church, and because the church has put its own reputation on the line, they have an additional incentive to perform. Like conventional capital for conventional borrowers, social capital serves as a kind of collateral for men and women who are excluded from ordinary credit or labor markets. In effect, the participants pledge their social connections, leveraging social capital to improve the efficiency with which markets operate.

The importance of social capital for America's domestic agenda is not limited to minority communities. Take public education, for instance. The success of private schools is attributable, according to James Coleman's massive research, not so much to what happens in the classroom nor to the endowments of individual students, but rather to the greater engagement of parents and community members in private school activities. Educational reformers like child psychologist James Comer seek to improve schooling not merely by "treating" individual children but by deliberately involving parents and others in the educational process. Educational policymakers need to move beyond debates about curriculum and governance to consider the effects of social capital. Indeed, most commonly discussed proposals for "choice" are deeply flawed by their profoundly individualist conception of education. If states and localities are to experiment with voucher systems for education or child care, why not encourage vouchers to be spent in ways that strengthen community organization, not weaken it? Once we recognize the importance of social capital, we ought to be able to design programs that creatively combine individual choice with collective engagement.

Many people today are concerned about revitalizing American democracy. Although discussion of political reform in the United States focuses nowadays on such procedural issues as term limits and campaign financing, some of the ills that afflict the American polity reflect deeper, largely unnoticed social changes.

"Some people say that you usually can trust people. Others say that you must be wary in relations with people. Which is your view?" Responses to this question, posed repeatedly in national surveys for several decades, suggest that social trust in the United States has declined for more than a quarter century. By contrast, American politics benefited from plentiful stocks of social capital in earlier times. Recent historical work on the Progressive Era, for example, has uncovered evidence of the powerful role played by nominally non-political associations (such as women's literary societies) precisely because they provided a dense social network. Is our current predicament the result of a long-term erosion of social capital, such as community engagement and social trust?

Economist Juliet Schorr's discovery of "the unexpected decline of leisure" in America suggests that our generation is less engaged with one another outside the marketplace and thus less prepared to cooperate for shared goals. Mobile, two-career (or one-parent) families often must use the market for child care and other services formerly provided through family and neighborhood networks. Even if market-based services, considered individually, are of high quality, this deeper social trend is eroding social capital. There are more empty seats at the PTA and in church pews these days. While celebrating the productive, liberating effects of fuller equality in the workplace, we must replace the social capital that this movement has depleted.

Our political parties, once intimately coupled to the capillaries of community life, have become evanescent confections of pollsters and media consultants and independent political entrepreneurs—the very antithesis of social capital. We have too easily accepted a conception of democracy in which public policy is not the outcome of a collective deliberation about the public interest, but rather a residue of campaign strategy. The social capital approach, focusing on the indirect effects of civic norms and networks, is a much-needed corrective to an exclusive emphasis on the formal institutions of government as an explanation for our collective discontents. If we are to make our political system more responsive, especially to those who lack connections at the top, we must nourish grassroots organization.

Classic liberal social policy is designed to enhance the opportunities of *individuals*, but if social capital is important, this emphasis is partially misplaced. Instead we must focus on community development, allowing space for religious organizations and choral societies and Little Leagues that may seem to have little to do with politics or economics. Government policies, whatever their intended effects, should be vetted for their indirect effects on social capital. If, as some suspect, social capital is fostered more by home ownership than by public or private tenancy, then we should design housing policy accordingly. Similarly, as Theda Skocpol has suggested, the direct benefits of national service programs might be dwarfed by the indirect benefits that could flow from the creation of social networks that cross class and racial lines. In any comprehensive strategy for improving the plight of America's communities, rebuilding social capital is as important as investing in human and physical capital.

Throughout the Bush administration, community self-reliance—"a thousand points of light"—too often served as an ideological fig leaf for an administration that used the thinness of our public wallet as an alibi for a lack of political will. Conservatives are right to emphasize the value of intermediary associations, but they misunderstand the potential synergy between private organization and the government. *Social capital is not a substitute for effective public policy but rather a prerequisite for it and, in part, a consequence of it.* Social capital, as our Italian study suggests, works through and with states and markets, not in place of them. The social capital approach is neither an argument for cultural determinism nor an excuse to blame the victim.

Wise policy can encourage social capital formation, and social capital itself enhances the effectiveness of government action. From agricultural extension services in the last century to tax exemptions for community organizations in this one, American government has often promoted investments in social capital, and it must renew that effort now. A new administration that is, at long last, more willing to use public power and the public purse for public purpose should not overlook the importance of social connectedness as a vital backdrop for effective policy.

Students of social capital have only begun to address some of the most important questions that this approach to public affairs suggests. What are the actual trends in different forms of civic engagement? Why do communities differ in their stocks of social capital? What *kinds* of civic engagement seem most likely to foster economic growth or community effectiveness? Must specific types of social capital be matched to different public problems? Most important of all, how is social capital created and destroyed? What strategies for building (or rebuilding) social capital are most promising? How can we balance the twin strategies of exploiting existing social capital and creating it afresh? The suggestions scattered throughout this essay are intended to challenge others to even more practical methods of encouraging new social capital formation and leveraging what we have already.

We also need to ask about the negative effects of social capital, for like human and physical capital, social capital can be put to bad purposes. Liberals have often sought to destroy some forms of social capital (from medieval guilds to neighborhood schools) in the name of individual opportunity. We have not always reckoned with the indirect social costs of our policies, but we were often right to be worried about the power of private associations. Social inequalities may be embedded in social capital. Norms and networks that serve some groups may obstruct others, particularly if the norms are discriminatory or the networks socially segregated. Recognizing the importance of social capital in sustaining community life does not exempt us from the need to worry about how that community is defined—who is inside and thus benefits from social capital, and who is outside and does not. Some forms of social capital can impair individual liberties, as critics of comunitarianism warn. Many of the Founders' fears about the "mischiefs of faction" apply to social capital. Before toting up the balance sheet for social capital in its various forms, we need to weigh costs as well as benefits. This challenge still awaits.

Progress on the urgent issues facing our country and our world requires ideas that bridge outdated ideological divides. Both

ROBERTLAMPHOTO /SHUTTERSTOCK.COM

Figure 6.5 One representation of community engagement

liberals and conservatives agree on the importance of social empowerment, as E. J. Dionne recently noted ("The Quest for Community (Again)," *TAP,* Summer 1992). The social capital approach provides a deeper conceptual underpinning for this nominal convergence. Real progress requires not facile verbal agreement, but hard thought and ideas with high fiber content. The social capital approach promises to uncover new ways of combining private social infrastructure with public policies that work, and, in turn, of using wise public policies to revitalize America's stocks of social capital.

READING REACTIONS

1. Putnam writes, "'social capital' refers to features of social organization, such as networks, norms, and trust, that facilitate coordination and cooperation for mutual benefit. Social capital enhances the benefits of investment in physical and human capital." Come up with your own definition of "social capital" along with an example that would make it easy to explain to a friend.

2. How might service learning or volunteering or becoming active in your own community increase your social capital?

3. In your own words, what did the Italian experiment teach Putnam and his coworkers?

4. According to Putnam, what is social capital's role in a community's economy?

5. Do some research about your own city or state. What kind of "government programs, such as urban renewal and public housing projects," have failed the community because they "ravage social networks" as Putnam suggests? Which projects have been successful? What are the differences?

6. How might churches, schools, community centers, and other such community networks add to the success of a community and its ability to prosper?

7. Putnam concedes some negative effects of social capital. What are they? What other dangers may be associated with social capital?

Technological Beginnings

This textbook has given you tips and tools for building and designing all types of digital projects, from images to videos. Early chapters asked you to start a blog and build a splash or home page for a website. For this project, you will apply some of your mediated skills to some of the more traditional writing you've done.

Using the rhetorical skills and technology tools you've learned in designing either a splash page or a blog, design a personal e-portfolio. The e-portfolio can include a link to your blog, a link to your video, the images you've created, links to

PDF versions of your essays, and anything else you think is relevant. Take a look at some sample e-portfolios (available at the English CourseMate for this text). for ideas of how to make your e-portfolio meaningful, personalized, and reflective.

First, choose a theme. Make sure the theme reflects your e-portfolio appropriately. Remember that color, font, and design choices matter. Think about your ethos as an author.

Next, add content. This may take up several pages. Keep in mind that your "splash" or "index" page is like the menu to the rest of your site. You can use free site builders like Moonfruit.com to guide you through the process. You can also access tutorials on website creation available on the English CourseMate for this text.

Some universities provide hosting space for student projects. If possible, publish your website in that hosting space. Otherwise, you can use a free hosting site. If you don't want to publish the website, you can simply save your website files to a disc or your computer.

TECHNOLOGY TIP   **Building a Brochure**

A brochure can help define the mission of student and volunteer organizations. Templates for brochures (such as the Apple template in **Figure 6.6**) are often available in word-processing and publishing software as well as online at free sites like http://www.hloom.com. Once you locate and open the brochure template you want, experiment with inserting images and text into the document.

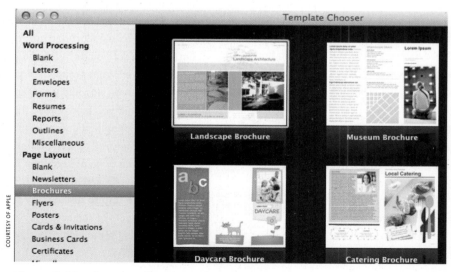

Figure 6.6 Brochure template options in Apple Pages

Additional Writing and Composing Activities

Proposal. Does your community have a recreational need? A splash park? A Frisbee golf park? A running trail? A mountain biking trail? A refurbished picnic pavilion? Write a proposal requesting the recreation addition to the city. It's often a good idea to begin with an executive summary, which uses 250 words or less to summarize your proposal, the benefits of the addition to the city, and the strategies toward completing the task.

Consider including the following common proposal features:

- A letter to the person in charge of such proposals
- A name for your project
- A complete argument for the project
- Specific strategies for completing the project. For example:
  - Buying material
  - Site location
  - Possible contractors
- A tentative budget draft

Look online for similar project proposals. Research how much similar projects have cost other cities, what the projects involved, and whether a similar proposal has ever been submitted (you can find this information by asking city-council members or checking city-council meeting minutes, usually available on a city website).

Flyer and Poster. Using Microsoft Publisher, Apple Pages, or open-source software, open a template for a flyer or poster. Create a flyer for a student organization or volunteer group you belong to. The flyer could announce a meeting or an activity. After you finish the flyer, ask someone on the organization's executive board or a sponsor to approve it. It's best to have two to three different versions of the flyer so the decision maker can choose which one he or she prefers.

Next, using the same software, design a poster that requests volunteer help for an activity presented by a community organization. It's always best to talk to someone at the organization who is in charge of public relations to find out what the flyer should include. Most organizations must use standardized logos, font, colors, and so on. Ask the organization representative about specifications you need to follow to maintain the integrity of the organization, or check the organization handbook for identity standards. For instance, a university most definitely has identity standards, so if you plan to use a university logo on your flyer or poster, check the official university website for usage specifications.

Reflective Essay. Writing a reflection on an experience helps solidify its meaning through critical thinking, analysis, and personal assessment. Reflect on a time when you engaged in some kind of volunteer work as part of a group like Boy Scouts or Girl Scouts, a religious group, your school, or a neighborhood group. What volunteer work did you do? Why did you do it? Where were you? What group were you with? Whom did it serve? How did you learn about the project? What did you learn about the people you helped and the people you were with? Did the activity encourage you to think differently about a group of people or an area of your community? Was it a worthwhile activity? Why? In your reflection, make sure to discuss any positive or negative aspects of the activity. Would you participate in this same kind of activity again? Why or why not?

Argument Essay Based on an Editorial Cartoon. Use the literacy skills practiced in this and other chapters to make an argument about **Figure 6.7**.

First, identify and analyze what is happening in the cartoon in order to ground your argument. Start by answering these questions:

- What is the artist's argument?
- What is the teacher in the cartoon saying about public service?
- What does "euphemism" mean?
- What is the significance of the American flag patch on the teacher's shirt?
- What is the students' attitude? How do you know?
- How does the artist use body language to indicate attitude?

Second, consider what argument you would make based on the attitudes shown in the cartoon. Use the following questions to help formulate an argument:

- How do the attitudes of the artist and teacher reflect on community engagement? How might a mandate affect the value of a service (e.g., diminish its meaning, cause negative responses)?
- Why might the artist, teacher, or students have different attitudes about service learning?

The argumentative essay is also a good place to use the definition skills you've practiced in this chapter or to prove your claim by using a narrative of a personal experience you've had in serving the community.

Figure 6.7 Mandatory public service cartoon

Online Resources

Resources available through the English CourseMate for this text include the following:

Websites

Hasbro's Community Relations page
Best Buy's Community Relations page
Nationwide's Community Relations page
"Social Capital." *CDC.*
"Social Capital." *Infed.*
"Library." *Learn and Serve America.*
"Kids in Action." *Learn and Serve Idaho.*

Articles

Beth A. Covitt. "Middle School Students'
Attitudes toward Required Chesapeake Bay
Service-Learning," *Corporation for National
and Community Service.*
Kimberly Fornek. "Even with Running Start,
State Struggles with Mandate," *Catalyst.*

Higher Education Network. "The Social and
Physical Capital of Women in Higher
Education," *The Guardian.*
Fran Smith. "Learning by Giving Community
Service as Classwork," *Edutopia.*
Emma Zink. "An Outsider's Mentality:
Community Projects Scream for Engaged
Volunteers," *The Daily Utah Chronicle.*

Videos

The Service Learning Channel. YouTube.com
"The Difference Between Service Learning and
Community Service." *Volunteer Global.*
Katherine Fulton. "You are the future of
philanthropy." *TED.*

Social Networks

There are many rules for dating—especially for first dates. There are rules for dress, appropriate activities, and even preferred conversation topics, like work and travel. Topics to avoid include politics and religion. How do these rules change when we meet online and seek partners in virtual communities?

According to Sandra Yin, an associate editor at *American Demographics*, Match.com (See Figure 7.1) is reportedly the nation's leading online dating site and a popular community among the estimated one-fourth of America's 98 million singles searching online for dates, relationships, sex, and spouses.[1] In an age of online shopping, education, and friendship, it seems logical that modern daters would seek out spaces where they

© NETPHOTOS/ALAMY

Figure 7.1 Match. com Home Page

[1]Sandra Yin, "Looking for Love," *American Demographics*, vol. 24, no. 2, p. 48. Copyright © by Crain Communications, Inc.

could craft and critique dating personas in a community of like-minded individuals. But how do we learn the rules of these communities?

Who tells us what is appropriate for a "first email" or how to demonstrate interest in the profile of a fellow dating-community member? In spaces like Match.com, PlentyOfFish.com and OkCupid.com, singles learn many rules for belonging to virtual communities through the templates they use to design an identity or space. In the Match.com community, for example, users can "wink" at prospective dates and can share a list of desirable interests and hobbies.

Virtual Communities

Scholars such as Henry Jenkins have talked about the ability of media-sharing sites such as YouTube to establish a participatory culture in which citizens produce and distribute media as much as they consume it. In his study of the 2007 CNN-YouTube presidential debates, for example, Jenkins concluded that "A closer look at the role parody videos played in American politics in 2007 may help us to understand how we are or are not realizing the potential of this new communication environment. Such videos give us an alternative perspective on what democracy might look like, though we have a long way to go."[1]

Since discovering new media's power to reach all kinds of voters, local and national political campaigns now rely on Facebook profiles and "causes" pages. Even traditional forums like debates often give audience members opportunities to tweet responses and questions to candidates. But both during and after the campaigns, social media holds promise and peril for government officials.

While such sharing and remixing foster copyright concerns, they also lead to the type of communal experience of culture that we have experienced in more mainstream genres of television, radio, and film. Yet, as the millions of YouTube video uploads indicate, such social networking also leads to differently mediated forms of communication that remix and remake all sorts of genres and contexts, from the e-greeting card to podcasting sites. The ways in which we participate, produce, and consume new media texts not only remake the sorts of media we encounter but also promote new kinds of community. Twenty years ago, Howard Rheingold introduced the concept of "virtual community":

---

[1]Henry Jenkins, "Convergence Culture: Where Old and New Media Collide," *New York University Press*, 2008.

COMMUNITIES In what ways have mobile technologies both helped, as suggested by **Figure 7.2**, and hindered communication across cultures and within communities? Address this question by interviewing diverse groups: student peers, teachers or family members, and older adults. Combine your interviews with articles and resources presented in this chapter and discovered in your own library research. Use your results to write an editorial for potential publication in your campus newspaper.

Figure 7.2 A nurse in Amman, Jordan, uses cell phone to send pictures of a patient to a doctor

worldwide forums for online affinity groups. Examples of virtual communities include Vimeo, a social network devoted to filmmakers, and DeviantArt.com, "a community of artists and those devoted to art." Today's virtual communities offer moral support for those who "tweet through chemo," as Halle Tecco of *The Huffington Post* reports, and help memorialize loved ones through videos like the one teenager Sarah Phillips posted on YouTube in March 2010.

Commonplaces Online

Online practices and conventions—friending, use of the "like" button, Rickrolling—are important for forming and sustaining community, both online and offline. They help teach us what a community values (humor, hipness, wit, and so on) and how the community operates. They also help identify users as insiders or outsiders in the community. Using the right lingo and actions suggests you have internalized what a given discourse community requires and offers.

A discourse community is a group or community that has shared goals and that uses language to reach those goals. Such groups may be professional, like lawyers using legal jargon, or personal, like *Twilight* fan groups that use shorthand slang and images. Discourse communities often share *commonplaces*—words, images, symbols, and other signifiers that quickly communicate the community's values and goals. An example might be the way an apple comes to stand in for good health when "an apple a day keeps the doctor away" or alternately symbolizes sin when in the Bible Eve plucked an apple from the tree of knowledge. Commonplaces are rooted in Aristotle's topoi (list of topics or instructions for constructing arguments) and are vital to communicating the specialized language, meaningful images, logos, and even videos and songs used as shorthand for discourse community members.

Language and visual rhetoric are common markers of virtual communities. While some cultures take access to virtual communities for granted, in many instances access is denied, as in China and Iran. Recently, a student from Beijing studying in the United States shared her amazement about being able to see pictures of the 1989 Tiananmen Square protests that were commonplace to world viewers. Yet even within the United States, the gap between who is "wired" and who isn't may be wider than people suspect, not only in terms of how much access various groups have but also in terms of what they do online once they are connected. NationMaster.com, a central data source that uses information gathered from the United Nations and other sources to graphically compare nations, indicates that the United States appears to be the most "connected" country, with more than 40 million people reported to have access to broadband. However, this figure says little about the wired population's daily online usage patterns or the speed and quality of their Internet connection. The Internet-access gap between the United States and other countries has led to the distinction between the traditional read-only concept of the Internet and the new era of Web 2.0, a read-write concept in which people constantly interact through Facebook, Twitter, Google, YouTube, and other popular tools. In places where Internet speed is slow or unavailable, citizens are denied access to the read-write texts and spaces that allow them to become producers of knowledge rather than just consumers. Thus, though many have access to computers, not everyone has access to the rich and dynamic worlds of Web 2.0.

Online Citizenship

Virtual communities offer many options for joining organizations, affinity groups, and spaces online. Like participation in any community, such membership has both privileges and costs. The theme of the 2010 conference of the Center for the Study of Citizenship at Wayne State University was virtual citizenship. Participants explored the similarities and the tensions between networks and citizenship in the past, present, and future. They also considered how networks have shaped citizenship and how citizenship has influenced the development of networks.

Just what does it mean to be a virtual citizen? In most cases, citizenship involves responsibility to act with good character within the understood social boundaries of the community. This notion goes back to the ancient Greek orators Quintilian and Cicero, who both taught that a good citizen acted with strong character, ethics, and knowledge. Citizenship is also tied to one's personal identity, which is now often constructed through a Facebook profile, a 140-character tweet, or a designed avatar.

Citizenship in the twenty-first century requires commitment not only to our own communities (as suggested in Chapter 8) and nation, but also to the nations of the globe. For some, modern citizenship may also mean an allegiance to nations and worlds that exist only in the imagination or on the screen. We see examples of virtual allegiances on the website FanPop.com, a site "where fans of anything" can create groups. People can also express commitments in Facebook "cause" groups.

Technology can foster citizens' best impulses for their communities. We can, in effect, be charitable members of any nation, group, or organization we want to. Texting has even become a means of charitable expression for many: *New York Times* technology reporter Jenna Wortham wrote that victims of the Haiti earthquake received $2 million in donations through texted donations. The company mGive (http://mgive.com), which helped coordinate the Red Cross's digital giving campaign for Haiti, reported more than $40 million in total donations for earthquake recovery.

COMMUNITIES Consider your Google+ or Facebook page (or a similar social networking space). Using analysis questions from Chapter 1 (p. 5), consider how you negotiate the page. What is important? Do you look at status updates first? How do you know where to click? What is the page design's hierarchy? (Is the page set up in a way that asks you to look at a particular design aspect first? What does the design seem to emphasize?) Who owns or produced the message? Does the page control how you use it? Under what contexts (political, historical, cultural) was the message created? What types of social knowledge should you have to use the site? What are the consequences for using and misusing the site?

Think about the way you use the site. How is the way you use your space on the site intended to affect other readers? Do you play games or use other applications? Do you spend most of your time looking at friends' pictures and posting to their spaces? What does this say about you as a Google+ or Facebook citizen?

Now spend a few days taking notes about how you use the site. Develop some criteria to guide your notes. Track yourself in areas like the amount of time spent on your pages or your friends' pages, and what types of activities you do in those areas. Then make a claim about what type of citizen you are. For instance, based on your activity, do you seem more concerned with your friends or yourself?

Write three to five paragraphs describing this experiment and discuss what kind of virtual citizen you seem to be based on the notes you gathered. Considering your observations, what claims can you make about the rules of Facebook citizenship and the ways you are given, use, and interpret those rules and conventions?

Membership and citizenship are exercised in various forms and forums but are often fully online experiences; we can exercise our membership, for example, by attending a virtual conference or conversing on a LISTSERV with people we will never meet face to face. Whether in place of or to augment offline communities and associations, we can use the power of technology to be virtual citizens.

Do real-world social rules differ from rules online? In your online world, how do you know how to be a good virtual citizen? What happens if you're not? What does it mean to act with character, ethics, and knowledge in our more modern virtual worlds? We know from our earlier exercise that cyberbullying is not tolerated in most online communities, but what of acts of aggression or retaliation that seem justified? In her article excerpted later in this chapter, Kim Zetter considers justice and consequences as she recounts cases of online vigilantism and the "firestorm that . . . illustrates what happens when the social imperative to punish those in a community who violate social norms plays out over the internet." Consider Zetter's quote. What are some of the consequences you can imagine when joining an online activism group? What sort of impact might result from donating time to a cause in a virtual setting? Is online activism motivated by different things than offline activism?

Choosing Your Online Citizenship

Online freedom is not limited to the choice of which communities we may join. It also extends to deciding whom we want to include and how we want to represent ourselves in those communities. Social networking, then, allows us to decide not only whom we want to "friend" but also how we want to be known. Just as rhetoric has always placed audience at the heart of all communication, digital identity is always bound up in whom you are performing your identity *with* and *for*.

Scholars Jay David Bolter and Richard Grusin, in their 1999 book *Remediation: Understanding New Media*, remind us that "we see ourselves today in and through our available media."[1] The media we use does not control our identity, but it is one way we act out who we are and who we want to be. This new-media identity performance (how we act out our identity in new media spaces) may result in a *virtual self* (one completely immersed in a digital space) or a *networked self* (a self who simultaneously lives both online and offline identities). This hybrid persona is presented in feminist scholar Donna Haraway's *Cyborg Manifesto*. Haraway believes people are becoming increasingly connected

---

[1]Jay David Bolter and Richard Grusin, "Remediation: Understanding New Media," 2000, Cambridge, MA: The MIT Press.

to technologies and increasingly drawn to "partial identities." Similarly, media scholar Sherry Turkle takes up this cyborg idea as she examines our "tethered" relationship to technology and ways this relationship collapses many of the barriers between online and offline worlds and identities (see chapter readings).

We are all always multiple people in multiple settings. Think about how you might build your personal profile on a dating site as opposed to on the Blackboard online learning platform. How does a professional site like LinkedIn encourage you to be a certain "you" that is quite different from the "you" on Facebook?

These online identities are often a mix of performance and associations. Like it or not, we make judgments about people because of how they dress, what bands they listen to, what TV shows they watch, and how they vote. Similarly, the types of media and online communities we engage in say a lot about us. The photographs we choose, witty sayings we post as updates, and videos we link to all say something both about the conventions and commonplaces of our online communities and also about how we want others to read us as digital beings.

The media we use is obviously not the only way others form opinions about who we are online and offline. Despite hopes that the Internet would erase gender, race, class, and other social barriers and differences, issues like hate speech, cyber rape, and discrimination continue online. Because we are always involved with both our media and our culture, society's problems often follow us to online spaces. The ability to form affinity groups, for example, offers voice and opportunity for change for diverse individuals. However, such groups might also unintentionally deepen stereotypes that are applied to them.

Unfortunately, stereotyping can be common within online communities. Because we cannot know the "whole" person online, we are often forced to categorize and prejudge others based on visual cues ranging from photos to fonts and color choices (see Chapter 4 for more discussion on visual literacy).

Schemas and rules direct us on how to act in online communities. Think about "girly layouts" for MySpace or profile settings in LinkedIn. Both communities make assumptions about what it "looks like" to be a certain gender or class in an online space. But just like in offline spaces, stereotypes are often misleading. Membership in an online community requires an awareness of cultural norms for a community but also requires the knowledge that people—maybe especially online—are always more than those norms.

Living with Fellow Citizens

The choices we make in online communities say a great deal about us, but we aren't the only ones controlling our identities. Communal or group authoring is vital to many Web texts (think of how Wikipedia entries are built by a community of readers rather than a single author who might pen a print encyclopedia entry). Group authoring is also important to the formation of digital identity. Although you may control the images, videos, and text on your Facebook profile, consider how much of your profile is authored by your friends. Wall posts, suggested fan groups, recommended videos, Pieces of Flair, and tagged photos are all part of your online identity in these spaces although you didn't create or choose all of them. Digital citizenship, then, implies a willingness not only to shape a virtual community but also to be shaped by that community.

What benefits and drawbacks come from a willingness to be identified with and through others and through specific media? A willingness to be forthcoming and honest about yourself online might yield rich friendships, budding romances, and even professional opportunities. The film *The Social Network* (2010) chronicles the meteoric rise of Facebook creator Mark Zuckerberg and his idea of "taking the entire social experience of college and putting it online." Many have questioned and criticized Facebook's emphasis on "oversharing" and its possible negative impact on offline interpersonal relationships. But others see advantages to being always connected. In his *New York Times* article "Brave New World of Digital Intimacy," Clive Thompson explores the idea that "ambient awareness"—getting meaningless or mundane "little snippets" of others' experiences—gives "a surprisingly sophisticated portrait of . . . friends' and family members' lives."

Thus, Facebook and other social media may actually increase our relationship bonds by making us more often—perhaps always—aware of the inner workings of others' lives.

This connection might also result in misunderstandings, hurt feelings, and in some cases, lost jobs. Consider the case of Stacy Snyder, a teaching major who alleges she was denied her teaching credentials just weeks before graduation at Millersville University when she posted a photo of herself on MySpace labeled "drunken pirate." Despite being twenty-seven and legally entitled to drink, posting these photos may have projected a less than "teacherly" identity for Snyder. It was considered at least a factor in her not becoming credentialed, and courts sided with the university. In a similar case, an associate professor of sociology at East Stroudsburg University was escorted off campus after her Facebook status update reported she "didn't want to kill even one student—Now Friday was a different story. . . ." On another day she asked, "does anyone know where I can find a very discrete[sic] hitman?" Although she was able to return to her job eventually, the Facebook jokes resulted in months of paid administrative leave.

Participating in online communities clearly has consequences. What should virtual citizens keep in mind about information, images, and details

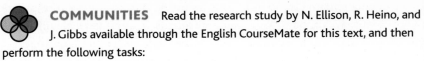

COMMUNITIES Read the research study by N. Ellison, R. Heino, and J. Gibbs available through the English CourseMate for this text, and then perform the following tasks:

1. Annotate the study, with special consideration to:

    material you question

    material you agree with

    material you want to learn more about

    material you can identify with

2. Specifically consider the ways the authors see online daters building identity and ethos in online dating communities. Make sure to mark each strategy they noticed.

3. Based on your analysis, summarize the ways in which the authors establish their conclusions about online identity.

    What is the authors' main argument?

    What types of research methods do they employ to establish their conclusions?

    To what extent do you agree with their findings?

    How do their findings align with your own efforts or those of your friends to craft online identities and impressions?

we share with others in our online communities? How do these online artifacts build for others—and for ourselves—our online personas? With consequences, digital media is constantly blurring the lines between public and private, work and leisure, private jokes and public comments.

Technological Beginnings: Using Online Videos as Commonplace

In every chapter of this book, you've practiced an invention strategy or a process or instrument you can use to help you develop ideas about a subject. It's important to remember that even videos on YouTube can give you ideas about subjects you already have some sort of knowledge about. Digital archives like YouTube are often valuable ways to supplement, challenge, and confirm findings found in other resources like the library or online databases. If you practice responding to the media around you with your opinion and experience, you'll find you have a lot more to say about a subject than you think.

CULTURES The video "Think before You Post," accessible through the English CourseMate for this text, strongly argues that people, especially adolescents and young adults, should consider the consequences of what they post online.

List five to seven ideas that came to your mind during or after viewing the video. Try to list them in question form. For instance: Is posting pictures really a problem? When does posting pictures become a problem?

Now think of a story about a friend, acquaintance, or family member that provides a good explanation of your idea. Write it down in about four paragraphs. For instance you might start the story like this: My brother's friend posted a picture of him on his Facebook page. The picture wasn't bad or anything, but the comments in response to the picture got so dirty that he got in trouble from my parents.

Answer one of the questions you listed by using the story you've written. For example: Posting pictures of your friends on sites like Facebook is risky because it can lead to big problems with their parents. I know because it happened to my brother.

Readings

As many of the readings and online resources in this chapter stress, our online lives are as vital as our real-time lives. The boundaries between the two become very blurry when it comes to things like dating and voting. Sherry Turkle, in her piece "Always-On/Always-On-You: The Tethered Self," considers ways our lives are constantly mediated by the ever-present technologies surrounding us and what those technologies teach us about ourselves and the communities we belong to. Social networking reaches into even traditional aspects of our lives, including local and national government efforts to reach citizens, as Zachary Sniderman suggests in his article "How Governments Are Using Social Media for Better and for Worse." But although we may engage in many worthwhile activities in our online life, some aspects of social networking challenge the boundaries of ethical behavior, and we are prone to question the limits of free speech online. Indeed, even as the Obama administration was one of the first to rely heavily on social networking, membership in anti-Obama groups such as the Facebook group "Praying for the President's Death" surpassed one million. A countergroup that called on Facebook to remove of the anti-Obama group gained more than six hundred thousand members. These sorts of ethical dilemmas are taken up in both Barbara Ortutay's "Don't Post That," Kim Zetter's "Cyberbullying Suicide Stokes the Internet Fury Machine," as well as Paul Smalera's blog entry, "What Real Internet Censorship Looks Like."

● Sherry Turkle

Always-On/Always-On-You: The Tethered Self

> Sherry Turkle is a professor of social studies of science and technology, and she is Director of the MIT Initiative on Technology and Self. She has authored several books and articles, including seminal works *The Second Self: Computers and the Human Spirit* (1984) and *Life on the Screen: Identity in the Age of the Internet* (1995). Her work also appears in *The New York Times*, *Scientific American*, and *Wired Magazine*.

In the mid-1990s, a group of young researchers at the MIT Media Lab carried computers and radio transmitters in their backpacks, keyboards in their pockets, and digital displays embedded in their eyeglass frames. Always on the Internet, they called themselves "cyborgs." The cyborgs seemed at a remove from their bodies. When their burdensome technology cut into their skin, causing lesions and then scar tissue, they were indifferent. When their encumbrances led them to be taken for the physically disabled, they patiently provided explanations. They were learning to walk and talk as new creatures, learning to inhabit their own bodies all over again, and yet in a way they were fading away, bleeding out onto the Net. Their experiment was both a re-embodiment—a prosthetic consummation—and a disembodiment: a disappearance of their bodies into still-nascent computational spaces.

Within a few years, the cyborgs had a new identity as the Media Lab's "Wearable Computing Group," harbingers of embedded technologies while the rest of us clumsily juggled cell phones, laptops, and PDAs. But the legacy of the MIT cyborgs goes beyond the idea that communications technologies might be wearable (or totable). Core elements of their experience have become generalized in global culture: the experience of living on the Net, newly free in some ways, newly yoked in others.

Today, the near-ubiquity of handheld and palm-size computing and cellular technologies that enable voice communication, text messaging, e-mail, and Web access have made connectivity commonplace. When digital technologies first came onto the consumer market in the form of personal computers they were objects for psychological projection. Computers—programmable and customizable—came to be experienced as a "second self" (Turkle 2005a). In the early twenty-first century, such language does not go far enough; our new intimacy with communications devices compels us to speak of a new state of the self, itself.

A New State of the Self, Itself

For the most part, our everyday language for talking about technology's effects assumes a life both on and off the screen; it assumes the existence of separate worlds, plugged and unplugged. But some of today's locutions suggest a new placement of the subject, such as when we say "I'll be on my cell," by which we mean "You can reach me; my cell phone will be on, and I am wired into (social) existence through it." *On* my cell, *online, on* the Web, *on* instant messaging—these phrases suggest a *tethered* self.

We are tethered to our "always-on/always-on-us" communications devices and the people and things we reach through them: people, Web pages, voice mail, games, artificial intelligences (nonplayer game characters, interactive online "bots"). These very different objects achieve a certain sameness because of the way we reach them. Animate and inanimate, they live for us through our tethering devices, always ready-to-mind and hand. The self, attached to its devices, occupies a liminal space between the physical real and its digital lives on multiple screens (Turner 1969). I once described the rapid movements from physical to a multiplicity of digital selves through the metaphor of "cycling-through." With cell technology, rapid cycling stabilizes into a sense of continual co-presence (Turkle 1995).

For example, in the past, I did not usually perform my role as mother in the presence of my professional colleagues. Now a call from my fifteen-year-old daughter calls me forth in this role. The presence of the cell phone, which has a special ring if my daughter calls, keeps me on the alert all day. Wherever I am, whatever I am doing, I am psychologically tuned to the connections that matter.

The Connections that Matter

We are witnessing a new form of sociality in which the connectedness that "matters" is determined by our distance from working communications technology. Increasingly, what people want out of public spaces is that they offer a place to be private with tethering technologies. A neighborhood walk reveals a world of madmen and women, talking to themselves, sometimes shouting to themselves, little concerned with what is around them, happy to have intimate conversations in public spaces. In fact, neighborhood spaces themselves become liminal, not entirely public, not entirely private (Katz 2006, chapters 1 and 2).

A train station is no longer a communal space, but a place of social collection: tethered selves come together, but do not speak to each other. Each person at the station is more likely to be having an encounter with someone miles away than with the person in the next chair. Each inhabits a private media bubble. Indeed, the presence of our tethering media signal that we do not want to be disturbed by conventional sociality with physically proximate individuals.

When people have personal cell phone conversations in public spaces, what sustains their sense of intimacy is the presumption that those around them treat them not only as anonymous, but as close to disembodied. When individuals hold cell phones (or "speak into the air," indicating the presence of cells with earphone microphone), they are marked with a certain absence. They are transported to the space of a new ether, virtualized. This "transport" can be signaled in other ways: when people look down at their laps during meals or meetings, the change of gaze has come to signify attention to their BlackBerries or other small communications devices. They are focused on elsewhere.

The director of a program that places American students in Greek universities complains that students are not "experiencing Greece" because they spend too much time online, talking with their friends from home. I am sympathetic as she speaks, thinking of the hours I spent walking with my fifteen-year-old daughter on a visit to Paris as she "texted" her friends at home on her cell phone. I worry that she is missing an experience that I cherished in my youth, the experience of an undiluted Paris that came with the thrill of disconnection from where I was from. But she is happy and tells me that keeping in touch is "comforting" and that beyond this, her text mails to home constitute a diary. She can look back at her texts and remember her state of mind at different points of her trip. Her notes back to friends, translated from instant message shorthand include "Saw Pont D'Avignon," "Saw World Cup Soccer in Paris," and "Went to Bordeaux." It is hard to get in too many words on the phone keyboard and there is no cultural incentive to do so. A friend calls my daughter as we prepare for dinner at our Paris hotel and asks her to lunch in Boston. My daughter says, quite simply: "Not possible, but how about Friday." Her friend has no idea that her call was transatlantic. Emotionally and socially, my daughter has not left home.

Of course, balancing one's physical and electronic connections is not limited to those on holiday. Contemporary professional life is rich in examples of people ignoring those they are physically "with" to give priority to online others. Certain settings in which this occurs have become iconic: sessions at international conferences where experts from all over the world come together but do their e-mail; the communications channels that are set up by audience members at conferences to comment on speakers' presentations during the presentations themselves (these conversations are as much about jockeying for professional position among the audience as they are about what is being said at the podium). Here, the public presentation becomes a portal to discussions that take people away from it, discussions that tend to take place in hierarchical tiers—only certain people are invited to participate in certain discussions. As a member of the audience, one develops a certain anxiety; have I been invited to chat in the inner circle?

Observing e-mail and electronic messaging during conferences at exotic locations compels our attention because it is easy to measure the time and money it takes to get everyone physically together at such meetings. Other scenes have become so mundane that we scarcely notice them: students do e-mail during classes; business people do e-mail during meetings; parents do e-mail while playing with their children; couples do e-mail at dinner; people talk on the phone and do their e-mail at the same time. Once done surreptitiously, the habit of electronic co-presence is no longer something people feel they need to hide. Indeed, being "elsewhere" than where you might be has become something of a marker of one's sense of self-importance.

Phoning It In

The expression "phoning it in" used to be pejorative. It implied a lack of appropriate attention to what might be novel about a task at hand. Now, as pure description, it provides a metric for status; it suggests that you are important enough to deliver your work remotely. The location of the high-status body is significant, but with connectivity comes multiple patterns for its deployment. In one pattern, the high-status body is in intensive contact with others, but spreads itself around the world, traveling. In another pattern, the high-status body is in retreat, traveling to face-to-face contact in order to maximize privacy and creativity. However the traveling body chooses to use its time, it is always tethered, kept in touch through technical means. Advertisements for wireless technology routinely feature a handsome man or beautiful woman on a beach. The ad copy makes it clear that he or she is important and working. The new disembodiment does not ask you to deny your body its pleasures, but on the contrary, to love your body, to put it somewhere beautiful while "you" work.

Our devices become a badge of our networks, a sign that we have them, that we are wanted by those we *know*, the people on our "contact lists" and by the potential, as yet *unknown* friends who wait for us in virtual places (such as Facebook, MySpace, or Friendster). It is not surprising that we project the possibility of love, surprise, amusement, and warmth onto our communications devices. Through them we live with a heightened sense of potential relationships, or at least of new connections. Whether or not our devices are in use, without them we feel adrift—adrift not only from our current realities but from our wishes for the future.

A call to a friend is a call to a known (if evolving) relationship. Going online to a social networking site offers a place to dream, sometimes fostering a sense that old relationships are dispensable. People describe feeling more attached to the site than to any particular acquaintances they have on them. In psychodynamic terms, the site becomes a transference object: the place where friendships come from. "I toss people," says Maura, thirty-one, an architect, describing how she treats acquaintances on Second Life, an elaborate online social environment. Second Life offers the possibility of an online parallel life (including a virtual body, wardrobe, real estate, and paying job). "I know it gives me something of a reputation, but there are always new people. I don't stay in relationships long." Maura continues: "There is always someone else to talk to, someone else to meet. I don't feel a commitment." People who have deployed avatars on Second Life stress that the virtual world gives them a feeling of everyday renewal. "I never know who I'll meet," says a thirty-seven-year-old housewife from the Boston suburbs, and contrasts this pleasurable feeling with the routine of her life at home with two toddlers.

From the early 1990s, game environments known as MUDs (for multiuser domains) and then MMRPGs (massively multiplayer role playing games) presented their users with the possibility of creating characters and living out multiple aspects of self. Although the games often took the forms of medieval quests, the virtual environments owed their "holding power" to the opportunities that they offered for exploring identity. (Turkle 1995). People used their lives on the screen to work through unresolved or partly resolved issues, often related to sexuality or intimacy. For many who enjoy online life, it is easier to express intimacy in the virtual world than in "RL" or real life. For those who are lonely yet fearful of intimacy, online life provides environments where one can be a loner yet not alone, environments where one can have the illusion of companionship without the demands of sustained, intimate friendship. Online life emerged as an "identity workshop" (Bruckman 1992).

Throughout our lives, transitions (career change, divorce, retirement, children leaving home) provide new impetus for rethinking identity. We never "graduate" from working on identity; we simply work on it with the materials we have at hand at a particular stage of life. Online social worlds provide new materials. The plain may represent themselves as glamorous; the introverted can try out being bold. People build the dreamhouses in the virtual that they cannot afford in the real. They plant virtual gardens. They take online jobs of great responsibility. They often have relationships, partners and what they term "marriages" of great emotional importance. In the virtual is this world the crippled can walk without crutches and the shy can improve their chances as seducers.

It is not exact to think of people as tethered to their *devices*. People are tethered to the gratifications offered by their online selves. These include the promise of affection, conversation, a sense of new beginnings. And, there is vanity: building a new body in a game like Second Life allows you to put aside an imperfect physical self and reinvent yourself as a wonder of virtual fitness. Everyone on Second Life can have their own "look"; the game enables a high level of customization, but everyone looks good, wearing designer clothes that appear most elegant on sleek virtual bodies. With virtual beauty comes possibilities for sexual encounters that may not be available in the physical real.

Thus, more than the sum of their instrumental functions, tethering devices help to constitute new subjectivities. Powerful evocative objects for adults, they are even more intense and compelling for adolescents, at that point in development when identity play is at the center of life.

The Tethered Teen

The job of adolescence is centered around experimentation—with ideas, with people, with notions of self. When adolescents play an online role playing game they often use it to recast their lives. They may begin by building their own home, furnishing it to their taste, not that of their parents, and then getting on with the business of reworking in the virtual world what has not worked so well in the real. Trish, a thirteen-year-old who has been physically abused by her father, creates an abusive family on Sims Online—but in the game her character, also thirteen, is physically and emotionally strong. In simulation, she plays and replays the experience of fighting off her aggressor. Rhonda, a sexually experienced girl of sixteen, creates an online innocent. "I want to have a rest," she tells me and goes on to recall the movie *Pleasantville* in which the female lead character, a high school teenager, "gets to go to a town that only exists from a TV show where she starts to be slutty like she is at home, but then she changes her mind and starts to turn boys down and starts a new life. She practices being a different kind of person. That's what Sims Online is for me. Practice."

Rhonda "practices" on the game at breakfast, during school recess, and after dinner. She says she feels comforted by her virtual life. The game does not connect her to other people. She is tethered to the game by a desire to connect to herself.

> ST: Are you doing anything different in everyday life [since playing Sims Online]? Rhonda: Not really. Not very. But I'm thinking about breaking up with my boyfriend. I don't want to have sex anymore but I would like to have a boyfriend. My character [in Sims Online] has boyfriends but doesn't have sex. They help her with her job. I think to start fresh I would have to break up with my boyfriend.

Rhonda is emotionally tethered to the world of the Sims technology that gives her access to a medium in which she can see her life through a new filter, and possibly begin to work through problems in a new way (Turkle 1995).

Adolescents create online personae in many ways: when they deploy a game avatar, design a Web page, or write a profile for a social networking site such as Facebook. Even creating a playlist of music becomes a way of capturing one's personae at a moment in time. Multiple playlists reflect aspects of self. And once you have collected your own music, you can make connections to people all over the world to whom you send your songs.

Today's adolescents provide our first view of tethering in developmental terms. The adolescent wants both to be part of the group and to assert individual identity, experiencing peers as both sustaining and constraining. The mores of tethering support group demands: among urban teens, it is common for friends to expect that their peers will stay available by cell or instant message. In this social contract, one needs good cause to claim time offline. The pressure to be always-on can be a burden. So, for example, teenagers who need uninterrupted time for schoolwork resort to using their parents' Internet accounts to hide out from friends. Other effects of the always-on/always-on-you communications culture may be less easily managed and perhaps more enduring.

Mark Twain mythologized the process of separation during which adolescents work out their identities as the Huck Finn experience, the on-the-Mississippi time of escape from the adult world. The time on the river portrays an ongoing rite of passage during which children separate from parents to become young adults, a process now transformed by technology. Traditionally, children have internalized the adults in their world before (or just as, or shortly after) the threshold of independence is crossed. In the technologically tethered variant, parents can be brought along in an intermediate space, for example, the space created by the cell phone where everyone is on speed dial. In this sense, the generations sail down the river together.

When children receive cell phones by their parents, the gift usually comes with a promise: children are to answer their parents' calls. This arrangement gives children permission to do things—take trips to see friends, attend movies, go to the beach—that would not be permitted without the phone-tethering to parents. Yet the tethered child does not have the experience of being alone with only him or herself to count on. There used to be a point for an urban child, usually between the ages of eleven and fourteen, when there was a "first time" to navigate the city alone. It was a rite of passage that communicated "You are on your own and responsible. If you are frightened, you have to experience those feelings." The cell phone buffers this moment; the parent is "on tap." With the on-tap parent, tethered children think differently about their own responsibilities and capacities. These remain potential, not proven.

New Forms of Validation

I think of the *inner history* of technology as the relationships people form with their artifacts, relationships that can forge new sensibilities. Tethering technologies have their own inner histories. For example, a mobile phone gives us the potential to communicate whenever we have a feeling, enabling a new coupling of "I have a feeling/Get me a friend." This formulation has the emotional corollary, "I want to have a feeling/Get me a friend." In either case, what is *not* being cultivated is the ability to be alone, to reflect on and contain one's emotions. The anxiety that teens report when they are without their cell phones or their link to the Internet may not speak so much to missing the easy sociability with others but of missing the self that is constituted in these relationships.

When David Riesman remarked on the American turn from an inner- to an other-directed sense of self by 1950 (Riesman 1950), he could not foresee how technology could raise other-directedness to a new level. It does this by making it possible for each of us to develop new patterns of reliance on others and transference relationships to a suite of devices that makes the others available to us at literally a moment's notice. Some people experienced this kind of transference to the traditional (landline) telephone. The telephone was a medium through which to receive validation, and sometimes the feelings associated with that validation were transferred to the telephone itself. The cell phone takes this effect to a higher power because the device is always available and there is a high probability that one will be able to reach a source of validation through it. It is understood that the validating cell conversation may be brief, just a "check-in," but more is not necessarily desired.

The cell phone check-in enables the new other-directness. At the moment of having a thought or feeling, one can have it validated. Or, one may *need* to have it validated. And further down a continuum of dependency, as a thought or feeling is being formed, it may *need validation to become established.* The technology does not cause a new style of relating, but enables it. As we become accustomed to cell calls, e-mail, and social Web sites, certain styles of relating self to other feel more natural. The validation (of a feeling already felt) and enabling (of a feeling that cannot be felt without outside validation) are becoming commonplace rather than marked as childlike or pathological. One moves from "I have a feeling/Get me a friend" to "I want to have a feeling/Get me a friend."

The psychoanalyst Heinz Kohut writes about narcissism and describes how some people, in their fragility, turn other persons into "self-objects" to shore up their fragile sense of self (Ornstein 1978). In the role of self-object, the other is experienced as part of the self, thus in perfect tune with the fragile individual's inner state. They are there for validation, mirroring. Technology increases one's options. One fifteen-year-old girl explains: "I have a lot of people on my contact list. If one friend doesn't get it, I call another." In Kohutian terms, this young woman's contact or buddy list has become a list of spare parts for her fragile adolescent self.

Just as always-on/always-on-you connectivity enables teens to postpone independently managing their emotions, it can also make it difficult to assess children's level of maturity, conventionally defined in terms of autonomy and responsibility. Tethered children know that they have backup. The "check-in" call has evolved into a new kind of contact between parents and children. It is a call that says "I am fine. You are there. We are connected."

In general, the telegraphic text message quickly communicates a state, rather than opens a dialogue about complexity of feeling. Although the culture that grows up around the cell is a talk culture (in shopping malls, supermarkets, city streets, cafés, playgrounds, and parks cells are out and people are talking into them), it is not necessarily a culture in which talk contributes to self-reflection. Today's adolescents have no less need than previous generations to learn empathic skills, to manage and express feelings, and to handle being alone. But when the interchanges to develop empathy are reduced to the shorthand of emoticon emotions, questions such as "Who am I?" and "Who are you?" are reformatted for the small screen, and are flattened in the process. High technology, with all its potential range and richness, has been put at the service of telegraphic speed and brevity.

Leaving the Time to Take Our Time

Always-on/always-on-you communications devices are seductive for many reasons, among them, they give the sense that one can do more, be in more places, and control more aspects of life. Those who are attached to BlackBerry technology speak about the fascination of watching their lives "scroll by," of watching their lives as though watching a movie. One develops a new view of self when one considers the many thousands of people to whom one may be connected. Yet just as teenagers may suffer from a media environment that invites them to greater dependency, adults, too, may suffer from being overly tethered, too connected. Adults are stressed by new responsibilities to keep up with email, the nagging sense of always being behind, the inability to take a vacation without bringing the office with them, and the feeling that they are being asked to respond immediately to situations at work, even when a wise response requires taking time for reflection, a time that is no longer available.

We are becoming accustomed to a communications style in which we receive a hasty message to which we give a rapid response. Are we leaving enough time to take our time?

Adults use tethering technologies during what most of us think of as down time, the time we might have daydreamed during a cab ride, waiting in line, or walking to work. This may be time that we physiologically and emotionally need to maintain or restore our ability to focus (Herzog et al. 1997; Kaplan 1995). Tethering takes time from other activities (particularly those that demand undivided attention), it adds new tasks that take up time (keeping up with e-mail and messages), and adds a new kind of time to the day, the time of attention sharing, sometimes referred to as *continuous partial attention* (Stone 2006). In all of this, we make our attention into our rarest resource, creating increasingly stiff competition for its deployment, *but we undervalue it as well*. We deny the importance of giving it to one thing and one thing only.

Continuous partial attention affects the quality of thought we give to each of our tasks, now done with less *mind share*. From the perspective of this essay with its focus on identity, continuous partial attention affects how people think about their lives and priorities. The phrases "doing my e-mail" and "doing my messages" imply performance rather than reflection. These are the performances of a self that can be split into constituent parts.

When media does not stand waiting in the background but is always there, waiting to be wanted, the self can lose a sense of conscious choosing to communicate. The sophisticated consumer of tethering devices finds ways to integrate always-on/always-on-you technology into the everyday gestures of the body. One BlackBerry user says: "I glance at my watch to sense the time; I glance at my BlackBerry to get a sense of my life." The term *addiction* has been used to describe this state, but this way of thinking is limited in its usefulness. More useful is thinking about a new state of self, one that is extended in a communications artifact. The BlackBerry movie of one's life takes on a life of its own—with more in it than can be processed. People develop the sense that they cannot keep up with their own lives. They become alienated from their own experience and anxious about watching a version of their lives moving along, scrolling along, faster than they can handle. It is the unedited version of their lives; they are not able to keep up with it, but they are responsible for it (Mazmanian 2005).

Michel Foucault wrote about Jeremy Bentham's Panopticon as emblematic of the situation of the individual in modern, "disciplinary" society (Foucault 1979). The Panopticon is a wheel-like structure with an observer (in the case of a prison, a prison guard) at its hub. The architecture of the Panopticon creates a sense of being always watched whether or not the guard is actually present. For Foucault, the task of the modern state is to construct citizens who do not need to be watched, who mind the rules and themselves. Always-on/always-on-you technology takes the job of self-monitoring to a new level. We try to keep up with our lives as they are presented to us by a new disciplining technology. We try, in sum, to have a self that keeps up with our e-mail.

Boundaries

A new complaint in family and business life is that it is hard to know when one has the attention of a BlackBerry user. A parent, partner, or child can be lost for a few seconds or a few minutes to an alternate reality. The shift of attention can be subtle; friends and family are sometimes not aware of the loss until the person has "returned." Indeed, BlackBerry users may not even know where their attention lies. They report that their sense of self has merged with their prosthetic extensions and some see this as a new "high." But this exhilaration may be denying the costs of multitasking. Sociologists who study the boundaries between work and the rest of life suggest that it is helpful when people demarcate role shifts between the two. Their work suggests that being able to use a BlackBerry to blur the line is problematic rather than a skill to be celebrated. (Clark 2000; Desrochers and Sargent 2003; Shumate and Fulk 2004). And celebrating the integration of remote communications into the flow of life may be underestimating the importance of face-to-face connections (Mazmanian 2005).

Attention-sharing creates work environments fraught with new tensions over the lack of primacy given to physical proximity. Face-to-face conversations are routinely interrupted by cell phone calls and e-mail reading. Fifteen years ago, if a colleague read mail in your presence, it was considered rude. These days, turning away from a person in front of you to answer a cell phone has become the norm. Additionally, for generations, business people have grown accustomed to relying on time in taxis, airports, trains, and limousines to get to know each other and to discuss substantive matters. The waiting time in client outer offices was precious time for work and the exchange of news that created social bonds among professional colleagues. Now, things have changed: professionals spend taxi time on their cell phones or doing e-mail on their PDAs. In the precious moments before client presentations, one sees consulting teams moving around the periphery of waiting rooms, looking for the best place for cell reception so that they can make calls. "My colleagues go to the ether when we wait for our clients," says one advertising executive. "I think our presentations have suffered." We live and work with people whose commitment to our presence feels increasingly tenuous because they are tethered to more important virtual others.

Human beings are skilled at creating rituals for demarcating the boundaries between the world of work and the world of family, play, and relaxation. There are special times (the Sabbath), special meals (the family dinner), special attire (the "armor" for a day's labor comes off at home, whether it is the businessperson's suit or the laborer's overalls), and special places (the dining room, the parlor, the bedroom, the beach). Now always-on/always-on-me technology accompanies people to all these places, undermining the traditional rituals of separation.

There is a certain push back. Just as teenagers hide from friends by using their parents' online accounts to do homework, adults, too, find ways to escape from the demands of tethering: BlackBerries are left at the office on weekends or they are left in locked desk drawers to free up time for family or leisure (Gant and Kiesler 2001). "It used to be my home was a haven; but now my home is a media center," says an architect whose clients reach him on his Internet-enabled cell. No longer a safe space or refuge, people need to find places to hide. There are technically none except long plane rides where there is no cell or Internet access, and this, too, may be changing.

A Self Shaped by Rapid Response

Our technology reflects and shapes our values. If we think of a telephone call as a quick-response system enabled by always-on/always-on-you technology, we can forget there is a difference between a scheduled call and the call you make in reaction to a fleeting emotion, because someone crossed your mind, or because someone left you a message. The self that is shaped by this world of rapid response measures success by calls made, e-mails answered, and contacts reached. This self is calibrated on the basis of what the technology proposes, by what it makes possible, and by what it makes easy. But in the buzz of activity, there are losses that we are perhaps not ready to sustain.

One is the technology-induced pressure for speed, even when we are considering matters over which we should take our time. We insist that our world is increasingly complex, yet we have created a communications culture that has decreased the time available for us to sit and think uninterrupted. BlackBerry users describe that sense of encroachment of the device on their time. One says, "I don't have enough time alone with my mind." Other phrases come up: "I have to struggle to make time to think." "I artificially make time to think." "I block out time to think." In all of these statements is the implicit formulation of an "I" that is separate from technology, that can put it aside and needs time to think on its own. This formulation contrasts with a growing reality of our lives lived in the continual presence of communications devices. This reality has us, like the early MIT "cyborg" group, learning to see ourselves not as separate but as at one with our the machines that tether us to each other and to the information culture. To put it most starkly: to make more "time" in the old-fashioned sense means turning off our devices, disengaging from the always-on culture. But this is not a simple proposition since our devices have become more closely coupled to our sense of our bodies and increasingly feel like extensions of our minds.

In the 1990s, as the Internet became part of everyday life, people began to create multiple online avatars and used them to shift gender, age, race, and class. The effort was to create richly rendered virtual selves through which one could experiment with identity by playing out parallel lives in constructed worlds. The world of avatars and games continues, but now, alongside its pleasures, we use always-on/always-on-you technology to play ourselves. Today's communications technology provides a social and psychological GPS, a navigation system for tethered selves. One television producer, accustomed to being linked to the world via her cell and Palm device, revealed that for her, the Palm's inner spaces were where her self resides: "When my Palm crashed it was like a death. It was more than I could handle. I felt as though I had lost my mind."

Tethered: To Whom and to What?

Acknowledging our tethered state raises the question of to whom or to what we are connected (Katz 2003). Traditional telephones tied us to friends, family, colleagues from school and work, and commercial or philanthropic solicitations. Things are no longer so simple. These days we respond to humans and to objects that represent them: answering machines, Web sites, and personal pages on social networking sites. Sometimes we engage with avatars that anonymously "stand in" for others, enabling us to express ourselves in intimate ways to strangers, in part because we and they are able to veil who we "really are." And sometimes we listen to disembodied voices—recorded announcements and messages—or interact with synthetic voice recognition protocols that simulate real people as they try to assist us with technical and administrative problems. We no longer demand that as a person we have another person as an interlocutor. On the Internet, we interact with bots, anthropomorphic programs that are able to converse with us, and in online games we are partnered with nonplayer characters, artificial intelligences that are not linked to human players. The games require that we put our trust in these characters. Sometimes it is only these nonplayer characters who can save our "lives" in the game.

This wide range of entities—human and not—is available to us wherever we are. I live in Boston. I write this chapter in Paris. As I travel, my access to my favorite avatars, nonplayer characters, and social networking sites stays constant. There is a degree of emotional security in a good hotel on the other side of the world, but for many, it cannot compare to the constancy of a stable technological environment and the interactive objects within it. Some of these objects are engaged on the Internet. Some are interactive digital companions that can travel with you, now including robots that are built for relationships.

Consider this moment: an older woman, seventy-two, in a nursing home outside of Boston is sad. Her son has broken off his relationship with her. Her nursing home is part of a study I am conducting on robotics for the elderly. I am recording her reactions as she sits with the robot Paro, a seal-like creature, advertised as the first "therapeutic robot" for its ostensibly positive effects on the ill, the elderly, and the emotionally troubled. Paro is able to make eye contact through sensing the direction of a human voice, is sensitive to touch, and has "states of mind" that are affected by how it is treated—for example, it can sense if it is being stroked gently or with some aggression. In this session with Paro, the woman, depressed because of her son's abandonment, comes to believe that the robot is depressed as well. She turns to Paro, strokes him, and says: "Yes, you're sad, aren't you. It's tough out there. Yes, it's hard." And then she pets the robot once again, attempting to provide it with comfort. And in so doing, she tries to comfort herself.

Psychoanalytically trained, I believe that this kind of moment, if it happens between people, has profound therapeutic potential. What are we to make of this transaction as it unfolds between a depressed woman and a robot? The woman's sense of being understood is based on the ability of computational objects like Paro to convince their users that they are in a relationship. I call these creatures (some virtual, some physical robots) "relational artifacts" (Turkle 1999; 2003a; 2003b; 2004a; 2004b; 2004c; 2005b; 2005c; 2006b; Turkle et al. 2006a). Their ability to inspire a relationship is not based on their intelligence or consciousness but on their ability to push certain "Darwinian" buttons in people (making eye contact, for example) that cause people to respond *as though* they were in a relationship.

Do plans to provide relational robots to children and the elderly make us less likely to look for other solutions for their care? If our experience with relational artifacts is based on a fundamentally deceitful interchange (artifacts' ability to persuade us that they know and care about our existence), can it be good for us? Or might it be good for us in the "feel good" sense, but bad for us in our lives as moral beings? The answers to such questions are not dependent on what computers can do today or what they are likely to be able to do in the future. These questions ask what *we* will be like, what kind of people are *we* becoming, as we develop increasingly intimate relationships with machines.

In *Computer Power and Human Reason*, Joseph Weizenbaum wrote about his experiences with his invention, ELIZA, a computer program that engaged people in a dialogue similar to that of a Rogerian psychotherapist (Weizenbaum 1976). It mirrored one's thoughts; it was always supportive. To the comment "My mother is making me angry," the program might respond "Tell me more about your mother," or "Why do you feel so negatively about your mother?" Weizenbaum was disturbed that his students, fully knowing they were talking with a computer program, wanted to chat with it, indeed, wanted to be alone with it. Weizenbaum was my colleague at MIT; we taught courses together on computers and society. At the time his book came out, I felt moved to reassure him about his concerns. ELIZA seemed to me like a Rorschach; users did become involved with the program, but in a spirit of "as if." The gap between program and person was vast. People bridged it with attribution and desire. They thought: "I will talk to this program 'as if' it were a person"; "I will vent, I will rage, I will get things off my chest." At the time, ELIZA seemed to me no more threatening than an interactive diary. Now, thirty years later, I ask myself if I underestimated the quality of the connection. Now, computational creatures have been designed that evoke a sense of mutual relating. The people who meet relational artifacts are drawn in by a desire to nurture them. And with nurturance comes the fantasy of reciprocation. People want the creatures to care about them in return. Very little about these relationships seems to be experienced "as if."

Relational artifacts are the latest chapter in the trajectory of the tethered self. We move from technologies that tether us to people to those that are able to tether us to the Web sites and avatars that represent people. Relational artifacts represent their programmers but are given autonomy and primitive psychologies; they are designed to stand on their own as creatures to be loved. They are potent objects-to-think-with for asking the questions, posed by all of the machines that tether us to new socialities: "What is an authentic relationship with a machine?" "What are machines doing to our relationships with people?" And ultimately, "What is a relationship?"

Methodology Note

I have studied relational artifacts in the lives of children and the elderly since 1997, beginning with the simple Tamagotchis that were available at every toy store to Kismet and Cog, advanced robots at the MIT Artificial Intelligence Laboratory, and Paro, a seal-like creature designed specifically for therapeutic purposes. Along the way there have been Furbies, AIBOS, and My Real Babies, the latter a baby doll that like the Paro has changing inner states that respond to the quality of its human care. More than two hundred and fifty subjects have been involved in these studies. My investigations of computer-mediated communication date from the mid-1980s and have followed the media from e-mail, primitive virtual communities, and Web-based chat to cell technology, instant messaging, and social networking. More than four hundred subjects have been involved in these studies. My work was done in Boston and Cambridge and their surrounding suburbs. The work on robotics investigated children and seniors from a range of ethnicities and social classes. This was possible because in every case I was providing robots and other relational artifacts to my informants. In the case of the work on communications technology, I spoke to people, children, adolescents, and adults, who already had computers, Web access, mobile phones, BlackBerries, et cetera. This necessarily makes my claims about their lives in the always-on/always-on-you culture not equally generalizable outside of the social class currently wealthy enough to afford such things.

REFERENCES

Bruckman, A. 1992. Identity workshop: Emergent social and psychological phenomena in text-based virtual reality. Unpublished paper written in partial completion of a doctoral degree at the Media Lab, Massachusetts Institute of Technology. http://www-static.cc.gatech.edu/~asb/papers/old-papers. html.

Clark, S. Campbell. 2000. Work/family border theory: A new theory of work/family balance. *Human Relations* 53(6): 747–770.

Desrocher, S., and L. D. Sargent. 2003. Work-family boundary ambiguity, gender and stress in dual-earner couples. Paper presented at the Conference "From 9-to-5 to 24/7: How Workplace Changes Impact Families, Work, and Communities," 2003 BPW/Brandeis University Conference, Orlando, Fla.

Foucault, M. 1979. *Discipline and Punish: The Birth of the Prison*. New York: Vintage Books.

Gant, D. B., and S. Kiesler. 2001. Blurring the boundaries: Cell phones, mobility and the line between work and personal life. In *Wireless World: Social and International Aspects of the Mobile Age*, edited by N. G. R. H. Barry Brown. New York: Springer.

Herzog, T. R., A. M. Black, K. A. Fountaine, and D. J. Knotts. 1997. Reflection and attentional recovery as distinctive benefits of restorative environments. *Journal of Environmental Psychology* 17: 165–170.

Jones, C. A. 2006. Tethered. In *Sensorium: Embodied Experience, Technology, and Contemporary Art,* edited by C. A. Jones. Cambridge, Mass.: List Visual Art Center and MIT Press.

Kaplan, S. 1995. The restorative benefits of nature: Toward an integrative framework. *Journal of Environmental Psychology* 15: 169–182.

Katz, J. E. 2006. *Magic in the Air: Mobile Communication and the Transformation of Social Life*. New Brunswick, N.J.: Transaction.

Katz, J. E., ed. 2003. *Machines that Become Us: The Social Context of Personal Communication Technology*. New Brunswick, N.J.: Transaction.

Mazmanian, M. 2005. Some thoughts on blackberries. In Memo.

Ornstein, P. H., ed. 1978. *The Search for the Self: Selected Writings of Heinz Kohut: 1950–1978*: 2. New York: International Universities Press, Inc.

Riesman, D., R. Denney, and N. Glazer, 1950. *The Lonely Crowd: A Study of the Changing American Character*. New Haven: Yale University Press.

Shumate, M., and J. Fulk. 2004. Boundaries and role conflict when work and family are colocated: A communication network and symbolic interaction approach. *Human Relations* 57(1): 55–74.

Stone, L. 2006. Linda Stone's thoughts on attention, and specifically, continual partial attention. http://www.lindastone.net.

Turkle, S. 1995. *Life on the Screen: Identity in the Age of the Internet*. New York: Simon and Schuster.

Turkle, S. 1999. Toys to change our minds. In *Predictions*, edited by S. Griffiths. Oxford: Oxford University Press.

Turkle, S. 2003a. Sociable technologies: Enhancing human performance when the computer is not a tool but a companion. In *Converging Technologies for Improving Human Performance*, edited by M. C. Roco and W. S. Bainbridge. The Netherlands: Kluwer Academic Publishers.

Turkle, S. 2003b. Technology and human vulnerability. *Harvard Business Review*.

Turkle, S. 2004a. *NSF Report: Relational Artifacts*. National Science Foundation. (NSF Grant SES-01115668).

Turkle, S. 2004b. Spinning technology. In *Technological Visions*, edited by M. Sturken, D. Thomas, and S. Ball-Rokeach. Philadelphia: Temple University Press.

Turkle, S. 2004c. Whither psychoanalysis in computer culture. *Psychoanalytic Psychology: Journal of The Division of Psychoanalysis* 21(1): 16–30.

Turkle, S. 2005a. *The Second Self: Computers and the Human Spirit* (20th anniversary ed.). Cambridge, Mass.: MIT Press [1984].

Turkle, S. 2005b. Computer games as evocative objects: From projective screens to relational artifacts. In *Handbook of Computer Games Studies*, edited by J. Raessens and J. Goldstein. Cambridge, Mass.: MIT Press.

Turkle, S. 2005c. Relational artifacts/children/elders: The complexities of cybercompanions. IEEE Workshop on Android Science, Stresa, Italy.

Turkle, S., C. Breazeal, O. Dasté, and B. Scassellat. 2006a. First encounters with kismet and cog: Children's relationship with humanoid robots. In *Digital Media: Transfer in Human Communication*, edited by P. Messaris and L. Humphreys. New York: Peter Lang Publishing.

Turkle, S. 2006b. Tamagotchi diary. *The London Review of Books*, April 20.

Turkle, S. 2006c. Tethering. In *Sensorium: Embodied Experience, Technology, and Contemporary Art*, edited by C. A. Jones. Cambridge, Mass.: List Visual Art Center and MIT Press.

Turner, V. 1969. *The Ritual Process: Structure and Anti-structure*. Chicago: Aldine.

Weizenbaum, J. 1976. *Computer Power and Human Reason: From Judgment to Calculation*. San Francisco: W. H. Freeman.

READING REACTIONS

1. Key to Turkle's argument about ubiquitous computing is the idea of the "tethered self." What are we tethered to?

2. How do some technologies make us avatars even offline? How does the concept of "cyborg" trouble our notions of identities?

3. Turkle notes the phenomenon of "continuous partial attention" in our always-on society. What is this? How do you see this in your own life or in the lives of those around you?

4. What are the challenges of living in an "always on" culture? What are the benefits?

5. How does this sort of tethering to technology encourage certain social action? How does it ask us to engage with other people or our own online identities? Consider especially Rhonda's story from the article. What makes us invest in online identities and relationships?

6. There are clear ways to play and to be in online spaces whether in a video game or another online-only community. But how do you "play yourself" offline with the help of "always-on" technologies? What are the contexts or conditions (historical, political, or cultural) under which we play such roles?

7. What strategies and types of proof or data does Turkle employ to create her overall persuasive point about the ways technology impacts us as users?

8. What role does narrative play in this scholarly argument? What is the intended impact on the reader? What are we as readers "supposed to" do or feel?

● Zachary Sniderman

How Governments Are Using Social Media for Better and for Worse

Zachary Sniderman is an assistant features editor at Mashable.com. He has also written arts and culture articles for *Maclean's Magazine* and GreenShoelace.com. Sniderman holds a BA from Harvard and an MS from Columbia. He currently resides in New York City.

Social media has become a crucial part of how we interact with our friends, community and even run our cities. Governments are starting to take serious notice and incorporate social media into their own day-to-day actions.

Governments may not be early adopters but the proliferation of social in national media has ramped up its importance for governments around the world. While this initial stance kept politicians on the defensive, enough time has passed that individual politicians and even entire governments are starting to use social media to connect with their communities in new, open ways.

We've chosen a few examples to illustrate some of the many ways government is embracing social media. [. . .] The list is neither exhaustive nor does it try to summarize the entirety of a government's social outreach. It is instead meant to start a conversation.

AMERICA GETS SOCIAL

Social media has a strange role in America as both kingmaker and career wrecker. For every social media success story like President Barack Obama's 2008 grassroots campaign there is another of a career-crippling gaffe, like Weinergate, when New York Rep. Anthony Weiner accidentally tweeted a picture of his crotch.

Social media, and particularly Twitter, have become a type of soapbox in America, on which many politicians are able to speak directly to their constituents. "I know the overall importance of reaching out through the social media, because I have 31 grandchildren and they are on all of these things," said U.S. Rep. Buck McKeon, R-Calif. "This is mostly a young person's game and I'm an old person, but I'm young at heart . . . the only advice I'd give is 'get involved' and then use it in the right way."

In fact, Republicans have been encouraging their members to get on social media with a friendly NCAA-style knock-out contest called the New Media Challenge, run by the House Republican Conference. Republicans are also using social media to reach out through initiatives like Youcut, a crowd-sourced platform where the public can debate and vote on how to lower the national debt. "If you ignore [social media] and you just keep doing things the way you did when I first came to congress, you do so at your own peril," McKeon said.

Of course the White House itself has taken to social media to help push some of its initiatives. Obama recently held a Twitter town hall where he received and answered questions through Twitter and pledged to start tweeting from his own official account. Social networks like Twitter and Facebook have also been used in presidential debates and forums. The White House has even set up several verified Twitter accounts for state entities such as the secret service (@SecretService), the Open Government Initiative (@OpenGov), a Spanish White House account (@lacasablanca) and an official account for White House Press Secretary Jay Carney (@presssec). Social media has become a place where politicians large and small can register their support in a public way, for example, when Hilary Clinton, Nancy Pelosi and Rep. Rosa DeLauro, D-Conn., called for the release of Chinese artist Ai Weiwei from police custody.

Social media has also been used in national campaigns such as ChooseMyPlate.gov, for healthier eating, Serve.gov, for organizing and coordinating national volunteer efforts and for the White House blog.

CANADA CROWDSOURCES

America's friendly neighbor to the North is also taking advantage of social media. Most Canadian politicians have a social presence, which they or their teams manage. Some governmental departments are even taking steps to integrate social media into actual government operations.

Glen Murray is the Minister of Research and Innovation for the province of Ontario. Following a social innovation summit, Murray wanted to find a way to bring the public into the discussion. Murray and two other ministries created a crowdsourced wiki to help create an official policy paper on what the government's approach to social innovation should be. Like Wikipedia, any user can add articles or edit submissions in a collaborative effort to create official policy.

"We are adjusting and trying to get ahead of the curve of a generation of social media users who more and more see social media as a way of affecting social change," said a spokesperson for Murray's office. "People are engaging with social policy in a way that they haven't before and government will either adjust or be adjusted."

Social media played a huge role in the 2011 federal election, though it exposed that social media alone can still not win an election. Michael

Ignatieff, the liberal party leader, was widely thought to own the social space but ultimately lost by a significant margin. "It was incredibly exhilarating and stressful and energizing and overwhelming," said a member of Ignatieff's social media team. "Every instant of every day we were completely absorbed, in addition to all the other aspects of campaigning that haven't changed, we were involved with what people were saying in the Twitterverse."

Twitter became another branch of the media arm which required monitoring and attention. Questions that appeared on social sites needed to be treated the same as traditional media calls, the aide said.

"Political figures can't work without engaging their constituents using social media," the aide said. "It's an expectation as much as it's an opportunity. It's changing the onus from working for people to working with people."

RUSSIA TRIES A LITTLE OPENNESS

Of course, North America isn't the only place where social media is making its way into the government. After Facebook's January 2010 launch in Russia, the number of users in the country grew by 376%, most of which are under 27 years of age. There is a young generation of socially active Russians asking their government to follow suit. A ComScore global study last summer showed Russia had the most engaged social networking audience in the world.

A year ago, Dmitri Medvedev, Russia's then and current president, paid a visit to Twitter's offices, created an account and sent out his first official tweet. He is now a prolific user with more than half a million followers across four verified accounts.

His tweets are as much a way of sharing updates on the government as they are about humanizing the president, and the trend is being seen government wide, according to Russia Beyond the Headlines:

> Opinion polls and electronic communications, which until recently were recipient-specific, are gradually becoming discussion forums where anyone can speak out. It has never been easier for people in Russia to observe government at work and to actively participate in discussions with officials through social networks and blogs.

Since last fall, Russians have been able to participate in meetings of the Presidential Commission for Modernization and Technological Development of Russia's Economy through online tools. When discussions came up around a new law on police, the government created a forum, called i-Russia.ru, where people can post comments and connect their social networks. The commission is also the first government body in Russia to get its own mobile app.

CENSORSHIP AND CONTROL

Social media isn't always sunshine and roses. Questions of censorship come up even in governments where a free press and public media are encouraged. In France, for example, the government banned the use of the words "Twitter" and "Facebook" on broadcast news saying that it constituted unsolicited advertising.

In the U.K., a government known for its support of personal privacy, social media has presented a challenge in protecting and controlling individual privacy rights. A recent ad campaign warned British soldiers about how they use social media lest that information also end up in enemy hands.

"Control works both ways," said Adam Clark Estes, a writer at *The Atlantic* and former social media editor at the *Huffington Post*. "The government can control what people are doing [on] Twitter, but they can't get rid of the services because even in China, where there are restrictions on [social media], they're finding a way to get around the firewall." Estes said governments are using social media as a kind of customary service tool to handle negative sentiment while at the same time humanizing the face of government. The goal is to give the illusion that social media is making the government more open, Estes said, while the government still retains control over their message.

"The kind of idea behind it, that you want to reach people and convince them of your opinion is really no different than the way governments have always used [the media]," said Weldon Kennedy, Change.org's director of organizing. For Kennedy, governments are using social media the same way they use more traditional outlets like the print press and broadcast. More open communities have more open social policies, whereas more restrictive or totalitarian communities place tighter reigns on social media. "You don't see dictators get on Facebook," Kennedy said. "[Former Egyptian president Hosni] Mubarak wasn't on Facebook, but the military council that's been in charge ever since was."

Kennedy was quick to point out that social media is still a bit of a luxury in parts of the Middle East and Africa. Social media there is often less a way to lobby the government as it is to network and organize protests.

CONCLUSION

Governments and social media have reached a tentative partnership. While the Internet is no longer a "Wild West," people in power are still trying to figure out how best to approach online communities and their social tools. There may not be any clear answers, but social is certainly not going to go away.

READING REACTIONS

1. What is Sniderman's claim about government agencies and social media?
2. Research the "Presidential Records Act" and explain how the law impacts the archiving of social networking sites.
3. Sniderman writes that social media might be useful for elections, but candidates cannot rely on it. Why?
4. According to the article, many government agencies have Facebook pages. Locate one of those pages and discuss how it differs in style, tone, and information from personal or group pages.
5. How does Sniderman build his case that social media is both good and bad for government?
6. How does the United States compare with other countries in the use of social media?
7. What do you think about how the U.S. government uses social media? How does using Twitter and similar media affect the White House ethos?

● Barbara Ortutay

'Don't Post That!': Networking Etiquette Emerges

Barbara Ortutay is a technology reporter for the Associated Press who focuses on social media and games. She received her MA from Columbia University and her BA from UCLA.

Stephanie Kahn wanted to bask in her engagement for a few hours before diving into the task of calling aunts, uncles and good friends with the big news. And even before she could call them, she had a surprise party to attend, one that her fiance had set up for their parents and her "closest group of girlfriends."

That party was when Kahn lost control of her news. Some of the guests took photos and were "uploading them on Facebook before I could even post anything," Kahn said from Smyrna, Ga., where she lives. "Of course the next morning I get a couple of calls, text messages from people I didn't call. They found out on Facebook. I think some people were a little upset."

In an age in which instant news and constant life streams from Facebook and Twitter change the way we communicate, the rules of etiquette surrounding these interactions are still evolving.

Figure 7.3 Like other private and public institutions, the White House now has a robust online presence.

What happens when I expected a phone call about something and read about it in a status update instead? What's the polite response to a distant friend posting bad news on Facebook? What to do with sensitive information?

Making matters trickier, good etiquette on Facebook might not apply on Twitter or in an e-mail. These days, milestones like marriage, pregnancy, breakups and divorce are being described over more forms of communications than ever.

"Because it's so new, there is sort of a gray area of what the manners are," said Brian McGee, a 33-year-old father-to-be in Charlotte.

He'd just gotten his first BlackBerry when he and his wife were driving to a doctor's appointment to learn the baby's sex. He had the BlackBerry out and was thumbing something.

"I was like, 'What are you doing?" recalled his wife, Megan Gelaburt-McGee. "He was posting that we were on the way to the doctor's office to find out the baby's sex. I said, 'Don't post that!'"

She said she wanted to tell her close friends the baby's gender personally, though she didn't mean an in-person visit. She didn't even mean a phone call. Instead, she drew the universal female symbol on her belly, had a friend take a photo and sent it in an e-mail to as many as 20 people: cousins, aunts and uncles, bridesmaids, friends she'd known for a very long time.

"We (weren't) going to keep the sex of the baby a secret," she said. "But I don't want to have my cousin find out through Facebook."

Online social networks haven't been around long enough to develop hard and fast etiquette rules, but general guidance is emerging. Just as most people learned that it's annoying to yell on a cellphone in public or to hit "reply all" when responding to just one person in a mass e-mail, social media-savvy folks are finding it's unwise to, say, post unflattering images of friends without their consent.

Etiquette adviser Anna Post, the great-great-granddaughter of manners icon Emily Post, recommends taking a step back before rushing to type, whether it's good news about you or a response to someone else's bad news.

Indeed, tweets and status updates posted in the heat of a moment can quickly backfire. In July, a New York City government aide resigned after posting inflammatory Facebook comments about the arrest of Harvard professor Henry Louis Gates Jr. The aide, Lee Landor, had called Gates a racist and referred to President Obama as "O-dumb-a." The lesson? Know your audience, especially if they will complain to your boss.

A decade or two ago, communicating important news electronically rather than in a letter was frowned upon. Now an e-mail is considered acceptable for many situations, but even people comfortable with that might draw the line at social networks, which feel more like public or semipublic venues.

After all, the average person has 120 "friends" on Facebook, according to the company. In real life, the average North American has about three very close friends and 20 people they are pretty close to, said Barry Wellman, a sociologist at the University of Toronto. This means people may sometimes forget just who is reading their status updates, and can let their guard down.

"The word Facebook uses, 'friend,' of course isn't true," Wellman said. "Many people Facebook calls friends are not friends but maybe acquaintances or former friends."

Facebook has done some studies on how people decide what information they share and how to share it. In one, Cameron Marlow, a research scientist at Facebook, explored with his team what tends to dictate the number of photos that people upload on the site. It turns out the number wasn't based on how many of their friends showed approval for the photos by clicking that they liked them, or how many comments were left on each.

"Rather, it was based on how many photos your friends uploaded," he said. "Social norms are constantly being developed based on what friends do."

READING REACTIONS

1. Who was Emily Post, and why is she important to the discussion of social mores?
2. What topics or events would you share in person, by email, or on a social networking site such as a blog or Facebook?

3. As Ortutay notes, "Just as most people learned that it's annoying to yell on a cellphone in public or to hit 'reply all' when responding to just one person in a mass e-mail, social media-savvy folks are finding it's unwise to say, post unflattering images of friends without their consent." Based on your social interactions online, what are some of the new rules of etiquette that govern online communication?

4. Ortutay reports a Facebook researcher's data that suggest that social norms are being developed based on what friends do. In this case, social norms might be playing games, taking quizzes, sharing links, or uploading images. Conduct your own informal study in which you trace your own Facebook friends' trends for a week. What are some of their most common activities?

5. Who owns the messages posted on social networking sites and other new media spaces?

6. How are Ortutay's message and ethos shaped by the decision to write about specific technologies within other technologies (traditional alphabetic text in this case) or genres? How would this piece differ if it were published on a Facebook page or as a blog post?

Kim Zetter

Cyberbullying Suicide Stokes the Internet Fury Machine

Kim Zetter is an American freelance journalist who has written on a wide variety of subjects, from the Kabbalah to cryptography and electronic voting. Her work has been published in newspapers such as the *Los Angeles Times*, the *Jerusalem Post*, and the *Sydney Morning Herald*.

Sarah Wells makes an unlikely cyber-vigilante. But the middle-aged mother in Virginia was outraged when she read a *Saint Charles Journal* article on Megan Meier, a 13-year-old Missouri girl driven to suicide by relentless online bullying. The fact that the bullying appeared to be instigated by the mother of one of Megan's friends through a fake MySpace account enraged Wells all the more.

When Wells learned that the woman had filed a police report against the dead girl's father—who had destroyed the woman's foosball table in anger and grief—she resolved to take matters into her own hands. The newspaper account didn't identify the perpetrator of the deadly hoax by name, but included enough detail to track her down through online property-tax records. With a few minutes of sleuthing, Wells identified the woman as Lori Drew, of O'Fallon, Missouri. After confirming it with someone in the O'Fallon area who she says was "in a position to know," she posted the name to her blog.

"It was outrageous enough what she had done, but dragging (Megan's father) into the courts, calling the police and bringing the charges against the family whose daughter had suffered a great deal because of her . . . for her to do that, it was like, OK, it's coming back to you," Wells says.

Experts say the firestorm that followed illustrates what happens when the social imperative to punish those in a community who violate social norms plays out over the internet. The impulse is human nature, say experts, and few can imagine an offense more egregious than a trusted adult preying on the emotions of a vulnerable child. Shunning wrongdoers, especially in the absence of legal redress, helps maintain order and preserve a community's moral sense of right—think church excommunications and the Amish tradition of *Meidung*.

But the drive for social shaming—to right a wrong and restore social balance—can run amok and create paradoxical consequences, especially on the internet where people instigate mobs in ways they wouldn't do offline.

"Internet shaming is done by people who want actually to enforce norms and to make people and society more orderly," says Daniel Solove, professor of law at George Washington University and author of *The Future of Reputation: Gossip, Rumor and Privacy on the Internet*. "The problem is that internet shaming actually destroys social control and makes things more anarchic, and it becomes very hard to regulate and stop it."

Wells published only Lori Drew's name, but her readers and other bloggers followed by finding and posting her husband's name, the family's address and phone number, a cellphone number, the name of the family's advertising company, and the names and phone numbers of clients with whom they worked.

As Megan's story raced across the internet and was picked up by national media, more people joined in the cause, including Wired News readers.

Many were outraged that Drew, a middle-aged woman with a teen daughter of her own, fabricated the MySpace identity of a 16-year-old named "Josh Evans" to woo the emotionally fragile Megan, in order to learn what the girl was saying about her own daughter. Once Megan was lured in, "Josh" turned on her, heaping verbal abuse until the teen went over the edge.

In retaliation, readers called Drew's advertising clients to urge them to withdraw their business from her. But it wasn't long before there were death threats, a brick through a window and calls to set the Drews' house on fire. Police have reportedly increased patrols to guard the family against attack. A peaceful protest is scheduled to occur on the family's street this weekend.

Solove isn't surprised. He points to a story two years ago about a man whose camera phone was stolen from his unlocked car. The apparent thief took pictures of himself and friends, which automatically uploaded to the camera owner's Sprint web account.

The owner discovered the thief's name and posted it online with the photos. Netizens superimposed the thief's picture onto pornographic images and posted racist remarks about him. After a Wired News story revealed that the alleged thief was 16 and that his mother claimed she'd bought the camera from a street seller, Solove says the owner regretted the fury he'd unleashed and asked the online mob to back off. Instead, the mob turned on him. "When you have a bunch of people together all trying to achieve the same goal, the whole starts to take on a mind of its own," Solove says, "and people start to act in extreme ways that they might not otherwise act."

It's no surprise that many people who posted Drew's name and personal details online have done so under a cloak of anonymity, with the exception of Wells and a few others. "People don't mind doing (this kind of thing) as long as it doesn't cost them anything, as long as there's very little risk of retribution," says Robert Kurzban, professor of psychology at the University of Pennsylvania and the author of works on social exclusion and stigmatization. "But when people actually have to pay a cost to punish other people, they prefer not to do that."

Wells says she doesn't condone calls for violence and has removed any that appeared on her blog. There are many who agree that the punishment fits the crime in this case. But online vigilantes have been known to react just as strongly to lesser grievances.

Two years ago a college girl in South Korea was harassed after her tiny dog defecated on the floor of a subway car, and she ignored passengers' requests to clean it up. Someone on the train snapped her photo and posted it online. She was quickly dubbed Dog Poop Girl, and within days a cyberposse had discovered her name and was digging up information about her and her family. The public humiliation reportedly led her to withdraw from her university, and the pictures of her and the feces are still online today.

Wells acknowledges that such a case can make it seem as if the internet is "a perpetual outrage machine," where people are simply looking for the next injustice to get worked up about. But she feels the reaction to Dog Poop Girl was unique to Korean culture and wouldn't have caused the same stir here, although Americans were as amused by the story as others around the world.

Still, she thinks the circumstances of Megan's story dictated the depth of the reaction here.

The fact that it involved an adult targeting a child, and that Megan's father—and not Lori Drew—was facing criminal charges, made it a clear-cut cause for cybermob outrage.

Kurzban agrees and disagrees. He says it's not really the details of a particular social violation that determine the strength of a community's reaction to it, but the degree to which a community agrees in its perception of the violation.

In other words, if many people reading the same facts didn't believe that Lori Drew violated a social norm, then the response against her would have been more muted. Indeed, a minority of people on the blogs said that Megan should have ignored the insulting messages, and that her parents should have monitored her online activity better. But they were swiftly shouted down by the mob.

In this way, the stories of Poop Girl and Megan are wildly different on the surface, yet essentially the same, Kurzban says, since both involved actions that the majority of people in their respective communities reacted to in the same way.

For her part, Wells thinks Drew deserves to be a pariah.

"I think this should follow her wherever she goes," Wells says. "There should be pressure on her to be sorry and to do something to make it better."

Wells herself felt the capricious hand of internet justice on Tuesday, when another blogger condemned her as a "vigilante" and posted *her* address and phone number online.

READING REACTIONS

1. Describe the concept of vigilantism.
2. Research the cyber vigilante cases that Zetter profiles in her article. What makes them similar despite differences in context and culture?
3. What role does anonymity play in cyber vigilante cases?
4. Zetter quotes Robert Kurzban, who states that "it's not really the details of a particular social violation that determine the strength of a community's reaction to it, but the degree to which a community agrees in its perception of the violation." To what extent do you agree with this view? What examples can you cite to support your position?
5. How does Zetter develop the idea of "social shaming"? Consider the examples and explanations she offers.
6. The author uses specific terms like *cybermob*, *cyberposse*, and *Netizen*. How does the use of new-media lingo build the author's ethos and persuasive point?

● Paul Smalera

What Real Internet Censorship Looks Like

Paul Smalera is the deputy opinion editor of Reuters. He previously worked for Fortune.com, and his work has appeared in *The New York Times* and *The Washington Post*.

Lately Internet users in the U.S. have been worried about censorship, copyright legalities and data privacy. Between Twitter's new censorship policy, the global protests over SOPA/PIPA and ACTA and the outrage over Apple's iOS allowing apps like Path to access the address book without prior approval, these fears have certainly seemed warranted. But we should also remember that Internet users around the world face far more insidious limitations and intrusions on their Internet usage—practices, in fact, that would horrify the average American.

Sadly, most of the rest of the world has come to accept censorship as a necessary evil. Although I recently argued that Twitter's censorship policy at least had the benefit of transparency, it's still an unfortunate cost of doing global business for a company born and bred with the freedoms of the United States, and founded by tech pioneers whose opportunities and creativity stem directly from our Constitution. Yet by the standards of dictatorial regimes, Internet users in countries like China, Syria and Iran should consider themselves lucky if Twitter's relatively modest censorship program actually keeps

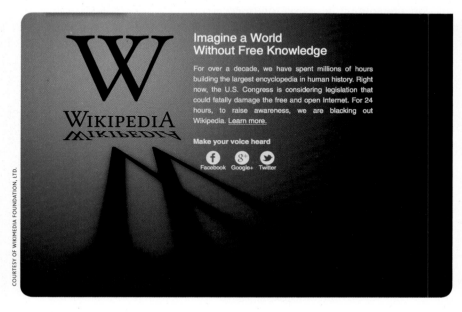

Figure 7.4 Wikipedia's blackout page in protest of SOPA/PIPA

Paul Smalera, "What Real Internet Censorship Looks Like," *Reuters.com*, February 27, 2012.

those countries' governments from shutting down the service. As we are seeing around the world, chances are, unfortunately, it won't.

Consider the freedoms—or lack thereof—Internet users have in Iran. Since this past week, some 30 million Iranian users have been without Internet service thanks to that country's blocking of the SSL protocol, right at the time of its parliamentary elections. SSL is what turns "http"—the basic way we access the Web—into "https", which Gmail, your bank, your credit card company and thousands of other services use to secure data. SSL provides data encryption so that only each end point—your browser and the Web server you're logging into—can decrypt and access the data contained therein.

By blocking SSL, Iran has crippled Tor, a program that enables Internet users to anonymize not just their content but their physical location as well. Tor is a very common workaround for users in totalitarian regimes to access Twitter, Gmail, Facebook and other services. It's hard to come up with an apt analogy for Iran's unprecedented blockage—it's not just that the letters you send are read by the Post Office and photocopied for their records, it's that the Post Roads themselves have been closed off, so you can't even send a letter in the first place. That's the net effect of blocking SSL in Iran.

The hacking group Anonymous has brought down all kinds of websites in protest, mostly over copyright, in the U.S. and Europe. I don't advocate their targeting any country's servers for retribution, but where is the outrage or public demonstration or media attention over the denials of Iranians' basic freedoms to communicate, via the Internet?

Unfortunately, it's still too easy for Internet companies and even the Internet's founding fathers to dismiss the importance of the tools they created in fostering free and open public dialogue, especially in places like Iran. Recently, legendary engineer and Google Vice-President Vint Cerf published a New York Times op-ed entitled "Internet Access is Not a Human Right," where he wrote: "Internet access is always just a tool for obtaining something else more important." How wrong he is. Cerf's line of thinking eviscerates the Internet—the wonder of the modern world he helped build. Cerf argues that humans have the right to "lead healthy, meaningful lives," including having "freedom from torture or freedom of conscience." Yet, we live in the 21st century: It's hard to see how, among people whose economies are developed enough to afford them communication devices, Cerf would excuse governments that curtail their citizens' freedom and right to use the ultimate communications tool—the global network of the Internet. In fact, in underdeveloped parts of the world, the cost to have a cell phone that connects to the Web can be quite affordable.

I'm not arguing semantics here—if our society excludes the Internet from the fundamental rights of human communication, we also excuse totalitarian regimes like Iran's from any repercussions when it comes to blocking that avenue of human contact. It's a dangerous compromise to make in a world that only gets more digital with each passing day. And it also conveniently excuses the free world from having to do much of anything about it. We wouldn't forgive Iran if it threw 30 million citizens into solitary confinement—so why would we ignore it when the Iranian government effectively cuts the entire population off from the outside world, to stifle their voices during a critical electoral cycle?

AP PHOTO/VINCENT THIAN

Figure 7.5 Flowers at Google's headquarters in Beijing

The U.S. and the free world have often engaged in global humanitarian missions in cases of genocide, famine and natural disaster. At what point will the deprivation of freedom of communication warrant such an intervention? The U.S. is already on guard itself against hacking attempts from Russia and China—intrusions by both rogue and government-sponsored actors—so how long will we tolerate countries' depriving their citizens of Internet access?

It's a tricky question, with no easy answer. However, contemplating it may prepare us for the possibility that the world's first cyber-war could be fought not to cut off a country's Internet hookup, but to restore it. After all, the Obama administration's State Department petitioned Twitter to stay online during one recent Iranian uprising and has used the service to communicate with citizens there during another. Iran has now essentially shut down Twitter with its SSL blocking. Will the U.S. respond? If we do, we will set a precedent that calls into question the rights of any government to silence its citizens on a global communications network, putting us into thorny conflicts with China and other 21st century frenemies. But if we don't, we are condoning the silencing of dissent and turning our backs on a century-long pledge to foster democracy wherever it might flourish—even if it's online.

READING REACTIONS

1. Based on your reading of Zetter's article on cyberbullying and Smalera's article about censorship and rights, what are some of the pros and cons of anonymity online?

2. Research Iran and China's Internet rules. Discuss how different or similar they are to rules in the United States. Do any of the online resources you found in your search have common features?

3. Interview an international student for his or her perceptions on access to online information in their country as opposed to the United States. Are there differences in the amount of access or types of censorship?

4. Recently, Google chose to close its Google.cn site in response to what were seen as deliberate attempts to censor information. Google redirected Chinese users to its Google Hong Kong version of the world's most popular search engine. As an experiment, use a range of search engines (such as Google, Bing, Yahoo, MSN, AOL, or Ask.com) to research a topic of interest. Do these search engines differ in the way they filter or prioritize information? What might this say about the reliability and equality of various search engines?

5. Who owns the messages on Chinese or Iranian websites?

6. Consider the context in which this U.S.-based writer reports on new Internet regulations. How does his context differ from that of a journalist writing from within China or Iran?

TECHNOLOGY TIP ✳ Using Twitter as an Academic Resource

Whether the subject is your favorite celebrity or your own university, tweeting seems to be a wildly favorite pastime. Although Twitter certainly plays a social role in our online lives, more and more people are using it to access and share news and information, even in academic settings.

If you don't already have a Twitter account, sign up for one at Twitter.com (see **Figure 7.6**), and "follow" several classmates in your peer review group. Brainstorm possibilities for your next writing or research project, and seek feedback from your peers. Compare this invention process of using 140 characters or less to sharing similar ideas on a discussion board or chat room. What are the advantages and disadvantages of using Twitter for academic work? In a blog post or other journaling space, reflect on what tools work best in your own writing and research process.

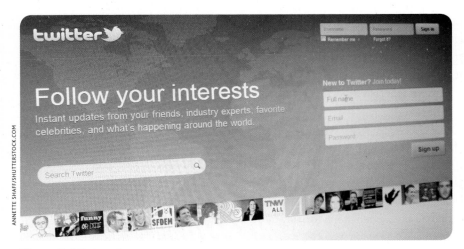

Figure 7.6 Twitter homepage

CULTURES   As both a work of art and a cultural artifact, Ruggieri's cell phone artwork makes a statement for viewers to interpret. How do you "read" this work? What positive and negative interpretations can result from your analysis? What details from the design, images, and structure of the painting lead you to these competing interpretations?

Consider too some of the questions posed in Chapter 1:

Under what contexts or conditions (historical, political, or cultural) was the message created?

What is the work's intended impact on viewers? What are we "supposed to do"?

How does the text appeal to diverse groups, including genders, ethnicities, sexual orientation, age, class?

ALBERTO RUGGIERI/GETTY IMAGES

Figure 7.7 Alberto Ruggieri. *People Talking on Cell Phones*

TECHNOLOGIES   The readings and resources in this chapter make it clear that the socially networked life has both pros and cons. Engage in a class debate about these pros and cons by dividing into groups and developing several arguments and counterarguments. What examples from the news or from various social networks themselves can you use to support your points? Address some of the questions we have been considering throughout the book:

- **Why is the** given technology or virtual space preferable to or more appropriate than others? Does the technology have limits?

- **How does the** message help shape membership within a community or create common goals and values?

- **What are the** technology's social and cultural associations or values?

- **How does the** technology affect how viewers think about content? How does it change or challenge cultural assumptions?

Use a tool such as Google Docs to collaboratively develop your ideas. Be prepared to present your argument to your classmates in the form of a Microsoft PowerPoint presentation.

Additional Writing and Composing Activities

1. **Online Identity Performance.** Ever wonder what George Washington's Facebook page might have looked like or who would have read Madame Bovary's Tumblr? For this project, choose a historical or fictional person or character—someone you can learn about and gather facts and research on—and create a Facebook, MySpace, Bebo, or Pinterest (or similar social networking site) profile for them. To accurately capture their identity and perform this research in a new medium, you will need to consider not only design choices you think they might make but also how others might decode those choices.

   The profile you create should include at least three media (music, video, links, still images, blog posts, and so on) to perform the identity. Then consider the following: Does the profile perform a cohesive identity? Would the character approve of the profile? (Support your answer with research about the character.)

2. **Position Argument.** How do social networks influence digital identity, virtual citizenship, or social activism? Argue your position, concentrating on the following questions to help with development:

   - What background information is important to your narrowed topic?

   - What specifically are you arguing about the topic?

   - Why does this matter to you, and why should it matter to your audience?

   - What two or three good reasons support (that is, provide evidence for) your claim?

   - What are the objections or counterarguments to your claim?

   - Do you, through language choices, indicate your authorial ethos as well as the ethos of your sources?

   - Have you considered ethos, pathos, and logos as well as the rhetorical triangle (author, audience, and text) in your development?

3. **Cause-and-Consequence Analysis.** Think about contemporary American popular culture (especially television, movies, video games, and so on) or social events (parties, concerts, and so on). What causes trend(s) in your topic? What are the trend's effects? In other words, why do we like the things we like, what are some possible consequences, and what does the trend say about our identity as citizens?

Online Resources

Resources available through the English CourseMate for this text include the following:

Videos

CNN YouTube Republican Debates

CNN YouTube Democratic Debates

Kitchen: Cyberbullying Prevention commercial, Ohio Commission DRCM

Think Before You Post, Ohio Commission DRCM

Sarah Phillips. Tribute to her dying mother, "Autumn by Paolo Nutini."

Olga Kay. My Ford Fiesta Story

Blogs and videoblogs

"Twitterquette: Rules of Conduct on Twitter," Buzzle.com

Online Articles and Reports

A Day Without Media, International Center for Media & the Public Agenda (ICMPA)

Scott Michels. "Teachers' Virtual Lives Conflict With Classroom"

Mary Helen Miller. "East Stroudsburg U. Suspends Professor for Facebook Posts," "East Stroudsburg U. Professor Returns After Suspension for Facebook Posts"

"Twitter Therapy: Cancer Patients Tweeting Through Chemo," Huffington Post

Websites

Nation Master: World Statistics/Country Comparisons

mGive Mobile Donations via Text Message

Vimeo Homepage

Deviant Art Homepage

E-Waste

Human Ecologies

Our online lives affect both the material world in which we live and our own physical well-being. Previous chapters in *CrossCurrents* have focused on the many social and educational effects of technologies on our global and in our local cultures and communities. It is equally important to consider how those technologies impact our natural environment. The political and scientific study of the relationship between living things and their natural surrounding is often referred to as *ecology*. Today, the emphasis on "going green" and being "eco-friendly" is as much about our own day-to-day lives as it is about the future of our natural world. How do our online and offline habits contribute to a larger, human ecology in positive and negative ways? This final chapter of *CrossCurrents* explores this question through a series of readings and activities that allow you to question the possibilities and constraints of technology on our local and global environments.

Figure 8.1 Social commentary on the role of Internet

Figure 8.2 The Valley
of the Drums

VAN D. BUCHER/PHOTO RESEARCHERS, INC.

Most twentieth-century concerns about our human ecologies have focused on issues of pollution. Undoubtedly, images immediately come to mind when you hear the phrase "toxic waste"—perhaps the image of chemical runoff, maybe from large corporations, infiltrating our water supply. Attention to toxic waste began in the 1970s with chemical cleanup efforts for such places as Love Canal in Niagara Falls, New York, and the Valley of the Drums site near Louisville, Kentucky (see Figure 8.2).

The Real Costs of Digital Technologies

In the computer age, the focus on toxic waste has been replaced with a focus on "e-waste," the discarded and nonrecycled parts of computers, cell phones, and television monitors that can contain contaminants that are just as deadly to the twenty-first-century generation as chemical waste was for both past and present generations (see **Figure 8.3**). As the Environmental Protection

Figure 8.3 E-waste

STEPHEN GIBSON/SHUTTERSTOCK.COM

Agency has acknowledged, although a number of states regulate e-waste, no federal law in the United States mandates recycling e-waste or prohibits the computer and electronics industry from exporting electronic waste. The waste ends up in communities around the world, and poor communities are especially affected.

Although it may have been possible to blame the harmful effect of toxic waste on a faceless, anonymous corporation, more recently, society has better understood the role of all citizens in decreasing our individual carbon footprint—"the measure of the impact our activities have on the environment"

CULTURES Reflect on both literal and figurative meanings of the term "e-waste." In what social and environmental ways does our time online impact our time offline?

CULTURES In what ways has concern over e-waste replaced our earlier concerns with toxic waste? Is the problem as visible in our culture as the Love Canal and the Valley of the Drums were nearly four decades ago? What efforts are increasing awareness of e-waste contamination and our role in the problem?

(CarbonFootprint.com). Foremost among these activities are driving and air travel, but according to the website CarbonFootprint.com, carbon-dioxide emissions result "from the whole lifecycle of products we use"—emissions associated with the products' "manufacture and eventual breakdown."

As Figure 8.1 suggests, our carbon footprint extends to both the mental and the physical energy we spend on our online routines, which increasingly seem to happen twenty-four hours a day, seven days a week. These routines can include online banking, home shopping, and even online courses. But regardless of who or what is collectively responsible for how modern technologies impact the environment, events such as Earth Day every April 22 evidence our global concern about and commitment to improving the environment. A number of recent books and films, such as Bill McKibben's *Eaarth: Making a Life on a Tough New Planet* (2011), Colin Beavan's *No Impact Man* (2009), and former Vice President Gore's *An Inconvenient Truth* (2006), have helped make the environment not just a political issue but a social and educational one as well. Both McKibben and Beavan, for example, have websites (http://350.org and http://noimpactman.com) to encourage social solidarity and financial support for their initiatives. Another useful resource is The Story of Stuff Project, based on Annie Leonard's 2010 book *The Story of Stuff*. The site includes educational videos and social commentary on the impact of consumer spending on everything from bottled water to cosmetics and electronics.

That these continuing concerns are necessary is evident from recent reports and the outrage that more hasn't been done to improve China's environmental problems since the 2008 Olympics in Beijing. In this case, because most Chinese citizens believe the Chinese government was being dishonest about air quality when it attributed recent flight cancelations to "weather conditions." Many Chinese citizens follow a Twitter feed created by the U.S. embassy in Beijing, @BeijingAir, for current air quality levels. As the Twitter example shows, technology has the potential to enable not only social solidarity but also environmental awareness.

Readings

Whereas more than a century ago, the theme of the day was journalist Horace Greeley's 1865 advice to "Go West, young man" to conquer new agricultural and economic frontiers, today's advice might be "Go online, young and old" to consume the world of information. We explore that world through our iPads, Blackberries, and desktop systems until the next great gadget comes along to replace our quickly obsolete technological toys. Indeed, Sherry Turkle, an internationally recognized scholar whose excerpt we feature from her book *Alone Together: Why We Expect More from Technology and Less from Each Other*, concludes that our time online, which is all the time, has led to a "new state of the self." In this new state, those of us from a generation who remember what it was like not to have such access never want to go back, and those from the current generation think "that's just how it is." Although Turkle's earlier work celebrated some of the identity play that's possible online, more recently she has asked what's gained and what's lost in our constant connection. She concludes her book by writing her daughter who's away at college, a regular letter to be mailed—something most of us rarely, if ever, do.

Even as we acknowledge the limits of our online existence, the @BeijingAir Twitter feed suggests that communities can tap the Internet in numerous ways to advocate for environmental awareness. For example, British journalist Damian Carrington, in his article "'Farmville' Project with Real Animals Launched by National Trust," profiles the way in which the United Kingdom creates ecological awareness by having people from around the world play an online but very real version of the popular Facebook game *Farmville*. And as University of Michigan professor Andrew Hoffman suggests in his blog post "Climate Debate in Word Clouds: The Conflicting Discourse of Climate Change," some reliance on technology can actually help us better understand conflicting positions on climate change by identifying dominant themes.

For writers such as Thomas Hayden, in his article "Ixnay on the iPod: In Praise of Crap Technology," our rush to replace one gadget with another is part of a larger plan to drive our consumer purchasing habits in ways that negatively impact the environment. Hayden advocates hanging on to our older, "crappier" tools that do fewer things but last just as long as their "smarter" counterparts, including the Apple iPod. Nevertheless, the ongoing demand for such toys has created a multibillion-dollar industry dependent on the labor of factory workers in corporations such as China's Foxconn, whose reputation in producing the Apple iPhone and other popular mobile devices is now as well known as the tragic suicides of young workers who have little else to do but assemble the gadgets that we use to consume information, goods, and services and to simply entertain ourselves.

For technology journalists such as Joel Johnson, these suicides serve as reminder that our increased ability to live a digital existence requires a critical awareness of the impact on our global community, as he makes clear in his article featured in this chapter, "1 Million Workers. 90 Million iPhones. 17 Suicides. Who's to Blame?" And what happens to those toys when we discard them? According to the United Nations Environment Programme, the United States produces nearly three million tons of e-waste, much of it exported to developing countries, including China, India, and Africa.

In the case of Ghana, Emmanuel Dogbevi laments the lack of regulation policies in his country in his online article "E-waste Is Killing Ghanaians Slowly." Although Dogbevi is writing in 2007, his 2010 YouTube video interview indicates that nothing in Ghana has changed to raise awareness of the dangers of e-waste on those who pillage dumping sites and burn hardware to extract the valuable metals for later sale. These writers make clear that unlike the toxic waste tragedies of the 1970s and 80s, we as citizens are as responsible as the corporations for e-waste, and thus we can do something in our own communities to heed the global call for change.

This chapter on human ecologies is a fitting way to conclude *CrossCurrents*, as it provides an important reminder that despite the book's overview of the significant impact of technology on our cultures and communities, this impact has negative consequences that we must acknowledge as well. Many of the writing, reading, and communication contexts in this chapter allow you to address this impact by developing the types of projects and media genres we have featured in previous chapters.

Figure 8.4 iPhone showing Chinese factory workers on production line

TECHNOLOGIES   What aspects of the iPhone image in **Figure 8.4** make it a visual argument? What is the point of this particular image? What other types of images would make as strong of a point about our role in the Foxconn's working conditions?

● Sherry Turkle

Walden 2.0

Sherry Turkle is Abby Rockefeller Mauzé Professor of the Social Studies of Science and Technology in the Program in Science, Technology, and Society at the Massachusetts Institute of Technology. She is an internationally recognized scholar on social networks and their impact on identity, relationships, and society. In this excerpt from her most recent book, *Alone Together: Why We Expect More from Technology and Less from Each Other*, Turkle questions whether the Internet can be a space for deliberation and a life well lived.

WALDEN 2.0

In his essay about his two years of retreat, Thoreau writes, "I went to the woods because I wished to live deliberately, to front only the essential facts of life, and see if I could not learn what it had to teach, and not, when I came to die, discover that I had not lived. I did not wish to live what was not life, living is so dear; nor did I wish to practise resignation, unless it was quite necessary." Thoreau's quest inspires us to ask of our life with technology: Do we live deliberately? Do we turn away from life that is not life? Do we refuse resignation?

Some believe that the new connectivity culture provides a digital Walden. A fifteen-year-old girl describes her phone as her refuge. "My cell phone," she says, "is my only individual zone, just for me." Technology writer Kevin Kelly, the first editor of *Wired*, says that he finds refreshment on the Web. He is replenished in its cool shade: "At times I've entered the web just to get lost. In that lovely surrender, the web swallows my certitude and delivers the unknown. Despite the purposeful design of its human creators, the web is a wilderness. Its boundaries are unknown, unknowable, its mysteries uncountable. The bramble of intertwined ideas, links, documents, and images create an otherness as thick as a jungle. The web smells like life."

But not everyone is as refreshed as Kelly. Brad talks about the "throwaway friendships" of online life. Hannah wonders what she really has to show for the time she has spent hanging out with a small, sarcastic in-crowd and with a best friend who she fears will simply not show up again. It is hard to accept that online friends are not part of your life; yet, they can make themselves disappear just as you can make them vanish. Anxiety about Internet friendships makes people cherish the other kind. The possibility of constant connection makes people value a bit of space. Pattie, fourteen, no longer carries her cell phone. "It feels good," she says, "to have people *not* reach you."

That bit of space could leave room for a child to be a child a bit longer. One of the privileges of childhood is that some of the world is mediated by adults. Hillary, sixteen, is taking a long break from her cell phone. She doesn't want to be on call, and so she leaves it at home. "I don't like the feeling of being reachable all the time . . . of knowing about everything in real time." For a child—and for this purpose, adolescents are still children—one cost of constant connectivity is that adults lose the ability to act as a buffer against the world. Only a few months before, Hillary was at a party to celebrate the release of a new volume in the Harry Potter series when her father suffered a seizure. She didn't learn about it until she was at home and with family. She was glad for this. Without a cell phone, the bad news waited until there was an adult there to support her, to put it in context. She didn't want to hear it alone, holding a phone.

Hillary is fond of movies but drawn toward "an Amish life minus certain exceptions [these would be the movies] . . . but I wouldn't mind if the Internet went away." She asks, "What could people be doing if they weren't on the Internet?" She answers her own question: "There's piano; there's drawing; there's all these things people could be creating." Hillary talks about how hard it is to keep up "all the different sites you have to keep up," and above all, how time-consuming it is to feed Facebook. These tiring performances leave little space for creativity and reflection: "It really is distracting." There is not much room for what Thoreau meant by a life lived deliberately.

There is nothing more deliberate than the painstaking work of constructing a profile or having a conversation on instant messenger in which one composes and recomposes one's thoughts. And yet, most of the time on the Net, one floats and experiments, follows links, and sends out random feelers. One flips through the photo albums of friends—and then the albums of their friends. One comments on the postings of people one hardly knows. Thoreau complained that people are too quick to share an opinion. Online, social networks instruct us to share whenever there's "something on our mind," no matter how ignorant or ill considered, and then help us broadcast it to the widest possible audience. Every day each of us is bombarded by other people's random thoughts. We start to see such effusions as natural. So, although identity construction on the Net begins in a considered way, with the construction of a profile or an avatar, people can end up feeling that the only deliberate act is the decision to hand oneself over to the Net. After that, one is swept along.

For those so connected, there may be doubts (about life as performance, about losing the nuance of the face-to-face), but there is the pleasure of continual company. For those not connected, there can be an eerie loneliness, even on the streets of one's hometown. Kara, in her fifties, feels that life in her hometown of Portland, Maine, has emptied out: "Sometimes I walk down the street, and I'm the only person not plugged in. It's like I'm looking for another person who is not plugged in." With nostalgia—which can come with youth or age—for the nod that marks a meeting in shared streets and weather, she adds a bit wistfully, "No one is where they are. They're talking to someone miles away. I miss them. But they are missing out." Nostalgia ensures that certain things stay before us: the things we miss.

There are no simple answers as to whether the Net is a place to be deliberate, to commit to life, and live without resignation. But these are good terms with which to start a conversation. That conversation would have us ask if these are the values by which we want to judge our lives. If they are, and if we are living in a technological culture that does not support them, how can that culture be rebuilt to specifications that respect what we treasure—our sacred spaces. Could we, for example, build a Net that reweights privacy concerns, acknowledging that these, as much as information, are central to democratic life?

The phrase "sacred spaces" became important to me in the 1980s when I studied a cohort of scientists, engineers, and designers newly immersed in simulation. Members of each group held certain aspects of their professional life to be inviolate. These were places they wanted to hold apart from simulation because, in that space, they felt most fully themselves in their discipline. For architects, it was hand drawings. This was where design implicated the body of the architect. This was where architects were engineers, certainly, but they were also artists. This was where the trace of the hand personalized a building. And this was where architects, so often part of large teams, experienced themselves as authors. The most enthusiastic proponents of computer-assisted design defended hand drawing. When their students began to lose the skill, these professors sent them off to drawing class. It was not about

GIRISH KULKARNI

Figure 8.5 Walden Pond

rejecting the computer but about making sure that designers came to it with their own values. A sacred space is not a place to hide out. It is a place where we recognize ourselves and our commitments.

When Thoreau considered "where I live and what I live for," he tied together location and values. Where we live doesn't just change how we live; it informs who we become. Most recently, technology promises us lives on the screen. What values, Thoreau would ask, follow from this new location? Immersed in simulation, where do we live, and what do we live for?

READING REACTIONS

1. Who was Henry David Thoreau, and what does Walden signify in his work and in Turkle's essay?
2. One of Turkle's interviewees, Hillary, asks, "What could people be doing if they weren't on the Internet?" Answer that question for yourself: What would you be doing if you weren't online?
3. What does Turkle mean by a "sacred space"?
4. In your opinion, is it possible to create a digital Walden?
5. Turkle writes, "Where we live doesn't just change how we live; it informs who we become. Most recently, technology promises us lives on the screen. What values, Thoreau would ask, follow from this new location? Immersed in simulation, where do we live, and what do we live for?" Attempt to answer this question in a reflective essay or blog post about how your time online or offline represents or impacts who you are.

Damian Carrington

"Farmville" Project with Real Animals Launched by National Trust

Damian Carrington is a journalist and head of the environment at *The Guardian* newspaper. He reports on issues of renewable energy, the oil and gas industry, and ethical accountability on the part of corporations and individuals. In this article from May 2011, Carrington chronicles the ways social networking can help to foster global awareness about where our food comes from.

A large working farm will be taken over for the first time by web users across the world on Wednesday, who will vote on every key decision taken on its cattle, pigs, sheep and crops.

The MyFarm experiment hands over power at the National Trust's 2,500-acre Wimpole Estate farm in Cambridgeshire, UK. Up to 10,000 farming novices will choose which bull to buy, which crop to plant and whether to spilt fields to resurrect lost hedgerows.

"I will put in here whatever the online farmers want to grow," said Richard Morris, Wimpole's manager, standing on the edge of Pond Field, currently green with grass and clover rippling in the wind. "Farming is always a compromise—there is never a right or a wrong answer. If I choose one thing, my neighbour will be leaning over the fence shaking his head.

"The online farmers will not be able to choose to grow cannabis or bananas, but undoubtedly there will be some strange decisions, some decisions I would not have made."

The National Trust is the UK's biggest farmer, said Fiona Reynolds, its director-general. "This is all about reconnecting people to where their food comes from. Our TNS poll showed that only 8% of mothers feel confident talking to their children about where their food comes from. That's really poignant."

Farmville, the virtual farming game that currently has 47 million players a month and is Facebook's second most popular game, was one inspiration, said project manager John Alexander, who came up with the MyFarm idea while working in a previous job at an advertising agency. "But this is a real farm," he added.

Online farmers will run the farm through discussions that end in votes, with the first option past the post the winner. Morris will set out the context for the decision, in the first instance what to grow in the 21-hectare Pond Field, and propose options.

Information to help people decide will come through blogs and videos. Other decisions could include choosing the new bull for one of the rare-breed herds or reinstating an old pond to encourage wildlife.

Morris says all major decisions will be put to the MyFarm users.

There will be one big vote each month, but these could trigger more frequent votes. In Pond Field, for example, if wheat is chosen, should it be bread-making wheat or biscuit wheat? "I am making decisions every day," he says. "The first thing I do after getting up is look at the weather out of the window, and that sets the day going."

Right now, with 300 new lambs delivered and scampering in the fields, Morris is bringing in grass to make silage for next winter's feed. But the dry weather has left the fields short of grass, so the young cattle are being left in the barns for a while, to make sure the sheep have enough.

In the future, Morris says, there will be a smartphone app which will allow him to get near instant decisions from the online farmers. "For example, if I have wheat in the field, ripe and ready, but rain in the morning means it is damp, do we risk waiting and losing some of the crop, or combining [harvesting] it now and incurring some extra drying costs?"

From the ginger-bristled pig snoring in the spring sunshine, to the free range hens, to the oats, barley or wheat in the fields, the online farmers will have to learn to juggle the competing factors that Morris faces each day, financial, ethical and environmental.

Arthur Potts Dawson, co-founder of the mutual business, the People's Supermarket which now has 1500 members, said: "MyFarm is brave, even mad, but the People's Supermarket was considered mad when we started. Both help prevent you blindly walking around a supermarket not knowing where your food comes from." The online farmers will need to pay a one-off £30 fee to join, which also allows them to visit the farm in person. Reynolds defended the fee. "We are a charity and there is a big upfront cost we need to cover. It feels like a reasonable cost. If we get many more [than 10,000] we could reduce the fee in the future conceivably."

But Nicholas Lovell, a games consultant and founder of the Gamesbrief blog, is yet to be convinced: "There is something in the idea that people like to grow, nurture and beautify things. But Farmville's success is down to the craftsmanship of hooking into basic human psychology: the need to finish things we've started, to return gifts when we're given them and many, many more.

"A Farmville for which people had to pay £30 to access would have flopped miserably. By charging for access, the National Trust is taking the success of Farmville as being about farming, when I think it was about bringing accessible, cost-effective, well-designed gaming to a new audience."

Alexander acknowledged: "The fee is where the comparison with Farmville falls on its cow-like bottom." Zynga, creators of Farmville, declined to comment.

For Morris, the MyFarm experiment continues the tradition of innovation on the Wimpole Estate that dates to the 1790s when the Earl of Hardwick [implemented] new machinery, crops and breeding techniques. "If we are going to find a [sustainable] way to feed 9 billion people by 2050 farming needs to change, but it can't do it on its own, it needs public opinion to change too."

But, however successful MyFarm turns out to be, Morris's 10,000 new bosses may not be able to direct him every moment of the day: the mobile signal on Wimpole farm is very patchy. "I know where I am heading" if things get tough, he joked.

READING REACTIONS

1. Carrington reports that the very popular Facebook game *Farmville* had 47 million players as of May 2011. Why would such a game attract so many online players? How is *MyFarm* based on *Farmville*?

2. What is the National Trust, and why would it rely on a gaming interface to educate the public?

3. What is the environmental purpose of the site? What initiatives in the United States are similar to *MyFarm* and the National Trust?

4. According to sources from the article, how does charging for access both help and hinder *MyFarm*'s environmental mission?

5. Visit the *MyFarm* site, available through the English CourseMate for this text. How does the website work to appeal to its multiple audiences and establish a sense of community?

Andrew Hoffman

Climate Debate in Word Clouds: The Conflicting Discourse of Climate Change

Andrew Hoffman is the Holcim Professor of Sustainable Enterprise at the University of Michigan, where he codirects the Erb Institute. He holds a Ph.D. in Management and Civil and Environmental Engineering from MIT, and he has published more than ninety articles and nine books, two of which have been translated into five languages.

Like it or not, climate change is now part of the "culture wars." Like abortion, gun control, and health care, climate change divides conversations along political battle lines of left versus right. But if you listen closely to what is being said, you will find that people are talking past each other, engaged in a debate that has little to do with an evaluation of climate science. Instead, it is a clash about values, beliefs, and worldviews. Opinions are based largely on ideological filters that people use to understand complex issues, influenced strongly by the cultural groups of which they are a part and the opinions of thought-leaders and pundits whom they trust. The arguments are constructed around the frames by which people view the science, not the science itself.

To explore this further, I studied the language used by opposing sides of this debate (what I call the *skeptical* and *convinced* positions) as it took place in U.S. newspapers between September 2007 and September 2009. In that period, 795 editorials and letters to the editor were written on the topics of climate change or global warming. Seventy-three percent were convinced, and 20 percent were skeptical, which is in line with numerous polling results (the remaining 7 percent were neutral or unclear). Then I looked at what they were saying and drew a word cloud for each side of the debate, with word size representing each word's relative use. These word clouds tell an interesting story, one that can help explain the terrain of the debate if you choose to engage it.

Figure 8.6 Word cloud—Convinced

First, note that the two sides do not use the same terms to define the debate. Skeptical authors use "global warming" three times as much as "climate change" while convinced authors use the terms equally. This is not an accidental artifact as the two terms take on very different meanings depending on who you are talking to. Recent work published in *Public Opinion Quarterly* found that Republicans were less likely to endorse that the phenomenon was real when it was referred to as "global warming" rather than "climate change" while Democrats were unaffected by the term. Corroborating research in *Climatic Change* concluded that global warming is a far more politicizing term than climate change, preferred most by people already concerned about the issue and least by those who don't believe it is occurring.

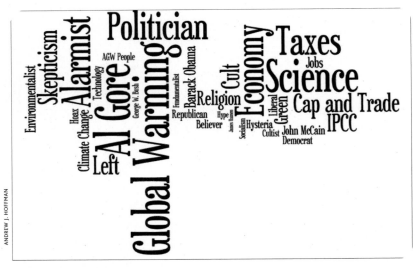

Figure 8.7 Word cloud—Skeptic

So, before you engage in the debate, consider who you are talking to and what effect you want to have. Words have meaning, and the terms you use trigger intended and unintended reactions on those you are trying to reach. You may find yourself losing the debate before it begins.

The second point to notice in the word clouds is the focus of the issue. For the skeptical editorials, the issue is primarily about the science, or more precisely, the flaws in the scientific process, which they see as corrupt. The sentiment, in the words of a skeptical speaker at the Heartland Conference, that "peer review has turned into pal review" reflects the skeptical belief that only research supporting the reality of climate change will get published. As a result, skeptical authors talk about a "hoax" and "hype" and refer to those who endorse such "hysteria" as "alarmist," "cultist," "fundamentalist," "AGW people" (in reference to Anthropocentric Global Warming), and "socialist" (as a threat to freedom, capitalism and democracy).

In direct contrast, the convinced editorials de-emphasize the "science" and the nature of the problem to focus instead on solutions, such as "technology," "nuclear power," "biofuels," "clean tech," "clean coal" and "carbon capture and sequestration."

And this leads to the topics of the "economy" and "risk," which both sides discuss, but in far different ways. Skeptical editorials warn that proposals to limit greenhouse gas emissions (like cap and trade, or what they call "cap and tax") will destroy the economy while convinced editorials predict that they will boost it by creating "jobs."

These differences point to an important landmark on the terrain of the debate; choose the battlefield of your choice—you can choose to debate the nature of the problem or the nature of the solutions.

Next, note who the two sides are referencing. Both sides like to spend more time attacking a prominent figure on the other side than citing a supporter on their own. Convinced editorials like to criticize George W. Bush and his opposition to climate legislation. With far less politeness, the skeptical editorials attack Al Gore with accusations that he fabricated the problem for ideological and personal gain. In fact, given that nearly 40 percent of all skeptical articles mention the former Vice President, it is apparent that he is the man that the climate skeptical love to hate. As such, he is not likely to win over many converts.

In the end, why is all this important? The short answer is that lots of small conversations add up to one big conversation. "All politics is local" as Tip O'Neill would say. We need to pull climate change out of the culture wars and keep it from devolving into a "logic schism," a breakdown in communication where the two sides are talking about completely different issues, only seeking information that confirms their position and disconfirms the other, and developing positions that are relatively exclusive and rigid. The rigidity of either side of the debate closes avenues of examination, such that resolution of the issue becomes intractable.

To help avoid this outcome, engage in vigorous debate over climate change. But first, consider the rhetorical landscape and the goal of avoiding a logic schism. One side may be talking about scientific data and the other may be talking about freedom, scientific corruption, or distrust of government. And never the twain shall meet. But if you are careful, you may find a common language and a way to communicate towards some kind of neutral ground.

READING REACTIONS

1. Hoffman refers to the environment as one of the "culture wars." What does he mean by this term?
2. What types of evidence does Hoffman rely on to document the difference in opinion about climate change?
3. Who are the "convinced" and who are the "skeptical"?
4. Why does Hoffman rely on the word cloud to make his point? Is the word cloud effective as a form of evidence?
5. What is the "logic schism" that Hoffman refers to, and why does it exist? What does Hoffman suggest we do to avoid it?

● Thomas Hayden

Ixnay on the iPod: In Praise of Crap Technology

Thomas Hayden is a visiting lecturer at Stanford University, where he teaches communication, environmental journalism, and sustainability in the Emmett Interdisciplinary Program in Environment and Resources (E-IPER) in the School of Earth Sciences.

I've been thinking about my Zune a lot since Steve Jobs passed away. You know, the revolutionary portable music device that lets users carry thousands of digitized songs around in a pocket or a purse? Oh wait, what am I saying— it's not a Microsoft product I've been thinking about. I don't have a Zune. I don't even have an iPod. I have a Coby.

That's right, a Coby. A cheap plastic mp3 player—basically a $19.99 flash drive with a headphone jack, a pixilated little screen, and controls that look a lot like the original iPod scroll wheel, without actually scrolling or being a wheel. It's a piece of crap, really. And I love it.

I mean no disrespect to Jobs or his legacy of attractive, functional design at Apple. I actually did have an iPod once, a sleek 30-gig number with a brilliant video screen and space for nearly half of my comically large music collection. I watched a video on it exactly once—Breaking Bad, season one—cringed with horror every time I dropped it and felt the $400 hole in my wallet for longer than I'd owned the thing when I inevitably lost it.

But I don't miss it. The iPod's much-lauded shuffle function was apparently designed to highlight the far corners and aesthetic lapses of my song library. Ironic curios such as Hasselhoff, Shatner and the suppressed first Alanis Morissette CDs recurred frequently enough to constitute harassment. Having a dinner party? iTunes selected powwow drumming. Looking for a jolt of energy in the morning? Say hello to mediocre Canadian whinge-rock from 20 years ago.

My portable audio technology needs are simple. A few hundred well-chosen—by me, dammit—songs and a half-dozen episodes of the WTF podcast and I'm good to go. My trusty Coby does all that, with an FM radio tuner included. (I do wish it had AM too—the crap technology of the air—but why gripe?) Most important, it's worth next to nothing so I'm virtually assured never to lose it—unlike apparently every iPhone prototype ever—and I don't cringe at all when my toddler flings it across the room. And because the next Coby is sure to be just as mediocre, I'll never need to upgrade—I've stepped off the escalators of feature creep and planned obsolescence, and all the expense and toxic e-waste that come with them. Crap technology, it turns out, is green technology.

My love of the technological mediocrity goes back at least to 1980. My birthday present that year was a new bike—a 12 speed no less. Oh sure, my friends on their Peugeots and Raleighs mocked, but the Roadace 404 has outlasted them all. I'm not sure I ever saw another bike of its (off-) brand on the road, but it saw me through more than a decade of heavy use, and my sister still rides it today.

Me, I ride a 1995 mountain bike—practically new, I know, but blissfully free of shock absorbers and disk brakes. I've experimented with a variety of advanced travel mugs to tote a dose of morning coffee on my bike-train-bike commute. They were beautifully designed, and capable of keeping the contents plenty hot enough to scald each time their complicated drinking lids dripped slowly into my lap or dumped wholesale into my backpack. I've given up, reverting to an old pasta sauce jar with a fail-proof lid and the decency to let the coffee cool enough to be drinkable by the time I'm ready for it.

Cell phones present the greatest challenge for the dedicated non-technologist. After losing three or four earlier models, I've settled on a not-smart-at-all Samsung that makes and receives phone calls (I don't pick up) and has a non-virtual qwerty keyboard that is forgiving of my sausage-fingered texting. The devilish thing apparently also has the power to connect to the Internet, but I refused to walk out of the store with the device until that feature was safely shut down. Here's what's smart about my humble Samsung: I spend approximately zero hours a day fumbling around with silly games, or trying to enjoy the latest from longreads.com on a screen the size of child's tongue.

My favorite piece of also-ran technology though is a simple pair of glasses. They were the rump-end of a buy one, get one free deal back in the '90s—the least awful of an almost perversely unlovely selection. I soon found that their vast, full moon plastic lenses made them a perfect substitute for safety goggles in the chemistry lab, and thanks to the unlosability law of lousy gear, they never went overboard during months of oceanography fieldwork, and I deploy them still whenever I'm doing a little handy work around the house. (Ask me about my collection of cast-off power tools.)

Does second-rate technology have a future? It's not for me to say. But my son, at 18 months, seems to think so. Not only does he love my "Zune"—easier for a toddler to say than "Coby" I suppose—but his own favorite technology is a little crappy, too. It's a second-hand wooden garbage truck, hand assembled by its previous owner and re-glued any number of times by me. Our kid loves the thing like the rest of us are supposed to love the new iPhone. I suspect that means crap technology has a future as bright and shiny as anything Steve Jobs ever imagined.

• • •

11/17/2011. I've heard from a lot of people since this post first went up, and I'm delighted to discover how many kindred spirits I have. Several people have pointed out though that it can be hard to tell the difference between "crap" technology—functional stuff with no cachet—and the truly "crappy." No one wants the latter, and there's nothing green about using something once and throwing it out because it doesn't work. But how can you tell the difference? Fortunately, I have a crack team of super-smart Stanford students who are standing by, waiting to answer this and all of your environmental questions. We call it SAGE: Sound Advice for a Green Earth. You can read through scores of answers in our archive, or ask your own questions here.

READING REACTIONS

1. What is the significance of Hayden beginning his article with a reference to the late Apple CEO, Steve Jobs? What do Apple and Jobs represent for him?

2. Why does Hayden prefer his obsolete Coby to his lost iPod? What other technological choices reflect his value system?

3. Hayden refers to the student group SAGE. What is SAGE, and what is its purpose? How might you develop a similar program devoted to informing the public about eco-friendly choices?

4. Hayden uses the term "planned obsolescence." What does this term mean, and how does it affect the environment?

5. Hayden asks "does second-rate technology have a future?" How would you answer that question? What technology did you purchase most recently? What is your typical rate of replacement?

● Joel Johnson

1 Million Workers. 90 Million iPhones.
17 Suicides. Who's to Blame?

Joel Johnson is a media writer and editor at Gizmodo, a consumer electronics blog. He has also written for *Boing Boing* and *Wired Magazine*. In this piece, Johnson describes life at Foxconn, the Chinese electronics company known for its employees' suicides.

It's hard not to look at the nets. Every building is skirted in them. They drape every precipice, steel poles jutting out 20 feet above the sidewalk, loosely tangled like volleyball nets in winter.

The nets went up in May, after the 11th jumper in less than a year died here. They carried a message: You can throw yourself off any building you like, as long as it isn't one of these. And they seem to have worked. Since they were installed, the suicide rate has slowed to a trickle.

My tour guides don't mention the nets until I do. Not to avoid the topic, I don't think—the suicides are the reason I am at a Foxconn plant in Shenzhen, a bustling industrial city in southern China—but simply because they are so prevalent. Foxconn, the single largest private employer in mainland China, manufactures many of the products—motherboards, camera components, MP3 players—that make up the world's $150 billion consumer-electronics industry. Foxconn's output accounts for nearly 40 percent of that revenue. Altogether, the company employs about a million people, nearly half of whom work at the 20-year-old Shenzhen plant. But until two summers ago, most Americans had never heard of Foxconn.

That all changed with the suicides. There had been a few since 2007. Then a spate of nine between March and May 2010—all jumpers. There were also suicides at other Foxconn plants in China. Although the company disputes some cases, evidence gathered from news reports and other sources indicates that 17 Foxconn workers have killed themselves in the past half decade. What had seemed to be a series of isolated incidents was becoming an appalling trend. When one jumper left a note explaining that he committed suicide to provide for his family, the program of remuneration for the families of jumpers was canceled. Some saw the Foxconn suicides as a damning consequence of our global hunger for low-cost electronics. Reports from inside the factories warned of "sweatshop" conditions; old allegations of forced overtime burbled back to life. Foxconn and its partners—notably Apple—found themselves defending factory conditions while struggling to explain the deaths. "Suicides in China Prompt Damage Control," blared *The New York Times*.

I seem to be witnessing some of those damage-control efforts on this still-warm fall day as two Foxconn executives—along with a liaison from Burson-Marsteller, a PR firm hired to deal with the post-suicide outcry—lead me through the facility. I have spent much of my career blogging about gadgets on sites like Boing Boing Gadgets and Gizmodo, reviewing and often praising many of the products that were made right here at Foxconn's Shenzhen factory. I ignored the first Foxconn suicides as sad but statistically inevitable. But as the number of jumpers approached double digits, latent self-reproach began to boil over. Out of a million people, 17 suicides isn't much—indeed, American college students kill themselves at four times that rate. Still, after years of writing what is (at best) buyers' guidance and (at worst) marching hymns for an army of consumers, I was burdened by what felt like an outsize provision of guilt—an existential buyer's remorse for civilization itself. I am here because I want to know: Did my iPhone kill 17 people?

My hosts are eager to help me answer that question in the negative by pointing out how pleasant life in the factory can be. They are quick with the college analogies: The canteens and mess halls are "like a college food court." The living quarters, where up to eight workers share rooms about the size of a two-car garage, are "like college dorms." The avenues and boulevards in the less industrial parts of the campus are "like malls."

For all their defensiveness, my guides are not far off the mark. The avenues certainly look more like a college campus than the dingy design-by-Communism concrete canyons I half expected to find. Sure, everything on the Foxconn campus is a bit shabby—errant woody saplings creep out of sidewalk cracks, and the signage is sometimes rusty or faded—more community college than Ivy League, perhaps. But it's generally clean. Workers stroll the sidewalks chatting and laughing, smoking together under trees, as amiable as any group of factory workers in the first world.

But "college campus" doesn't quite capture the vastness of the place. It's more like a nation-state, a gated complex covering just over a square mile, separated from the rest of Shenzhen's buildings by chain link and concrete. It houses one of the largest industrial kitchens in Asia—perhaps the world. Shenzhen itself was developed over the past three decades as one of party leader

Deng Xiaoping's Special Economic Zones—a kind of capitalist hot spot. The experiment was a rousing success. Millions of workers, gambling that low but dependable wages would be more readily found in Shenzhen, migrated from the poor, rural western provinces, packing into the tenement complexes that soon riddled the city. Factory work offered a chance to change their lives and the lives of their families back home, but it offered little in the way of security. Many companies did not supply housing, leaving workers to find shelter in dodgy slums or encouraging them to sleep on the assembly line. When they did provide lodging, it was typically a dorm room crammed with bunk beds.

According to company lore, Foxconn founder Terry Gou was determined to do things differently. So when the firm built its Longhua factory in Shenzhen, it included onsite dormitories—good ones, designed to be better than what workers could afford on their own. Terry Gou built on-campus housing, I am told, because Terry Gou cared about the welfare of his employees.

Up went a factory, up went a dorm. Up went an assembly line, up went a cafeteria. While other companies' workers fended for themselves or slept under the tables they worked at, Gou's employees were well fed, safe from the petty crime of a growing metropolis, and surrounded by peers and advocates.

It rings as unalloyed munificence—until a man puts his foot on the edge of a roof, looks across the campus full of trees and swimming pools and coffee shops, and steps off into nothing.

In the part of our minds where Americans hold an image of what an Asian factory may be, there are two competing visions: fluorescent fields of chittering machines attended by clean-suited technicians, or barefoot laborers bent over long wooden tables in sweltering rooms hazed by a fog of soldering fumes.

When we buy a new electronic device, we imagine the former factory. Our little glass, metal, and plastic marvel is the height of modern technological progress; it *must* have been made by worker-robots (with hands like surgeon-robots)—or failing that, extremely competent human beings.

But when we think "Chinese factory," we often imagine the latter. Some in the US—and here I should probably stop speaking in generalities and simply refer to myself—harbor a guilty suspicion that the products we buy from China, even those made for American companies, come to us at the expense of underpaid and oppressed laborers.

From what I can tell, though, the reality is more banal than either of those scenarios. This is what it's like to work at the Foxconn factory: You enter a five- or six-story concrete building, pull on a plastic jacket and hat, and slip booties over your shoes. You walk up a wide staircase to your assigned floor, the entirety of which lies open under unwavering fluorescent light.

It's likely that your job will require you to sit or stand in place for most of your shift. Maybe you grab components from a bin and slot them into circuit boards as they move down a conveyer. Or you might tend a machine, feeding it tape that holds tiny microprocessors like candy on paper spools. Or you may sit next to a refrigerator-sized machine, checking its handiwork under a magnifying glass. Or you could sit at a bench with other technicians placing completed cell-phone circuit boards into lead-lined boxes resembling small kilns, testing each piece for electromagnetic interference.

If you have to go to the bathroom, you raise your hand until your spot on the line can be covered. You get an hour for lunch and two 10-minute breaks; roles are switched up every few days for cross-training. It seems incredibly boring—like factory work anywhere in the developed world.

You work 10 hours or so, depending on overtime. You walk or take a shuttle back to your dorm, where you share a room with up to seven other employees that Foxconn management has selected as your bunkmates. You watch television in a common room with bench seating, on an HDTV that seems insultingly small compared with the giant units you and your coworkers make every day. Or maybe you play videogames or check email in one of the on-campus cybercafes, perhaps sharing a semiprivate "couple's booth" with a girlfriend or boyfriend.

In the morning, you clean yourself up in your room's communal sink or in one of the dorm's showers, then head back to the production line to do it all over again.

A report by the UK's *The Mail on Sunday* in 2006 accused Foxconn of forcing workers to pull long shifts to meet unrealistic quotas. That report prompted an audit from Apple, which found "no instances of forced over-time" but noted that "employees worked longer hours than permitted by our Code of Conduct"—over 60 hours a week. (Apple has performed such audits every year since.)

Last April, the Chinese newspaper *Southern Weekend* sent a young reporter into Foxconn to work undercover for a month; he returned with bleak tales of hopelessness and "voluntary overtime affidavits." An October report by Students and Scholars Against Corporate Misbehavior, a Hong Kong-based labor rights group, found that workers at Foxconn's Shenzhen plant worked 13 days straight, 12 hours a day, to produce the first generation of Apple's iPad. Foxconn has denied the reports and said it complies with all Chinese regulations regarding working hours and overtime.

That 17 people have committed suicide at Foxconn is a tragedy. But in fact, the suicide rate at Foxconn's Shenzhen plant remains below national averages for both rural and urban China, a bleak but unassailable fact that does much to exonerate the conditions at Foxconn and absolutely nothing to bring those 17 people back.

But the work itself isn't inhumane—unless you consider a repetitive, exhausting, and alienating workplace over which you have no influence or authority to be inhumane. And that would pretty much describe every single manufacturing or burger-flipping job ever.

I walk one afternoon to the brassiest concentration of Shenzhen's manufacturing power, the SEG Square electronics market in the Futian district. My Taiwanese guide, Paul, has spent the better part of a decade in Shenzhen as a steward for Western electronics companies seeking to procure components or goods from one of the city's thousands of suppliers. Here in SEG Square, the products of those suppliers fill glass cases and hang from pegboards in vast, low-ceilinged grottoes that would echo if they weren't crammed wall to wall with vendors' stalls. Elsewhere in Shenzhen, such markets are stocked with bamboo knickknacks and counterfeit puffy vests; this one is filled with obviously fake iPhone chargers.

SEG Square's markets are crowded, loud, and mildly mephitic from cigarette smoke and the odor of fresh-baked electronics. Whole floors are dedicated to knockoffs, not just at-first-glance-perfect clones of popular products but also cargo-cult evocations, like FM radios cast from a third-generation iPhone mold that probably wasn't convincingly accurate in the first place. It all looks like so much junk, but there is something touching about it. Each item was once the moment's work of a human being.

Paul has seen his share of factories in Shenzhen over the years. I ask him about Foxconn, and he echoes the sentiment I've heard from others: Whatever problems Foxconn has, it's still one of the top places to work in the area. "In terms of infrastructure, Foxconn is by far the best factory in China," he says. We stop to haggle with a vendor over five nonfunctional dummy iPhones (in mythic white) that I want to buy as gag gifts for friends back home. "But how much of that is a facade?" Paul asks, citing the LCD monitors that grace the company's assembly lines—ostentatious symbols of modernity that provide little benefit to the worker. "Pointless waste of electricity."

As for the Cyberfox Café, Foxconn's onsite Internet lounge, where I recently ate a fine bowl of bitter melon soup? "It might look huge, but considering the size of Foxconn's workforce," Paul says, "it can't even serve 5 percent of the employees."

Even if it is one of the better places to work in Shenzhen (at least for entry-level factory jobs), by the middle of 2010 [...] it was clear to Foxconn management that they were no longer running an anonymous manufacturing company. Foxconn was now a billion-dollar avatar of globalization, and they were feeling the rubbernecked gape of international scrutiny.

The living quarters on the Shenzhen campus were recently handed off to property management companies that are more experienced at addressing the living needs of employees. Foxconn hopes the outside firms will be quicker to respond to tenant complaints, although some critics suggest that the company hopes to outsource some of the blame as well. (When Foxconn constructs new inland factories, the living quarters will be managed in partnership with local governments.)

Foxconn has also built onsite counseling facilities, which are staffed by psychologists and counselors. I toured two such facilities. One, sharing storefront space on a busy avenue, has agents who can help workers replace lost keycards or buy prepaid mobile-phone cards to call home; this place was fairly busy. Another, off the main drag, was a full-on care center with music-therapy rooms, private counseling, and lounge areas; when I visited, it was nearly empty. In one room, a life-size Weeble Wobble with a scowling face could be smacked with a padded baseball bat. (It relieved my own stress for a moment.)

But the most ambitious effort to address worker morale is a modest-looking electronics store on the Foxconn campus, right next to a shop selling fresh fruit. It's called Ten Thousand Horses Galloping. (I'm assured the name has more pizzazz in Chinese.) Inside, you can buy rice cookers and desk fans and phones. It's like a RadioShack without the DIY components, or a Best Buy without the large appliances or racks of media. And according to Foxconn executives, it's the future of their company.

Foxconn campuses already have company stores where workers can buy the products they manufacture at discounted prices. Ten Thousand Horses Galloping is designed to be an electronics store for the rest of China. Foxconn plans to offer franchises to employees and even grant them a little startup capital.

The idea is to give some lucky, hard-working employees a way to bring a touch of entrepreneurial spirit back to their home provinces, especially in the poorer west. The workers get to own their own businesses; Foxconn gets to supply the stores with goods. To date, Foxconn has granted franchises to 60 employees and several more to outsiders.

Foxconn positions Ten Thousand Horses Galloping as a new direction for the company, one that allows it to shift into retail while tapping into the cream of the roughly million-strong workforce it has cultivated in China. But the store also offers another benefit to Foxconn, one that wasn't even needed until recently: employee retention. In recent years, factories have been sprouting up in China's interior to take advantage of cheaper labor.

Workers aren't flocking to Shenzhen as they did a decade ago, when it was one of the only places to get a manufacturing job. "Now that work opportunities are increasing in the interior regions of the country, would-be migrants are willing to take a lower salary at home to stay with their families," says Benjamin Dolgin-Gardner, general manager of Shenzhen CE and IT Limited. Even Foxconn itself is building a facility in Hunan, after being lured by multibillion-dollar tax and investment incentives from the provincial government.

Shenzhen may soon relinquish its role as the stoked furnace of the Chinese dream. But will that mean even greater expansion of the middle class, with commensurate benefits—or just the same old system shifted a thousand miles to the west?

In America, we have wrestled with the idea of divine sanction since the country's inception. Some of us believe we have a God-given dominion over the earth; others argue that we're bound to a larger Gaian system and are, at our best, caretakers.

My heart is with the caretakers. But I believe that humankind made a subconscious collective bargain at the dawn of the industrial age to trade the resources of our planet for the chance to escape it. We live in the transitional age between that decision and its conclusion.

In this middle age, the West built a middle class. It's now eroding and may be less enduring than the American Dream itself—a dream we exported to the rest of the world by culture and conquest. Nevertheless, most Americans have food, cars, gadgets. How can we begrudge a single person these luxuries if we want them ourselves?

By many accounts, those unskilled laborers who get jobs at Foxconn are the luckiest. But eyes should absolutely remain on Foxconn, the eyes of media both foreign and domestic, of government inspectors and partner companies. The work may be humane, but rampant overtime is not. We should encourage workers' rights just as much as we champion economic development. We've exported our manufacturing; let's be sure to export trade unions, too.

I've written thousands of posts, millions of words, about *things*. Usually things with electricity in them. Doing this for a living, on and off, for the better part of a decade, has greatly—perhaps fundamentally—changed how I perceive the world around me. I can no longer look at the material world as a collection of objects but instead see interfaces, histories, and materials.

To be soaked in materialism, to directly and indirectly champion it, has also brought guilt. I don't know if I have a right to the vast quantities of materials and energy I consume in my daily life. Even if I thought I did, I know the planet cannot bear my lifestyle multiplied by 7 billion individuals. I believe this understanding is shared, if only subconsciously, by almost everyone in the Western world.

Every last trifle we touch and consume, right down to the paper on which this magazine is printed or the screen on which it's displayed, is not only ephemeral but in a real sense irreplaceable. Every consumer good has a cost not borne out by its price but instead falsely bolstered by a vanishing resource economy. We squander millions of years' worth of stored energy, stored life, from our planet to make not only things that are critical to our survival and comfort but also things that simply satisfy our innate primate desire to possess. It's this guilt that we attempt to assuage with the hope that our consumerist culture is making life better—for ourselves, of course, but also in some lesser way for those who cannot afford to buy everything we purchase, consume, or own.

When that small appeasement is challenged even slightly, when that thin, taut cord that connects our consumption to the nameless millions who make our lifestyle possible snaps even for a moment, the gulf we find ourselves peering into—a yawning, endless future of emptiness on a squandered planet—becomes too much to bear.

When 17 people take their lives, I ask myself, did I in my desire hurt them? Even just a little?

And of course the answer, inevitable and immeasurable as the fluttering silence of our sun, is yes.

Just a little.

READING REACTIONS

1. Johnson suggests that there are larger cultural stereotypes about Chinese factories. Explain those assumptions and how they impact our perceptions of working conditions in the global electronics industry.
2. What conditions in China result in the migration of workers to urban areas such as Shenzhen for jobs at Foxconn and other companies?
3. Describe a day in the life for workers at Foxconn. How does Foxconn try to enhance the working conditions of its employees?
4. What is Johnson's point in stating that "the work itself isn't inhumane—unless you consider a repetitive, exhausting, and alienating workplace over which you have no influence or authority to be inhumane. And that would pretty much describe every single manufacturing or burger-flipping job ever."
5. Johnson states of his time in China: "I am here because I want to know: Did my iPhone kill 17 people?" Reflect on Johnson's changing attitude toward gadgetry in light of the Foxconn suicides.

● Emmanuel K. Dogbevi

E-waste Is Killing Ghanaians Slowly

Emmanuel Dogbevi is online managing editor at *Ghana Business News* and National Coordinator for the Programme for African Investigative Reporting (PAIR) Ghana project. With a bachelor's degree in sociology from the University of Ghana, Dogbevi is an award-winning journalist and an early opponent of e-waste dumping in Ghana. In his 2007 article on ModernGhana.com, Dogbevi shows the consequences of absent e-waste regulation in his home country.

There is presently no direct evidence to show that e-waste related diseases are increasing in Ghana, because no such study has been done.

But from the scientific evidences available in other parts of the world, the probability that e-waste could be a large contributing factor to some illnesses in Ghana is high.

Indeed, the issue of e-waste has not attracted any serious concern yet in Ghana and therefore, nothing is being done about it.

Meanwhile, concerns about e-waste or computer waste are growing around the world, particularly in developed countries. However, in developing countries including Ghana the need to take a serious look at the issue of e-waste has not caught up yet.

E-waste is the generic name for electronic or computer wastes. These are discarded electronics devices that come into the waste stream from several sources.

They include gadgets like televisions, personal computers (PCs), telephones, air conditioners, cell phones, and electronic toys.

The list can further be widened to include appliances such as lifts, refrigerators, washing machines, dryers, kitchen equipment or even aeroplanes.

The problems posed by e-waste are becoming more challenging, because the increase in the quantity of e-waste in the system is largely due to the speed of technological advancement and innovation coupled by a high obsolete rate. And because of the very critical role of technology in social and economic development, the issue of e-waste has become a complicated one.

Countries of the world are racing against each other in developing new technology, but technological advancement comes at some costs.

Indeed, no nation can develop without technological know-how and expertise. And some of the costs technology leaves in its trail include e-wastes and associated consequences.

These consequences reverberate in potential environmental as well as health hazards that put the globe at risk.

Among industrial waste campaigners the world over, electronics equipment is one of the largest known sources of heavy metals, toxic materials and organic pollutants in city waste.

Due to the speed at which technology is changing, people change their electronic equipment within short periods.

In the US alone, an estimated 30 million computers are thrown out every year. According to the United States Environmental Protection Agency (EPA), of this number, only 14% are recycled.

Available records show that by the end of 2004, over 314 million computers were obsolete and by the year 2007 the cumulative number of obsolete computers in the US is expected to rise to 500 million.

Due to this rapid advancement, the average life-span of computers has shrunk to less than two years. For most people, the lure of new technology is so strong that, they would rather buy a new computer than upgrade an old one, and those PCs that can not be upgraded add up to the waste pile.

Another estimate suggests that by 2010, 100 million cell phones and 300 million PCs will end up on the dumping site.

Sadly, because accurate statistics are often hard to obtain in Ghana and in most cases figures do not exist, estimates of PCs in Ghana are not readily available.

Moreover, the rate at which electronic gadgets become obsolete in Ghana is not known, taking into account the fact that a good number of PCs and other electronics gadgets that are imported into the country are already old.

E-waste is known to contain dangerous chemical pollutants that are released into the atmosphere and underground water.

The modes of disposal, which include dumping old gadgets into landfills or burning in smelters, also expose the environment and humans to a cocktail of toxic chemicals and poison.

These chemicals contain substances like lead, mercury and arsenic.

The cathode ray tubes (CRTs) in most computer monitors and television screens have x-ray shields that contain 4 to 8 pounds of lead, mostly embedded in glass.

Flat screen monitors that are mostly used in laptops do not contain high concentrations of lead, but most are illuminated with fluorescent lights that contain some mercury.

A PC's central processing unit (CPU), the module containing the chip and the hard disk, typically contains toxic heavy metals such as mercury (in switches), lead (in solder on circuit boards), and cadmium (in batteries).

Plastics used to house computer equipment and cover wire cables to prevent flammability often contain polybrominated flame retardants, a class of dangerous chemicals. Studies have shown that ingesting these substances may increase the risk of cancer, liver damage, and immune system dysfunction.

Lead, mercury, cadmium, and polybrominated flame retardants are all persistent, bio-accumulative toxins (PBTs), that can create environmental and health risks when computers are manufactured, incinerated, landfilled or melted during recycling. PBTs, in particular are a dangerous class of chemicals that linger in the environment and accumulate in living tissues.

And because they increase in concentration as they move up the food chain, PBTs can reach dangerous levels in living organisms, even when released in minute quantities. PBTs are harmful to human health and the environment and have been associated with cancer, nerve damage and reproductive disorders.

Looked at individually, the chemicals contained in e-waste are a cocktail of dangerous pollutants that kill both the environment and humans slowly.

Lead, which negative effects were recognized and therefore banned from gasoline in the 1970s causes damage to the central and peripheral nervous systems, blood systems, kidney and the reproductive system in humans.

Effects of lead on the endocrine system have been observed, including the serious negative effects it has on children's brain development. When it accumulates in the environment, it has high acute and chronic effects on plants, animals and micro-organisms.

Cadmium compounds are also toxic with a possible risk of irreversible effects on human health and accumulate in the human body, particularly the kidneys. Cadmium occurs in certain components such as SMD chip resistors, infra-red detectors, and semi-conductor chips.

Mercury on the other hand, can cause damage to various organs including the brain and kidneys as well as the fetus. More especially, the developing fetus is highly susceptible through maternal exposure to mercury.

These are only few of the chemicals used in the manufacture of electronics equipment. Other chemicals are Hexavalent Chromium which is used as a corrosion protection of untreated and galvanized steel plates and as a decorative or hardener for steel housings. Plastics including PVC are also used. Plastics constitute about 13.8 pounds of an average computer.

The largest volume of plastics 26% used in electronics is PVC. When PVC is burned, dioxin can be formed because it contains chlorine compounds. Barium is a soft silvery-white metal that is used in computers in the front panel of a CRT, to protect users from radiation.

Studies have shown that short-term exposure to barium has caused brain swelling, muscle weakness, damage to the liver, heart and spleen.

Considering the health hazards of e-waste, another ubiquitous computer peripheral scrap worth mentioning is toners. The main ingredient of the black toner is a pigment commonly called carbon black—the general term used to describe the commercial powder form of carbon.

Inhalation is the primary means of exposure, and acute exposure may lead to respiratory tract irritation.

These facts and factors are well documented, and it would not be far fetched to say that it is surprising that the agencies responsible for the welfare of Ghana's environment and the health of the people of this beloved country have not taken the necessary steps and measures to establish mechanisms as is done elsewhere to safeguard the environment and human health.

Checks at Ghana's Environmental Protection Agency (EPA) drew blank. Sources at the EPA said there is no policy regarding the handling of e-waste in Ghana!

The EPA is poorly resourced and not motivated enough to do its job of monitoring Ghana's environment.

Besides, Ghana's health institutions, apart from facing acute shortage of qualified health professionals, lack the equipment required to handle known and possible side effects of e-waste.

When one takes a walk around Accra, especially Agbogbloshie, and the area around the Abossey Okai mosque, where scrap dealers do their businesses, one would find piles of discarded television sets, PCs and other electronics equipment put out for sale.

Some people buy these items and use some of the parts to fix faulty equipment, but what happens to the other unwanted parts is anyone's guess. Others are also known to burn these parts, under unhygienic and unsafe circumstances to remove some of the parts for use in other ways.

In the absence of any clear policy on e-waste in Ghana, the situation in the country becomes grim.

What is even more surprising is that, in spite of the currency of environmental issues in today's globalized world, which has lead to the formation of political parties with ideological leanings that seek to pursue environmental issues in some countries, in Ghana, politicians hardly raise environmental issues in their campaign for political power.

It is high time we as a country looked seriously at the growing trend in e-waste and take a decisive step to deal with the problem, before we are slowly, but surely submerged in this cocktail of poisonous chemicals which can only mean disaster which is sure to come.

Environmental campaigners believe that a good heap of the e-waste discarded in developed countries land in developing countries, further exposing our people to health hazards we are hardly prepared to handle.

1. Who is the audience for Dogbevi's article? Are there potentially multiple audiences?

2. What are some of the factors that have contributed to Ghana's e-waste problem?

3. According to Dogobevi, what accounts for the lack of interest in or awareness of e-waste in Ghana?

4. Compare Dogbevi's print article to his recent YouTube interview, available through the English CourseMate for this text. Are both communication modes equally persuasive? If you were to construct a similar article on an environmental topic, what types of figures, images, and media would you use to support your position?

5. View the Greenpeace Guide to Greener Electronics, available through the English CourseMate for this text. Download the "report card" for the manufacturer of your computer or cell phone, if available, or the computers used on your campus. What criteria does Greenpeace use to evaluate the electronics industry? How does failure to meet criteria impact the e-waste problem in Ghana and other parts of the world?

COMMUNITIES Review the public service announcement shown in **Figure 8.8**. Who is the target audience? How are the needs of this audience addressed visually and textually? Consider the relationship between appeals in the PSA and the subjects figured. What has the message creator presumed about the target audience?

Figure 8.8 EPA Public Service Announcement

TECHNOLOGIES Construct your own visual argument about the environment in your life or in your community, similar to the visual argument made in **Figure 8.9** and in "Looks Clean, Doesn't It" from Chapter 1 (p. 10). What claim are you trying to establish, and how do the components (context, people, actions) of your image support your claim?

Figure 8.9 Stop global warming poster

A word cloud or tag cloud visually represents textual content, using text size and color to distinguish the dominant ideas. In this chapter, Andrew Hoffman uses word clouds (Figures 8.6 and 8.7, p. 340) to show some of the differences between two sides of the climate change debate. Similarly, you can use word-cloud programs to brainstorm directions for your own projects. Word clouds are an easy way to identify ideas that stand out and how major topics and subtopics interconnect. To create a word cloud, you can choose from a number of free programs, including TagCrowd(http://tagcrowd.com) and Wordle (http://wordle.net).

Spend fifteen minutes free writing about some aspect of the environment that is important to you, such as global warming. Paste the results of your free writing text into a program like Wordle.net to create a word cloud to share with your classmates or on your personal blog or Facebook profile. Reflect on what your word cloud reveals about your position on this environmental issue.

Technological Beginnings

Several resources in this and other *CrossCurrents* chapters show that in many cases, images, videos, and other visual formats communicate a persuasive message just as strongly as a print document. Although you might assume that developing a video clip requires an advanced skill set, tools such as Apple iMovie and Microsoft Movie Maker make desktop video editing easier than ever. And now that most digital cameras and many cell phones can capture video footage, you'll find that transferring footage to the computer has become equally convenient. This is why more students and citizens are sharing videos on a range of topics on sites like Vimeo and YouTube. Nevertheless, it is important that you develop basic understanding of the various composing technologies common to the videography process.

Rather than starting with advanced tools that are often more difficult to learn, you can try the YouTube Video Editor. Student Megan Adams developed documentation for Video Editor to show the ease of combining visual, textual, and audio elements in a movie format. One advantage of experimenting with this particular tool is that you can create a movie without actually having any footage of your own. Use the following documentation to get started.

YouTube Video Editor

1. Navigate to http://www.youtube.com and follow the instructions to create an account if you don't already have one.
2. Select the "My Videos" option from the menu, shown in **Figure 8.10**.

Figure 8.10

3. Select the Video Editor from the menu at the top of the screen.
4. You should have reached the Video Editor! Your screen should look like **Figure 8.11**.

Figure 8.11

5. YouTube automatically imports the video files you've uploaded to your account into the Video Editor, but you can upload videos from Creative Commons (see step 6) if you wish to edit with new videos. To begin editing your videos, simply drag a video clip onto your timeline.

Figure 8.12

6. If you would like to include video from Creative Commons, select the Creative Commons icon at the top of the screen. From there, you can search the Commons and upload video based on your needs.

Figure 8.13

7. To cut a video clip, hover over the clip on the Timeline and select the scissors icon.

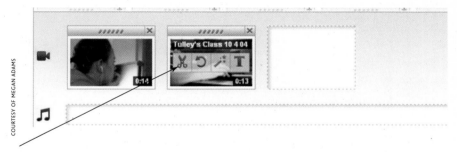

Figure 8.14

8. A box will pop up, allowing you to mark in and out points on your clip as you like.

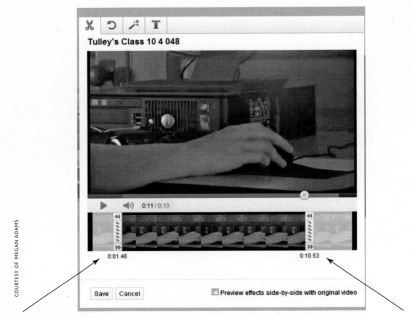

Figure 8.15

9. You can also add effects to your video clip by selecting the magic wand icon. Select the effect you like and they will be added to your clip.

10. If you would like to include music in your video, select the music note icon. From there, you can choose from the selections provided or search for music that you want by genre or artist. Once you've made a selection, simply drag the track to the timeline.

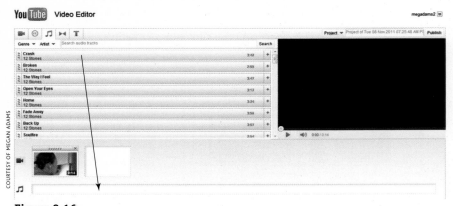

Figure 8.16

11. To add transitions to your video, select the transition icon, choose a transition, and drag it to the timeline.

YouTube Video Editor

Figure 8.17

12. You can also add text to your video by selecting the text icon, which looks like a "T".

13. Type in the text you like in the text box and drag it to the timeline, placing it wherever you like in the text.

Figure 8.18

14. When you are ready to publish your video, select "Publish" (located at top right-hand corner of the screen).

Most likely, it will take a few minutes before YouTube publishes the video and provides a link where it can be viewed. Once you receive the link, click on it to view your video!

TECHNOLOGIES Set up an account on YouTube, and use its video-editing tool to develop a one-minute public service announcement for a specific audience on some aspect of the environment that is important to you. As part of the process, you should rely on clips and music that are available from free public-domain sites such as Creative Commons (http://creativecommons.org). You may want to review both amateur and professional videos of public service announcements on YouTube by using various environmental search terms.

Additional Writing and Composing Activities

1. **Multimedia Presentation (Report).** Developed by a team of chemists, toxicologists, nutritionists, and lifestyle analysts, GoodGuide is an online resource that allows consumers to compare numerous products and companies on their environmental and social responsibility. Visit the GoodGuide site at http://goodguide.com, and use the site to compare consumer products that are part of your lifestyle, such as jeans or cell phones. Report your comparisons to the class in presentation form, using a tool such as Microsoft PowerPoint, Apple Keynote, Google Presentation, or Prezi.

2. **Proposal.** What happens to old computers on your campus? Interview an information technology specialist to learn about desktop and laptop replacement and recycling procedures on your campus. How do these procedures mesh with programs at other universities? Conduct an online search for best e-cycling practices on college campuses, and write a proposal for a similar recycling program on your campus if one doesn't already exist.

3. **Review.** Climate change, energy conservation, and sustainability have been a major part of our contemporary concern with environmental protection. Given this concern, many books have been published in the last several years to alert the public to our own role in going green. Select one book and write a review of it for other readers. Share your review on a blog, in your campus newspaper, or even on Amazon.com.

Online Resources

Resources available through the English CourseMate for this text include the following:

Online Articles:

Ecycling: From the Environmental Protection Agency

Grist: Environmental News, Commentary, Advice

Interview with Emmanuel Dogbevi

Edward Wong. "Outrage Grows Over Air Pollution and China's Response."

Resources:

Design Crave: Earth Day Graphics: 30 Creative Environment Ads

GoodGuide

TagCrowd

Wordle

Websites:

Climate Reality Project

EarthDay

Ecogamer

Enviromedia Greenwashing Index

Gardening SuperFund Site

Greenpeace Guide to Greener Electronics

MyFarm

Story of Stuff Project

Index